MARKETING MANAGEMENT

STRATEGIES AND PROGRAMS

MARKETING MANAGEMENT
STRATEGIES AND PROGRAMS

FOURTH EDITION

Joseph P. Guiltinan
University of Notre Dame

Gordon W. Paul
University of Central Florida

McGRAW-HILL, INC.

New York   St. Louis   San Francisco   Auckland   Bogotá   Caracas
Hamburg   Lisbon   London   Madrid   Mexico   Milan   Montreal   New Delhi
Paris   San Juan   São Paulo   Singapore   Sydney   Tokyo   Toronto

MARKETING MANAGEMENT
STRATEGIES AND PROGRAMS

2 3 4 5 6 7 8 9 0   DOC DOC   9 5 4 3 2 1

ISBN 0-07-048942-4

This book was set in Optima by the College Composition Unit
in cooperation with Ruttle Shaw & Wetherill, Inc.
The editors were Bonnie K. Binkert, Mimi Melek, and Bernadette Boylan;
the production supervisor was Richard A. Ausburn.
The cover was designed by Joan Greenfield.
New drawings were done by Hadel Studios.
R. R. Donnelley & Sons Company was printer and binder.

Cover Credit: Point/Counterpoint, machine-sewn quilt by Michael James.

Library of Congress Cataloging-in-Publication Data

Guiltinan, Joseph P.
    Marketing management: strategies and programs / Joseph P. Guiltinan, Gordon W. Paul.—4th ed.
        p.   cm.—(McGraw-Hill series in marketing)
    Includes bibliographical references and index.
    ISBN 0-07-048942-4
    1. Marketing—Management.   I. Paul, Gordon W.   II. Title.
III. Series.
HF5415.13.G84   1990
658.8—dc20   90-23270

ABOUT THE AUTHORS

JOSEPH P. GUILTINAN is Professor of Marketing and Associate Dean, College of Business Administration, University of Notre Dame. He holds the BBA degree from Notre Dame and both the MBA and DBA degrees from Indiana University.

Dr. Guiltinan has served on the faculties of the University of Massachusetts–Amherst and the Univesity of Kentucky. He was department chair at both Kentucky and Notre Dame.

Dr. Guiltinan's other books include *Marketing* (now in its fourth edition) published by Allyn & Bacon and *Pricing Bank Services* published by the American Bankers' Association. His research has appeared in the *Journal of Marketing, Journal of Consumer Research, Journal of Retailing,* and many other publications.

GORDON W. PAUL is a professor of Marketing at the University of Central Florida–Orlando. Professor Paul received his Ph.D. in marketing from Michigan State University. He has been on the faculty at Louisiana State University–Baton Rouge and the University of Massachusetts–Amherst. He has been a Fulbright lecturer in Greece and Portugal and has published numerous articles in a variety of journals and proceedings. Professor Paul has co-authored *Consumer Behavior: An Integrated Approach* (Richard D. Irwin, Inc.) and *Readings in Marketing Management: Strategies and Programs* (McGraw-Hill).

CONTENTS

PREFACE

This book is specifically designed for advanced undergraduate students and for those MBA students with some previous coursework in marketing. It is intended for use in those courses in which the application of marketing concepts, tools, and decision-making processes is emphasized. In addition, practicing managers should find it useful in providing guidelines for developing marketing plans and programs.

As with previous editions, this book presents concepts from a decision-making perspective rather than from a descriptive point of view. For example, it does not include survey chapters on consumer behavior or marketing research. Instead, these topics are covered in the context of their relevance to managers, so that students will gain an appreciation of their importance in making product, price, distribution, and promotional decisions.

This approach reflects our emphasis on the middle-management marketing decisions which students are most likely to confront in their careers. Accordingly, top management's strategic decisions have been distinguished from the strategic and operating decisions that middle managers make for a specific product or product line. Additionally, because marketing managers are held accountable for profits as well as sales, the budgetary considerations of marketing decisions are given extensive coverage.

The book has been organized around the **marketing planning process** to clearly delineate the relationship among marketing decisions. In Part One we present the marketing planning process, and we examine the corporate marketing planning decisions which top management must make to provide direction for middle-management decisions. Part Two presents the analytical tools that middle managers must use in analyzing the situation confronting the products or product lines for which they are responsible. Included in this section are chapters on market analysis (presenting approaches for analyzing the buying process and market segmentation), market measurement, competitive analysis, and profitability and productivity analysis (for budgeting decisions). Part Three presents systematic planning approaches for developing a marketing strategy for a product and for program decisions needed to implement the overall marketing strategy. The programs discussed include product development, pricing, advertising, sales promotion, and sales and distribution. Part Four examines the coordination and control mechanisms available to marketing managers. Included in this section are chapters on organizing and managing marketing and sales activities and on the annual marketing plan.

Users of previous editions will note that in terms of philosophy and perspective, this edition follows that of previous editions. However, there are some important substantive changes that have been made. For one, we have added a new chapter on "Competitive Analysis." Another important addition is the appendix on sources of market information. This appendix allows the student to identify and locate useful sources for performing market analyses and competitive analyses. The chapter on "International Marketing Strategies and Programs" has been eliminated in this edition. As the importance of international markets continues to expand, marketing managers can no longer examine multinational concerns as appendages to strategy. Instead, we have chosen to integrate the international dimensions of marketing throughout the text rather than treat them in an isolated manner.

In addition to these changes, we have enhanced existing chapters by incorporating new material. In particular there are readable but practical treatments of the important analytical tools for perceptual mapping and concept testing. Additionally, significant new issues such as brand equity, the shift in power from manufacturers to retailers, targeting regional markets, and the use of electronic scanning and single source data in market response measurement are given prominent attention in this edition. Additional emphasis has been given to services and industrial marketing practices in this edition. New end-of-chapter discussion cases and questions have been added to reflect this emphasis as well as to help integrate the international perspective.

To a large extent, these modifications reflect the comments and suggestions of faculty members who have used previous editions as well as the insightful evaluations by several reviewers. For their support and constructive comments we are especially indebted to the following individuals.

Hiram C. Barksdale, Jr., Georgia State University
Sharon E. Beatty, University of Alabama
Terry L. Childers, University of Minnesota
Eli P. Cox, III, University of Texas–Austin
Michael J. Dotson, Appalachian State University
William Gaidis, Arizona State University
Frederic B. Kraft, Wichita State University
Brian M. Meyer, Mankato State University
Marti J. Rhea, University of North Texas
Kenneth L. Rowe, Arizona State University
JoAnn K. L. Schwinghammer, Mankato State University

Rajan P. Varadarajan, Texas A&M University
Larry K. Yarbrough, University of Arkansas

We are particularly thankful to Sam Gillespie of Texas A&M University who has provided us with constructive suggestions and materials throughout several editions. Our thanks are due, too, to Greta Hoisington for her assistance in preparing the manuscript for publication. Her skill and attention to detail are most appreciated.

Joseph P. Guiltinan
Gordon W. Paul

MARKETING MANAGEMENT

STRATEGIES AND PROGRAMS

PART 1

MANAGERIAL PERSPECTIVES ON MARKETING

In today's world it sometimes seems that change is the only constant. Managers of both profit-oriented and not-for-profit organizations face an environment characterized by rapidly changing technology, by competition which is increasingly multinational in scope, and by shifting political and economic forces such as the economic unification of Europe, an international trend toward the deregulation of key industries, and dramatic growth in international trade and foreign investment.

These changes have important implications for marketing decisions in an organization. Decisions on the design of products and services, on prices, and on appropriate promotional methods and distribution systems must be made after considering environmental constraints and opportunities. Because the environment is dynamic and complex and because the range of marketing decisions, issues, and positions is extensive, organizations must develop processes for coordinating various decisions and activities to ensure a common purpose and direction. This is particularly important at what is generally called the *middle-management* level of an organization. The term *middle management* is generally applied to the vast area between first-line supervisors and vice presidents. In marketing, middle-management personnel include individuals with titles such as product or brand manager, advertising manager, market manager, and sales manager.

This book provides the concepts, tools, and decision-making approaches that prospective middle-level managers need to carry out their specialized job roles and responsibilities. However, each of these job roles represents only one or, at most, a few elements of the total marketing effort. Accordingly, so that a middle manager can fully appreciate and effectively utilize these concepts and tools, it is important to understand the relationship between top-management and middle-management decisions.

In Part 1, which includes Chapters 1 and 2, we examine the broad organizational setting in which the marketing function is performed, and we discuss the ways in which the organization as a whole can attempt to deal with broad environmental changes. Both of these issues are important to ensure that middle-management activities are integrated and well focused.

Chapter 1 presents the marketing planning process, which serves as the basis for *integrating* the various marketing activities. Chapter 2 discusses the role of top-management decision making, which is to develop a corporate marketing plan that establishes a basic *direction* for middle-management actions.

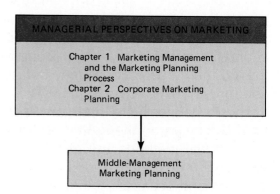

THE SCOPE OF MARKETING MANAGEMENT AND THE MARKETING PLANNING PROCESS

OVERVIEW

Few would argue with the statement that a business organization must be attuned to the marketplace in order to be successful. Nevertheless, time and time again, leading firms suffer economic losses (and even go out of business) because of a failure to fully meet customer needs. Consider, for example, the following:

> Overnight package delivery was not introduced by UPS, the airlines, or the principal freight forwarders. It was introduced by Fred Smith's Federal Express, an industry upstart.... The industry consensus seemed to be that consolidating packages in a single city [Federal's innovative operations process] was a foolish idea, and speed of delivery was not an important benefit.
>
> Vincent Marotta was a successful real estate developer.... He developed the first Mr. Coffee machine. The dominant makers of coffee percolators did not see the threat Mr. Coffee presented and reacted to Marotta's innovation slowly.... Marotta correctly

foresaw that it offered consumers many benefits: It was faster, brewed tastier coffee, and did not cost the consumer much more for those benefits.[1]

Why do large firms with experienced managers so often "miss the boat" on new opportunities? One possible answer was offered by former General Electric executive John B. McKitterick:

> So the principal task of the marketing function in a management concept is not so much to be skillful in making the customer do what suits the interests of the business as to be skillful in conceiving and then making the business do what suits the interests of the customer.[2]

It is certainly possible that, in the interest of lowering costs or achieving operational simplicity, firms may not ardently pursue some innovations that would enhance the buyer's welfare. However, it is the role of marketing to help an organization maintain a focus on the marketplace by

- Identifying needs
- Finding out which needs an organization can and should serve
- Developing an offering (something of value) which meets those needs

It is important, however, to recognize that the marketing function is *not* reserved for personnel with marketing management job titles. According to leading management thinker and writer Peter Drucker:

> Actually marketing is so basic that it is not just enough to have a strong sales force and to entrust marketing to it. Marketing is not only much broader than selling, it is not a specialized activity at all. It is the whole business seen from the point of view of its final results, that is, from the customer's point of view.[3]

This broader view—that marketing must permeate all business activity—can be illustrated by a recent action taken at the Inland Steel Company.

> Inland Steel executives developed a plan to enhance long-term growth by becoming stable, preferred suppliers to leading firms in the various steel-consuming industries. One of the target companies was Whirlpool, a leader in the appliance business. But Whirlpool was unwilling to make large commitments to Inland until they saw improved product quality. One of Inland's strategies for building quality was to take bus loads of steel workers and supervisors to Whirlpool's production facilities so they could meet Whirlpool's manufacturing personnel and gain a better understanding of *why* high quality steel was important in appliance manufacturing. The result was a substantial improvement in product quality and vastly expanded sales to Whirlpool.[4]

While marketing (in the broad sense) may indeed be everybody's business, there

[1]Steven P. Schnaars, "Why Do Outsiders See the Future Better," *Sales & Marketing Management,* April 1989, p. 94.
[2]John B. McKitterick, "What Is the Marketing Concept?" *The Frontiers of Marketing Thought and Action,* American Marketing Association, Chicago, 1957, pp. 71–82.
[3]Peter Drucker, *The Practice of Management,* Harper & Row, New York, 1954, p. 37.
[4]Based on discussions between one of the authors and sales and marketing personnel at Inland Steel.

are many specialized marketing management roles and functions. The goal of this book is to enable prospective middle-level marketing managers to understand the tools, concepts, and procedures that can be used in customer-creating activities. In order to have a complete understanding of marketing's role in the organization, however, managers must develop a perspective on the role of marketing at various decision-making levels. Accordingly, in the remainder of this chapter, we will examine the following:

- The *marketing concept* as a philosophy behind the role marketing plays in a *market-oriented* organization
- The nature of marketing decisions at the *top-management* and *middle-management* levels
- The *marketing planning* process as a systematic approach for developing and coordinating marketing decisions

THE MARKETING CONCEPT AND THE MARKET-ORIENTED ORGANIZATION

Perspectives on what constitutes marketing and on the place marketing holds in the firm have undergone substantial change in recent years. In earlier years, marketing was viewed as not much different from selling. Many companies believed that with enough effort and expense, almost any product could be sold by high-powered selling and aggressive advertising. In effect, this "selling concept" implied that marketing's role was to help dispose of whatever the factory decided to make.

With the maturing of the American economy over the past 40 years, an increasing number of suppliers and brands began to compete more intensively for the buyer's dollars. Increasingly, the successful firms became those who adopted the modern *marketing concept* as a guiding philosophy. The essential elements of this concept were[5]

1 Careful analysis of markets to understand needs
2 The selection of target groups of customers whose needs match up with the firm's capabilities
3 Tailoring the product offering to achieve customer satisfaction

While these policies seemed laudable, it has become apparent that, by themselves, they provide insufficient guidance. That is, they reflect key marketing tasks but usually involve the support of other functions. For example, marketing managers alone may be unable to assess whether the firm has the requisite abilities to meet certain needs and may lack information about the costs of tailoring products to achieve customer satisfaction. Accordingly, marketers (and managers in general) have come to recognize that there are important *organizational* dimensions that enable a firm to be *market-oriented*.

[5]Frederick Webster, Jr., "The Rediscovery of the Marketing Concept," *Business Horizons*, May–June 1988, p. 31.

Specifically, Harvard professor Benson Shapiro has identified three key characteristics of a truly market-oriented company:[6]

1 Information on all important buying influences permeates every corporate function so that manufacturing, research and development, and finance all understand the needs and problems of the buyer.

2 Decisions are made interfunctionally and interdivisionally so that each organizational unit is aware of the constraints and opportunities facing those units with whom they must coordinate.

3 Decisions are well coordinated and executed with a sense of commitment so that functional goals support the common goals of customer satisfaction and profitability.

An example of a market-oriented company that has achieved notable success recently is Motorola.

> Motorola has experienced success in recent years in a number of telecommunications and electronics markets. The company is the world's largest maker of modems (which enable computers to "talk" to each other over telephone lines) and has emerged as a leading innovator in cellular phones and electronic pagers. The MicroTac cellular phone which fits into a coat pocket and the company's wristwatch pager have both received technical as well as market acclaim. Additionally, Motorola is a leader in automotive electronics and in microprocessors and memory chips used in products such as computers and cameras.
>
> Motorola's success has been ascribed in large part to the firm's continuing strong emphasis on research and development which has enabled it to be responsive to customer demand. As Motorola sees things, customers want improved benefits, better quality, and lower prices. To achieve all of these first requires an understanding of the market. Consequently, Motorola customer service personnel work closely with customers, sometimes even helping to design customers' products (such as Canon's EOS 35 mm camera). Moreover, design, manufacturing, and marketing personnel work together on new product projects so that products are designed at the outset to be cost-effective to build and to provide the benefits and features customers want.[7]

Thus, Motorola has responded to the market with innovative products that satisfy target customers. The key to Motorola's success, however, lies in its market-oriented organization. Research and development still has a primary goal of enhancing technology and manufacturing must meet high-quality goals as well as lower costs. By identifying which needs the company can serve, given its manufacturing and design capabilities, Motorola is able to coordinate the marketing requirements posed by the marketing concept with its internal technical and manufacturing constraints and capabilities.

Figure 1-1 summarizes the relationship between the marketing concept and the requirements for successfully implementing the concept. The truly market-oriented organization is receptive to market information, attempts to match its

[6]Benson Shapiro, "What the Hell Is 'Market Oriented'?" *Harvard Business Review,* November–December 1988, pp. 119–125.

[7]Lois Therrien, "The Rival Japan Respects," *Business Week,* Nov. 13, 1989, pp. 108–118.

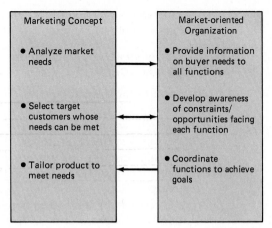

FIGURE 1-1 The marketing concept and the market-oriented organization.

capabilities and limitations with target market needs (hence the bidirectional arrow), and is able to tailor products to meet market needs only after all relevant business functions have been coordinated.

Probably the most controversial aspects of the marketing concept and of being market-oriented revolve around their applicability to not-for-profit organizations such as colleges, arts organizations, political groups, and social-action causes. Hospitals, for example, have really begun to recognize that patients expect more than just basic health care. Increasingly, hospitals are emphasizing pleasant "extras": friendly nurses and staff, faster service and attention, nicely decorated rooms, and even gourmet meals in some cases. Similarly, marketing has taken on greater importance for the U.S. Army.

> Between 1978 and 1986, the U.S. Army's recruitment advertising budget rose 85 percent to $100 million. At the same time, the quality of army recruits rose: 92 percent of 1986 recruits held high school diplomas compared to 54 percent in 1980. But advertising alone did not yield these results. Marketing research done in the 1970s showed that potential recruits simply did not like the army's "product": Enlistment periods (3 and 4 years) were considered too long and the traditional vocational training was perceived as inadequate. The army then developed a new product featuring a new 2-year enlistment period, a new college tuition fund, and bonuses of up to $8,000 for those selecting certain combat specialties such as the infantry.[8]

The primary controversy, however, revolves around the degree to which all organizations should focus on customer or client satisfaction when the essential mission of the organization cannot be changed (for example, an antiabortion or antinuclear group) or where production is based on personal norms and values. While businesses can move across products and markets to satisfy customers and still retain their core purpose of providing economic exchanges, not-for-profit or-

---

[8]"Atten-hut! The Army's Ad Business Is Up for Grabs," *Business Week*, Nov. 17, 1986, p. 132.

ganizations must consider the marketing concept within the limits imposed by their purposes.[9]

LEVELS OF MARKETING MANAGEMENT

Because the marketing concept requires a consumer-buyer orientation, middle managers' activities focus on specific customer needs and on adapting the firm's products, prices, promotional effort, and other activities to meet these needs. The marketing concept, however, is also a philosophy that provides long-range direction and purpose for the organization, and in a market-oriented organization, marketing must be coordinated with other functional activities. Therefore, marketing decision making takes place at the top-management level. We should emphasize that the distinction between top management and middle management is found in the types of decisions they make, not only in their job titles. In small- and medium-sized organizations, the same individual may have both kinds of responsibilities. (See Table 1-1 for a brief outline of the two levels of marketing management.)

Although top-management and middle-management marketing personnel focus on different decisions, their activities are equally related to the marketing concept. That is, top management must identify general, long-term positions to ensure future customer satisfaction in a changing environment. The responsibility of middle management is to identify more specific, short-term actions to achieve customer satisfaction.[10] For example, in the automotive industry, the top management in most companies has identified fuel efficiency and product quality as priority long-term positions, whereas the designing and marketing of specific

[9]For example, Elizabeth Hirschman, "Aesthetics, Ideologies and the Limits of the Marketing Concept," *Journal of Marketing,* Summer 1983, pp. 45–55.

[10]Paul F. Anderson, "Marketing, Strategic Planning and the Theory of the Firm," *Journal of Marketing,* Spring 1982, pp. 15–26.

TABLE 1-1   THE TWO LEVELS OF MARKETING MANAGEMENT

These personnel	At this level	Make these decisions
Chief executive officer	Top management	Markets to be served
Comptroller		Products to offer
Vice president of marketing		Product objectives
Other vice presidents		Allocation of resources
Marketing managers	Middle management	Product design
Product and brand managers		Prices
Sales managers		Advertising
Advertising managers		Sales promotion
Promotion managers		Selling and distribution
Customer service managers		Customer service

products and features that meet current customer preferences is a middle-management responsibility.

As a general rule, *middle-management* decisions focus on the sales and profitability of individual products, brands, or lines of closely related products marketed as a group (such as Maytag's line of dishwashers or the various versions of Buick Regal). Action-oriented programs regarding advertising campaigns, sales promotions, prices, and product development, as well as sales-force activities directed at buyers or distributors, are generally the responsibility of middle managers.

Top-management decisions are those which provide the long-term direction of the organization regarding the markets and needs that will be served and the kinds of products that will be produced. (Examples of such decisions include Sears' entry into the credit card business and Singer's exit from the sewing machine business.) These decisions, termed *corporate strategies*, have a clear marketing component because they indicate the general kinds of customers to be created. They also have implications for the other functional areas because they influence future financing needs, research and development (R&D), production planning, and personnel development. Although corporate marketing planning is discussed in greater detail in Chapter 2, we should note here the basic purposes of top-management decisions.

- Establishing a basis for resolving conflicts among the marketing, finance, production, and R&D functions by providing general, companywide objectives
- Providing a basis for allocating scarce human and financial resources among major products or product lines
- Identifying the specific role that each product line is expected to play in achieving corporate sales and profit objectives

Although top-management and middle-management marketing personnel focus on different decisions, their activities are interrelated. First, middle managers can and should provide top management with information on sales and profit trends and on problems and opportunities existing in the marketplace for each product. This information is useful to top management in developing the overall corporate strategy. Second, the decisions made by top management will influence the difficulty of the tasks faced by middle managers.

Consider, for example, the information in Table 1-2. The three well-known corporations listed in this table are typical of most business organizations in that they operate in multiple markets with multiple products (both goods and services). Moreover, the chosen mix of businesses and the allocation of resources among these businesses is continually being evaluated. For example, in 1989, RJR Nabisco was seeking to sell the Del Monte line and shift financial resources away from certain products (Planters nuts, Nabisco products, and Winston cigarettes) and toward others (such as Grey Poupon and Camels). Such decisions certainly will impact the goals that middle-level marketing managers will be able to achieve as well as the range of tactics available to them. Apparently, managers responsible for the Nabisco lines were expected to emphasize short-term profit

TABLE 1-2   SOME MAJOR BUSINESSES AT LARGE CORPORATIONS*

Sears
  Sears retail stores
  Sears catalog business
  Dean Witter Investments
  Discover card
  Allstate Insurance

IBM
  Mainframe computers
  Minicomputer systems
  Personal computers
  Printers
  Software for computer users
  Typewriters

RJR Nabisco
  Tobacco (Camel, Winston, Salem cigarettes)
  Nabisco cookies and crackers
  Butterfingers and Baby Ruth candy bars
  Planters peanuts
  Milk Bone dog biscuits
  Del Monte canned fruits and vegetables
  A-1 Steak Sauce
  Grey Poupon mustard

*The rapid rate of change in corporate strategies all but assures that some of these businesses will be eliminated and new ones added every year or so.

gains while those product managers handling Camel were being encouraged to build market share.[11] Thus, while brand-level decisions such as advertising, product improvement, or sales-force strategy are generally considered to be middle-management decisions, they are shaped by top management's views about the roles various products are expected to play in the organization's long-term plan and by the resources allocated.

Major Obstacles Facing Middle-Management Marketers

As we have seen, top-management decisions can be critical to the welfare of an organization. Choosing an effective corporate strategy is a difficult task because markets tend to be dynamic and because it is not always easy to determine the time and resources required for success. However, even a well-conceived corporate strategy can fail because middle managers face several major obstacles in implementing the corporate strategy on a product-by-product basis.

First, selecting the correct marketing actions is not an easy task because customer needs are not always easy to identify. And not all customers (or potential customers) will respond in the same way to such marketing variables as price,

[11]Christine Donahue, "At RJR Nabisco, New Owner KKR Is Already Wielding the Knife," *Adweek's Marketing Week,* Aug. 21, 1989, pp. 4–5.

advertising campaigns, and product modifications. Consequently, managers need to know which group of buyers to focus their efforts on in attempting to create customers.

Second, marketing costs money. The cost of advertising, product-development investments, sales salaries, and many other financial resources may be required to serve the customer satisfactorily. However, the available resources and the profitability requirements established by top management often constrain middle managers' actions (as we discussed in the RJR Nabisco example).

Third, it is often difficult to evaluate all the possible alternatives because there are so many possible combinations to test or consider. For example, a manufacturer of personal computers might easily consider five alternative designs, two possible advertising themes, and four price levels. This would mean $5 \times 2 \times 4 = 40$ alternative combinations to assess, yet this is only a small fraction of the number of possible decisions and variations that might be considered.

Fourth, the various marketing decision areas are not independent but are interrelated with one another. For example, a cut in price may reinforce a new advertising campaign, or it may undercut the campaign if the advertising was designed to build an image of quality.

Fifth, marketers have limited control over outcomes because of environmental factors such as changes in the cost or availability of components or raw materials or changes in economic conditions (such as inflation or employment rates) which may influence the level of demand. Additionally, the rapid pace of technology and changing political/legal restrictions (such as deregulation of long-distance phone rates or the planned elimination of all trade barriers among Western European nations in 1992) can change the competitive situation in a market. Because of these uncertainties, decisions must often be revised after the results have been examined.

The foregoing obstacles are by no means a complete list. However, they do point up some basic issues confronting middle managers. Specifically, they imply the need for systematic approaches to defining the specific markets to be served, clarifying the relative importance of sales and profit objectives, reducing the number of possible marketing actions to a manageable number, and monitoring results in order to make appropriate modifications to decisions. To a large extent, resolving these issues requires interaction with top management. So, any systematic approach must be capable of including not only multiple decisions but also multiple decision-making levels. The systematic approach most widely employed in such situations, and the one around which this book is structured, is known as the *marketing planning* process.

THE MARKETING PLANNING PROCESS

Planning is merely a systematic way for an organization to attempt to control its future. A plan is essentially a statement of *what* the organization hopes to achieve, *how* to achieve it, and *when* it will be achieved. Virtually every marketing manager acknowledges the importance of planning, because the logic behind it is undeniable. In practice, however, planning often does not take place. One reason for this is that the results of planning are often long-term, and top management places a premium on immediate results. Another is that, because they are under considerable time pressure, the middle managers are more action-oriented than planning-oriented. Some organizations still lack a decision-making structure that facilitates planning.

In other organizations, however, planning is the *basis* of the management process. In general, these firms believe that planning

- Encourages systematic thinking about the future
- Leads to improved coordination
- Establishes performance standards for measuring results
- Provides a logical basis for decision making
- Improves the ability to cope with change
- Enhances the ability to identify marketing opportunities

Marketing planning is the systematic process for developing and coordinating marketing decisions. Because marketing decisions are made at two major levels—top management and middle management—the marketing planning process must operate at two levels (see Figure 1-2). Corporate marketing planning provides overall direction for the organization by specifying the products the firm will make and the markets it will pursue and by establishing the objectives to be

FIGURE 1-2   Linking corporate marketing planning to middle-management planning.

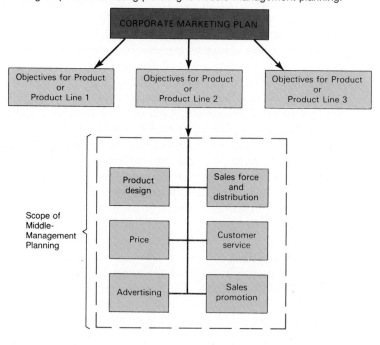

achieved by individual products. Often, firms use the term *strategic business units* (or SBUs) to represent these basic planning units. Middle-management planning specifies the details for implementing the corporate marketing plan on a product-by-product basis. Note that the corporate marketing planning process should provide the basic *direction* for middle management, and the middle-management planning process should *integrate* the various specialized marketing decisions made on behalf of each product. In other words, all marketing decisions should be made in the context of marketing plans. Only in this way can a firm coordinate the specialized middle-management roles and achieve its objectives.

Basic Steps in Planning

Although marketing planning takes place at both the corporate level and the middle-management level, four basic steps are involved at each level (see Figure 1-3).

1 *Conducting a situation analysis*. Before developing any action plan, decision makers must understand the current situation and trends affecting the future of the organization. In particular, they must assess the *problems and opportunities* posed by buyers, competitors, costs, and regulatory changes. Additionally, they must identify the *strengths and weaknesses* possessed by the firm.

2 *Establishing objectives*. Having completed the situation analysis, the decision makers must then establish specific objectives. Objectives identify the level of performance the organization hopes to achieve at some future date, given the realities of the environmental problems and opportunities and the firm's particular strengths and weaknesses.

3 *Developing strategies and programs*. To achieve the stated objectives, decision makers must develop both strategies (long-term actions to achieve the objectives) and programs (specific short-term actions to implement the strategies).

4 *Providing coordination and control*. Plans that are fairly comprehensive often include multiple strategies and programs. Each strategy and each program may be the responsibility of a different manager. Thus, some mechanism must be developed to assure that the strategies and programs are effectively implemented.

FIGURE 1-3 Basic steps in planning.

Conduct a Situation Analysis

Establish Objectives

Develop Strategies and Programs

Provide Coordination and Control

Organizational structures and budgets are the primary means for coordinating actions. Control is also essential because the success of strategies and programs can never be predicted with certainty. The purpose of control is to evaluate the degree to which progress toward an objective is being made and to pinpoint the causes of any failure to achieve objectives so that remedial actions can be taken.

One further point about planning must be noted. Planning is a *process*. Organizations operate in complex and dynamic environments. Therefore, as the situation changes, managers must be prepared to modify objectives and strategies to deal with those changes.

Marketing Management and the Marketing Planning Process

Marketing management encompasses all of the decisions involved in designing and executing marketing plans in order to implement the marketing concept. As we have indicated, marketing decisions are made by top management and by middle managers, and decisions made at these two levels are interrelated. Accordingly, both levels will be examined in this book, although our focus is primarily on decision making at the middle-management level.[12]

More specifically, subsequent chapters will examine the kinds of information, concepts, tools, and procedures marketing managers can employ in decision making. As Figure 1-4 indicates, these decision areas are treated within the framework of the marketing planning process. Chapter 2 examines procedures for developing the situation analysis, objectives, and strategies at the corporate level. Additionally, a major outcome of corporate marketing planning is the development of product objectives that guide decision making at the middle management level. This is also covered in Chapter 2.

In Chapters 3 to 6, we will examine techniques and procedures for conducting a situation analysis at the individual-product level.

Our primary focus in Chapters 7 to 13 is on developing marketing strategies and programs that will achieve the product objective and that take into account the problems and opportunities uncovered in the situation analysis.

Finally, Chapters 14 and 15 present procedures for coordination and control at both the middle-management and top-management levels.

In examining Figure 1-4, the reader should note the direction of the arrows linking the major sections. That some arrows go in both directions between two sections reflects two important points. First, in a well-managed organization, top management will use the insights of middle management as an important input to corporate strategy. Information on the situation analysis for a given product and on the feasibility of developing a successful marketing strategy for a product is

---

[12]For a more complex view of the planning process that incorporates a multilevel review, see Richard F. Vancil and Peter Larange, "Strategic Planning in Diversified Companies," *Harvard Business Review,* January–February 1975, pp. 81–90.

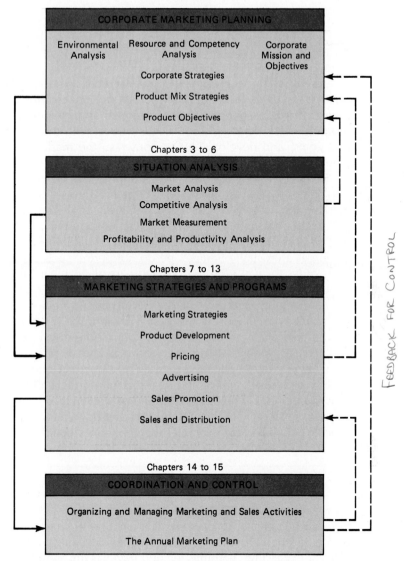

Marketing management and the marketing planning process: An overview.

usually more detailed at the middle-management level and should be communicated to top management.

Second, the control function has a primary purpose of alerting managers to the need for changes in objectives, strategies, or programs. This feedback is denoted by the dashed lines.

CONCLUSION

The marketing concept serves as our starting point for examining marketing management because this concept reflects the basic purpose of a business. Without giving effective attention to customer needs, marketing and the other business functions will lack the direction needed for success.

It is important to recognize, however, that a market-oriented organization is one that takes its lead from the *market,* not necessarily from the *marketing department.* Market-oriented firms acquire an understanding of their customers, determine which customers and needs fit best with the organization's capabilities and goals, and develop their responses to the marketplace in a highly coordinated fashion.

Even in a market-oriented organization, however, it is not a simple matter to implement the marketing concept. Organizations are faced with many alternative markets and customers and with a vast array of alternative policies and programs for meeting customer needs. Organizations cannot pursue *all* possible buyers, and *all* possible marketing actions cannot be taken because human and financial resources are usually limited and do not permit such extravagance.

In order to deal with the problems involved in implementing the marketing concept, a planning approach has been suggested. Conducting a situation analysis and setting objectives before developing strategies and programs improves the chances for choosing the best marketing policies. Further, planning really should take place on two levels. At the middle-management level, planning focuses on an individual product or on a line of related products. At the top-management level, planning focuses on the broad questions of "What business should we be in?" and on the total mix of products and product lines.

It is important to recognize that all firms, even those with a long-term record of success, must vigilantly maintain a market-orientation and an effective planning process. Consider, for example, the challenges confronting IBM.

IBM: Renewing a Market-Orientation*

Between 1979 and 1989, IBM's share of the worldwide computer market slipped from 44 percent to 30 percent. This decline in share coincided with a gradual decline in the industry's rate of growth in sales of computing hardware. As a result, the company's earnings fell and IBM has engaged in several early retirement incentive programs to reduce costs.

Industry analysts noted a number of problems that led to IBM's decline in

*Developed from Deidre A. Depke, Susan M. Gelfond, and John W. Verity, "Suddenly, Software Houses Have A Big Buddy," *Business Week,* Aug. 7, 1989, pp. 68–69; David Kalish, "IBM's Brand Stand," *Marketing and Media Decisions,* May 1989, pp. 71–73; Steve Kaufman, "IBM Cuts Show Computer Sector Woes," *Chicago Tribune,* Dec. 7, 1989, sec. 2, p. 3; Gary Levin and Alan Radding, "IBM Mulling Brand Setup," *Advertising Age,* Aug. 8, 1988, p. 1; Patricia Sellers, "How IBM Teaches Techies to Sell," *Fortune,* June 6, 1988, pp. 141–146; Gary McWilliams, "Selling IBM on Solutions Selling," *Datamation,* Jan. 1, 1988, pp. 57–59; Ira Sager, "IBM Ties U.S. Marketing, Manufacturing in Realignment," *Electronic News,* Feb. 1, 1988, pp. 1 and 4.

share. One problem often cited was that IBM's product-development organizations became isolated from emerging customer needs and were thus slow to bring new products to market. Another problem was a lack of coordination between marketing and research and development, resulting in a number of unsuccessful introductions. For example, the PCjr failed in part because consumers found the "chiclet" keyboard to be a problem; a laptop computer failed because of insufficient memory; and a technical workstation, the RT PC, lacked sufficient power to compete against products made by workstation specialists such as Sun Computer. Finally, while IBM had focused its marketing efforts on selling hardware, customers have been increasingly concerned with obtaining good advice and software to solve specific business problems and with networking—the development of systems by which different computer sizes and brands can communicate with one another. IBM was considered to be weaker than competitors such as Digital Equipment in the ability to develop networks, and had never been considered a leader in software development—especially for midsize and smaller computers.

IBM has attempted to respond to these developments in several ways. First, the company invested in or formed marketing arrangements with hundreds of small software companies in order to expand its software product line to provide the solutions desired by customers. Second, the company's development team established a systems application architecture, a set of technical rules and guidelines for designing interconnections among programs and various computers to enhance networking capabilities. Third, the company initiated a stronger emphasis on naming its products as part of a new advertising strategy in order to emphasize its sensitivity to customers' requirements. As a consequence new products will carry market-oriented names. (Thus, a new touch-sensitive screen is called *Info Window* instead of *4055 Display Unit*.) Fourth, market research has been stepped up. The new AS/400 midrange computer was pretested with customers then revised to incorporate use-related suggestions before its 1988 introduction.

Finally, a major reorganization of IBM was announced in 1988. Five divisions were established (instead of the previous four):

- IBM Enterprise Systems—focusing on large-scale mainframe computers
- IBM Applications Business Systems—covering midrange products like the AS/400
- IBM Personal Systems—including typewriters and all personal computers
- IBM Communication Systems—all communication products and operating systems software
- IBM Technology Products—responsible for semiconductors

Management hoped that the new organization would more closely integrate development, manufacturing, and marketing. It was anticipated that some units would be able to develop their own marketing and advertising strategies. Simultaneously, the IBM sales force was reorganized so that marketing representatives specialized in a type of customer such as retail, manufacturing, or finance. These

marketing representatives are backed up by a technical team charged with identifying software solutions for the needs of individual companies and industries.

1 Which of IBM's initiatives reflect top-management decisions and which reflect middle-management decisions?

2 Discuss how these two levels of decisions are related.

3 Which of IBM's organizational changes is most likely to lead to a turn-
around for the company?

4 If a customer-orientation is critical to success, how could IBM have become
a large, successful company and then later be viewed as a company that was not
customer-oriented?

Δ CUSTOMER NEEDS → S/W, NETWORKING, TIME TO MARKET — No LONGER H/W

QUESTIONS AND SITUATIONS FOR DISCUSSION

1 "If firms practiced the marketing concept, all new products would be based on extensive consumer research and few products would not be successful." Do you agree or
disagree? Explain your answer.

2 Why should the functions of finance, production, and research and development have
coequal status with marketing?

3 "Repair service is more a function of production than marketing, just as the extension
of credit is more a function of finance than marketing." Do you agree or disagree with
this statement? Explain.

4 How would you answer the business manager of the local symphony if he or she made
the following statement? "At times, I've thought about using marketing more in our
affairs, but I simply cannot afford the cost of surveys and advertising campaigns. Anyway, people will always come to hear good music. The quality of our programs is the
only important consideration."

5 How would you explain the marketing concept to a university official who is interested in applying it to noncredit programs offered in several urban communities?

6 The 3M Company has 50,000 products ranging from Scotch tape to heart-lung machines. How would formal marketing planning differ in 3M from a company having
only a few products?

7 In Chapter 1, several obstacles facing middle-management marketers were cited.
Which ones would be most significant in managing each of the following:
a One brand of toothpaste for a company producing five brands in the category?
b A hospital belonging to a national chain?
c A new line of high-definition television sets that offer far superior picture and sound
quality compared to existing models?

8 Develop a list of possible top-management issues that might be considered by the
McDonald's Corporation. What middle-management issues would this firm likely deal
with?

9 Would marketing planning be more difficult for the Ford Motor Company or for
Steelcase (a leading manufacturer of office furniture)? Why? For which company
would marketing planning be more important? Taking both answers into consideration, what generalization would you make about the usefulness of planning?

10 In 1917, the DeVries Brothers formed a chemical manufacturing company located in Holland, Michigan. This company grew over the years to become a major producer and manufacturer of fertilizers and chemicals. In many of the product lines, DeVries held the leading market share. Chemicals were sold under their own brand names and were added to various feeds to protect against diseases and to stimulate growth. Then the leading competitor (Chase Chemical) improved production facilities by installing modern processing equipment that was faster than that of DeVries. As a result, Chase Chemical was able to meet customer specifications so quickly that they soon replaced DeVries as the industry leader.

DeVries responded to the competitive change in several ways. Historically, they used the crystalline method of manufacturing their chemicals. Quickly they added new tablet, liquid, and powdered forms. They also ordered new process equipment to increase the speed of their production runs. At about the same time they brought in all of their salespeople from the six regions to a general sales meeting. At this meeting several things were covered. Among the major points were: (1) briefing on new forms of products, (2) briefing on new process machinery purchases, (3) review of new products and emphasis on the importance of increasing sales, (4) price lists and future advertising support for new product forms, and (5) motivation to restore DeVries to its leading position in the industry.

Initial (second-quarter) sales of the new forms were poor. Company officials had been optimistic that sales would be much higher and asked district managers to account for such low sales. District managers reported that potential buyers and purchasing agents asked highly technical questions about the new product forms which salespeople were unprepared to answer. To rectify this situation, technical people were assigned to assist salespeople when encountering such problems. Management felt this would correct the problem and anticipated a much higher level of sales for the third quarter of the year.

When sales figures were reviewed, results were disappointing. A 3 percent increase over the previous quarter was evidence to the national sales manager that new salespeople whose principal job would be to sell the product forms were necessary. This, combined with a series of advertisements emphasizing the greater effectiveness of the new product forms, as opposed to the crystalline products, was viewed as the solution to the poor reception by the market.

Fourth-quarter results indicated a 5 percent sales increase over the second quarter. Management felt that it was time to coordinate all marketing activities in the sale of their products and created a new position of marketing manager. Although they would have preferred to promote from within the company, they felt that no one had a broad marketing viewpoint and sought someone from outside. After a short search, Mr. Warren Brown was hired for the position.

Mr. Brown had previously worked in chemical sales with a leading industrial chemical firm. He had held a variety of staff positions with this same company, including marketing development and sales research and analysis and had been involved in the development and marketing of several new products as a member of a new product group. In reviewing the DeVries difficulties, he felt that it was necessary to undertake a study of actual sales as well as sales potential for the industry. This study was completed by a member of the staff and forwarded to Mr. Brown for his review.

Brown, after his review, concluded that DeVries should not have anticipated increased sales as a result of the new product variations as there had been inadequate identification of the appropriate target markets for these products. In addition, in reviewing production schedules, he found that scheduling these new variations had resulted in slowing down the production of the crystalline forms. Sales analyses showed that customers purchasing the new product variations were smaller operators and these products were a negligible portion of their operation. This resulted in higher costs for order processing and, in many cases, these orders appeared to be unprofitable.

Brown felt that it was necessary to concentrate on the original product line and phase out the new variations. In preparing his recommendation, he also felt it was necessary to establish procedures to avoid such a situation in the future.

a What do you think of DeVries's planning process?

b What do you think the proper approach should have been?

c Do you feel that the sales force's lack of technical expertise contributed to the lackluster performance and should this have been anticipated?

SUGGESTED ADDITIONAL READINGS

Bonoma, Thomas V., "Marketing Subversives," *Harvard Business Review,* November–December 1986, pp. 113–118.

Gilliatt, Neal, and Pamela Cuming, "The Chief Marketing Officer: A Maverick Whose Time Has Come," *Business Horizons,* January–February 1986, pp. 41–48.

Houston, Franklin S., "The Marketing Concept: What It Is Not," *Journal of Marketing,* April 1986, pp. 81–87.

Jackson, Barbara Bund, "Build Customer Relationships That Last," *Harvard Business Review,* November–December 1985, pp. 120–128.

Levitt, Theodore, "Marketing When Things Change," *Harvard Business Review,* November–December 1977, pp. 107–113.

Payne, Adrian, "Developing a Marketing-Oriented Organization," *Business Horizons,* May–June 1988, pp. 46–53.

Shapiro, Benson, "What the Hell Is 'Market Oriented'?" *Harvard Business Review,* November–December 1988, pp. 119–125.

Stasch, Stanley F., and Patricia Lanktree, "Can Your Marketing Planning Procedures Be Improved?" *Journal of Marketing,* Summer 1980, pp. 79–90.

Walker, Orville, and Robert Ruekert, "Marketing's Role in the Implementation of Business Strategies: A Critical Review and Conceptual Framework," *Journal of Marketing,* July 1987, pp. 15–33.

Wilson, Ian, William George, and Paul Solomon, "Strategic Planning for Marketers," *Business Horizons,* December 1978, pp. 65–73.

CHAPTER 2

CORPORATE MARKETING PLANNING

OVERVIEW

In Chapter 1, we noted that the successful marketing of a good or a service depends first of all on having a sound understanding of the market. Additionally, success depends on how many resources (human, technological, and financial) are applied in developing a market offer and on how effectively these resources are used.

In a small, highly specialized firm these decisions are relatively simple. However, in firms that offer an array of products serving a set of diverse markets, effective implementation of the marketing concept is complicated by two factors. First, some mechanism must be developed for allocating scarce resources across products. Second, the organization's effectiveness in applying these resources is not likely to be equal in all products and markets: Few firms will have the ability to be equally effective meeting the needs of all the markets they serve.

Corporate marketing planning is the process by which an organization sets its long-term priorities regarding products and markets in order to enhance the value of the overall company. Two kinds of top-management decisions are involved in corporate marketing planning—*corporate strategy* and *product mix strategy* (see Figure 2-1). In corporate strategy, management identifies the businesses in which the company will be involved in the future by specifying:

- The range of markets to be served
- The kinds of products to be offered

In making corporate strategy decisions, the critical question to be answered is "In

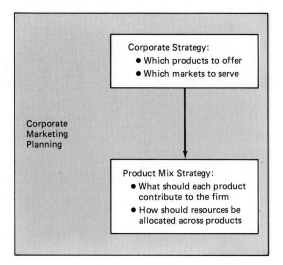

FIGURE 2-1 Elements of corporate marketing planning.

what markets will our particular resources be most effective in implementing the marketing concept?''

Once a corporate strategy has been chosen, management must develop a product mix strategy to identify the role each product is expected to play in building the value of the business. In particular, this strategy will usually specify

• The relative share of the firm's resources to be devoted to each product or product line
• The kind of contribution (such as rapid sales growth or high profitability) that each product or product line is expected to make toward building the company's value

Importantly, from the *middle* manager's perspective, the product mix strategy provides guidance concerning top management's expectations. As we discuss throughout this book, knowing the role the product is expected to play in the overall corporate picture is essential to the development of marketing strategies and programs.

The purpose of this chapter is to identify the various corporate strategies and product mix strategies available to top management and to present procedures and tools for developing a corporate marketing plan. We will also consider the relationship between corporate-level decisions and the marketing planning process at the middle-management level.

CORPORATE STRATEGY

When a new organization is formed, it is often oriented toward the production or sale (or both) of a single product, a single service, or a line of closely related products and services and, frequently, the name of the organization conveys the nature of the firm's business. Consider, however, the history of Stora Kopparberg AB.

> In 1988, the Swedish company Stora Kopparberg AB (The Great Copper Mountain Mining Company) celebrated its 700th anniversary as a continuously operating company. Actually, the mine had existed for 200 years when Bishop Peter of Vasteras purchased it in 1288 and applied "modern" water wheel technology to power the mine and greatly increase productivity. While the original mine remains open today for sentimental reasons, most of Stora's other mining and steel interests have been eliminated. Stora is now primarily devoted to the manufacture of packaging board and fine papers, and to a recently acquired consumer products company.[1]

Obviously, few companies have as storied a history as Stora Kopparberg AB. However, the experience of having a major change in products produced and markets served is shared by most large organizations. Goodyear produces chemicals and plastics as well as tires. Sears has an insurance business and also deals in automotive repair and financial services. Cigarette maker Philip Morris owns a leading beer company (Miller Brewing) and a line of razor blades. Even smaller, local firms are often multiproduct, multimarket operations; a Maine potato farmer may own an automobile dealership, or a Midwestern real estate firm, a nursery. In this section of the chapter, we discuss how corporate strategies are selected and why they change. Subsequently, we examine the major types of corporate strategy that a firm can pursue and the reasons why each type might be chosen.

Factors Affecting Corporate Strategy

As we indicated at the start of this chapter, corporate strategies are long-range plans designed to select the various businesses a company should be in. They identify the markets to be served (defining them in terms of needs or customers or both) and the product lines and services to be produced on the basis of an assessment of the company's environment, resources, and objectives.

As portrayed in Figure 2-2, corporate strategies should be derived from the analysis of three elements: environmental problems and opportunities, corporate mission and objectives, and organizational resources and competencies. A corporate strategy should be consistent with a company's objectives and achievable with existing (or anticipated) resources. Further, it should take into account prospective problems and opportunities in the environment.

Environmental Problems and Opportunities

All organizations operate in a dynamic environment which can create a variety of problems or opportunities in the firm's existing or potential markets. Specifically, managers should be aware of the possible impact of six major environmental forces.

---

[1]"1988 Concerns for 1288 Firm," *Chicago Tribune,* July 5, 1988.

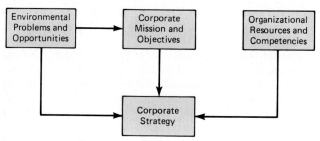

FIGURE 2-2   Factors influencing corporate strategy.

1 *Demographic characteristics,* such as the age distribution of the population, birth rates, population growth, regional population shifts, and the percentage of two-worker households.

2 *Social and cultural values,* such as attitudes toward health and nutrition, the need for self-expression, materialism, ecological concerns, product safety.

3 *Economic factors,* including inflation and unemployment rates, economic growth, raw material scarcities, energy costs, interest rates, import duties, and excise taxes.

4 *Technology,* particularly developing and anticipated changes that have an impact on the kinds of products available in a market and the kinds of processes (such as automation or the use of synthetic materials) used to produce these products.

5 *Legal and regulatory actions,* including such factors as regulations (and deregulation) regarding the type of advertising available to a product, product labeling and testing requirements, limitations regarding product contents, pollution control, restrictions or incentives with respect to imports or exports.

6 *Competition,* which to a large extent is a function of the other environmental forces. Specifically, both the *identity* of competitors and the type of focus (for example, price-oriented versus technology-oriented) of competition may change because of

- The entry of new firms (especially foreign firms)
- The acquisition of a small competitor by a large, well-financed organization
- Deregulation, changing economic conditions, or new production processes which foster increased price competition
- Changing social and cultural values or new technology which causes buyers to purchase products or services previously considered noncompetitive

An examination of these forces is essential to the development of corporate strategies because these factors will shape the attractiveness of various businesses. Often such factors will create new opportunities or lead to the rejuvenation of markets. Consider, for example, the recent developments in the market for lawn and garden products.

Sales of lawn and garden products grew 29% between 1985 and 1988. However, the changes taking place in this market go beyond the increased sales growth rate and do not simply reflect the aging U.S. population. While, traditionally, the average age of gardeners has been around 50, the recent spurt in growth has come from baby boomers in their 30's and 40's. Some observers have suggested that this is a reflection of social trends shaping babyboomers' lives: Many have recently bought new homes and started families that keep them closer to home, and gardening can be seen as an expression of the same concerns about health and the purity of food and water that have bolstered sales of bottled water and organic foods. Additionally, baby boomers have brought to this market the same buying concerns evident in their purchases of automobiles, clothing and many other products: a quality-orientation, a strong sense of design, and a desire for convenience. Meeting these needs requires many new products. Water soluble hose attachments permit spray fertilizing during watering to save time and the Teknor Apex company has begun selling garden hoses in a variety of colors so buyers can coordinate them with patio furniture.[2]

Additionally, multiple environmental influences are even more dramatic when a firm broadens its perspective globally.

Except in Japan, most Asian nations have populations in which young people are dominant. The percentages of "under-24" persons in China, Indonesia, and the Philippines are 48.5%, 56.3%, and 60% respectively. This has resulted in huge market opportunities for companies such as Coca-Cola, McDonald's, and Nike, all of whom have increased the attention given to these markets. But population changes seldom operate in a vacuum from other environmental changes. In Japan, younger women especially have different attitudes about their role in society and the purchase of some products (such as California wines) have been seen as symbols of their new independence.[3]

Finally, dynamic competitive forces are increasingly disrupting the established order of things, and are complicated by changes in technology and government actions.

In 1992, the European Common Market nations are scheduled to eliminate all remaining tariffs and other trade barriers among the member countries. For electronics firms such as West Germany's giant Siemen's, this means the loss of protective barriers at home for its telecommunications and information processing markets. Additionally, Siemen's has had to develop its own capability for designing and producing its key component, random access memory chips because it could not obtain the latest in high speed processors from its Japanese suppliers—the same firms it had begun to compete with in the telecommunications market. And in 1991, the company faced yet another "deregulatory" challenge as the German government deregulated all telecommunications prices. Previously, with its protection from both domestic and foreign competition, Siemens sold cordless phones through the state phone company for $665 vs. prices as low as $80 for some Japanese brands sold in the United States.[4]

Because environmental changes result in changing *opportunities* and changing *threats,* they are fundamental considerations in the development of corporate

[2]Nancy Youman, "The Lawn and Garden Boom," *Adweek's Marketing Week,* July 24, 1989, pp. 18–23.
[3]Jon Berry, "Asia Minors," *Adweek's Marketing Week,* July 17, 1989, pp. 32–40.
[4]Gail Schares, John J. Keller, Thane Peterson, and Mark Maremont, "Siemens: A Plodding Giant Starts to Pick Up Speed," *Business Week,* Feb. 20, 1989, pp. 136–138.

strategies. However, not all firms are equal in terms of their ability to take advantage of an opportunity or to avoid a threatening situation. A second fundamental consideration in selecting a corporate strategy is whether the firm possesses the resources and competencies required to take advantage of opportunities and to avoid damaging situations.

Resources and Competencies

In developing a corporate strategy, top management should also analyze the resources that will be available to the organization. In the broadest sense, resources include

- Financial resources, such as cash reserves
- Labor and managerial skills, such as the ability to produce high-technology products or to manage large advertising budgets
- Production capacity and the efficiency of equipment
- Research and development skills and patents
- Control over key raw materials, as in the ownership of energy resources
- Size and expertise of the sales force or distribution system

Too often firms limit their evaluation of resources to the more tangible ones, such as cash and facilities. Yet management and marketing capabilities are often more important. For example, Frito-Lay's success in the snack business is due primarily to effective advertising management and its extensive sales force which rotates and replenishes the stock in the retail stores. These competencies enhance the company's ability to continue to bring successful new products to the marketplace—a necessity in a market where product variety is important to the buyer.

The idea of relying on a firm's strongest resources is generally referred to as using a *distinctive competency*, and in selecting from potential corporate strategies, a firm should usually rely on its distinctive competencies or on competencies that it can acquire. Table 2-1 suggests some ways in which various distinctive competencies can be effectively employed.

TABLE 2-1   DISTINCTIVE COMPETENCIES AND POTENTIAL USES

Competency	Potential use
Financial resources	Acquiring other businesses
R&D capability	Emphasizing high technology in product development and diversification
Unique raw materials resources	Emphasizing products that require these resources
Company reputation for quality	Selecting markets where reputation is known
Strong sales force	Selecting new products that can be sold by same sales force

Corporate Mission and Objectives

In most organizations, strategic decisions are guided by some statements of corporate mission and/or corporate objectives. Corporate mission refers to the broad purposes the organization serves and provides general criteria for assessing *long-run* organizational effectiveness. Consider, for example, the following statements expressing the mission of Hershey Foods Corporation.

> As a major diversified company, we are in business to make a reasonable profit and adequate return on our investment and to enhance the value of our shareholders' investment.... In seeking to balance our desire for profitable growth with the obligations which we have to our other various constituencies...
>
> • We pursue profitable growth by maintaining excellence in our current businesses.
> • Growth opportunities are actively sought from within and outside the Corporation in areas which capitalize upon our strengths.
> • We constantly strive for positions of market leadership.[5]

Corporate objectives reflect management's specific expectations regarding organizational performance. Table 2-2 lists some of the more common types of corporate objectives which might be established. Remember that an organization

[5]Hershey Foods Corporation, "Statement of Corporate Philosophy" July 8, 1988.

TABLE 2-2   COMMON TYPES OF CORPORATE OBJECTIVES

Profitability

- Net profit as a percent of sales
- Net profit as a percent of total investment
- Net profit per share of common stock

Volume

- Market share
- Percentage growth in sales
- Sales rank in the market
- Production capacity utilization

Stability

- Variance in annual sales volume
- Variance in seasonal sales volume
- Variance in profitability

Nonfinancial

- Maintenance of family control
- Improved corporate image
- Enhancement of technology or quality of life

may have more than one objective at a given time. However, there is usually only one primary goal toward which the corporate strategy can be directed.

As the environment changes, organizations often modify their missions and objectives. For example, the elimination of many regulations in the banking industry and an increase in the number of types of financial investment products (such as Money Market Accounts) have led many firms to broaden their missions. Thus, many banks now view themselves as "financial institutions." Similarly, changes in technology or the natural extension of existing technology can create an opportunity for broadening the definition of a business. The regional telephone companies (the so-called Baby Bells) created from American Telephone and Telegraph Corporation's (AT&T's) old local telephone business are no longer "telephone companies" but telecommunications firms, with involvement in office automation, data systems, and a host of other goods and services with related technological bases.

It is important to recognize that there may be built-in conflict when a firm tries to achieve more than one objective. For example, a small business that sets sales growth as a primary goal may find that working capital and production facilities must be dramatically increased to meet rising demand. To acquire the investment funds to support this expansion, the firm may be forced to take on new investors—an action that could conflict with an objective of maintaining family control.

> Interlego A/S, the Danish company that makes Lego blocks for children, is a family-owned business that has stuck to a plan of slow, steady growth with a single product line. While many strategists would argue that it is risky to put "all your eggs in one basket," the company uses astute marketing and product enhancements to maintain its market position without resorting to costly investments in diversifications that would stretch the family's financial resources.[6]

Moreover, a long-range goal of profitability or increased sales may only be achieved if short-run sacrifices are made. For example, Greyhound Corporation sold its Armour Food subsidiary (which accounted for nearly one-half of its sales) in order to improve its return on investment and to generate funds for investing in businesses which promise higher long-range sales growth.

In sum, the process of developing a corporate strategy is based on

- Examining environmental problems and opportunities
- Selecting corporate objectives that are consistent with these problems and opportunities
- Examining the resources and distinctive competencies that can be used in implementing the strategy

Figure 2-2 portrays the relationship among these factors.

Although this process appears rather simple, any number of corporate strategies are available to top management. Only by understanding the different types

---

[6]Hesh Kestin, "Nothing Like a Dane," *Forbes*, Nov. 3, 1986, pp. 145–148.

of strategies available can managers effectively select the ones most appropriate for a particular firm's situation.

Types of Corporate Strategy

Organizations have two fundamental directions in which to proceed when selecting a corporate strategy: growth or consolidation. Traditionally, organizations have pursued *growth strategies,* even when sales growth was not the primary corporate objective. Essentially, a growth strategy is one in which sales growth (usually from new products and markets) becomes a vehicle for achieving stability or enhanced profitability, as well as sales growth.

In recent years, however, both large and small organizations have begun to realize that unbridled and random growth can create as many problems as it solves. *Consolidation strategies,* in which firms seek to achieve current goals (especially enhanced profits) through nongrowth means have, accordingly, become increasingly popular.

Table 2-3 summarizes the basic types of corporate strategy and shows the specific kinds of strategies in each category.

Growth Strategies for Current Markets

A firm that finds many opportunities and few problems in its present markets is likely to select some form of current-market strategy. Top management may find such problems as a scarcity of raw materials, new competition, or technological change, but if, in spite of these problems, the current markets are attractive in sales growth, sales stability, or profitability, the corporate strategy may still focus on the current market.

TABLE 2-3 BASIC TYPES OF CORPORATE STRATEGY

Growth strategies
For current markets:
• Market penetration
• Product development
• Vertical integration
For new markets:
• Market development
• Market expansion
• Diversification
• Strategic alliances
Consolidation strategies
• Retrenchment
• Pruning
• Divestment

The three strategies that focus on current markets are

- Market penetration
- Product development
- Vertical integration

Market Penetration   The term *market penetration* refers to a strategy in which a firm expands its marketing effort to increase sales of existing products in its current markets. Typically, market penetration is achieved by increasing the level of marketing effort (as by increasing advertising or distribution) or by lowering prices.

Indeed, the sales potential of many products goes unrealized because the company is too small to initiate such efforts. As a result, large firms often acquire such products and then engage in the proper market-penetration efforts. For example, sales of Gatorade expanded dramatically after Quaker Oats acquired the brand in 1983 and sharply expanded advertising and distribution.

Because market penetration requires no change in either a firm's products or markets, it is essentially a *status quo* strategy. As long as current performance is sound and as long as the environment remains supportive of growth and profit opportunities, a firm may want to stick with its basic business. But even in growing or highly profitable markets, some adjustments to the product offering will usually become necessary because of environmental changes.

Product Development   Product-development strategies involve the development of new products for existing markets in order to

- Meet changing customer needs and wants
- Match new competitive offerings
- Take advantage of new technology
- Meet the needs of specific market segments

Typically, this strategy involves replacing or reformulating existing products or expanding the product line. Usually, product development is appropriate when changing needs and tastes result in the emergence of new segments or when competitive and technological changes motivate firms to modify their product lines.

Consider, for example, the actions of firms in the automotive and battery markets.

Toyota and Nissan introduced their Lexus and Infiniti models in large part due to an increase in the relative demand for luxury sedans at the expense of compact cars. As the United States market matured, the Corolla buyer of the 1970's became the Camry buyer of the 1980's. As one Toyota executive saw things, the same group would be the heart of the luxury market in the 1990's.[7]

In March of 1989, Varta, a West Germany battery maker, introduced a new line of

[7]Wendy Zellner, "The Coming Jam in the Luxury Lane," *Business Week,* Jan. 30, 1989, p. 78.

batteries which contained no mercury or cadmium. Those chemicals can be hard to dispose of and are toxic in large quantities. Since this introduction, Varta's share of the $120 million British supermarket business has increased from 5% to 15%. Approximately at the same time, Swedish pulp and paper maker Svenske Cellulosa introduced Britain's first diapers made from pulp that is bleached without using toxic chlorine gas. The product quickly increased their market share from 10% to 13% of the British $500 million dollar market. Both of these decisions were responses to the "Green" Consumer Movement in Europe toward ecologically safe consumer products.[8]

Vertical Integration   To enhance a firm's effectiveness or efficiency in serving existing markets, vertical integration strategies are selected. Such integration is often accomplished when a firm becomes its own supplier (in *backward integration*) or intermediary (in *forward integration*). As a general rule, these strategies will be most appropriate when the ultimate markets are projected as having high growth potential, because the resources required to implement these strategies are usually extensive. Some specific types and purposes of vertical integration strategies can be seen in the following examples.

> Villeroy & Boch is a 240-year-old German maker of fine china. Although it is the world's largest ceramics manufacturer, it has been relatively unknown in the United States, partly because of weak marketing by its traditional department store retailers. Consequently, the company has opened its own retail stores to enhance the effectiveness with which its vast assortment is merchandised.[9]
>
> The forward integration strategy of Quaker State Corp. (a motor oil company) in acquiring the chain of stations owned by McQuik's Oilube Inc. assures the company of a high-volume outlet for its product.
>
> IBM continues to manufacture its own semiconductors to assure that it does not become dependent on Japanese producers with respect to prices or access to the latest technology because semiconductors are vital components of computers.

Although vertical integration seems to be a fairly low-risk strategy, in practice it is not nearly as simple as other current market strategies. For example, the managerial and marketing skills required for forward integration into retailing of clothing are far different from those involved in the manufacturing of clothing. Similarly, backward integration may backfire if a firm cannot produce its own supplies efficiently.

Growth Strategies for New Markets

In examining environmental forces and sales trends, top management may conclude that the sales growth, sales stability, or profitability of current markets will be unsatisfactory in the future. Such a conclusion will lead these firms to seek out new markets that will present better opportunities.

---

[8]Shawn Tully, "What the Greens Mean for Business," *Fortune International*, Oct. 23, 1989, pp. 46–52.
[9]Tatiana Pouschine, "We Will Remove the Cobwebs," *Forbes*, Aug. 22, 1988, pp. 56–58.

In entering new markets, four kinds of corporate strategies can be used: market development, market expansion, diversification, and strategic alliances.

Market Development   The market-development strategy represents an effort to bring current products to new markets. Typically, management will employ this strategy when existing markets are stagnant, and when market-share increases are difficult to achieve because market shares are already very high or because competitors are very powerful. This strategy can be implemented by identifying new uses or new users, as the following examples show.

> Arm & Hammer has long held a dominant market share of the baking soda market. However, this market had been growing very slowly until the company began to promote additional uses of its product (most of which were suggested by regular customers), such as cleaning toilets or deodorizing refrigerators.
>
> Apple Computer Inc. achieved its initial success in the home and education markets. During the middle and late 1980's the company found that the home computer market was really an extension of the business market—a market that Apple had largely ignored. At the same time, Apple's strong presence in the education market would be difficult to expand. Consequently, the company began to focus more attention on developing software that would enable its Macintosh line to meet the needs of new users such as lawyers, engineers, government agencies and others who could readily benefit from its graphics capabilities.[10]

Market Expansion   A market expansion strategy involves moving into a new geographic market area. Many firms originate as regional competitors and later move into other areas of the country. For example, Coors beer was sold only in the western part of the nation for many years and Borden's has recently taken its Creamette's line of pasta products from a Midwestern base to nearly national distribution.

Today, however, market expansion is more likely to be international in scope, and frequently this is the growth strategy most likely to achieve rapid gains in volume. Procter & Gamble officials expected overseas sales to reach 50 percent of total sales by the 1990s from 28 percent in 1978 and 38 percent in 1988, for instance.[11] International market expansion can be pursued at one of three levels: regional strategy, multinational strategy, or global strategy.[12]

A *regional* strategy implies that a company will concentrate its resources and efforts in one or two areas. Thus, Fiat of Italy has historically competed primarily in Europe and Latin America. This strategy generally is employed when a firm intends to rely primarily on its home base for business.

---

[10]Len Strazewski, "Apple Uses New Marketing Strategy to Take a Slice of Competition's Pie," *Marketing News,* June 19, 1989, p. 7.

[11]Alecia Swasy, "After Early Stumbles, P&G Is Making Inroads Overseas," *The Wall Street Journal,* Feb. 6, 1989, p. B1.

[12]This discussion is based in part on Jean-Pierre Jeannet and Hubert D. Hennessey, *International Marketing Management,* Houghton Mifflin, Boston, 1988, pp. 252–260.

Multinational strategies involve a commitment to a broad range of national markets including those in Europe, Asia, and the Americas. Such firms organize their businesses around nations or regions so that separate marketing strategies (including decisions on the range of products to offer) are largely left to the local subsidiary. IBM, Nestle, and Royal Dutch-Shell are among the firms that are considered multinationals.

A *global* strategy is employed when an organization operates in a broad set of markets but with a common set of strategic principles. Put another way, this strategy views the world market as a whole rather than as a series of national markets. Country strategies are thus subordinated to a global framework. Global strategies are most appropriate when a firm's competitors or customers are globalized. For example, Caterpillar competes with Komatsu for earth-moving equipment in virtually every market, and financial institutions like Morgan Guaranty Trust Company work with corporate clients who are themselves global or multinational.

Diversification   A strategy which involves both new products and new markets is termed diversification. This strategy is likely to be chosen when one or more of the following conditions exist:

• No other growth opportunities can be established with existing products or markets
• The firm has unstable sales or profits because it operates in markets that are characterized by unstable environments
• The firm wishes to capitalize on a distinctive competence.

German automaker Daimler-Benz (maker of Mercedes) has been transformed from a luxury car maker to a conglomerate firm with products ranging from vacuum cleaners to computers to aerospace. While the company was highly profitable, most of top management felt that the firm's strong cash position could best be used to develop new growth opportunities.[13]

Dow Chemical embarked on a diversification strategy in 1982 after watching earnings fall from $1.4 billion in 1979 to $287 million in 1982. The decline was a direct result of a recession and excess capacity in the industry which combined to send chemical prices plummeting. Throughout the 1980's, Dow expanded into pharmaceuticals through the acquisition of Richardson-Merrell, into consumer goods (Ziploc bags, Spray 'N' Wash stain remover) with the purchase of Texize, and into automotive plastics with the purchase of Essex Chemical. Additionally, Dow entered the agricultural chemicals market in 1989 through a joint venture with Eli Lilly & Co.[14]

When the markets for many of its most successful hardware products (such as drills and chain saws) began to level off, Black & Decker turned its attention to the development of housewares products. Relying on its expertise in cordless-appliance tech-

[13]Robert Ingersoll and Rose Brady, "The Banker Behind the Shakeup at Daimler-Benz," *Business Week,* July 27, 1987, pp. 36–37.
[14]David Woodruff, "Has Dow Chemical Found the Right Formula?" *Business Week,* Aug. 7, 1989, pp. 62–63.

nology, the company achieved success with its Dustbuster vacuum, Spotlighter (a rechargeable flashlight), and the cordless screwdriver. Based on these successes and its ability to manufacture products at low cost, Black & Decker continued its diversification into housewares products by purchasing General Electric's small-appliance business. Within three years, Black & Decker had become the market leader in irons.[15]

Strategic Alliances   Often a firm can only be successful in moving into a new market if it can acquire new resources or competencies. In such cases, the firm's strategy may be to form a strategic alliance with another firm. Importantly, a strategic alliance is more than a joint venture. In the case of a joint venture, two firms essentially create a third entity which develops on its own. In a true strategic alliance, two firms collaborate in a far more complete way by *exchanging* some key resources (although new entities may also be formed) to enable both parties to enhance their performance. Typically, alliances involve exchanges of one or more of the resources listed below:

- Access to sales and distribution networks
- Transfers of new product technology
- Production technology

In 1988, Black & Decker forged an alliance with Shin-Daiwa Kogyo to market Black & Decker power tools for the professional market in Japan. The alliance gives Black & Decker access to Shin-Daiwa's extensive sales force, distribution network and service operations. Shin-Daiwa, already well-known among Japan's professional builders and craftsmen for its two-cycle engine products and a variety of sawing tools, benefits by having a broader product line to offer.[16]

In the world of pharmaceuticals, new products are essential to success but the expansion of bio-technology has made it costly for firms to stay on top of all new developments. Because of the extraordinary costs required for R&D, few firms have the funds available to expand geographically through their own efforts. As a result, many have followed the pattern developed by the British company, Glaxo, which trades proprietary drug products with Japanese firms to broaden its product line and generate greater sales volume from its established European sales and distribution network.[17]

Fanuc, the Japanese firm that is the world's leading maker of electronic factory help, solidified its position through strategic alliances with General Electric and General Motors. General Motors formerly produced industrial robots for its own use while GE manufactured computerized numerical controls (the electronic systems that drive automated tools such as lathes and milling machines). While both GE and GM possess highly advanced technology, Fanuc's strength lies in its production processes which permit lower cost and higher volume production. Prior to its alliance with Fanuc, GM

[15]Mary Lu Carnevale, "Black & Decker Goes to Full Court Press," *The Wall Street Journal*, Nov. 10, 1988, p. A8.

[16]Mary Lu Carnevale, "Black & Decker in Alliance to Sell Its Tools in Japan," *The Wall Street Journal*, Dec. 10, 1988, p. B6.

[17]Kenichi Ohmae, "The Global Logic of Strategic Alliances," *Harvard Business Review*, March–April 1989, pp. 143–149.

could not produce enough robots to fill its own needs. Now production is sufficient so that GM (as well as GE) is able to sell hardware as Fanuc's distribution arm.[18]

Consolidation Strategies

A major strategic development (observable beginning in the mid-1980s) is the increased emphasis on consolidation. Led by large conglomerates, more and more firms are undoing some of their recent growth strategies. Basically, there are three types of consolidation strategies:

- Retrenchment
- Pruning
- Divestment

Retrenchment   Retrenchment is essentially the opposite of market development: A firm reduces its commitment to its existing products by withdrawing from weaker markets. Generally, this strategy is pursued when a firm has experienced uneven performance in different markets. For example, many oil companies have decided to concentrate their gasoline marketing efforts in a few regions of the country.

In 1988, Mobil traded 244 of its West Coast Mobil stations to BP America in exchange for 326 Sohio, Gibbs, Gulf and Gas 'n' Go stations in Michigan and seven other midwestern states. BP America also agreed to purchase Mobil's Washington state oil refinery. The move was expected to help solidify Mobil's strong presence in the East and Midwest where it held a much greater market share. In similar moves, Atlantic Richfield has left the East and Midwest, Texaco vacated the Chicago area, and Unocal has retreated from Florida.[19]

Pruning   Pruning occurs when a firm reduces the number of products offered in a market. In effect, pruning is the opposite of product development and occurs when a firm decides that some market segments are too small or too costly to continue to serve.

Although Black & Decker enjoyed immense success with product development in recent years, its core business—power tools—has had some profitability problems. In large part, these stemmed from an extraordinarily long product line. By the mid-1980's, the company produced over 100 different motor sizes in 25 plants. So from 1984 to 1987, the company began to streamline the product line, eliminating six plants and hundreds of product variations in the process. As a result, the utilization of individual production facilities was greatly improved.[20]

---

[18]Gene Bylinsky, "Japan's Robot King Wins Again," *Fortune,* May 25, 1987, pp. 53–58.
[19]Michael Arndt, "Mobil, BP America to Swap Gas Stations," *Chicago Tribune,* Oct. 21, 1988, p. B2.
[20]Christopher Eklund, "How Black & Decker Got Back in the Black," *Business Week,* July 13, 1987, pp. 86–90.

Divestment   Divestment occurs when a firm sells off a part of its business to another organization. Because this usually means that a firm is taking itself out of a product line and out of a particular market, divestment is essentially the opposite of diversification.

A firm typically pursues divestment strategies when management becomes aware that a particular business is not meeting the organization's objectives for it. Often, divestment occurs after an organization realizes that a diversification strategy has failed. This is more likely to occur when the business does not fit the organization's competencies and when top management fails to appreciate the kinds of skills central to success in that market.

> In an attempt to seek new avenues of growth away from the slow-growing food industry, General Mills diversified into clothing (with Izod sportswear), toys (Kenner Products), and fashion accessories (such as Monet jewelry). In most cases the diversifications proved unsuccessful as several of the acquired businesses experienced reductions in market share. According to critics, General Mills failed to appreciate the importance of timely new-product development in these faster-paced businesses where obsolescence was a fact of life.[21]

In other cases, the divestment is viewed as something that is necessary in order to make better use of resources.

> Hershey Foods sold its Friendly restaurant chain, composed of 850 family restaurants in the Northeast and Midwest, to Tennessee Restaurant Company. At the time, the chain contributed one-quarter of total Hershey sales. Although Friendly's slow growth was cited as a factor in the sale, the company's main reason for divesting it was to use the financial capital to acquire the U.S. operations of British candy maker Cadbury Schweppes, a move which would reinforce its position in its core market.[22]

PRODUCT MIX STRATEGY

A corporate strategy provides an organization with a basic direction by establishing the general product and market scope to be pursued. Given this scope, a firm usually elects to divest or prune businesses and products which do not fit the strategy and to commit resources to those products and businesses which do fit this strategic scope. However, in most organizations a number of products and businesses are likely to remain within the product market scope and management must have some basis for establishing priorities among those products of businesses that will remain.

A product mix strategy helps management solve the problem of establishing priorities. Specifically, a product mix strategy is a plan that specifies

• How various products or businesses will be prioritized for the purpose of allocating scarce resources

---

[21]"Splitting Up: The Other Side of Merger Mania," *Business Week,* July 1, 1985, pp. 50–55.

[22]Rachel Swarns, "Hershey, in Bid to Focus Only on Candy, to Sell Restaurant Unit for $375 Million," *The Wall Street Journal,* Aug. 9, 1988, p. 7.

• What objectives will be established for each product or business to ensure that the total corporate objectives will be met.

Top management can rely on two useful concepts in developing a product mix strategy: the *product life cycle* and *product portfolio models*. We will discuss each of these in turn.

The Product Life Cycle

The product life cycle (PLC) concept plays an important part in the development of a product mix strategy. It helps managers to identify the significance of sales trends and to assess the changing nature of competition, costs, and market opportunities over time.[23]

The product life cycle (PLC) represents a pattern of sales over time, with the pattern typically broken into four stages (see Figure 2-3). The four stages are usually defined as follows.

1 *Introduction*. The product is new to the market. Since there are therefore no direct competitors, buyers must be educated about what the product does, how it is used, who it is for, and where to buy it.

2 *Growth*. The product is now more widely known, and sales grow rapidly because new buyers enter the market and perhaps because buyers find more

[23]Alternative perspectives on the product life cycle are available in Theodore Levitt, "Exploit the Product Life Cycle," *Harvard Business Review,* November–December 1965, pp. 81–94; Bernard Catry and Michael Chevalier, "Market Share and the Product Life Cycle," *Journal of Marketing,* October 1974, pp. 29–34; N. Dhalla and Sonia Yuspah, "Forget the Product Life Cycle," *Harvard Business Review,* January–February 1975, pp. 102–111; and George S. Day, "The Product Life Cycle: Analysis and Applications Issues," *Journal of Marketing,* Fall 1981, pp. 60–67.

FIGURE 2-3   Stages of the product life cycle.

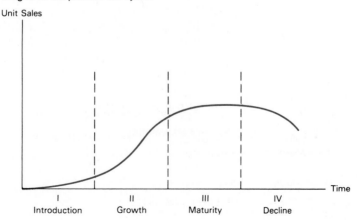

ways to use the product. Sales growth stimulates many competitors to enter the market, and the major marketing task becomes to build market share.

3 *Maturity.* Sales growth levels off as nearly all potential buyers have entered the market. Consumers are now knowledgeable about the alternatives, repeat purchasers dominate sales, and product innovations are restricted to minor improvements. As a result, only the strongest competitors survive: It is very difficult for the weaker firms to obtain distribution and to increase market shares.

4 *Decline.* Sales slowly decline because of changing buyer needs or because of the introduction of new products which are sufficiently different to have their own life cycles.

It is important to note that managers could select from more than one portrayal of a life cycle for a given product. As Table 2-4 indicates, for example, an executive at a company that makes tea could consider three different levels of the market in which that product competes when measuring unit sales: (1) beverages, (2) tea, or (3) a specific form of tea such as herbal tea. The decision involved in selecting a level is known as determining the relevant market and is treated in detail in Chapter 3. For our present purposes, however, it is important to recognize that one could arrive at a very different interpretation of the PLC depending on how the relevant market is defined.

Sales of herbal tea are growing much more rapidly than sales of tea, and sales of tea are growing somewhat more rapidly than all beverages taken as a group. Most important, however, herbal tea is in the growth stage of the life cycle, while tea itself is essentially in the maturity stage.

Generic-need life cycles are seldom useful for strategy purposes because (by definition) they seldom experience significant changes. But *product-form* and *product-class* life cycles are of substantial value to the process of developing strategies. In Chapters 4 and 7 we will see some of the implications of the product life cycle for the development of competitive marketing strategies for a product or product line. From the viewpoint of corporate marketing planning, however, the product life cycle has two major contributions. First, knowing the product-form life cycle stage tells more about the market opportunities than does the current brand growth rate. Low brand sales growth may occur because the market share is declining in the growth stage or because the market share is stable in a mature market. But knowing which state a product is in enables management to evaluate the opportunities for enhancing brand sales growth.

TABLE 2-4   DIFFERENT DEFINITIONS OF THE RELEVANT MARKET

Level	Illustrative measure(s)
Product-form	Sales of regular tea or decaffeinated tea or herbal tea
Product-class	Sales of tea
Generic-need	Sales of all beverages

Second, knowing the stage of the product life cycle enables a firm to project future costs and profits. Marketing costs (especially advertising) tend to be greatest in the introduction and early growth stages of the life cycle. In the introduction stage, extensive advertising and selling efforts are required to communicate the basic benefits to be derived from the new form or class. In the early growth stage, high marketing expenses for promotion and minor product modifications are necessary as firms jockey for strong market-share position in order to be strong enough to survive the shakeout of competitors that often comes at maturity.

The product life cycle concept can be a valuable tool in corporate marketing planning because it enables the manager to understand the growth and profit opportunities facing each product or business. As discussed later in this chapter, this information is useful in developing the growth and profit expectations for a product and for assessing the resource needs of various products. As such, the PLC is a useful adjunct to the widely used product portfolio models.

Product Portfolio Models

Serious investors usually have a *portfolio* of different kinds of financial investments, each with special characteristics regarding risk, rate of return, and appreciation. So, too, do organizations have a range of products with varying characteristics. Just as an investor attempts to balance the growth, risk, and yields of the various instruments, top management should strive to find a desirable balance among alternative products. In seeking this long-run balance, managers must recognize that some products will generate large amounts of cash over and above what is required for operating expenses or for additional investment in production facilities and inventory. However, other products will, at least in the short run, generate far less cash than is needed for operating expenses (including marketing efforts and research and development) and for additional investment.

Portfolio models are methods that managers can use to classify products in order to determine the future cash contributions that can be expected and the future cash requirements that will be appropriate for each product. Thus, in using a portfolio model, managers usually must examine the competitive position of a product (or product line) and the opportunities presented by the market.

To illustrate how portfolio models work, we shall examine two of the most widely known models: the BCG Growth-Share Matrix and the Directional Policy Matrix.

The BCG Growth-Share Matrix   The Boston Consulting Group (BCG) model assumes that cash flow and profitability will be closely related to sales volume. Accordingly, products are classified in terms of the product's market-share dominance and in terms of the rate of growth in that market. As Figure 2-4 indicates, a firm's relative market share is the ratio of its share to that of the largest competitor (X). If our share equals that of the largest competitor it would be 1.0X. Additionally, the rate of growth of the market can be interpreted as reflecting the

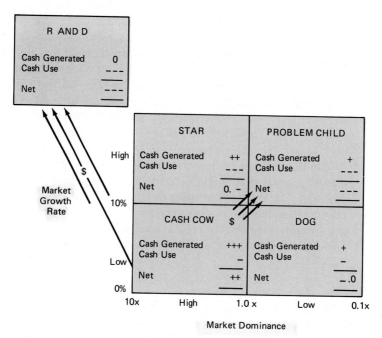

FIGURE 2-4   The Boston Consulting Group growth-share portfolio model. (*Source:* George Day, *Analysis for Strategic Market Decisions*, West Publishing, St. Paul, Minn., 1986, p. 174.)

stage in the PLC—high growth reflecting the first two stages and low growth reflecting maturity or decline.[24] The BCG model enables a manager to classify a firm's products into four basic types: stars, cash cows, dogs, and problem children.

Stars are products that hold a major market share in a high-growth market. Because such products can be expected to enjoy rapidly growing sales and profits, they will likely generate a large cash flow. However, high-growth markets are attractive to competitors. Consequently, stars must receive continuing cash resources to provide a level of marketing support that will enable middle-level managers to protect the market-share position. Moreover, because sales will grow rapidly, additional investment in production facilities and inventories may be needed. As a result, most of the cash flow generated by stars must be reinvested in these same products.

Cash cows are also market leaders, and so the sales volume from these products is usually large enough to generate substantial profits and cash flow. However, because cash cows are in low-growth markets, the cash generated will not

---

[24]Boston Consulting Group, *The Product Portfolio,* pamphlet no. 66, Boston, 1970; see also George S. Day, "Diagnosing the Product Portfolio," *Journal of Marketing,* April 1977, pp. 29–38.

typically have to be reinvested in additional marketing expenses or in expanded facilities. Consequently, these products are a firm's primary source of cash flow.

Dogs are low market-share products in low-growth markets and consequently are likely to be weak cash providers. If such products do have loyal core markets, they may yield consistent profits and cash. However, because the future contribution of these products is not likely to be very large, they normally should receive a relatively small share of the firm's scarce cash resources for marketing purposes.

Problem children are so named because they have great potential (being in high-growth markets) but require a good deal of attention (in order to build market share). To put it another way, a problem-child product may ultimately be a good cash provider if the firm can successfully build its market share. However, problem children will often be heavy users of cash because large dollar commitments for product reformulation, advertising, improved distribution, or other marketing activities will be necessary in order to achieve a profitable market-share level.

In practice, the BCG matrix is generally viewed as far too simplistic for managing the resource allocation process. Some of the reasons for this view are discussed in the following sections of this chapter. However, this matrix was an important contribution to management thought because it was the first systematic model for managing a large set of businesses in a modern, diversified corporation. Additionally, it introduced terms for important types of products (such as cash cows and problem children) that remain widely used in business strategy discussions.

Directional Policy Matrix   The BCG model suggests that market share and industry growth are the best predictors of profitability. However, strict reliance only on these two dimensions may not be appropriate for several reasons. First, some products will be "borderline" cases since they cannot clearly be classified as high- or low on at least one of the dimensions. Second, current market share says very little about the feasibility of increasing or maintaining that share. Third, some high-growth markets may not be attractive because of their lack of size or stability or because of other factors.

To overcome these limitations, managers will usually want to examine other competitive strengths (besides market share) and other dimensions of market attractiveness (besides industry growth). Table 2-5 lists some of the questions which managers should consider in evaluating the competitive strength and market attractiveness dimensions. These dimensions can be used to supplement market share and industry sales-growth information in implementing the BCG model. Alternatively, these dimensions are used in other portfolio models such as the Directional Policy Matrix (DPM).

In the DPM nine (rather than four) portfolio categories are employed. The overall rating of market attractiveness allows for a high rating—even if industry sales growth is low—when the overall size, stability, or cost of competing are positive enough to make the market attractive. The overall competitive strength

TABLE 2-5   EVALUATING COMPETITIVE STRENGTH AND MARKET ATTRACTIVENESS

Competitive strength dimensions

1. Does our *market share* suggest that we have a strong customer base?
2. Do we have the managerial skills needed to compete?
3. Are our production facilities modern and efficient?
4. Do we possess the technology required to maintain a competitive rate of innovation and product development?
5. Do customers have a positive image of our products?
6. Does our cost structure enable us to be competitive on price while maintaining profitability?
7. Are our distributors well established and supportive?
8. Do we have an adequate number of qualified sales and customer service personnel?
9. Do we have stable and reliable suppliers?

Market attractiveness dimensions

1. Is the industry sales-growth rate high?
2. Is the market size large enough to sustain many competitors?
3. Are industry sales susceptible to cyclical, seasonal, or other fluctuations?
4. Is the rate of product obsolescence high?
5. Does extensive government regulation constrain actions or pose uncertainties?
6. Is the industry demand very low relative to industry capacity?
7. Is there a risk of raw material or component shortages?
8. Are there a large number of well-financed competitors?
9. Do a small number of buyers account for a disproportionately large percentage of industry sales so that we will be heavily dependent on them?
10. Overall, does the industry present a strong potential for profit?
11. Does this industry have a high degree of fit with our corporate strategy?

rating reflects the firm's ability to compete successfully in building or maintaining market share. In general, products classified in the "maintain" or "challenge" categories can be viewed as problem children and stars, those on the diagonal will be comparable to cash cows, and the remainder can be considered dogs with those in the low business strength–low market attractiveness category being the leading candidates for elimination. Figure 2-5 portrays the DPM and shows some typical views of the role each type of product should play in the organization's portfolio.

Implications and Limitations

As the preceding discussion has indicated, portfolio models can provide insights into the appropriate allocation of resources and product performance objectives. According to these models, stars and problem-child products should emphasize market-share objectives while cash cows and dogs should be profit-focused.

These implications should be examined with care, however, because the models are founded on assumptions that are not always appropriate. Managers who use portfolio models should be especially aware of the following considerations:

COMPETITIVE POSITION

Market Attractivensss	Strong	Medium	Weak
High	Maintain leadership	Challenge leader	Overcome weakness, find a niche, or quit
Medium	Challenge leader	Manage for earnings	Harvest
Low	Cash generator	Harvest	Divest

FIGURE 2-5   The Directional Policy Matrix.

• Portfolio models implicitly assume that the portfolio must be in cash balance; therefore, there must be a sufficient number of cash cows and dogs to fund stars and problem children. In reality, firms may also generate resources through borrowing, and so it may not be necessary to extract all the cash flow from products in lower growth–less-attractive markets just because of high cash needs in attractive, higher-growth markets.

• Portfolio models suggest that cash cows can be milked with impunity because of their established market position and because they are in mature markets. In reality, many market-share leaders do experience extensive competitive challenges to their leadership position—especially in large, stable consumer goods markets. Thus, profitability objectives may have to be subordinated to an objective of market-share maintenance, at least in the short run.

• Portfolio models indicate that resources should be invested in stars and in problem-child products in order to enhance the market shares of these products. However, there is no assurance that the application of more resources will lead to increases in market share. The ability to maintain or increase market share is not only dependent on having adequate resources but also on the existence of competitive advantage. Thus, managers should only invest in high-growth markets if they can identify a feasible competitive marketing strategy.

• The BCG model is criticized for relying on only two elements while the Directional Policy Matrix accommodates a large number of factors. However, because each element of market attractiveness and competitive strength has a different degree of importance in each situation, it is impossible to have a standard method for weighing the importance of the various elements.[25] Additionally, the ratings are somewhat subjective, so different managers may not always rate a particular business the same way on every dimension.[26]

Additionally, portfolio models in general have been attacked for the view that the only interdependencies among the products or businesses in a portfolio are the cash flows. Harvard's Michael Porter points out that this perspective is part of the reason for the lack of success of so many diversification strategies. In successful diversifications, either the new business should be stronger by virtue of being associated with the parent firm or it should benefit the firm's other businesses by bringing some competitive strength to them (such as new technology or access to broader distribution channels).[27] The term *synergy* is generally applied to such relationships. Synergy means that the whole is worth more than the sum of its parts, that two or more product lines operating in the same firm will be more successful than if they operated in separate organizations because of some commonality in resources employed. Thus, in assessing the role each product line plays in the organization, managers should be careful to identify important synergistic relationships.

Specifying Product Objectives

The basic purpose of portfolio models and of product mix strategy is to establish some guidelines on how to manage each product or product line. Some classification process is necessary so that decisions can be made about the role each product can be expected to play in the organization's future. These roles are detailed through the statement of specific product performance objectives which provide middle managers with a focus for developing the marketing strategies and programs that are appropriate.

Based on the various product mix strategy models available to management, we can identify six basic types of product objectives.

Market-Share Growth   This objective is typically appropriate for problem-child products. Because market-growth rates are high, the opportunities for market-share growth are often good since brand or supplier preferences may not yet be firmly established and since much of demand is from new (first-time) buyers of the product form.

---

[25]Patrick McNamee, "Competitive Analysis Using Matrix Displays," *Long Range Planning,* June 1984, pp. 110–113.

[26]David Hussey, "Portfolio Analysis: Practical Experience with the Directional Policy Matrix," *Long Range Planning,* January 1978, pp. 2–8.

[27]Michael Porter, "From Competitive Advantage to Corporate Strategy," *Harvard Business Review,* May–June 1987, pp. 43–59.

Market-Share Maintenance   For stars that hold large shares in growing markets, market-share maintenance is a typical objective. Because markets are growing, new competitors are likely to emerge and existing competitors are likely to provide strong support for their products and brands in order to expand sales. For the dominant firm, a major consideration will be establishing brand or supplier loyalty to fortify its market position. Firms with low market-share products that have already established themselves in unique segments may also choose to work toward this objective.

Cash Flow Maximization   This objective is a common one for so-called cash cow products with large market shares in mature (or even slightly declining) markets. Such markets have stable market shares and few new competitors. Consequently, attention is focused on marketing expenditures that stimulate increases in product usage rates or on modifying price and expense structures so that profit margins can be increased.

Sustaining Profitability   Weak competitive position products which lack the resources to support significant market-share growth (dogs) may be best served with this objective. Essentially, this objective seeks solid profitability with only modest increases in marketing effort by seeking unique market positions that are not directly competitive with those of market-share leaders. This can often be achieved by focusing on a small segment of the market which has unique needs (that is, by becoming a *product market specialist,* or *market nicher*).

Harvesting   Products that cannot find profitable enclaves and yet require some valuable resources such as production capacity are candidates for harvesting or elimination. Harvesting reflects a *gradual* withdrawal of marketing resources on the assumption that sales will decline only at a slow rate and profitability will remain positive even at lower volume. In contrast, *divestment* means that a firm will immediately exit from the business. (Because divestment means the product or product line is to be eliminated, it is not really a relevant objective for managing the future strategy for a product.)

Establishing an Initial Market Position   This is a primary objective for new products just entering a market. However, a subtle but important difference exists in the objectives for new product forms and new brands. In the case of a new brand of an existing product form (such as the second or third brand of disposable diapers), the product objective is to build market share. For a new product form (where no direct competitors exist), the product-form market share will be 100 percent. Thus the critical objective is to build sales volume.

THE CORPORATE PLAN AND MIDDLE MANAGEMENT

The corporate marketing plan is important to marketing managers in two respects. First, in most organizations, marketing plays a major role in influencing corporate and product mix strategy. Second, all marketing personnel are responsible in one way or another for developing and implementing the marketing strategies and programs necessary for achieving corporate objectives and product objectives.

Figure 2-6 summarizes the major elements in the corporate marketing planning process and indicates that middle managers can provide two basic kinds of inputs to this process. First, middle managers can provide the most detailed information on each individual product regarding the size of the market, the profitability of the product, and the likely sales results of increasing the marketing expenditures on a product. Second, middle managers must identify the kinds of marketing strategies and programs that can be used to achieve the product objective. In identifying these strategies and programs, it frequently will become apparent that the cost of achieving a product objective will be excessive or that there is no feasible way to achieve the objective because of a lack of resources or because of competitors' strengths or other factors. Consequently, corporate marketing plans may need to be revised once feasibility has been assessed.

Chapters 3 to 13 examine the analytical tools and procedures for performing the situation analysis and for selecting strategies and programs. As we shall see, the starting point for these analyses and decisions must always be an examination of the needs of the marketplace. Accordingly, we will focus on this topic in Chapter 3.

FIGURE 2-6 Relationship between corporate marketing planning and middle-management activities.

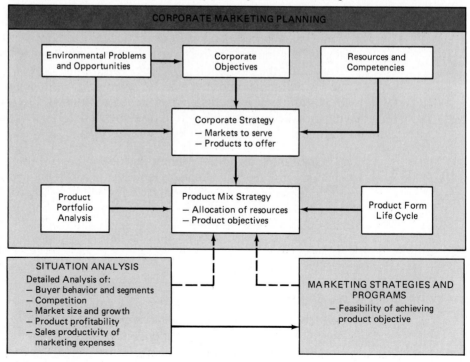

CONCLUSION

Corporate strategies provide the blueprint for the long-term development of a viable, profitable organization by establishing the markets to be served and the products and services to be offered. In this chapter, a variety of types of corporate strategies were presented, and the reasons for selecting each type of strategy were established. In general, corporate strategies are selected on the basis of an analysis of environmental factors (especially market growth), corporate resources, and long-run objectives. Further, in deciding which corporate strategy to select, it is important to identify a firm's distinctive competencies. That is, an organization must have the specific resources required to be successful in the specific product and market arenas in which it will compete.

Product mix strategy is an essential element in corporate marketing planning because it forms the bridge between corporate strategy and the development of marketing strategies and programs on a product-by-product basis. The foundation for this bridge is the development of product objectives, which indicate the role each product is expected to play in meeting the firm's future growth and profitability requirements. Further, the product objectives provide a general format for allocating resources among products. In selecting these objectives, portfolio models and the product life cycle are useful tools. In general, product objectives should be determined on the basis of a firm's competitive strength in the market and on the attractiveness of the market as measured by opportunities for growth and profitability.

In order to more clearly appreciate the scope and significance of corporate marketing, consider the decisions made by top management at American Express.

American Express: Dynamic Corporate Marketing Planning*

American Express was founded in 1850 as a delivery company but today it is known for the variety of financial services it offers. Beginning in the business of traveler's checks, the firm is now a $20 billion enterprise in terms of annual revenue.

The largest element in American Express is the travel related services business whose product line includes the traveler's check and American Express cards (in green, gold, and platinum versions depending on a customer's income and spending habits). While these cards account for only 10 percent of the credit cards in the United States, they account for 30 percent of the charge volume. Additionally, the company also now offers the Optima card (for green and gold card customers who wanted a separate card for revolving credit).

*Developed from Monci Jo Williams, "Synergy Works at American Express," *Fortune*, Feb. 16, 1987, pp. 79–80; Frederic Miller, "How Amex Is Revamping Its Big Beautiful Money Machine," *Business Week*, June 13, 1988, pp. 90–92; Harlan Byrne, "Profitable Partnership: American Express Connection Revives IDS," *Barron's* Nov. 7, 1988, pp. 72–74; and "Amex Charges Ahead," *The Economist*, Nov. 28, 1987, pp. 85–86.

While many observers have argued that the credit card market in the United States is now saturated, American Express has continued to commit large advertising resources to it. Additionally, the company is broadening the range of outlets that will accept the card, even to the point of trying to get Domino's Pizza and K-Mart on the list of participating outlets. At the same time, extensive efforts are being made to build card volume in Europe and Japan. Finally, the card holders' base is also a growing source of revenue from American Express merchandising activities. Using direct mail and targeting cardholders with specific buying patterns, the company sells over half a billion dollars per year of furniture, jewelry, luggage, and other goods.

American Express also is the primary stockholder in Shearson Lehman Hutton (investment banking and stock brokerage), and owns the American Express Bank (which operates outside the United States and focuses on private banking—managing wealthy individuals' portfolios and lending them money for personal investing in areas such as art or real estate).

In 1984, the company purchased Investors Diversified Services (IDS), the giant Minneapolis-based financial services firms specializing in providing financial planning services and selling mutual funds. Under IDS's previous owner, the company's growth had been seriously curtailed as it was treated like a cash cow. American Express has poured over a $100 million into IDS, attempting to expand its base of 1.2 million investors whose incomes generally range from $40,000 to $90,000. The objective is to gain a greater presence in higher income households and on the east and west coasts where IDS had fewer salespeople.

Not all of American Express's new ventures have worked out. The company did divest its Fireman's Fund property and casualty insurance company after poor performance. However, the company is still building new business opportunities. It recently established a significant link with the Japanese insurance giant Nippon Life by selling it a minority share in Shearson Lehman Hutton.

1 What are the various corporate strategies that American Express has been pursuing?

2 What insights do these strategies suggest about the firm's corporate mission and objectives?

3 If you were asked to do a portfolio analysis for American Express using the Directional Policy Matrix, what are some of the dimensions that you think would be most important in assessing competitive strength and market attractiveness?

QUESTIONS AND SITUATIONS FOR DISCUSSION

1 In 1989, Federal Express held a 45 percent share of the domestic overnight delivery market. However Federal's growth had slowed due to increasing competition from UPS and the boom in facsimile machines. Additionally, price competition had squeezed domestic profits while the company was actually losing millions on its international business. On January 31, 1989, the company received government approval to acquire Tiger International, the world's largest heavy cargo airline, well known for its Flying Tiger

Line airfreight service. Federal Express had not yet cracked the heavy freight business. Additionally, the company looked forward to using Flying Tiger planes for overseas package delivery, reducing the need to subcontract its deliveries to other carriers as they had previously had to do in many countries.

What corporate strategies is Federal Express pursuing? What do these strategies suggest about Federal's environment, competencies, and objectives?

2 Dunkin' Donuts shops have to be open between 20 and 24 hours a day since part of their appeal is coffee and donuts ready whenever they are wanted. However, over 50 percent of sales are between 6 and 10 a.m. If the operating hours cannot be changed, what alternative growth strategies could be pursued?

3 Portfolio management theory suggests that management should assemble a collection of businesses in different industries and different states of maturity to diversify risk. What would be some of the reasons that these same managements may later have to utilize consolidation strategies?

4 Maytag Company's acquisition of Magic Chef broadened its product line to include virtually every segment of the home appliance market. For instance, Maytag's refrigerators are sold under the Magic Chef, Admiral, Norge, Warwick, and Jenn Air brands. What type of corporate strategy would Maytag seem to be following? What are the problems and limitations of such a strategy?

5 Sales of FAX machines in 1989 were 1.4 million units and are projected to reach 3.2 million units in 1993. In 1983 there were seven manufacturers and nine brands and by 1989 there were twenty-five manufacturers offering over sixty brand names in the American market. What inferences would you draw from this information about the product life cycle and the appropriate product objective for a competitor in this market?

6 What if, after charting your business on a growth share matrix, you found you had only cows and dogs. Does a portfolio model tell you where new business should come from?

7 In the 1980s Coca-Cola Company sold its Wine Spectrum properties to Seagram Company. Growth in the wine industry had slowed dramatically and Wine Spectrum's shipments had actually declined. Some industry observers suggested that Coca-Cola Company sold because wine had reached the maturity stage of the life cycle. Do you think this is enough information to support this suggestion? What other explanations might account for the leveling in sales?

8 Europe is a growth market for soft drinks. The average European now drinks only 15 gallons of carbonated drinks per year compared to the U.S. consumers' 50 gallons, and European growth is expected to double the rate for the United States in the 1990s. With the European Economic Community's unified market in 1992, Coca-Cola Europe has begun to buy back distribution rights in some countries and form joint ventures with bottlers in others. Previously, Coke had relied upon licensees and independent regional bottling companies for much of its manufacturing and distribution in Europe. By centralizing bottle filling and distribution, Coke feels it can cut costs and lower its prices to increase sales. In order to do this, Coke standardized on "convenience packaging"— the plastic bottles and aluminum cans that are less expensive, lighter, and easier to transport than bottles. In some European countries such as Britain, 90 percent of all soft drinks are now sold in cans or plastic. However, in countries such as West Germany and Switzerland, most beverages come in reusable bottles. In West Germany there are 1100 brewers who also produce soft drinks and local grocery stores collect and return bottles to local plants. A recent law in West Germany prohibits plastic beverage containers by putting a 25-cent deposit on each bottle.

Discuss the corporate strategy options facing Coca-Cola Europe.

SUGGESTED ADDITIONAL READINGS

Anderson, Paul, "Marketing, Strategic Planning and the Theory of the Firm," *Journal of Marketing,* Spring 1982, pp. 15–20.

Cravens, David W., "Strategic Forces Affecting Marketing Strategy," *Business Horizons,* September–October 1986, pp. 77–86.

Feldman, Laurence P., and Albert L. Page, "Harvesting: The Misunderstood Market Exit Strategy," *Journal of Business Strategy,* Spring 1985, pp. 79–85.

Gray, Daniel H., "Uses and Misuses of Strategic Planning," *Harvard Business Review,* January–February 1986, pp. 89–97.

Hall, George E., "Reflections on Running a Diversified Company," *Harvard Business Review,* January–February 1987, pp. 84–92.

Haspeslagh, Philippe,"Portfolio Planning: Uses and Limits," *Harvard Business Review,* January–February 1982, pp. 58–73.

Lambkin, Mary, and George Day, "Evolutionary Processes in Competitive Markets: Beyond the Product Life Cycle," *Journal of Marketing,* July 1989, pp. 4–20.

Lenz, R. T., "Managing the Evolution of the Strategic Planning Process," *Business Horizons,* January–February 1987, pp. 34–39.

Raymond, Mary Anne, and Hiram C. Barksdale, "Corporate Strategic Planning and Corporate Marketing: Toward an Interface?" *Business Horizons,* September–October 1989, pp. 41–48.

Thorelli, Hans B., and Stephen C. Burnett, "The Nature of Product Life Cycles for Industrial Goods," *Journal of Marketing,* Fall 1987, pp. 97–108.

Varadarajan, P. Rajan, "Marketing Strategies in Action," *Business,* January–March 1986, pp. 11–23.

PART 2

SITUATION ANALYSIS

As we demonstrated in Part 1, middle-management decisions should be consistent with the broad decisions that top management makes regarding the long-term purpose and direction of an organization. Specifically, top management is responsible for identifying the role each product or product line should play in achieving an organization's long-run objectives, and for effectively communicating what this role is to be through the formulation of a *product objective*.

Essentially, middle managers have the basic task of achieving the product objective. Later on, in Part 3, we will present some fundamental tools and approaches for selecting marketing *strategies* and action *programs* that can be used to achieve the various types of product objectives. However, in order to develop a logical, planned approach to selecting the marketing strategies and programs that are appropriate, managers must not only be aware of the product objective but also understand the specific problems and opportunities confronting a product or a product line.

By performing a *situation analysis,* managers should be able to identify the major problems and opportunities that can be employed to guide the selection of marketing strategies and programs. The chapters in Part 2 are designed to provide the most important and useful analytical procedures and concepts for performing a situation analysis.

Generally, the most significant problems and opportunities are those related to the market for a product. Accordingly, in Chapter 3, we examine the process of market analysis. In particular, we examine the issue of identifying possible target markets and we present a sequential approach for understanding how buyers (and potential buyers) are likely to respond to different marketing actions.

Because the extent of a market opportunity also depends on competition, managers must assess the current and potential competitive situation in a market. In Chapter 4 we examine ways of identifying the sources of competition, of predicting the nature and intensity of competition over time, and of assessing the relative strengths and weaknesses of competitors attempting to serve the same market.

In Chapter 5, alternative procedures for measuring the size of a market and for forecasting sales are presented. By understanding the uses, assumptions, and limitations of these procedures, managers will be more capable of identifying the size of a market opportunity and the potential problems that are involved in achieving sales growth.

Chapter 6 examines the relationship between sales and profitability. Because marketing activities cost money, middle managers must know how to determine the sales and profit impact of proposed marketing expenditures. Accordingly, in this chapter we present some basic tools for identifying the problems and opportunities associated with budgeting decisions in marketing.

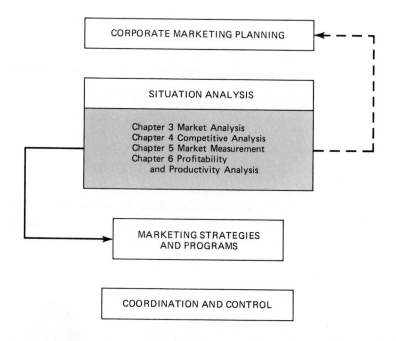

CHAPTER 3

MARKET ANALYSIS

OVERVIEW

In our discussion of the marketing concept in Chapter 1, we noted the central importance to an organization of understanding the customer. The ultimate objective of market analysis is to determine which needs of a buyer the firm hopes to satisfy and how to design and target the offer to satisfy these needs. In order to achieve this objective, managers must develop an understanding of

- The choices available to potential customers
- The processes potential customers use in making buying decisions

In this chapter, we present a general, five-step approach for analyzing the market. In addition, we also present some specific methods and guidelines for carrying out these steps, and we discuss how managers can use the information obtained from this approach to develop marketing strategies and programs. The five-step approach is portrayed in Figure 3-1.

1 *Define the relevant market.* Managers cannot analyze a market unless they first define it, and frequently there are a very large number of products and services available for satisfying basic needs and wants. A market can be defined very narrowly (for example, to include a variety of different types of products). It is important to remember that the way a market is defined will have a major impact on the specific findings we can expect in the subsequent steps.

2 *Analyze primary demand for the relevant market.* In this step, managers attempt to understand the common dimensions of the buying process for all brands and products in the relevant market. Specifically, we provide a series of questions to help managers diagnose who the buyers (and nonbuyers) in the relevant market are and why they buy (or don't buy).

3 *Analyze selective demand within the relevant market.* In this step we examine the process by which buyers select specific alternative brands or suppliers within the boundary of the relevant market.

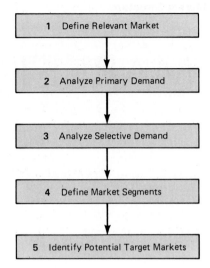

FIGURE 3-1   Steps in market analysis.

4 _Define market segments_. There are few buying situations in which all customers have similar motivations and undergo similar choice processes. The concept of market segmentation explicitly recognizes this reality. This step in the process presents some alternative ways of separating buyers into segments whose members are similar in their response to marketing programs.

5 _Identify potential target markets_. Ultimately, the goal of market analysis is to identify the best opportunities for creating customers. This final step demonstrates how the information from preceding steps can be used to identify the specific markets (and market segments) which managers should consider as targets when selecting marketing strategies.

DEFINING THE RELEVANT MARKET

DSP

The _relevant market_ is the set of products and/or services (within the total product market structure) that management considers to be strategically important. As we noted in Chapter 2, a product mix strategy can change substantially depending on how the relevant market is defined. For example a specialized brand of decaffeinated herbal teas may have a relatively large share of that market but a very small share of the total tea market. Moreover, the total tea market is not growing nearly as rapidly as the herbal tea market. Thus, this product might be viewed as a "star" if the relevant market is herbal tea but a "cash cow" or even a "dog" if the relevant market is tea.

Defining the relevant market usually involves two steps. First, management will attempt to describe the product market structure. Subsequently, the relevant market boundaries within that product market structure will be defined.

Describing the Product Market Structure

A market can only exist when both sellers and buyers are present. Consequently, in order to define a market, managers must identify both the *needs of the buyers* and the *goods and services offered by the sellers* to meet those needs.

A *product market structure* is a representation of the degrees of substitutability that exist among a set of products and/or services which satisfy similar needs. By describing the product market structure, managers can more readily identify the various ways in which the market for a product *might* be defined. Specifically, managers can use the product market structure to identify the types of products and services they must compete with in various need-satisfaction situations.

In Chapter 2, we suggested that managers could classify competing alternatives at three levels:

1 Competing brands (or suppliers) within a product form
2 Competing product forms within a product class
3 Competing product classes serving a generic need

In describing the product market structure, our immediate concern is to classify product forms and classes in order to identify possible ways of defining the market to be analyzed. Because brand or supplier competition can best be analyzed *after* the relevant market is defined, the classification of brand alternatives is discussed in the third step of the market analysis process.

In identifying and classifying alternative product forms and product classes, several methods are available.[1] Typically, however, classification is based either on the similarity of *characteristics or functions* among alternatives or on the similarity of the *usage situations*.

Similarity of Characteristics or Functions In this approach, managers classify products as highly similar if they share physical or chemical characteristics or if they function technically in the same way. For example, within the generic-need "breakfast foods," cereals, pastries, and eggs would be considered as distinct product classes based on the differences in their composition and in the processes used to prepare them. Cereals could be subsequently divided into product forms (nutritional cereals, presweetened cereals, and so on) which share some technical characteristics but which still exhibit some differences.

Similarity of Usage Situations Consumers do not always select the most functionally similar alternative when switching product forms or classes. Accordingly, managers may want to obtain customers' judgments of similarity among various product alternatives. However, when asking what products are most substitutable, managers should attempt to account for differences in usage situations. For example, although hot cereal and cold cereal may be more similar to each

---

[1]An extensive review of approaches for describing product market structures is available in George Day, Allan Shocker, and Rajendra Srivastava, "Customer-Oriented Approaches to Identifying Product Markets," *Journal of Marketing*, Fall 1979, pp. 8–19.

other than cold cereal and frozen waffles, consumers may elect to substitute frozen waffles (rather than oatmeal) for cold cereal if the usage situation calls for fast preparation.

An example of the importance of carefully describing the product market structure is Procter & Gamble's assessment of the competition for its Metamucil laxative.

> In 1989, Procter & Gamble petitioned the Food & Drug Administration to pull a new General Mills cereal (named Benefit) from store shelves. P&G does not compete in the cereal market. But General Mills claimed that Benefit could reduce cholesterol levels by up to 6%.
>
> This feature made Benefit a potential competitor of P&G's Metamucil laxative because, like Benefit, Metamucil contains husks of the high-fiber grain psyllium and clinical studies suggest that psyllium lowers blood-borne cholesterol levels. P&G also wanted to advertise Metamucil as a cholesterol reducer. Unlike cereals, however, laxatives are considered drugs so all advertising claims must receive FDA approval.[2]

While Benefit and Metamucil are not used at the same usage times and while they appear very different physically, they share important chemical and functional characteristics and they share a common benefit. Thus, they are likely to compete to a degree. However, the competition is indirect in the sense that each product also provides different benefits and is used in different situations. Indeed, a great many products may compete to a degree with Benefit and with Metamucil. Consequently, managers must decide on the degree of relevance of each group of products in the product market structure.

Defining Broad Relevant Market Boundaries

Generally top management will be interested in taking a broad perspective of the relevant market. Specifically, top management will be concerned with identifying long-run growth opportunities (especially via product development) and with identifying potential threats to the firm's growth due to a changing environment. For example, soft-drink manufacturers have been increasingly concerned with shifts in beverage preferences toward natural and health-oriented products. Similarly, manufacturers of large computers have been concerned about the way the increasing use of personal computers by business firms will influence demand for larger machines.

Specifically, it is appropriate that managers (especially at the top-management level) define the relevant market *broadly* when the following conditions occur:

• Regulatory and technological changes are expected to create new alternatives on the seller's side of the market.

• Economic, demographic, and/or social and cultural changes are likely to change the type or frequency of usage situations on the buyer's side of the market.

---

[2]Russell Mitchell, Zachary Schiller, and John Carey, "Does This Cereal Belong in the Medicine Cabinet?" *Business Week,* July 24, 1989, pp. 22–23.

• A company's sales gains and losses are coming increasingly from alternative forms and classes (rather than merely from brand competitors).

• Competitors do not exist at the product-form level (often because the product is an innovative form).

When these factors are considered, we can see why Procter & Gamble viewed the market for cholesterol-reducing products broadly: technological change is still occurring, buyers are becoming more interested in solutions to cholesterol problems, and there appear to be no direct brand competitors in the low-cholesterol laxative market. Similarly, McDonald's has maintained a broad view of its relevant market.

Rather than defining its business as strictly fast food hamburgers, McDonald's has gradually broadened its market to fast food in general, adding chicken and salad offerings, and apparently contemplating entry into the pizza business. Changing consumer preferences have made the chicken and pizza markets faster growing than the burger market. Additionally, new cooking technologies allow virtually error-free pizzas to be made in five minutes, a factor that would allow McDonald's to utilize its drive-through capacity.[3]

Defining Narrow Relevant Market Boundaries

Middle managers are more likely to define the relevant market in terms of a product form rather than a product class. This focus is most likely to be appropriate to the extent that the planning focus is on short-run decisions and when

• Brand or company competition is far more significant than competition among forms and classes.

• Major environmental changes are not anticipated or are not expected to lead to major changes in alternative forms or in usage situations. (Although it is often dangerous to assume a no-change situation, the assumption may be reasonable in the short run.)

• The product form or the product class is used for a unique set of usage situations so that there are no easily substitutable products.

In the automotive industry, for example, product-form competition (compact versus subcompact versus luxury) exists as does product-class competition (public transportation versus motorcycles versus recreational vehicles versus automobiles). However, the environmental changes influencing product-form choice are usually gradual, and the cost and time involved in responding with major product changes are extensive. For middle managers, then, the primary focus is usually on developing marketing strategies and programs for individual brands and models at the product-form level. On the other hand, top management will be more concerned with long-range strategies reflecting the product mix growth potential of various product forms and of the automobile product class.

[3]Brian Bremmer, "Two Big Macs, Large Fries—And a Pepperoni Pizza, Please," *Business Week*, Aug. 7, 1989, p. 33.

The major steps involved in selecting a relevant market and the consequences of the choice of broad or narrow boundaries are portrayed in Figure 3-2. As suggested in this figure, managers who are concerned with narrow relevant market boundaries will be focusing their attention on brand or supplier choice, otherwise known as *selective* demand. On the other hand, when management sets broad relevant market boundaries, their primary next concern is the analysis of *primary* demand. Figure 3-3 identifies some of the issues in analyzing these two forms of demand.

ANALYZING PRIMARY DEMAND

By defining the relevant market, a manager will have identified the set of relevant competing products and services within which the buying process should be analyzed.

Primary demand is the demand for the product form or product class that has been defined as the relevant market. By analyzing primary demand, managers can learn why and how customers buy a product form or class and who the buyers are in the relevant market. For example, if we define the relevant market as herbal teas, the analysis of primary demand should reveal who buys herbal teas (and who does not), and why some people buy and some do not.

FIGURE 3-2   Elements and implications of the process of defining the relevant market.

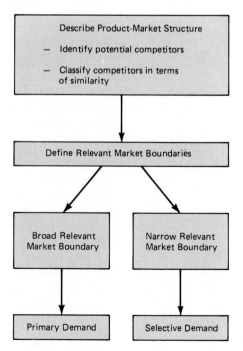

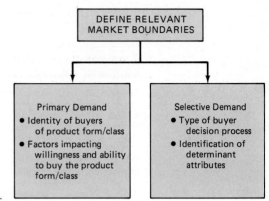

FIGURE 3-3   Analyzing primary and selective demand.

Key Elements in Analyzing Primary Demand

The most important reason for analyzing primary demand is to identify the growth opportunities for the product form or class. This information is of special importance to managers of new product forms (in the initial stages of the product life cycle) and to managers of products in low-growth markets who are seeking ways of revitalizing product-form or product-class sales. In order to identify growth opportunities and the actions that should be taken to realize these opportunities, managers should attempt to answer a series of diagnostic questions about the buying process. These questions fall into two categories:

- Buyer-identification questions
- Willingness-to-buy and ability-to-buy questions

Buyer-Identification Questions

By identifying the existing buyers of a product form or class, managers can obtain insights about the potential growth opportunities in a market and about appropriate means of communicating to the market. Specifically, by identifying the current buyers, managers can learn which types of buyers are likely to have a need for the product form or class. To the extent that these buyers can be described in terms of age, location, and similar characteristics, managers can also project changes in primary demand based on population trends for different groups. Additionally, by identifying the heavier users in a product category, managers can select communications media that are efficient in reaching buyers or can identify individuals the sales force should call on. Table 3-1 lists the major diagnostic questions that might be used in buyer identification.

Buyer or User Characteristics   The characteristics of customers provide managers with a variety of insights into what communication programs are appropriate. In particular, three kinds of characteristics are useful for describing buyers of a product form or class: location, demographics, and lifestyle.

TABLE 3-1   DIAGNOSTIC QUESTIONS ON BUYER IDENTIFICATION

1 Characteristics of buyers or users
Can buyers of this product category be classified by location, demographics, or lifestyle and psychographics?

2 The buying center
Who is involved in the buying process (reference groups; colleagues; family members)?

3 Customer turnover
Is there a high degree of customer turnover due to mobility or because purchase is tied to age or other demographic factors?

Location   Rates of purchase of various product forms may be influenced by climate, population density, cultural traditions, and other factors that vary according to region or urban-suburban-rural distinctions. For example, weather conditions result in a greater demand for ski equipment in New England and in other Northern and Western states. Accordingly, it may be appropriate for manufacturers of ski equipment to spend a greater share of the advertising budget and to have more retail outlets in those regions.

Demographics   Age, sex, education, occupation, and family size are among the characteristics that may typify buyers of a product form. Demographics are useful because most advertising media measure these characteristics in describing their audiences and make this information available to prospective advertisers. Consequently, if we know that the majority of buyers are aged 25 to 44, media can be selected to efficiently reach these customers. Similarly, knowing the characteristics of buyers is considered important by many industrial and retail store managers. These managers often believe that buyers will more likely buy from someone who is viewed as similar in age, education, or other demographic traits. Accordingly, they may assign salespeople to accounts partly on the basis of similarity with the buyer.

Lifestyle   Measures of lifestyle (also called *psychographics* by some marketers) attempt to reflect the way in which products fit into a consumer's normal pattern of living by examining how people spend their time, what things are important to them, and what opinions they have about themselves and the world around them.

In effect, lifestyle measures reflect the influence of social forces on consumption processes. To the extent that lifestyles are related to product-purchase behavior, they may provide clues about why people do or do not use a product regularly. Additionally, the media and advertising setting will be most effective in reaching buyers if it is at least somewhat consistent with customer lifestyles.

To illustrate the usefulness of buyer characteristics for the analysis of primary demand consider the demand for goods and services dominated by consumers over fifty.

> Men over 50 are the heaviest purchasers of many financial investment services. This group is 57% more likely to own mutual funds, 64% more likely to own money market funds, and 107% more likely to own retirement real estate than other groups. This group also shares common media habits. They are 76% more likely to view Sunday news and interview shows, 54% more likely to watch golf on television, and 35% more likely to watch the early evening network news.[4]

The Buying Center   The buying center for a product consists of all the individuals who are involved in the buying decision. In fact, the actual buyer is frequently not the user of a product or service. Accordingly, managers should identify all the individuals who may be involved in the buying process and understand the kind of influence exerted by each one. In the case of some nutritional cereals, for example, advertisements have been directed at parents as well as children, since both are involved in the decision-making process in many homes. Similarly, a manufacturer of sophisticated medical diagnostic equipment found that the sales force was paying too much attention to the purchasing agent and not enough to the chief of surgery, the pathologist, the head nurse, and others with an interest in the product and an influence on the purchase decision.

Customer Turnover   This term refers to the rate at which an organization must replace all or a substantial part of the individuals in its market because of a change in some aspect of the buyer's characteristics. For example, the high rate of geographic mobility in the United States means that a large proportion of the customers of local retail institutions (such as banks) will be newcomers. In other cases, age may be a key factor in customer turnover. For example, buyers of disposable diapers are usually in the market for only a short time. In these situations, managers should recognize that a large part of the marketing effort must be directed toward continually identifying and reaching first-time users or patrons. And since these targets will be less knowledgeable about the product, different marketing strategies and programs must often be designed for them. Thus, a number of major ski resorts such as Vail in Colorado and Waterville Valley in New Hampshire have recognized that as skiers get older they often decrease their skiing activity. Specifically, skiers in their late twenties and thirties are often parents and have less money for ski vacations, and older skiers often drop out altogether for safety reasons. Accordingly, such resorts have begun to revise their advertising and promotional programs, targeting an increasing proportion of their messages to these demographic groups.

As this example demonstrates, the potential market for a product form is often larger than the current level of demand when some potential customers do not buy the product or service or do not buy as frequently as they might. But knowing

---

[4]*Niche Marketing*, Mediamark Research Inc., New York, 1988, pp. 20 and 45.

that a market can be expanded because other potential users exist is not suffi-cient—even if managers can identify such prospects. In addition, managers must understand the factors influencing the willingness and ability to buy the product form or class.

Questions Concerning Willingness and Ability to Buy

Customers cannot be created for a company unless potential buyers are first will-ing and able to purchase the product form or class. To the extent that managers can identify ways of improving the willingness and ability to buy, primary de-mand can be increased either because potential buyers become actual buyers or because actual buyers increase their rate of use. Table 3-2 lists the major diag-nostic questions that might be used to answer these questions.

Willingness to Buy   The main determinant of the willingness to buy a product form or class is the buyer's perception of a product's utility for one or more usage situations. Presumably, a manager's analysis of the product market structure will identify the usage situations for which a product form is potentially applicable. However, in order to determine why some potential buyers do not use the prod-uct for one or more of these purposes, several specific questions should be raised.

1 *Related products and services.* Usage may be limited because the related products and services which are essential to satisfactory usage are inadequate. Manufacturers of personal computers have found that the lack of programs for applications that are not job-related serves as a barrier to sales growth for in-home computers. In contrast, the market for videocassette recorders was ex-panded when consumers became able to rent cassettes of a variety of movies rather than having to buy them. Similarly, managers involved in the marketing of arts organizations are recognizing that related services are important in luring convenience-oriented customers.

The marketing director of Minneapolis' Guthrie Theater successfully lured more sub-urban subscribers to the theater series by adding valet parking with pre-packaged

TABLE 3-2   DIAGNOSTIC QUESTIONS ON WILLINGNESS AND ABILITY TO BUY

1 Willingness to buy
Would new or improved related products and services increase utilization?
What usage problems exist or are perceived to exist?
Is the product or service compatible with the values and experiences of the buyer?
What types of perceived risks are significant in the purchase of the product form?

2 Ability to buy
To what extent do purchase prices and other acquisition or maintenance costs inhibit purchase?
Are product size or packaging factors creating space problems for customers?
Is the spatial availability of the product inadequate?

parking vouchers and a complete dinner package (with either valet parking or limo service to the theater) as optional features.[5]

2 *Usage problems.* Some products are not perceived as performing equally well under all circumstances. It is important to identify situations in which these problems occur and to determine whether the problem lies in the product features or in the user's lack of knowledge about how to use the product correctly. In the first case, new product features may have to be designed; while, in the second case, customer training or technical assistance is necessary to overcome perceived deficiencies. To a large extent, the growth of microwave ovens was due to the efforts of manufacturers and retailers to educate consumers about the correct use of the product so that they could avoid overcooking or undercooking various foods.

3 *Value or experience compatibility.* When a new product requires a change in buying or usage behavior that conflicts with customers' prior usage experiences or with broader value systems, the rate of adoption will be slower. To overcome this source of resistance, managers should design communications that stress not only the advantages of the product but also the advantages of the change in values or usage experiences that go with the product. For example, although earlier low-calorie beers were market failures, Miller's Lite was extremely successful even though it had essentially the same features. In large part, this success reflected the company's foresight in associating a low calorie count with the positive advantage of being *less filling* to appeal to the heavy beer drinker. Values are also tied to cultures, so primary demand for some products can vary dramatically across cultures.

> The Japanese penchant for saving is legendary and one byproduct of this attitude is a tremendous demand for life insurance. Per capita life insurance premiums in Japan are now in excess of $1,000 per year and growing. By contrast, per capita premiums in France are less than $300 and in Greece and Spain less than $100. While insurance demand is dependent on income, the primary source of these differences is culture.[6]

4 *Perceived risk.* The willingness to buy a product form or product class will also depend on the types of risks perceived by potential buyers. Perceived risks will exist when buyers believe there is a strong likelihood of making a poor decision and that the consequences of a poor decision are significant. Specifically, there are six types of risk that may exist when purchasing a product form or class.

a Economic or financial risks—if the purchase price, maintenance costs, or operating costs are high

b Time or convenience risks—if there is the potential for using up a large amount of time in purchasing or using a product

c Performance risks—if there is concern about how well the product's basic function is performed

---

[5]Andrew Feinberg, "Gettin' Culture," *Adweek's Marketing Week,* Aug. 7, 1989, pp. 18–20.
[6]Resa King, Larry Armstrong, Steven J. Dryden, and Jonathon Kapstein, "Who's That Knocking on Foreign Doors? U.S. Insurance Salesmen," *Business Week,* Mar. 6, 1989, pp. 84–85.

d Physical risks—if there is a threat to the health or appearance of the buyer

e Social risks—if the purchase or use of the product may affect the attitudes of reference groups toward the buyer

f Psychological risks—if the purchase or use of the product may influence the buyer's self-image or self-esteem

By knowing the types of risk perceived by buyers, managers will be able to design marketing programs to reduce these risks and thus enhance the willingness to buy. For example, bottled-water suppliers offer home delivery to reduce the convenience risk that a consumer may not want to bring home large, heavy jugs of water. Similarly, some firms offer special trial sizes or money-back guarantees to reduce economic risks. Social risks may be reduced if products or services are advertised in a way that emphasizes that they are socially acceptable.

Ability to Buy The ability to buy a product may be limited by a number of factors, many of which are not under the direct control of managers.

1 *Cost factors.* If a product is a discretionary item, or if less expensive product-form alternatives exist, the price and/or associated buyer costs (operating cost, credit cost, installation cost, maintenance cost) are likely to inhibit primary demand. For example, the demand for solar collectors to heat homes has been limited by the large initial investment required of a homeowner even though solar energy is often very price-competitive viewed in the long run. Similarly, high interest rates on home mortgage loans and automobile loans were partly responsible for declines in new home and automotive sales during the late 1970s and early 1980s.

2 *Packaging and size factors.* Product-form sales may be limited by virtue of space and size requirements. Some potential buyers of home computers, big screen televisions, and similar products simply have a space problem in accommodating these items. Similarly, space limitations may inhibit the purchase of a product in large volumes.

3 *Spatial availability.* The cost of acquiring a product may be a function of locational factors. For example, people in very rural communities have less access to health care and, consequently, visit physicians less frequently. Similarly, the rate of purchase of low-value, postponable purchases can be enhanced by improved access. Consider, for example, the impact on soft-drink sales if vending machines were not available.

Although our discussion of the willingness and ability to buy has focused on the implications for assessing opportunities for building primary demand, these forces can often be important in analyzing selective demand as well. Certainly a firm that gains an advantage on cost or location or which does a better job of reducing perceived risk or offering related services will enhance its ability to acquire customers. Indeed, by developing a thorough analysis of primary demand, managers will usually be in a better position to understand the processes determining brand or supplier choice.

ANALYZING SELECTIVE DEMAND

Selective demand is the demand for a specific brand or supplier within the relevant market. (Note that a supplier could be a retail store, a wholesale business, or a manufacturer selling directly to final users or to wholesale or retail distributors.) In analyzing selective demand, managers are primarily interested in understanding how buyers make choices from the alternative brands or suppliers within the relevant market. However, not all buyers are alike in their choices. Rather, choice is a function of buyers' needs (desired benefits) and buyers' perceptions of alternatives in the context of the specific usage situation.

In this section, we present an approach for examining selective demand. The first step in this approach is to identify the type of decision-making process likely to be used. The second step is to identify the determinant attributes. Table 3-3 summarizes the diagnostic questions used in analyzing selective demand.

Identifying the Types of Decision Processes

Buying decisions are typically categorized in terms of three types: (1) extensive problem solving, (2) limited problem solving, (3) routinized response behavior.[7]

Extensive problem solving occurs when buyers have no prior experience (or at least no recent prior experience) in purchasing a product or service and when the product or service carries a high degree of perceived risk. Because of these conditions, such buying decisions involve extensive information search and deliberation. Buyers must develop an understanding of what the alternatives are and what the important considerations in making a choice should be. The purchase of a house by a consumer or a corporate jet by an organization are illustrative of situations in which extensive problem solving probably occurs.

Limited problem solving characterizes situations in which the buyer has a generally sound knowledge of the product category and is familiar with the important considerations in making a choice, but still takes time to compare and eval-

[7]See William Wilkie, *Consumer Behavior*, Wiley, New York, 1986, chap. 18, for a detailed treatment of the topics in this section.

TABLE 3-3   DIAGNOSTIC QUESTIONS ON SELECTIVE DEMAND

1 Decision processes
How extensive is the search for information?
Do buyers use personal or impersonal sources of information?
Do buyers seek information about brand or supplier characteristics?

2 Determinant attributes
What are the benefits buyers hope to obtain from usage or ownership of the product?
What product attributes (characteristics) are viewed as providing these benefits?
What is the relative importance of the various benefits desired?
How much variation is perceived among the alternatives on each of the important attributes?

uate alternatives. This form of problem solving usually occurs on products for which the buyer has some experience but where the alternatives may change over time or where buyers change their preferences for different attributes. For example, the set of alternatives may change owing to the market introduction of new brands of suppliers, modifications to existing products, or price changes. Preferences may change because of changes in buyers' financial circumstances, changes in products usage, or simply because the buyer is seeking variety. Thus, a buyer may purchase different wines or shirts on different purchase occasions because of changes on the supply side of the market and/or because of changes in the buyer's needs.

Finally, *routinized response behavior* occurs when the decision deals with frequently purchased items. In such cases, buyers have experience with the brands in the product category and perceive no need to search among the alternatives. In some cases of routinized behavior, strong brand loyalty exists so brand choice decisions are reached almost immediately.

Traditionally, these three types of decision processes have been used to describe decisions made by consumers. For organizational buyers, a parallel set of processes (see Figure 3-4) can be identified. The *new task* is a situation in which extensive problem solving will occur because the product is being purchased for the first time. The *modified rebuy* is the term used for limited problem solving in organizational purchases. *Straight rebuys* are essentially routinized response behaviors in that little active search will take place (although for many products in the straight rebuy category, some buyers divide their orders among two or more established suppliers).

There are two reasons why the distinction among types of decision processes is important. First, an understanding of the type of decision process involved in the purchase of a product enables managers to understand buyer search behavior. The more extensive the problem solving required, the greater the amount of

FIGURE 3-4   Types of decision processes.

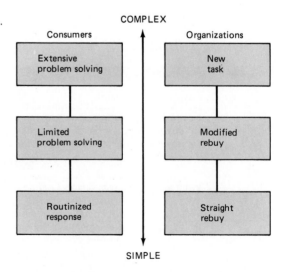

search and the more likely customers will be to rely on personal sources of information (including family members, friends, and salespeople). At the other extreme, routinized decision making leads to limited (even perhaps zero) search with impersonal sources of information likely to play a stronger role than personal sources.

Second, the kind of information required by buyers will vary according to the type of decision process. In routinized decision making, additional information may not even be needed: Buyers may simply respond to those brands or suppliers that have the greatest levels of buyer awareness. In limited problem solving, the key information sought is that which relates to brand or supplier characteristics (attributes). In extensive problem solving, it is necessary to acquire information not only on brand or supplier characteristics but to learn what the important considerations should be in making a choice. Stated differently, in extensive problem solving, buyers must learn the determinant attributes.

Identifying Determinant Attributes

A basic assumption of choice behavior is that buyers will choose the brand or supplier that best fits the buyer's needs. However, because needs represent internal drives and motives, they are difficult to observe and measure. Instead of needs and drives, therefore, marketers use the concept of *benefits sought*. The functional and psychological benefits that buyers hope to receive are generally considered to reflect these underlying needs. Frequently, marketers use the term *attributes* interchangeably with benefits. Attributes represent the specific features or physical characteristics that are designed into a good or service. Benefits are the results the customer receives from using or owning the product. For example, the size and gasoline mileage rating of an automobile are attributes which buyers can use to evaluate the *economy of operation* benefit.

Managers should be aware that, often, the attributes governing choice are not attributes of the physical product but, rather, are those of the broader offering. For example, quick or reliable delivery of raw materials are critically important attributes to many industrial firms. Convenience is generally the most important factor in determining where people have their checking accounts. Similarly, access to related products is often the determinant factor in choice as the following example demonstrates.

> Airstream Inc. has manufactured travel trailers for over 50 years. The company's trailers are easily distinguished by their "silver-bullet" look and Airstream has a good reputation for product durability. However, the decision by many people to buy an Airstream—especially among those buying their second or third Airstream—is the "lifestyle fulfillment" the company offers through its Wally Byam Caravan Clubs. The clubs bring more than 18,000 Airstream owners together to socialize, compare trailers, and share notes on their travels. The clubs are especially popular among older couples whose children have left home and who enjoy the family atmosphere of the clubs, helping Airstream build a large and faithful following.[8]

[8]Jeff Ostroff, "Reaching the 50+ Consumer," *Adweek's Marketing Week,* July 31, 1989, pp. 18–24.

Frequently, several products are similar on a large number of attributes. In such cases, it is important to distinguish one or more determinant attributes—attributes that are most likely to determine the buyer's choice. The preferred supplier or brand will generally be the one that enjoys the buyer's best overall rating on determinant attributes. Two dimensions help make an attribute a determinant attribute: importance and uniqueness. An attribute will be considered important if it provides very desirable benefits; however, if all competing alternatives have the same feature, then other attributes will determine brand choice. For example, buyers may be asked whether safety is of low, medium, or high importance when buying a lawn mower. Further, this feature can be rated according to how much alternative brands vary in providing safety. Figure 3-5 illustrates the potential kinds of responses an individual can make.

If a large number of buyers evaluate the attribute as being in the high-variation–high-importance cell, the attribute is likely to be a major factor influencing brand selection and accordingly will be determinant. Alternatively, a large number of consumers may respond by describing the attribute as high in importance but low in variation if all (or most) competitors are perceived as very similar in providing this attribute. An attribute that is high in importance and low in variation can be considered potentially determinant.[9] If a company can differentiate itself by redesigning the product or promoting an existing advantage on a potentially determinant attribute, then it may be able to turn a potentially determinant attribute into a determinant attribute. For example, assume that lawn mower safety features are perceived as important but all alternative brands are perceived as equal in safety. If the firm can design and promote a unique safety

[9]Robert Hansen, "Heuristic Crosstabulation: A Managerially Oriented Method of Analyzing Consumer Attitude Information," in *The Changing Marketing Environment: New Theories and Applications*, Kenneth Bernhardt et al., eds., pp. 5–8, American Marketing Association, Chicago, 1981.

FIGURE 3-5   A framework for assessing if an attribute is determinant.

Perceived Variation among Alternatives on this Attribute

	Low	Medium	High
Low	Nondeterminant attribute	Nondeterminant attribute	Nondeterminant attribute
Medium			
High	Potentially determinant attribute		Determinant attribute

Perceived Importance of This Attribute

feature, buyers will be more likely to consider this attribute when making brand choices.

The most difficult problem that marketers have in assessing determinant attributes is that not everyone is alike. Indeed, in most product categories, a broad array of brands of suppliers offering different benefit combinations is available. The ability of all of these alternatives to exist is testimony to the fact that different attributes are determinant for different buyers. In effect, the relevant market is segmented.

DEFINING MARKET SEGMENTS

Once the diagnostic questions regarding selective demand have been answered, it usually becomes apparent that not all buyers are alike. Different groups of buyers are likely to respond in different ways to prices, promotional appeals, and product features. Further, different advertising media or distribution systems may be needed to reach different customers. Since buyers may vary along each of the dimensions of the buying process, it is often difficult to decide just how to segment the market operationally. That is, it is often difficult to choose a basis for grouping customers.

In this section, we offer an operational approach for defining market segments that might serve as potential target markets. There are three steps in this process.

1 Establish the specific decision-making purpose of segmenting the relevant market.
2 Select the basis for segmenting that best serves that purpose.
3 Describe the membership and behavior of segment members.

Because the purposes and bases for segmenting consumer markets are quite different from those for segmenting organizational markets, we examine these two types of markets separately.

Purposes and Bases for Segmenting Consumer Markets

Because market segmentation is a managerial tool, the most important consideration in selecting a basis for segmenting is to determine the decision-making purpose of the segmentation effort.[10] The most typical decisions in the case of consumer markets are displayed in Table 3-4 along with the bases most appropriate for each type of decision.

Product Design Product-design decisions should be made with an understanding of the attributes the product must have in order to fulfill buyer usage requirements properly and to provide the desired benefits. Therefore in designing

---

[10]Yoram Wind, "Issues and Advances in Segmentation Research," *Journal of Marketing Research,* August 1978, pp. 317–337.

TABLE 3-4   PURPOSES OF AND BASES FOR SEGMENTING CONSUMER MARKETS

Decision-making purpose	Appropriate bases for segmentation
Product design	Benefits or attributes sought Product usage situation
Advertising message	Benefits or attributes sought Product usage situation
Advertising media	Buyer characteristics Heavy user characteristics
Packaging	Volume or size of purchase Product usage situation
Distribution	Shopping patterns Significance of purchase
Price	Price sensitivity Volume or size of purchase

different product features, models, or options for different segments, the most appropriate bases for segmentation will be benefits or attributes desired.

Remember that differences in benefits or attributes desired are often caused by differences in the product usage situation.[11] As we suggested earlier, most products can be used in a variety of situations. (Orange juice may be drunk with breakfast or after exercise, or it may be mixed in a cocktail. A large computer may be used to perform research, to control a production process, or to process an organization's payroll records.) Accordingly, alternative brands or suppliers within a relevant market may be used in different situations, and as the situation differs, the specific needs (benefits) that buyers hope to satisfy from buying or using a product may also differ.

Of course, differences in benefits or usage may be closely associated with differences in other buying-process variables (such as demographics or lifestyle). While it will be useful for managers to know that such relationships exist (for communications purposes), it is often dangerous to infer buying motives from demographics. Buyer characteristics may be useful for predicting who will purchase a product form or product class but are generally much less useful in predicting brand choice.

Advertising   Advertising programs entail a number of different decisions, each of which requires a different basis for segmentation. As Table 3-4 indicates, managers responsible for advertising-message decisions should segment the market on the basis of benefits and attributes or product usage. This is because the appeals to be used should focus on the benefits most desired or on buyer usage problems. On the other hand, in selecting media, buyer characteristics are ap-

[11]Peter Dickson, "Person-Situation: Segmentation's Missing Link," *Journal of Marketing,* Fall 1982, pp. 56–64.

propriate bases for segmentation, because many magazines and TV shows reach audiences with specific demographic characteristics or lifestyles.

Packaging and Distribution   Decisions about packaging and distribution should be made after considering purchase and shopping patterns. Accordingly, if the purpose of segmenting is to examine alternative package sizes and designs or alternative kinds of distribution outlets, these patterns will be useful bases for grouping customers. However, differences in purchase and shopping patterns may also be closely associated with differences in buyer characteristics. For example, age and family-size differences will be associated with differences in the use of large-sized packages in the case of soft drinks, while income and lifestyle differences will be associated with the selection of different types of retail outlets (for example, discount stores versus specialty stores) for clothing.

Price   Decisions about price should be made after examining the price sensitivity of the buyer. In Chapter 9, we will examine some approaches for attempting to estimate price sensitivity. In addition, price segmentation often is used when large differences in purchase volume exist across customers.

When considering any of these segmentation purposes in a multicultural relevant market it is important to recognize that cultural forces can have an important impact on segmentation structure by influencing the importance of different benefits. Consider, as examples, the following:

> Although potato chips seem to have universal appeal tastes vary from country to country. In Korea, Frito-Lay sells a wheat, squid and peanut ball called cuttle fish. In Great Britain salt and vinegar and prawn cocktail flavored chips are best sellers.[12]
>
> The rapid growth of the Hispanic population in the United States has led marketers in a number of product categories to examine specific preferences and needs of this portion of the market. For grocery retailers, the growth of the Hispanic population poses special challenges since a large portion of this market does not read the English language daily newspapers where supermarkets advertise most. Additionally, the benefits desired by Hispanic shoppers are different. The Tianguis chain in Southern California has been successful by recognizing that most Hispanics view shopping as a social event involving browsing, chatting, listening to music, and eating. At Tianguis, the stores feature live mariachi music, food stands, and outdoor patios for dining.[13]

Purposes and Bases for Segmenting Organizational Markets

In the previous section we suggested that the basis for segmentation should be selected according to the decision to be made. This guideline also holds for organizational markets. However, the actual bases employed in organizational market segmentation will differ because of differences in the typical uses of seg-

---

[12]"Frito-Lay's Cooking Again, and Profits Are Starting to Pop," *Business Week*, May 22, 1989, pp. 66–70.

[13]Alfredo Corchado, "Hispanic Supermarkets Are Blossoming," *The Wall Street Journal*, Jan. 23, 1989, p. B1.

mentation and because of some major differences between organizational and consumer buying processes.

In particular, several major distinctions are important in contrasting organizational market segmentation with consumer market segmentation. First, the cost of using personal selling and the relative importance of personal selling generally far outweigh advertising in the promotion mix. Thus, it is more critical for managers to be efficient in allocating salespeople to customers than in allocating advertising expenditures to media. Accordingly, in segmenting organizational markets, management must have segmentation bases that will enable it to make sales-force allocation decisions.

Second, compared with consumer decision making, organizational decision making frequently involves a number of individuals. Consequently, choice criteria may be known only if the seller can identify the individual influences and relationships involved in a buying center. As a result, segmenting according to the organization of the buying center will often be necessary.

Finally, organization buyers are more likely to intentionally limit the amount of search. That is, organizations often choose to consider only a few of the available suppliers in order to receive preferred treatment from these suppliers on delivery and price by maintaining strong ongoing relationships with them. Similarly, in order to reduce the risk of shortages in supply (due to contingencies such as strikes) or in order to maintain price competition among suppliers, large buyers may maintain a policy of spreading purchases of the same item among several qualified sources, rather than use only a single supplier. Consequently, managers must understand the factors that determine the set of sellers that a buyer will consider. This means that the type of search process will often be an important element in segmentation.

Table 3-5 specifies the most common purposes of and bases for segmenting organizational markets.

Sales-Force Allocation   Decisions on allocating the sales force can require a number of different bases for segmentation. Account size or volume is frequently a useful basis because a small percentage of industrial buyers and resellers typically account for a large percentage of sales. Generally this will lead manage-

TABLE 3-5   PURPOSES OF AND BASES FOR SEGMENTING ORGANIZATIONAL MARKETS

Decision-making purpose	Appropriate bases for segmentation
Sales-force allocation to accounts	Volume Location Product usage (industry type)
Product design and communications appeals	Product usage (application type) Benefits and attributes sought
Communications targets	Buying-center members

ment to design its sales-force policies so that large accounts are called on more frequently than small accounts.

Product Design and Communications Appeal Decisions   Frequently the features that a firm should design into the product and the basic sales appeals that marketing managers should emphasize in communications will vary from one customer to another. In such cases, segmentation on the basis of product usage may be appropriate, because the same basic product may be used to perform different functions. For example, a computer may be used for accounting and payroll purposes, for inventory control, for production processing, or for research and development. Knowing how different segments will use a product will help managers to determine the product features (such as quality levels and options) and related services to be offered and to specify the sales message to be emphasized in each segment.

Benefit segmentation may be employed for the same purposes. As in the case of consumer goods, benefits usually provide the clearest directions for designing products and for selecting appeals, since they most closely reflect buying motives and needs. As Table 3-6 indicates, a large number of possible benefits can be considered by management in defining market segments.

However, the process of identifying benefit segments in organizational markets is complicated by the fact that many individuals may be involved in the buying center. To effectively use benefit segmentation, the sales force must usually spend a good deal of time learning about the organization in order to identify the benefits desired by the various buying-center members.

TABLE 3-6   POTENTIAL TYPES OF BENEFITS USEFUL
FOR SEGMENTING ORGANIZATIONAL MARKETS

Industrial buyers
Price
Financing terms
Availability of lease or buy options
Delivery time
Quality control and reliability of performance
Ability to meet technical specifications
Other product-performance characteristics
Technical advice on usage
Maintenance, repair, operating services provided

Distributors
Gross margin
Promotional support
Inventory investment required
Space requirements
Impact on store image
Impact on customer traffic
Number of competitors carrying the same product

Communications Targets Organizational customers often differ in terms of who makes or influences the buying decision. In selecting advertising programs, media designed to reach purchasing agents may be appropriate in one segment, while media designed to reach line supervisors, design engineers, or controllers may be required in more complex buying-center segments. Similarly, before a selection can be made of the buying-center members that the sales force should call on when visiting an organization, it is important to identify the most influential persons in the buying center.

Describing Segment Membership and Behavior

By defining market segments in terms of buyers' ideal combinations of determinant attributes, managers can isolate the key choice criteria used in different segments in order to design market offerings. However, managers are also interested in knowing what potential sales opportunities are presented by each segment and how the members in each segment can best be targeted in attempting to influence their choice. Table 3-7 lists some of the types of questions managers should try to answer in assessing sales opportunities and targeting options.

Potential Sales Opportunities Not every segment of the market will present the same potential sales opportunity and, because organizations operate with limited resources, the relative importance of different segments should be considered in determining how resources will be allocated. For example, managers in industrial firms must determine how to allocate the time and effort of the sales force to different segments and among specific accounts within each segment. Similarly, decisions regarding whether to design specific features or special advertising programs for a given segment should only be made after the sales opportunity is known.

Frequently, firms find that the variations among customers in terms of potential sales opportunities are so large that potential sales opportunity becomes the ma-

TABLE 3-7 DIAGNOSTIC QUESTIONS FOR DESCRIBING SEGMENTS

1. Assessing potential sales opportunities

How many buyers are there in each segment?
How frequently does the usage situation occur?
In the case of durable goods, how frequently is the product replaced?
In what volumes or quantities do segment members buy?
What is the potential for selling related products and services to these customers?

2. Targeting segment members

What are their demographic/lifestyle characteristics?
Who are the key decision makers in the family or organization?
What media are they exposed to?
Where do they shop?

jor element in segmentation. For example, many banks have directed special efforts toward "upscale" customers who are able to maintain very large account balances and who use a variety of bank services. These special efforts have included new products (such as special checking-type accounts which earn high rates of interest if large minimum deposit levels are maintained) and special services (such as "personal bankers"—individual bank personnel who are assigned to work on all of the needs of selected high-balance customers). Similarly, most industrial firms offer quantity discounts to large-volume buyers and many have established *national account* programs in which selected personnel are assigned to provide special technical assistance and/or service to all offices or facilities of large customers which operate in a variety of locations.

Targeting Segment Members   In order to make the most effective use of the segmentation concept, it is useful to determine if segments differ in terms of the identity of the buyers and/or in terms of the search processes they use. If, in fact, the members of a segment are similar in terms of characteristics or search processes, managers can use this information in several ways:

- To select appropriate advertising media
- To identify the individuals to be called on by the sales force
- To develop special methods for presenting a sales message
- To determine the types of retail outlets through which to sell

Specifically, managers should attempt to identify similarities among the members of each segment by answering the questions listed in Table 3-7. In considering this information, managers must recognize that the purpose is to examine similarities within benefit or attribute segments. That is, demographics may well give clues as to the buyer's determinant attributes, but seldom do all individuals with a given set of demographic characteristics have the same determinant attributes.

For example, if we were to find that the low-caffeine segment of the cola market is heavily composed of adults over 50 years of age, this is useful in deciding how to select media for marketing a low-caffeine cola. But this information does not mean that all (or even most) adults over 50 years of age prefer caffeine-free colas. There may be other segments of the cola market that actually have more buyers in the over-50 age group. The key point is that within a relevant market, demographics are generally more useful for *describing* a benefit segment than for *defining* a target market segment because specific benefits sought usually vary among people with similar traits.

IDENTIFYING POTENTIAL TARGET MARKETS

The process of market analysis is the first step in designing a marketing strategy for a product or a line of related products. Specifically, a market analysis enables managers to identify potential target markets toward which the marketing effort might be focused.

Note that there are two types of target markets. If the market analysis indicates that there is an opportunity to substantially increase the willingness or ability to purchase a product form or class, then a firm could consider the total product-class or product-form market as a potential target market. If the market analysis indicates that there are one or more market segments where the firm could offer the benefits desired and could effectively target the members of such segments, these segments would constitute potential target markets. As examples, consider the following:

> The suncare products market is estimated to be worth $500 million and growing rapidly as consumers become increasingly aware of the hazards of unprotected exposure to the sun. Sun screens represent about 44% of that total and are growing at 15% per year. In spite of this growth, a small Pennsylvania firm, Solar Care Inc. has found a new opportunity to expand sun screen sales. The company found that certain potential usage situations were being passed over by consumers because existing sun screens come in large bottles and are messy to handle. Consequently, the company developed Sun Sense, a greaseless sun screen in a disposable towelette that the consumer simply wipes on. A towelette can fit in a wallet and one towelette covers the face, neck, arms and legs and lasts a full day. The product was designed to meet the needs of people who enjoy outdoor sports such as tennis, golf, skiing and bicycling.[14]

The diagnostic questions discussed in this chapter provide the kinds of information that would be needed to identify the needs of markets or segments such as the one Solar Care found. However, not all potential market needs can be profitably met by every competitor. The success of a marketing strategy ultimately depends not just on being able to meet a need revealed by market analysis but also on other factors that influence the market opportunity and the ability to meet the requirements for success in that target market.

Figure 3-6 portrays the relationship between market analysis and the other sources and types of information that will influence the final selection of a target market and marketing strategy. As this figure suggests, managers must also consider the other elements of the situation analyses in order to obtain answers to questions like

- What are competitors' capabilities, and how do consumers evaluate our offerings versus those of competitors?
- What is the size and what are the growth prospects for this market?
- What costs are involved in meeting market needs and in targeting our offer, and are these reasonable relative to the expected sales payoff?

Answers to these questions can be obtained from the analyses discussed in Chapters 4, 5, and 6. Additionally, as we discussed in the preceding chapter, the final decision on a marketing strategy will also be consistent with the product objective.

---

[14]Frank Allen, "Tiny Solar Care Seeks Place in the Sun as a Start-Up in a Competitive Market," *The Wall Street Journal,* May 13, 1988, p. B1; and Laurie Freeman, "Suncare Baby," *Advertising Age,* Apr. 3, 1989.

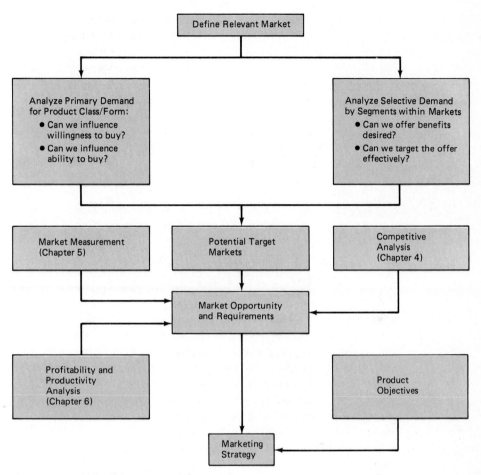

FIGURE 3-6   The process of identifying target markets.

CONCLUSION

If an organization is to achieve customer satisfaction, it must first and foremost understand its market. In this chapter, we have presented an approach for analyzing markets which is useful for managers concerned with long-term corporate planning and for those concerned with short-term marketing strategies. Specifically, we examined the process of defining the relevant market—the primary competitive arena of concern to a manager. Subsequently, we presented diagnostic questions and concepts which managers can employ to analyze primary and selective demand within the relevant market and to define market segments. Finally, we discussed how the information from these various analyses could be used to identify potential target markets and to define the kinds of market offerings needed to achieve customer satisfaction in these target markets. Each of these steps is of critical importance to the selection of a market strategy, as is demonstrated by the market situation confronting appliance makers in Western Europe.

Analyzing the Domestic Appliance Market for Western Europe*

On August 18, 1988, Whirlpool Corporation announced a joint venture with Philips, Europe's number two appliance maker. At that time, the chairman of Whirlpool indicated this joint venture was undertaken to take advantage of Whirlpool's management expertise and well-established brands. With the elimination of trade barriers within Europe's common market countries expected by 1992, the company hoped that establishing business there through a joint venture would give Whirlpool the chance of becoming a leader in the world appliance industry.

The European market for home appliances was growing faster than the market in the United States but was far more complex. No company has been able to sell identical appliances worldwide because appliance markets are so different from country to country. For instance, the French prefer to cook their food at high temperatures and the resulting splattering of grease on oven walls leads most French customers to want self-cleaning ovens. On the other hand, in West Germany where cooking is done at lower temperatures, there is not much demand for self-cleaning ovens. Hot-water heating systems vary from country to country and automatic washing machines may have up to sixteen different combinations of fabric types and cycles to choose from. In addition, the French prefer top-loading machines while Britons prefer front loaders. West Germans like machines with high spin speeds while Italians prefer slower spinners. While the Spanish wash in cold water and the Italians with water that is nearly boiling, Germans and the British prefer tepid water.

The complexity of the European market has contributed to the existence of over 300 local appliance manufacturers. In the past, large international appliance makers have attempted to reach broader markets with their products. However, consumers have viewed these products as compromises that are neither German, Italian, nor French.

Merloni Elettrodomestici of Faboriano, Italy, has about 10 percent of the European market. Merloni's Ariston and Indesit brands are produced in ten plants in Italy and Portugal. Merloni executives feel the market trend is toward steady globalization but at the same time away from mass production due to the need to quickly adapt new lines to demand. In recent years, Merloni has focused attention on more automated production which provides them with greater speed in

*Based on "The Myth of the Euro-Consumer," *The Economist,* Nov. 4, 1989, pp. 91–92; Zachary Schiller, Joyce Heard, Karen Wolman, and Thane Peterson, "Whirlpool Plots the Invasion of Europe," *Business Week,* Sept. 5, 1988, pp. 70–72; Giacomo Ferrari, "The Personal Touch," *Business Week: International,* Oct. 30, 1989, special advertising section: Italy.

adapting new lines to meet small consumer demand changes. In Merloni's plants, production planning, handling supplies, and deliveries to clients are highly automated. Production planning for each model now only requires one week's advance notice compared to 2 years ago when this required up to 2 months.

1 How would you describe the way top management at Whirlpool and Merloni have defined the relevant market boundaries for household appliances in Western Europe?

2 What would you select as the principal purposes and bases for segmenting the consumer market for major appliances in Western Europe?

3 What specific questions would you ask if you were a marketing manager for Whirlpool/Philips or Merloni charged with the task of selecting potential target markets in Western Europe?

QUESTIONS AND SITUATIONS FOR DISCUSSION

1 Reynolds Metals Co. introduced a new line of colored plastic food wrap in transparent shades of red, green, yellow, and blue. Research had indicated women were very favorably disposed toward the product but men didn't see the point of color differences in a plastic food wrap. Since men comprised the majority of supermarket purchasing staffs, initial distribution was difficult to obtain. What diagnostic questions seem to have been overlooked in conducting a market analysis of the plastic food wrapper market?

2 Sub-Zero manufactures expensive, custom-finished refrigerators built into fancy kitchens. Sub-Zero's best-seller is a 30.5-cubic foot side-by-side refrigerator-freezer which costs $2000 more than the top-of-the-line unit made by Amana. Is the relevant market for Sub-Zero the same as that for Amana? How would you explain how a buyer would select either the Sub-Zero or the Amana brand?

3 The athletic director at your university has asked you to help identify ways of improving attendance at home baseball games. Discuss the diagnostic questions you would try to answer and illustrate how the answers you might obtain would lead to the development of specific marketing strategies and programs.

4 Psychographics reveal BMW automobile owners to be (or to want to be) aggressive, athletic, high-achieving types who buy high-risk stocks and graphite tennis rackets. In addition, they have fewer children than owners of Saab and Mercedes Benz cars. How would information such as this be useful to the manufacturers of BMWs and to the local BMW dealer?

5 As a rule, most firms that sell to organizational buyers would prefer to be able to segment their markets on a basis of product usage rather than on benefits. Why do you think this is the case?

6 What factors would you use in segmenting the market for a new word processing software package developed to compete with the leading software packages on the market? Why?

7 Indicate some ways of segmenting the market for printers used with personal computers. How would these various potential target markets differ from the viewpoint of marketing strategy?

SUGGESTED ADDITIONAL READINGS

Aaker, David A., and J. Gary Shansby, "Positioning Your Product," *Business Horizons,* May–June 1982, pp. 56–62.

Day, George S., Allan Shocker, and Rajendra Srivastava, "Customer-Oriented Approaches to Identifying Product Markets," *Journal of Marketing,* Fall 1979, pp. 8–19.

Dickson, Peter, "Person-Situation: Segmentation's Missing Link," *Journal of Marketing,* Fall 1982, pp. 56–64.

Forbis, John L., and Nitin T. Mehta, "Value-Based Strategies for Industrial Products," *Business Horizons,* May–June 1981, pp. 32–42.

Green, Paul E., Abba M. Krieger, and Catherine M. Schaffer, "Quick and Simple Benefit Segmentation," *Journal of Advertising Research,* June–July 1985, pp. 9–17.

Holak, Susan, and Donald Lehman, "Purchase Intentions and the Dimensions of Innovation," *Journal of Product Innovation Management,* March 1990, pp. 59–73.

McQuiston, Daniel, "Novelty, Complexity, and Importance as Causal Determinants of Buyer Behavior," *Journal of Marketing,* April 1989, pp. 66–79.

Morden, A. R., "Market Segmentation and Practical Policy Formulation," *Quarterly Review of Marketing,* January 1985, pp. 1–12.

Wells, William, "Psychographics: A Critical Review," *Journal of Marketing Research,* May 1975, pp. 196–213.

Young, Shirley, Leland Ott, and Barbara Feigin, "Some Practical Considerations in Market Segmentation," *Journal of Marketing Research,* August 1978, pp. 405–412.

CHAPTER 4

COMPETITIVE ANALYSIS

OVERVIEW

In Chapter 3 we discussed the forces that influence primary and selective demand and presented a five-step approach for analyzing a market. The final step in that approach was the identification of potential target markets. As we suggested in that discussion, achieving success in a target market involves more than just the ability to satisfy customer needs: Consideration must also be given to the competitive situation in a market.

In this chapter, we present a five-step approach for performing a competitive analysis. The steps in this approach are portrayed in Figure 4-1.

1 *Define the target market.* This step is the result of the market analysis discussed in Chapter 3. Recall that by performing this step we establish the product-market boundaries of interest and identify any specific target segments within those boundaries.

2 *Identify direct competitors.* Direct competitors are those who are most likely to take customers away from us (or to be sources of new customers) because they serve the same target market.

3 *Assess the competitive dynamics of the market.* Markets vary in terms of the degree to which changes in the competitive structure are likely to occur. Accordingly, we discuss how competition may change over time because of the product life cycle, technological breakthroughs, and the entry of new competitors.

4 *Assess the intensity of competition.* In this step we employ some basic concepts of economic theory used to describe the degree of competition and the extent to which competition is likely to be price-oriented.

5 *Assess competitive advantage.* Ultimately, managers must have a sense for what relative advantages are possessed by each competitor. This entails examin-

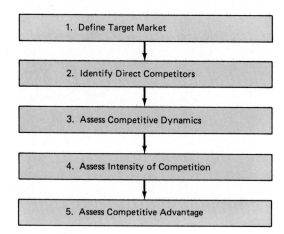

FIGURE 4-1   Steps in competitive analysis.

ing both the *positions of advantage* achieved (from the customer's perspective) and the skills and resources that constitute the *sources of advantage*.

DEFINING THE TARGET MARKET

As we discussed in Chapter 3 the relevant market is the set of goods and/or services (within the total product market structure) that management considers to be strategically important. Additionally, we noted that the relevant market could be defined at various levels such as,

1 Competing brands (or suppliers) with a product form
2 Competing product forms within a product class
3 Competing product classes within a generic need

A target market is the relevant market or the portion of the relevant market that a firm is most interested in serving. The target market might be defined in terms of a generic need (recreation), a product class (bicycles), a specific product form (ten-speed, touring bikes), or a target customer segment for one of those markets (safety and price-oriented buyers between 21 and 40 years of age).

The determination of the target market should help management identify the current direct competitors—those perceived as presently serving the target market.

IDENTIFYING DIRECT COMPETITORS

We define direct competitors as firms who are likely to gain or lose a substantial share of customers from each other over time because they serve the same customers and offer similar benefits. A consequence of this definition is that the delineation of direct competitors should be made by customers in the target market.

That is, two firms are direct competitors if customers (or potential customers) *say* they are.

Consider, for example, Figures 4-2 and 4-3. Figure 4-2 portrays the product-market structure of the product class *cookies,* indicating some of the various product forms and subforms in this category. If a firm were to identify the "moist and chewy" cookie market (which represents about 15 percent of total packaged cookie industry sales) as the target market, the five most direct competitors can be identified by management based on the technical characteristics "moist" and "chewy."

But do consumers view all of these cookies as equal competitors? Because there may be a very large number of brands in a category and because many products have highly subjective characteristics, managers usually rely on some *perceptual mapping* techniques. This class of techniques is designed to portray how consumers perceive the various potential competitors in a market.

Perceptual Mapping Techniques

Figure 4-3 is an example of a perceptual map generated by a technique called *multidimensional scaling.* In this technique, consumers are asked to rate each pair of products in terms of their degree of similarity using a scale such as that in Figure 4-4. These similarity judgments are then analyzed by statistical programs that determine the relative closeness of the brands from the perspective of the target market customers as a whole. Because traditional multidimensional scaling approaches map only the similarity judgments, the reasons why some pairs of

FIGURE 4-2   Alternative ways of defining competition in "the cookie market."

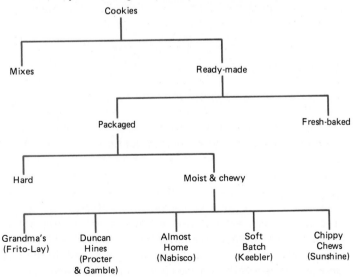

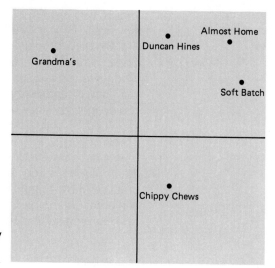

FIGURE 4-3   A perceptual map of the moist and chewy cookie market using multidimensional scaling.

	Very Similar				Very Different
	1	2	3	4	5
Grandma's/Duncan Hines	—	—	—	—	—
Grandma's/Almost Home	—	—	—	—	—
Grandma's/Soft Batch	—	—	—	—	—
Grandma's/Chippy Chews	—	—	—	—	—
Duncan Hines/Almost Home	—	—	—	—	—
Soft Batch/Chippy Chews	—	—	—	—	—

FIGURE 4-4   Measuring perceived similarity.

brands are more similar than other pairs must be inferred. So, the axis in Figure 4-3 will normally have to be labeled based on the researcher's judgment.

A second basic approach to perceptual mapping is *factor analysis based*. Rather than using similarity judgments, buyers are asked to rate each competitor on each of the determinant attributes, using a scale such as the one in Figure 4-5. These ratings are then subjected to a statistical factor analysis which examines the correlations among the ratings. Based on this examination, the procedure usually finds that the various attributes can be reduced to a very small number of underlying "factors" (e.g., economy, stays fresh in the box, appeals to the whole family, and so forth) that are used to evaluate alternatives.

Attribute no. 1

_____cookies stay fresh in the package

	Strongly Agree				Strongly Disagree
	1	2	3	4	5
Grandma's	—	—	—	—	—
Duncan Hines	—	—	—	—	—
Almost Home	—	—	—	—	—
Soft Batch	—	—	—	—	—
Chippy Chews	—	—	—	—	—

Attribute no. 2

You get your money's worth with_____cookies.

.
.
.

FIGURE 4-5   Rating alternatives on attributes.

Figure 4-6 is a hypothetical perceptual map developed from a factor analysis. As we can see, the factor analysis method not only portrays which brands are closest competitors (based on their nearness to one another) it also gives some clues as to *why* some brands are close to each other and others are not. Table 4-1 summarizes some advantages and disadvantages of the two alternative methods.

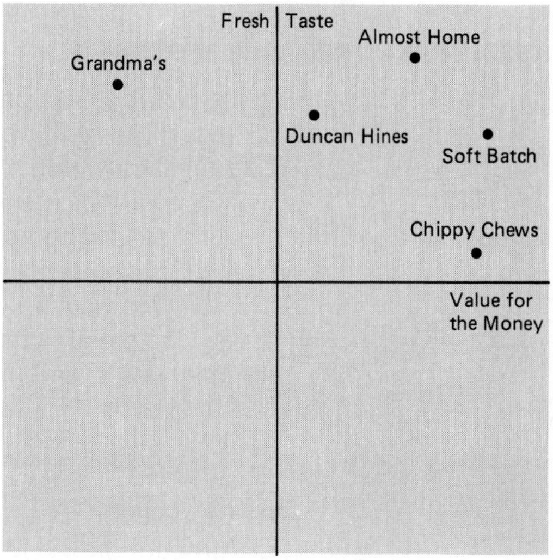

FIGURE 4-6   A perceptual map of the moist and chewy cookie market using factor analysis.

TABLE 4-1 COMPARING PERCEPTUAL MAPPING TECHNIQUES

Factor analysis	Multidimensional scaling
Input	
Consumer's ratings of brands on attributes	Consumer's direct judgments of similarity
Advantages	
Can understand why brands are perceived as similar	Does not require list of benefits
Disadvantages	
Require that all benefits and attributes are known	Reasons for similarity must be inferred
Some subjective benefits are hard to measure	Maps often change if we add or delete brands from process

Source: Adapted from Glen L. Urban, John R. Hauser, and Nikhilesh Dholakia, *Essentials of New Product Management*, Prentice-Hall, Englewood Cliffs, N.J., 1987, p. 117.

Importantly, perceptual mapping techniques are readily available and can be performed on most current personal computers. Because they enable managers to obtain the consumer's perception of the market, they can be of tremendous help in understanding the competition. It is also important, however, to recognize a key assumption underlying these techniques: uniformity of perceptions. To the extent that members of the target market are familiar with all of these brands or suppliers (at least through advertising), they are more likely to share similar perceptions. However, when buyers vary widely in their awareness of alternative brands within a product form or product class, their perceptions will also vary. In the latter case, separate analyses should be conducted to determine how perceptions vary across segments.

ASSESSING COMPETITIVE DYNAMICS

In the previous section, we discussed perceptual mapping, a procedure for taking a "snapshot" of the competitive structure of a market (as perceived by buyers). Like the family album, new pictures are necessary over time if we want to know what the various members look like today.

But assessing competitive dynamics is much more than the process of tracking changes in competition; it really involves attempting to *project* what the competitive environment will look like down the road. Specifically, managers need to assess potential changes due to the product life cycle, technological discontinuities, and the likelihood of new market entrants.

Pioneering Advantage

As we noted in Chapter 2, competition changes substantially over the course of the product life cycle. In the introductory stage, the innovator (or *pioneer*) that initiated the life cycle may be a virtual monopolist. But during the growth phase, a number of new competitors enter the market, lured by the prospects for rapid sales growth. When growth levels off as the life cycle approaches maturity, a shakeout occurs, with only the strongest brands surviving.

From the perspective of competitive analysis, the critical questions confronting management are: "What are the forces that will enable our firm to succeed in the growth stage?" and "What will determine survival (long-term market share) in this market?"

Critical to answering these questions is the issue of the *pioneering advantage,* the market advantage that results from being the innovator in a market.

Table 4-2 provides a very strong picture of the advantages of pioneering. This table shows that the average market share attained by a consumer product depends substantially on when it enters a market. (The study was designed to hold product performance and advertising effects equal for all competitors.) For example, if a market contained five brands, on average the first brand to enter (that is, the *pioneer*) held a 30.8 percent share, while the fifth brand held a 13.9 percent share.

Why do pioneers hold such an advantage? There appear to be several factors involved.

1 Because they are the *prototypes* for all products that follow, the pioneer influences judgments about which attributes are important.[1]

2 The first brand has more of an opportunity to build loyalty through repeat purchasing.

3 Later entrants will have more difficulty in getting distribution and consumer awareness and trial. Unless the late entrant has some clearly unique attribute there will be little incentive for distributors to stock it or for consumers to try it.

---

[1]See Gregory Carpenter and Kent Nakamoto, "Consumer Preference Formation and Pioneering Advantage," *Journal of Marketing Research,* August 1989, pp. 285–298, for a detailed discussion of this point.

TABLE 4-2 SHARE POTENTIAL VERSUS ORDER OF ENTRY

Number of brands in market	Market share held by					
	1st	2d	3d	4th	5th	6th
1	100	—	—	—	—	—
2	58.5	41.5	—	—	—	—
3	43.6	31.0	25.4	—	—	—
4	35.7	25.4	20.8	18.1	—	—
5	30.8	21.9	17.9	15.5	13.9	—
6	27.3	19.4	15.9	13.8	12.4	11.2

Source: Adapted from G. L. Urban, T. Carter, S. Gaskin, and Z. Mucha, "Market Share Rewards to Pioneering Brands: An Empirical Analysis and Strategic Implications," *Management Science,* June 1986, p. 654.

The pioneer's advantage depends heavily on the rate of trial for the product category, however. Thus, while Apple was really the pioneer in personal computing, IBM was able to catch up and take the lead because the rate of adoption was modest in the introductory stage of the life cycle.

Additionally, other research has shown that the pioneering advantage is not automatically maintained into maturity. A pioneer's ability to maintain the leadership position depends on

- Maintaining a high level of quality relative to price
- Offering a breadth of product-line options to meet the needs of different segments
- Maintaining superior distribution
- The rate of change in the product (with few seasonal or periodic model changes being favorable to the pioneer).[2]

Consider, for example, the situation confronting Jiffy Lube.

> Jiffy Lube pioneered the quick oil change business in 1979 with seven stores. By 1986, the chain had grown to 350 stores and had attracted the attention of potential competitors such as major oil companies and rental car companies. Because of the far greater financial resources possessed by these firms, Jiffy Lube's founder, Jim Hindman, had to decide how to preserve his pioneering advantage. Hindman chose to seek additional funding to continue expanding as fast as possible in order to obtain the best locations before competitors could reach them. He also closely monitored dealer performance to insure that quality service was being delivered. By 1989, Jiffy Lube had retained its leading position, holding a 3 to 1 advantage over its nearest competitor, Minit Lube.[3]

Indeed, many firms choose to be followers instead of pioneers. Although they are mindful of the pioneering advantage, they also recognize that there are three advantages from being a follower.

1 Followers usually incur fewer initial marketing costs because the pioneer has performed the task of educating the market about the product class or form. For example, Kimberly Clark allowed Procter & Gamble to spend millions pioneering the concept of disposable diapers before entering the market.

2 Followers can learn from competitors' actions regarding the selection of distribution channels, pricing, demand estimates, or user problems. IBM's success as a follower in the personal computer market was aided by the company's observation of the importance of developing a strong network of retail dealers.

3 Followers can apply the latest in technology. Sony was the pioneer in videocassette recorders, but eventually was overtaken by followers who employed the newer VHS technology instead of the beta technology.

---

[2]William T. Robinson and Claes Fornell, "Sources of Market Pioneer Advantages in Consumer Goods Industries," *Journal of Marketing Research*, August 1985, pp. 305–317.
[3]Paul B. Brown, "Looking Out for Number One," *Inc.*, April 1989, pp.165–166.

Technological Discontinuities

Ultimately, most product life cycles end—often abruptly—because of a technological innovation. Thus, if the future competitive structure of a market is to be understood, managers should attempt to determine the potential for a technological discontinuity.

A technological discontinuity results when a major enhancement of a consumer benefit occurs due to new technology. In effect, the new product form totally eliminates the life cycle of an existing product. For example, the share of total automotive tire sales held by glass-belted radial tires dropped by 40 points in 18 months when steel-belted radials were introduced. Similarly, sales of electromechanical cash registers slid from 90 percent of the market in 1972 to 10 percent in 1976.[4]

Being able to predict the decline and fall of a product life cycle due to changing technology is not always easy. However, there is a greater motivation for competitors and potential competitors to pursue an innovative technology when the current technology (the foundation for the current product line) is close to its limits. Based on studies conducted by McKinsey & Co. consultants, there appear to be several warning signs that a technology is approaching its limits.

- Greater efforts are needed to produce even small improvements in performance.
- R&D shifts more toward process improvement and away from product improvement.
- Sales growth comes more from serving new segments and less from "across the board" improvements in market position.
- There are wide differences in R&D spending among competitors with apparently minor differences in market effects.
- Some market leaders begin to lose share to smaller rivals in selected market segments, a possible indicator that the small firms have a new technology enabling them to be more productive with their dollars.[5]

New Market Entrants

While the identity of current direct competitors is important, it is equally essential to be able to identify likely future competitors. However, in many cases the identity of all potential competitors may not be immediately obvious. Sometimes consumer usage patterns will change, creating different industry and market boundaries. Consider, for example, the following:

> The publisher of the trade journal *Confectioner* recently noted that "Candy isn't an industry in itself anymore." Indeed, the lines between candy, ice cream bars, and other snacks are becoming less distinct. When consumers want something sweet, they consider a whole range of choices.[6]

---

[4]Richard N. Foster, *Innovation: The Attacker's Advantage*, Summit Books, New York, 1986, p. 162.
[5]Ibid., pp. 215–217.
[6]"Candy May Be Dandy but Confectioners Want a Sweeter Bottom Line," *Business Week*, Oct. 6, 1986, p. 66.

As market boundaries change, firms find themselves competing with different product forms and classes and with different organizations. Often these organizations produce a variety of different products and may compete on several fronts. For example, Mars Inc. now markets Snickers candy bars and Dove Bar ice cream products. Nestlé Foods competes with Mars in both markets. However, when Nestlé and Mars entered the ice cream business, they also began competing with a variety of non-candy-producing firms. New competition can also arise from firms with which a company does business.

> Kroy Inc., sold a patented machine that puts letters onto transparent tape. The tape can then be applied to folders or drawings or other items. In 1982, Kroy opened direct sales centers, bypassing its independent dealers. Two former Kroy employees then decided to organize a competing firm, Varitronic, found someone to develop a competing machine and capitalized on the disenchantment of Kroy's dealers to gain an effective entry into the market.[7]

Table 4-3 lists some of the most likely directions from which new competitors may come. The probability that these potential competitors actually enter the relevant market will be a function of the *barriers* to entry to that market.

Barriers to Entry

In general terms, barriers to entry refer to the conditions that make it difficult to become a significant competitor in a new market. Table 4-4 lists some of the more typical barriers to entry.

An economies of scale barrier exists when a very high volume of production is necessary to be cost-competitive. As we discuss in detail in Chapter 6, a high volume of production allows a firm to spread fixed costs (such as advertising and production overhead costs) across a greater number of units. Thus, when fixed costs are very high (as is the case in the beer industry, for example) existing firms with large market shares will have a strong cost advantage over new entrants.

---

[7]Alyssa Lappen, "How to Exploit Someone Else's Mistake," *Forbes*, Nov. 14, 1988, pp. 164–168.

TABLE 4-3   IDENTIFYING COMPETITORS: LIKELY SOURCES OF NEW COMPETITORS

Source	Example
1. Competitor in segment which we don't serve	Regional airline goes national
2. Indirect (product form or product class) competitors	Chocolate granola bar is developed to compete with ice cream bars
3. Customers	Brewer decides to produce own cans
4. Suppliers	Manufacturer of contact lenses opens optical products stores

TABLE 4-4 TYPICAL BARRIERS TO ENTRY

1. Economies of scale in production, delivery, advertising, selling
2. Initial financial investment requires extensive resources
3. Lack of access to sources of production (raw materials, technology, labor skills)
4. Limited access to distribution channels
5. Government regulation
6. Customer loyalty to existing sellers

Additionally, the initial financial investment involved in facilities, equipment, or initial marketing expenses just to get started may constitute barriers to entry. For example, to bring its brand new Saturn line of automobiles to the market, General Motors originally budgeted $5 billion, a sum far beyond the reach of most business organizations.[8] Similarly, Gillette Co. launched its new Sensor razor with a North American and European rollout estimated to cost $175 million. The Sensor razor comes equipped with 13 moving parts and 22 patents and took 10 years and $200 million to develop.[9]

In other markets, entry may be thwarted even if investment and production barriers are low. It is difficult to successfully enter the detergent market because retailers are not likely to be easily persuaded to carry yet another brand. In other markets consumer loyalty may be well established, and so the marketing costs required in acquiring competitors' customers are prohibitive.

Moreover, innovative attempts at market entry may meet with resistance by suppliers or distributors. For example, Hillmark Casket Gallery attempted to enter the retail market for coffins by undercutting funeral home prices by 30 to 40 percent. But Hillmark's discounting tactics have met with resistance by coffin manufacturers and funeral homes. The world's largest coffin maker, Batesville Casket Company, and most of its competitors refuse to sell to distributors other than funeral homes. Additionally, many funeral directors have increased fees for their services to families who purchase coffins from Hillmark.[10]

International Entry Barriers Table 4-5 lists some barriers that can be troublesome when attempting to enter new international markets. These barriers may increase the costs of doing business, make a firm's product more costly to the consumer, or encourage favoritism on behalf of locally owned competitors.

While tariff barriers have declined in importance in recent years, nontariff barriers appear to be gaining in prominence and can be very costly. Ford, for example, claimed that the price of its Escort was 50 percent higher in Japan than in the

[8]William J. Hampton, "Will Saturn Ever Leave the Launchpad?" *Business Week,* Mar. 16, 1987, p. 107.
[9]"Gillette's Sensor: New Salvo in Cutthroat Market," *USA Today International,* Oct. 5, 1989, pp. 20–21.
[10]John Emshwiller, "Independent Coffin Sellers Fight Established Industry," *The Wall Street Journal,* July 5, 1989, p. B1.

TABLE 4-5 INTERNATIONAL ENTRY BARRIERS

1. Tariffs and duties paid as fees to import a product
2. Quotas (voluntary or involuntary) on the amount or type of products that can be imported
3. Product requirements regarding health and safety, product standards and testing, packaging and labeling
4. Customs and entry procedures including inspection and licensing
5. Government participation through subsidies, procurement policies favoring domestic firms, level of intervention in competition
6. National attitudes toward domestic versus foreign products
7. Access to distribution channels may be limited by preference for established local suppliers, shortages of space for new products

United States because of licenses and other nontariff barriers.[11] Similarly, while the United States allows foreigners to make industrial investments at will and poses few limits on the expansion of foreign banks, Japan requires foreigners to seek a license prior to investing and limits foreign banks to one or two new branches per year.[12]

Significance of New Entry In assessing changes in the identity of competitors, managers must determine whether new entrants will have a significant impact on competition. Of particular concern is the new entrant who threatens to create a major disruption by creating improved *price performance tradeoffs,* by bringing *new skills* to the industry, or by virtue of *cross-subsidization.*

A classic example of an improved price performance tradeoff occurred in the domestic airline industry during the early 1980s. Several new airlines (such as People Express) were successful in disrupting the industry pricing structure because of cost advantages associated with their newness: their flight crews were younger and thus lower-paid, their aircraft were often newer and more efficient, and they were not encumbered by the need to continue serving low-profit routes.[13]

Philip Morris is a classic example of the impact of bringing new skills to an industry. The firm acquired Miller Brewing and a small, regional, "low calorie" beer, and employed its skill at segmenting markets and managing large advertising budgets to make Miller Lite a market leader.

Cross-subsidization occurs when a competitor uses the profits from a dominant position in one market to support an entry into a new market. For example, AT&T holds a dominant position in the residential segment of the long-distance telephone market. This position could be used to subsidize price cuts directed to the markets for large business and toll-free 800 numbers. However, the Federal Communications Commission still oversees AT&T rates and requires the com-

---

[11]Sak Onkvisit and John Shaw, "Marketing Barriers in International Trade," *Business Horizons,* May–June 1988, pp. 64–74.

[12]Robert Neff, Paul Magnusson, and William Holstein, "Rethinking Japan: The New, Harder Line Toward Tokyo," *Business Week,* Aug. 7, 1989, pp. 44–52.

[13]George S. Yip, *Barriers to Entry,* Lexington Books, Lexington, Mass., 1982, p. 26.

pany to base rates separately on the profits of each segment.[14] Similarly, Procter & Gamble spent tens of millions of dollars to enter the cookie market with its Duncan Hines brand. This entry was financed by its profits from a strong position in other snack-food segments. The potential for cross-subsidization is important to recognize because firms who have such opportunities are likely to be persistent and significant competitors. The existence of potential competitors who bring improved price or performance or cross-subsidization is an important consideration in understanding the intensity of competitive rivalry and in analyzing competitive strengths and weaknesses.

ASSESSING THE INTENSITY OF COMPETITION

Competition is a matter of degree in business as well as in games: competition in some markets is simply more intense (and thus more costly) than in other markets. The importance of assessing competitive intensity is twofold: to determine the likely cost of meeting competition and to recognize the bases and types of competition that are likely to be most important.

Several basic conditions foster intense competition:

- Competitors are numerous or are roughly equal in size and power.
- Industry growth is slow, leaving market-share gains as the only avenue to growth.
- Products and services are essentially undifferentiated.
- The cost to buyers of switching from one supplier to another is low because sellers have not developed a way to tie their customers into long-term relationships.
- Economies of scale are significant or the product is perishable, creating the temptation to cut prices to build volume.
- The industry is characterized by frequent periods of overcapacity.
- Companies remain in the market in spite of low profits because of management's loyalty to a business or because the business involves specialized assets which are difficult to sell.[15]

Fundamentally, the importance of assessing competitive intensity is to understand the degree to which price competition will be a factor. To the extent that most of the foregoing conditions exist, price competition will be severe. Such conditions characterize industries such as airline travel, steel, basic chemicals, paper plates, and long-distance telephone service.

A second purpose of this analysis, however, is to identify the factors which cause competitive intensity in a given industry. By recognizing which conditions apply in a given instance, firms can often develop strategies to change those conditions or to respond to them. For example, a firm might try selling off part of its excess capacity and focusing on making specialty products for small market

[14]"FCC Eases AT&T Rate Guidelines," *Chicago Tribune*, Mar. 17, 1989, p. C2.
[15]Michael Porter, "How Competitive Forces Shape Strategy," *Harvard Business Review*, March–April 1979, pp. 137–145.

niches as many steel manufacturers did in the 1980s. In the long-distance telephone market, efforts to deal with competitive intensity have focused on product differentiation, with AT&T emphasizing its reliability and experience, and U.S. Sprint its fiber-optic network for enhanced sound clarity. Airlines have attempted to tie their customers into long-term relationships through frequent-flyer programs.

As these examples suggest, an understanding of the forces shaping competitive intensity can help identify the company capabilities necessary for success. Usually, however, a firm needs to develop a thorough assessment of competitive strengths and weaknesses in order to determine where a competitive advantage lies.

ASSESSING COMPETITIVE ADVANTAGE

The ultimate purpose of performing a competitive analysis is to identify possible avenues for attaining a sustainable advantage over competitors to achieve the objectives set for a product or product line. Specifically, managers are concerned with achieving certain performance outcomes such as repeat-purchase loyalty, market-share growth, and profitability.

Market success depends in large part on the firm's ability to deliver the benefits desired by customers more effectively or at lower cost than the competition. Consequently, the first step in assessing competitive advantage is to identify the *positions* and *sources* of advantage that lead to desired market performance outcomes as shown in Figure 4-7.

Positional Advantages

As Figure 4-7 suggests, positional advantages are the immediate causes of performance outcomes. These positional advantages can include any of the following:

- Lowest delivered price
- Superior product benefits

FIGURE 4-7 The elements of competitive advantage. (*From* George S. Day and Robin Wensley, *"Assessing Advantage: A Framework for Diagnosing Competitive Superiority,"* Journal of Marketing, April 1988, p. 3.)

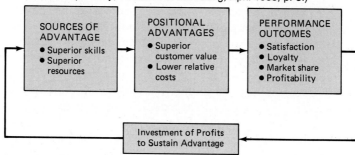

- Superior customer service
- Established brand name or company reputation for quality
- Innovative features of options
- Better spatial availability to the buyer (due to delivery policies or distributor locations)

Importantly, it is the customer's perception of these advantages that counts. We may have built a better product but only the customer's judgment about our relative position is important in terms of the performance results. This underscores the importance of perceptual mapping as a vehicle for understanding positional advantages. Additionally, managers should recognize that the only positional advantages of consequence are those that occur on the determinant attributes for the target market.

Sources of Advantage

Three basic types of sources can be identified: the *skills* of people within the organization, the *systems or arrangements* that have been developed for responding to the market, and the organization's *resources*. All positional advantages derive from one or more of these sources.

Superior skills exist when one competitor has the ability to perform a function more effectively than its competitors. Among the most important of these skills (and some firms known for each one) are the following:

- The ability to generate innovative new products (3M Company)
- Precision manufacturing to assure quality (Gillette)
- Ability to manage large advertising budgets (Philip Morris)
- Obtaining dealer cooperation in display and retail promotion (Frito-Lay)

Systems or arrangements are often developed which enhance company skills. Usually such arrangements result in enhanced positions of advantage by virtue of strengthening a company's ties with a customer. Among the kinds of systems or arrangements most important to a competitive analysis are

- Long-term contractual arrangements whereby customers receive special prices or services in exchange for buying in specified quantities
- Complementary products and services (including software or systems) that enhance the value or utilization of the main product
- Customized product specifications or customized, on-line computer ordering systems that simplify customer reordering

One of the most effective systems for developing a strong customer-supplier relationship was developed by Baxter Healthcare Corp. Baxter, which resulted from a merger between Baxter Laboratories and American Hospital Supply, offers a huge variety of healthcare equipment and supplies to hospitals. Not only do they offer a wide range of complementary products, but the company was a pioneer in offering computer-linked systems to speed reordering of routine supplies. Additionally, Baxter recently signed a 3-year contract with Daughters of Charity National Health System in which the hospitals run by that system will purchase about $270 million worth of products. In exchange, the hospitals receive discounts and a series of special services designed to help control costs.[16]

Clearly such arrangements have a major impact on the ability of other firms to compete in this industry.

Superior resources can enable a firm either to underprice the competition or to offer better or unique performance. Two kinds of resources are relevant: intangible and tangible.

Intangible resources can be used to give a business a differential advantage. The two most useful of these resources are *intellectual property rights* (such as patents and copyrights) and *brand equity*.

Intellectual property rights can confer a strong technological advantage on a company especially in industries such as pharmaceuticals or electronics, and indeed are necessary to justify much of the huge research and development expenditures in such industries. Products such as Crest toothpaste and Polaroid's instant camera succeeded in large part because a patent helped preserve their pioneering advantage. In contrast, IBM's inability to patent the technology of its original personal computer allowed many competitors to develop lower-priced "clones," a practice the company hopes to avoid on its new PS/2.[17] However, even tough patents have a 17-year life, much of that time frame can elapse before a patent results in a commercial product. For example, Monsanto's patent on aspartame (which is marketed under the trademark NutraSweet) expires in 1992 but did not receive approval from the Food and Drug Administration until 1981, a process that reduced its commercial life by one-third.[18]

Brand equity is the added value that a brand name brings to a product beyond its functional qualities. Typically, strong brand names (such as Kraft, Jell-O, Vaseline, or IBM) enable firms to resist competitive attack on a product quality basis, assist firms in building distributor support, and enhance the likelihood of trial when the brand name is used on new products. It appears as though a strong brand equity results from three elements: the delivery of superior performance, the building of strong associations between a brand name and the product category (for example the link between Sunkist and orange products), and the development of a consistent imagery through spokespersons (such as Bill Cosby for Jell-O) or characters (such as the Jolly Green Giant).[19]

Tangible resources include the physical assets of the firm, financial resources, and marketing resources such as the number of salespeople and distributors available to cover the marketplace. Such resources influence the amount of effort that can be exerted in support of positions of advantage. Consequently, an understanding of competitors' resources should help management predict the kinds of competitive advantage that firm will have. For example a commercial

[16]Steven Morris, "Baxter Deal Wins Over Care Group," *Chicago Tribune,* Jan. 19, 1989, pp. C1 and C4.

[17]Paula Dwyer, Laura Jereski, Zachary Schiller, and Dinah Lee, "The Battle Raging Over Intellectual Property," *Business Week,* May 22, 1989, pp. 78–90.

[18]Darral G. Clarke, G. D. Searle, (A) Harvard Business School Case 9-585-010, 1984.

[19]Peter Farquhar, "Managing Brand Equity," *Marketing Research,* September 1989, pp. 24–29.

bank's ability to generate deposits will be greatly enhanced if it has more branches, more automatic tellers, more human tellers, and a larger advertising budget.

Additionally, understanding a competitor's resource base enables a manager to better predict how a major change in strategy will be reacted to by competitors. Knowing the potential resources available to competitors and being able to estimate their reaction is especially important when contemplating a challenge to a market leader. Some scholars have likened such a marketing strategy to the military strategy of a frontal assault where the rule of thumb is that the attacker needs a 3-to-1 advantage in firepower to be successful.[20] Accordingly, managers must have some idea of the ability and motivation of competitors to build resources for retaining or acquiring customers.

In general, managers should expect a competitor to support a product or brand aggressively through price cutting or by expanding marketing expenditures when the competitor has

• A distinct cost advantage because of higher sales volume and economies of scale, modern or automated production facilities, lower labor costs, ownership of its sources of components or raw materials, or superior production processes
• A large number of profitable products in other markets which can serve as cash cows to provide funding for this product
• The reputation of being a single-industry competitor and thus highly committed to maintaining a strong presence in this market
• Recently made major investments in research and development in this market
• A financial position enabling it to generate extensive additional funding through borrowed funds as needed

To illustrate, in the domestic wine industry, Gallo has a substantial resource advantage. Gallo grows its own grapes, and owns a glass bottle plant, an aluminum cap business, and a large fleet of trucks, all of which enable it to be cost-competitive. Additionally, in those states where it is permitted, Gallo owns its own distributors who call on retail stores, which helps assure it a positional advantage in terms of retailer service and availability.[21]

But price is not the only positional advantage, because not all markets are highly price-sensitive. Where competitive reactions to a new entrant or a new strategic initiative are concerned, the positional advantage that will be sought will be that which a firm views as most effective. If a firm believes that advertising is its most effective weapon, that is how it is likely to respond to a competitive threat.[22]

---

[20]Philip Kotler and Ravi Singh Achrol, "Basic Military Strategy for Winning Your Marketing War," *Journal of Business Strategy*, Winter 1981, pp. 30–41.

[21]Jaclyn Fierman, "How Gallo Crushes the Competition," *Fortune*, Sept. 1, 1986, pp. 24–31.

[22]Hubert Gatignon, Erin Anderson, and Kristiaan Helsen, "Competitive Reactions to Market Entry: Explaining Interfirm Differences," *Journal of Marketing Research*, February 1989, pp. 44–55.

Implementing a Competitive Analysis

One way to summarize the results of a competitive analysis is through a competitor strength grid. Figure 4-8 presents a competitor strength grid for the gourmet frozen foods market. The relevant skills and resources in the grid are listed in approximate order of importance. Then the major competitors are positioned on each dimension. Based on this grid, Stouffer's Lean Cuisine would appear to hold the greatest overall position of strength.[23]

An important issue in developing and using competitive grids is the relative importance of each dimension. In some cases, managers may want to assign weights to different dimensions to reflect their differential importance, rather than just rank ordering them. In any event, it is critical to recognize that there is little to be gained by being best on unimportant factors.

While the idea of a competitive grid has great appeal, the grid is only as useful as it is accurate. Thus, consumer perceptions should be obtained when making judgments on dimensions like quality. These can then be combined with other sources of competitive intelligence.

OBTAINING COMPETITIVE INTELLIGENCE

Information on many dimensions of a strengths-and-weaknesses analysis can be readily obtained by simple observation. However, more and more organizations

[23]David Aaker, *Strategic Market Management,* 2d ed., Wiley, New York, 1988, pp. 85–86.

FIGURE 4-8   A competitor strength grid. (*From David Aaker, Strategic Market Management, 2d ed.,* Wiley, New York, 1988, p. 86.)

Assets and Skills	Weakness → Strength
Product quality	W V B A G L M
Market share/share economies	V B W A G M L
Parent in related business	B W V G A M L
Package	W B V L G A M
Low-calorie position	V G M B A L W
Sales-force/distribution	V B W G A M L
Advertising/promotion	V B G W A M L
Ethnic position	W A L M G V B

L	Stouffer's Lean Cuisine (Nestle's—also makes Stouffer "Red Box" line)
M	Le Menu (Campbell's Soup—also makes Swanson's, Mrs. Paul's)
W	Weight Watchers (Heinz)
A	Armour Dinner Classic/Classic Lite (Conogra—also makes Banquet)
V	Van deKamp Mexican Classic and other ethnic lines
B	Benihana
G	Green Giant Stir Fry Entrees (Pillsbury)

are establishing formal processes for collecting competitive intelligence. The procedures rely on sources which fall into three basic categories.

Published Material and Documents   Electronic data bases such as those published by Business Research Corporation and Economic Information Systems can be accessed by personal computer and provide information such as the production volume of competitors' industrial facilities and research reports on competitors compiled by investment bankers. Simpler, but often more useful, sources include labor contracts negotiated by competitors (which yield clues as to competitors' labor costs), speeches given by company officers, and press releases. There is even a company which monitors help-wanted ads which can be used to track expansion plans or new engineering directions. Some important specific sources of information that can be used to assess the competition are also general market measurement sources. These are discussed in the next chapter, and many are summarized in the Appendix to this book.

Competitors' Employees, Suppliers, or Customers   Many firms flirt with ethical questions (and sometimes legal questions) in using these sources. While "picking a competitor's brain" about general industry problems is a legitimate way to project competitors' thinking, hiring competitors' key employees can be construed as illegal if it can be proved that the sole purpose in making the hire was to acquire trade secrets. Less obvious, but sometimes questionable, are techniques designed to use competitors' suppliers and customers to provide information about competitors' new-product development activities, forthcoming promotions, or sales levels.

Direct Observation   It is often said that the first ten buyers of any new product are competitors' salespeople. The technique of *reverse engineering* involves taking apart a new competitive product to analyze the product's attributes, to determine the cost of production, and, sometimes, to even copy the technology. Even simple plant tours can, to the trained observer, yield useful insights regarding plant capacity and costs.

CONCLUSION

Both for-profit and not-for-profit organizations operate in a complex environment in which there is competition for the attention, patronage, and financial resources of customers and clients. Accordingly, it is essential to have a clear understanding of the alternatives from which potential customers can choose and of potential customers' assessments of those alternatives. As summarized in Figure 4-9, organizations must assess the competitive environment in which they will operate and the competitive advantages (and disadvantages) they will have in a potential target market. (Note the bidirectional arrow in Figure 4-9 between competitive dynamics and intensity and market measurement. This reflects the fact that industry sales are influenced by competitive dynamics and, at the same time, competitive intensity is influenced by the market potential and the growth in industry sales.)

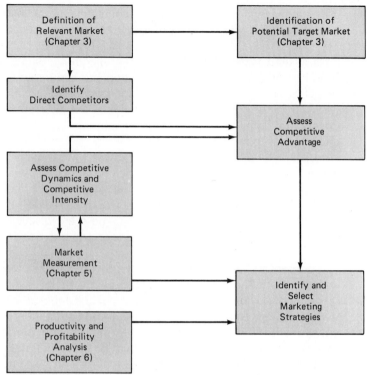

FIGURE 4-9   Steps in competitive analysis and their relationship to other aspects of the situation analysis.

Clearly, the process of competitive analysis is of critical prerequisite to the selection of a marketing strategy as the ACME division's situation demonstrates.

ACME Division: Designing a Competitive Analysis

Mr. John Veitch, General Manager of ACME division of the Simplimatic Engineering Co., was in the process of developing an annual marketing plan for his company. ACME manufactured and marketed a line of high-speed, fully automatic palletizing and depalletizing machines. Automatic palletizers were used by container and packaging manufacturers to load empty containers such as aluminum cans and 2-litre plastic bottles on pallets for shipment to beverage and food bottlers and processors. Depalletizers automatically unload empty containers off stacked pallets and move them to high-speed filling and packaging lines. In addition to these industries, palletizers and depalletizers were purchased by customers in several other industries requiring high-speed materials handling equipment. For instance, Ford Motor Company used depalletizers to unload oil filter cartridges to auto assembly lines. Pennzoil and Quaker State used depalletizers to sweep empty containers to their consumer oil container filling lines. However, ACME had concentrated its design and marketing efforts on food and beverage container manufacturers and on bottlers and processors in those same industries. Companies such as Continental Can, Ball Container, Budweiser, Coca-Cola, and PepsiCo used ACME machines in their plants. In some cases, these and other customers used two or more different types and sizes of packaging.

Automated palletizing and depalletizing products had been around for years. Generally, they were used as a part of an overall production system with a variety of other automated production equipment. These systems were becoming increasingly sophisticated in the way they monitored and controlled the flow of packaging and filling operations. Often, the efficiency of the operation was limited by the speed of the packaging process and the downtime involved for maintenance and repair.

While market-share information was not published, prior research had identified over 50 manufacturers of various types of palletizers ranging in size from very small to large, multinational organizations. Customer loyalty was not believed to be especially high. An analysis of the United States packaging industry suggested that this industry would grow at a slower rate than the economy as a whole.

As Mr. Veitch began thinking about his marketing plan he began to realize the importance of gaining more insights on the competition prior to setting a strategy. For instance, field sales managers had often expressed to him the problems they encountered when competing on a price basis for a customer's order. Lack of price competitiveness was a frequent reason given by the sales force for not obtaining an order. But Veitch felt that ACME had a superior reputation for engineering and on-time delivery that would more than offset competitors' lower prices (if, in fact, they were lower).

1 Based on this information, would you expect competition to be intense in this industry? Explain.

2 Do you think tangible resources would be more important than intangible resources in developing a competitive advantage in this market? Or is the reverse more likely?

3 What dimensions would be useful to Mr. Veitch if he wanted to construct a competitive strength grid? How could he obtain the information for completing this grid?

QUESTIONS AND SITUATIONS FOR DISCUSSION

1 In 1989, Toyota and Nissan introduced their Lexus and Infiniti luxury automobiles. A major element in both introductory strategies was the decision to establish separate dealerships for these cars rather than marketing them through existing Toyota and

Nissan dealers. Which steps in competitive analysis could have been used by Toyota and Nissan that would have led to this decision?

2 If you were working for a manufacturer of consumer electronics, what types of information about competitors would you expect to obtain from each of the following sources: consumers, distributors, trade shows?

3 Discuss some difficulties that a firm operating only in the United States would have in developing a competitive analysis as it prepares to expand into the Far East.

4 Many firms have begun their overseas operations by developing joint ventures with a local firm (for example, Toyota and General Motors developed a joint venture called NUMMI to produce Corollas and Novas in California). What special resources would you look for in a joint-venture partner to help be more competitive overseas? Would your answer differ if you were selling industrial versus consumer goods?

5 How important would the United States dollar's strength (measured against foreign currencies) be in a competitive analysis undertaken by
  a A manufacturer of personal computers?
  b A travel agency selling "see America" tour packages in Western Europe?
  c A manufacturer of Portland cement?

6 The sun can burn the cornea of the eye as it does skin and long-term exposure to sunlight can cause cataracts. Your company has recently developed clear eyedrops that will block 98 percent of ultraviolet rays for up to 4 hours. How would you proceed to develop a competitive analysis for this product? What are the major difficulties you would anticipate in analyzing the competitive situation for this new product?

7 In 1990, the ready-to-eat cereal market was expected to be worth over $6.5 billion. After many years of very slow growth, this market has been propelled at a double-digit growth rate in recent years, primarily due to the growth of adult cereals. By the end of the 1980s, adult cereals accounted for 40 percent of the ready-to-eat market.

In the late 1980s, industry leader Kellogg dominated the adult cereal business with over a dozen brands. During the early 1980s Kellogg doubled spending on research and development and on advertising. This resulted in a string of successful new products such as Nutri-Grain (Kellogg's first cereal with whole grain, no sugar, and no preservatives), Mueslix (an upscale version of granola with a European heritage), Nutrific (combining barley, bran, almonds, and raisins), and Pro-Grain (another multigrain cereal). Along with traditional mainstays like Raisin Bran, Product 19, and All-Bran, Kellogg's seemed to have the adult cereal business blanketed—especially in the bran/fiber varieties. Six firms competed in the cereal market. Of these only Kellogg's and General Mills relied on this business for a dominant share of earnings and sales. In 1986, Kellogg was estimated to have 48 percent of the fiber and adult nutritional cereal market compared to General Foods Post division's 29 percent share. General Mills, Nabisco, Quaker, and Ralston-Purina trailed with 16, 3, 2, and 2 percent, respectively. Overall, Kellogg's total share of the cereal market was around 41 percent. However, Kellogg's share declined to 39 percent over the ensuing 3 years, as General Mills expanded its adult lines with an especially heavy emphasis on oat bran, a substance that had been the subject of numerous positive health claims recently.[24]

a What are the key positional advantages and sources of advantage in this industry?

[24]Developed from Julie Erickson, "Kellogg Pours Out More Cereals," *Advertising Age*, July 25, 1988, pp. 2 and 66; Rebecca Fannin, "Crunching the Competition," *Marketing & Media Decisions*, March 1980, pp. 70–74; Paula Schnorbus, "Brantastic," *Marketing & Media Decisions*, April 1987, pp. 93–96; Julie Franz, "Cereals Growing Up," *Advertising Age*, Feb. 9, 1987, p. 3; and Janet Key, "Kellogg Wises Up to Health Ads," *Chicago Tribune*, Aug. 31, 1989, pp. B1 and B4.

b What problems must be overcome if perceptual mapping is to be a useful analytical tool in this market?

c How strong is the pioneering advantage in this market?

d Is intensive price competition likely to surface in this industry?

e As market leader, does Kellogg's fit the profile of an aggressive defender/reactor?

SUGGESTED ADDITIONAL READINGS

Coyne, Kevin P., "Sustainable Competitive Advantage—What It Is. What It Isn't," *Business Horizons,* January–February 1986, pp. 56–68.

Day, George S., and Robin Wensley, "Assessing Advantage: A Framework for Diagnosing Competitive Superiority," *Journal of Marketing,* April 1988, pp. 1–20.

Devine, Hugh, and John Morton, "How Does the Market Really See Your Product," *Business Marketing,* July 1984, pp. 70–79, 131.

Farquhar, Peter, "Managing Brand Equity," *Marketing Research,* September 1989, pp. 24–33.

Gatignon, Hubert, Erin Anderson, and Kristiann Helsen, "Competitive Reactions to Market Entry Explaining Interfirm Differences," *Journal of Marketing Research,* February 1989, pp. 44–55.

Henderson, Bruce, "The Anatomy of Competition," *Journal of Marketing,* Spring 1983, pp. 7–11.

Karakaya, Fahri, and Michael J. Stahl, "Barriers to Entry and Market Entry Decisions in Consumer and Industrial Goods Markets," *Journal of Marketing,* April 1989, pp. 80–91.

Porter, Michael, "How Competitive Forces Shape Strategy," *Harvard Business Review,* March–April 1979, pp. 137–145.

Robinson, William, "Marketing Mix Reactions to Entry," *Marketing Science,* Fall 1988, pp. 368–385.

Robinson, William, and Claes Fornell, "Sources of Market Pioneer Advantages in Consumer Goods Industries," *Journal of Marketing Research,* August 1985, pp. 305–317.

MARKET MEASUREMENT

In Chapters 3 and 4, we discussed some fundamental steps that managers should take in analyzing buyers and competitors within markets in order to understand the underlying processes influencing primary and selective demand. Chapter 5 also focuses on primary and selective demand. However, in this chapter our primary concern is with measuring the amount of primary or selective demand in a market in order to determine the size of various sales opportunities within it.

Market measurements are critically important in a number of management decisions. Top management must be aware of the size and rate of growth of various markets in order to select corporate strategies. Middle-management decisions regarding marketing strategies, programs, and budgets for individual products cannot be made effectively without some estimate of the expected levels of industry and company sales. Additionally, in order to evaluate the performance of a company, a product, a sales territory, or a distributor some benchmark (such as a sales goal or quota) must be established. And both top management and middle managers will use benchmarks that are based on some estimate of market demand.

Managers need to understand market measurement procedures for several reasons. In some cases, managers may have to do their own measurement because the firm does not have qualified staff researchers. However, even if the manager is only the user of this kind of information, an understanding of these procedures is important. In order to specify the information they will need, managers must be aware of the kinds of measures that are available. Further, before using the information, a manager should be familiar with the limitations of these measurements and the potential sources of error or bias inherent in them. Market measurements are estimates, and few are so reliable that a manager can simply accept a single number as perfectly accurate. By understanding the assumptions used to develop any measure, managers can better evaluate by how much such measures are optimistic or pessimistic and how much such measures should be relied on. The purposes of this chapter are to demonstrate the uses of the various types of market measurements and to point out the assumptions and limitations of the most widely used techniques for developing these measurements.

Basic Types of Market Measurements

Before examining the basic approaches to market measurement, it is important to define the major kinds of measures that are useful to managers.

1 *Actual sales* represent either the past or current levels of demand realized. Those realized by a firm come under the category of *company and product sales,* and those of a group of sellers are known as *industry sales.*

2 *Sales forecasts* are estimates of future levels of demand. Industry sales forecasts indicate the level of demand that is expected to be achieved by all firms selling to a defined market in a defined period of time. A statement such as "Automobile sales in the United States between the years 1995 and 2000 are expected to be 100 million units" is an industry sales forecast. Similarly, company (or product-line or brand) sales forecasts indicate the expected level of demand that will be met by an individual supplier.

3 *Market potential* represents the upper limit of demand in a defined period of time. That is, market potential is either the maximum sales opportunity that can be achieved by all sellers at the present time (called *current market potential*) or the one that can be achieved during some future period of time (*future market potential*).

Figure 5-1 portrays the relationship among company sales, industry sales, and market-potential measurements. As the figure suggests, company sales will generally be lower than industry sales. (The only exception to this rule is the case of a monopoly. If a firm has no competitors, company sales will equal industry sales.) The ratio of company sales to industry sales is the firm's market share. Additionally, as Figure 5-1 suggests, industry sales will usually be below market potential.

In developing the three types of measurements, managers should normally be concerned with the forecasted rate of growth in the measurements over time and the size of the *strategic gaps* among the measurements. More specifically, market potential may increase because the number of potential buyers or the rate of purchase may increase over time. Industry sales may increase over time for several reasons:

- Prices may decrease, improving potential customers' ability to buy
- Industry marketing efforts (regarding product quality, advertising and selling expenditures, and extent of distribution) may become more extensive so that a

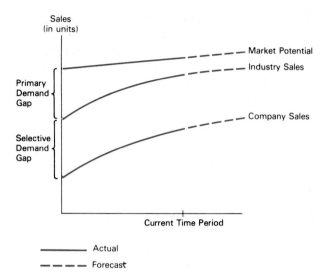

FIGURE 5-1   Basic kinds of market measurements.

greater number of potential customers fully perceive or obtain the product's benefits

• Environmental factors (such as economic conditions or changing social values) may stimulate the willingness or ability to buy the product

Company sales may increase over time for one of two reasons. First, the sales of all firms competing in a given industry may increase because of an overall increase in industry sales. Second, some firms may gain sales at the expense of competitors by offering and communicating superior combinations of benefits and thus increasing market share.

The most important strategic implications of these three measures can be isolated by comparing market potential to industry sales and by comparing industry sales to company sales. If a large difference exists between market potential and industry sales, then a large *primary demand gap* exists. This means that managers should examine the factors influencing primary demand (discussed in Chapter 3) to determine how industry sales may be increased. If a large difference exists between industry sales and company sales, then a *selective demand gap* exists. In such situations, managers should examine buyers' choice processes to identify opportunities for increasing market share.

Defining What to Measure

Managers must clearly identify the market to be measured in order to accurately measure industry sales and market potential. That is, the relevant market must be defined (in terms of product form, product class, or generic needs). Further, if only certain segments of the relevant market (such as geographic areas or age groups) will be served, this should be stated as well. (For example, a cereal manufacturer may be interested in determining industry sales or cereals among single-person households in New England.) Additionally, the time frame must be established. For some kinds of decisions our concern is with current levels of sales or potential. In other cases, estimates of sales or potential at some specific future time may be required.

In the remainder of this chapter, we will examine four basic kinds of market measurements: absolute market potential, relative market potential, industry sales forecasts, and company sales forecasts. Our discussion of each measure will begin by indicating how each measure can be used in decision making.

ABSOLUTE MARKET POTENTIAL

Absolute potential is an estimate of maximum potential demand, usually based on two factors: the number of potential users and the rate of purchase. For a given market, absolute potential indicates the total dollar or unit volume that could be sold by all suppliers. There are three kinds of decisions that generally require an estimate of absolute market potential:

1 *Evaluating market opportunities:* In order to decide what market opportunities to pursue in the future, a firm will want to assess the market potential. This is particularly true in the case of new-product-form or new-product-class markets. Consider, for example, the large resource commitments made by companies entering the market for products such as videotape recorders, personal computers, and industrial robots. These commitments could not have been economically justified if the companies had not been able to identify a large potential demand. In the case of existing products, market opportunities can be more easily examined if the market potential can be measured and compared with industry sales. If the market potential is significantly larger than industry sales, then all suppliers have an opportunity to increase sales volume by pursuing policies (such as lower prices) to close the market-potential industry-sales gap. However, if industry sales are already close to market potential, then a firm will know that the only avenue for company sales growth is to improve market share. Consequently, in the latter case, the market opportunity is generally smaller (unless of course a firm believes it has some unique advantage that can be used to build market share).

2 *Determining sales quotas and objectives:* Market potential must usually be considered in order to establish reasonable objectives for the sales force and for distributors. Potential demand in some sales territories may be growing so rapidly that sharp yearly increases in sales objectives are appropriate. However, other territories may be stagnant in the number of potential buyers and purchase rates. Consequently, a fair evaluation of sales-force and distributor performance should be based on the potential for sales.

3 *Determining the number of retail outlets:* Firms that sell through retailers generally will have a desired number of retail distributors for a market of a given size. For instance, an automobile manufacturer may want to have one dealer for every 2000 units per month of market potential in order to assure adequate coverage of the market. Accordingly, the potential in a given retail market area will be a major input into these decisions.

Measuring Absolute Market Potential

There are essentially two components of market potential: the *number of possible users* and the *maximum rate of purchase* that can reasonably be expected. Frequently, managers can obtain estimates of market potential (often broken down by geographic area, industry type, or household type) from trade associations or commercial research firms specializing in such estimates. More typically, managers themselves must estimate at least one of these two components of market potential.

Estimating Potential in Consumer Markets When the characteristics of all potential buyers are known and readily measurable, the easiest way of estimating the number of buyers is to use secondary sources. If potential buyers for consumer goods can be described in terms of basic demographic or locational factors (such as age, county, home ownership, or income) both government and private industry data sources can be employed. For example, the annual *Survey of Buying Power* (published by *Sales and Marketing Management* magazine) provides data on the size and the distribution of the population by age group and income category for each county and for metropolitan areas within each county.

Managers often use data obtained from trade associations, from government, or from commercial publications in estimating purchase rates. Particularly in cases where they are estimating current market potential, managers may use the existing ratios of sales per household or sales per person. These kinds of ratios can often be obtained directly from secondary sources. For example, the Conference Board, a New York–based, industry-supported organization, publishes a distribution of household expenditures on various product categories. Alternatively, if data on total industry sales are available, average demand per household (or per person) may be calculated by dividing total sales by the number of households.

Although a wide variety of sources of data are used in estimating market potential, the following example is typical of the approach used in estimating potential for consumer markets.

Penn Sport Sales is a company that serves as a manufacturer's representative for a variety of sports equipment and sports apparel firms in the Mid-Atlantic states. Recently, the company was asked to represent a golf shoe firm in the state of Pennsylvania, so the company's Vice President for Sales decided to estimate the market potential for golf shoes.

Based on industry data, the manager knew that 2.2 percent of the adult population bought golf shoes in the previous year. Given that Pennsylvania's adult population was about 9,093,000 the market potential could have been estimated as 2.2 × 9,093,000, or 200,046 pair.

As with most consumer products, however, golf shoes are not bought at the same rate by all population segments. Examining data on golfing and golf shoe purchase rates obtained from the syndicated research firm Mediamark Research Inc. leads to the calculations given in Table 5-1. This estimate (205,750) is higher and likely to be more accurate because Pennsylvania's population profile is older than that of the United States on average and because golf shoe sales are higher among golfers who are older.

As the previous example suggests, if different buyer types are likely to differ extensively in their purchase rates, total market potential should be measured by summing the potentials for each group of customer types. In addition to improving accuracy, this allows the manager to more readily account for the effects of projected demographic changes on future market potential levels.

This example is typical of many market potential estimates in that the current average rate of purchase is a good approximation for the maximum rate of purchase. Although this assumption will be valid in many cases, managers should examine the diagnostic questions on willingness and ability to buy (discussed in Chapter 3) to determine if the current rate of purchase could be increased. For example, across markets, the actual rate of golf shoe purchases may vary because of the relative popularity of golf. If secondary data were available on a statewide basis to adjust the national estimates, then the estimate of potential could be refined. Additionally, it may be possible to increase golf shoe purchases if manufacturers offer lower prices, broader styles, or innovative features. Thus, to the extent that the maximum rate of purchase can be realistically increased, managers should modify this rate to more accurately reflect the gap between actual usage rates and potential usage rates.

Estimating Potential in Organizational Markets   Secondary data sources such as the U.S. Department of Commerce's *County Business Patterns* and the *Annual Survey of Industrial Buying Power* are useful in projecting market potential for organizational markets. Each of these two sources is especially useful in identifying the number of buying organizations.

But secondary sources of data are usually less useful in measuring purchase rates in organizational markets than in consumer markets. There are two major

TABLE 5-1   ESTIMATING MARKET POTENTIAL FOR GOLF SHOES IN PENNSYLVANIA (in thousands)

Age group	% of adults buying golf shoes in year*	×	Pennsylvania adult** population	=	Potential shoe sales
18–24	1.5%		1369		20.54
25–34	1.2%		1934		23.21
35–49	2.3%		2186		50.28
50+	3.1%		3604		111.72
Total			9093		205.75

*Source: Mediamark Research Inc., Report P-12, Spring 1986, p. 196.
**Source: 1986 *Sales Management Survey of Buying Power*, July 28, 1986, p. C-160.

reasons for this. First, many manufacturers sell highly specialized product lines, but industry sales data are usually available only for broad product categories. For example, a manufacturer of envelopes will not be able to measure industry envelope sales per customer because industry sales will be available only for the broader category "paper products." Second, buyer purchase rates usually vary substantially according to the size of the organization and from one buying industry to another. This is a point of particular concern if market potential is being estimated for a limited geographical area. That is, in a local market a small number of buyers of widely varying sizes and purchase rates may exist. Some of these firms may buy much more than the national average sales per customer and some may buy much less than the average simply because of the size of the organization.

Because of the first problem—lack of industry sales data—estimates of purchase rates must often be made through primary marketing research. Because of the problem caused by the widely varying sizes of organizational buyers, managers usually attempt to *weight* the potential of each prospective buyer in order to account for differences in size.

Two measures that are widely used to account for size differences are the *number of employees* and the *value of shipments,* a measure of the value of the production output of a specific industrial plant or facility. The value of shipments and the number of employees usually are closely correlated with the rate of purchase (at least within a given industry). Additionally, these measures are reported annually and are reported for different industries, classified through the Standard Industrial Classification code (SIC code). The SIC code, established by the U.S. Department of Commerce, is a method for classifying individual business establishments (such as stores or manufacturing plants) in each county into industry categories. Data on the number of employees and the value of shipments are then aggregated at the county level for each industry code. Government publications (such as *Census of Retailing, Census of Manufacturing, County Business Patterns,* and *U.S. Industrial Outlook*) and commercial publications (such as *Sales and Marketing Management* magazine's *Survey of Industrial Buying Power*) rely on SIC codes to report such data along various geographic lines. Data are aggregated

TABLE 5-2   SOME SIC CODES FOR APPAREL AND
TEXTILE PRODUCTS MANUFACTURING

Code			Industry
23			Apparel and textile products
	231		Men's and boys' suits, coats
	232		Men's and boys' furnishings
		2321	Men's and boys' shirts
	233		Women's and misses' outerwear
		2335	Dresses
		2337	Coats and suits
	234		Women's and children's undergarments

at what are called two-digit, three-digit, and four-digit levels, as indicated in Table 5-2.

In order to understand how this type of data can be used in estimating potential in organizational markets, consider the following example.

Rockmorton Chemical Corporation is a manufacturer of various inks that are used in many types of printing operations. In planning to establish sales quotas for his district, the Midwest sales manager wanted to first determine the market potential for his product line. His five salespeople were located in Pennsylvania, Ohio, Michigan, Indiana, and Illinois. Upon reviewing past sales history for the company, he felt that the primary ink-using industries were SIC 2711 (newspapers), SIC 2721 (periodicals), SIC 2732 (book printing), and SIC 2751 (letterpress commercial printing). Close inspection of his sales records combined with his knowledge of the industry led him to conclude that the cost of printing ink comprises about .1 percent of the value of shipments for the ink-using industries. Using Sales and Marketing Management's most recent *Survey of Industrial Purchasing Power,* he calculated the value of shipments in each SIC group for each state as indicated in the following table.

	Value of shipments, millions of dollars				
SIC	**Illinois**	**Indiana**	**Michigan**	**Ohio**	**Pennsylvania**
2711	$ 810.8	$121.5	$397.6	$606.2	$ 262.4
2721	1638.5	0	0	264.1	689.3
2732	0	358.0	71.3	0	0
2751	1031.7	0	45.1	36.0	53.3
Total	$3481.0	$479.5	$514.0	$906.3	$1005.0
×.001 Estimated potential	$3.481	$0.479	$0.514	$0.906	$ 1.005

For the five-state area, the total value of all shipments was $6385.8 million. When this total was multiplied by .1 percent, the estimated potential was calculated at $6,385,800.

Projecting Future Market Potential

Many of the uses of market-potential information require management to obtain estimates to cover a number of future years. Estimating the *number of potential users* is not generally a difficult problem in the case of consumer goods, because projections regarding the number of households, age-group populations, and many other demographic factors are readily available from secondary sources.

In the case of industrial goods, the number of customers may change rather slowly. However, some buying industries may grow more rapidly than others. Further, geographic movements (such as the recent trend in some industries to shift facilities to the Sunbelt) may change the distribution of potential among sales territories. Government publications (such as *Current Industrial Reports* and *U.S. Industrial Outlook*), trade association data, and commercial publications (such as *Predicasts*) are easily obtained and are generally sufficient for projecting buying industry growth patterns in output and employment.

More difficult is the problem of estimating changes in purchase rates. As a practical matter, management generally assumes that these rates will remain stable. However, managers often project rate changes judgmentally—on the basis of sales-force opinions or of recent trends in usage rates.

In the case of durable goods (such as appliances or industrial machines) the future market potential will also depend on the rate at which owners scrap a product because of wear out or obsolescence. Managers can estimate scrappage rates either by examining the technical service life of a product or the historical long-term rate of voluntary scrappage. That is, some products must be scrapped on account of technical failure. However, the time until scrappage (or resale) is often a function of economic conditions. For example, new-car lending rates, other economic conditions, or changes in automotive product design (leading to new features, greater efficiency, or improved capability) may influence the voluntary rate of replacement of a durable item. If historical data on scrappage rates can be calculated from a sample of users, managers can use actuarial methods to estimate the replacement potential for products of different ages.

To see how replacement potential for videocassette recorders might be estimated, for example, consider the data in Tables 5-3 and 5-4. Assume that a VCR manufacturer is attempting to estimate replacement market potential for 1991 and is armed with past industry sales data plus data from a consumer survey of VCR owners who purchased their products between 1980 and 1990.

Table 5-3 shows the scrappage rates of VCRs purchased between 1980 and 1986. (Because none of the units bought between 1987 and 1990 had been scrapped as of the end of 1990, none of the data for those years is relevant to the calculations in Table 5-3.) The table indicates that 1 percent of those who purchased VCRs in 1986 scrapped their 4-year-old VCRs during 1990. This means

TABLE 5-3   CALCULATING SURVIVAL RATES

Year product was purchased	Age of product	Percent of units scrapped in 1990	Annual survival rate	Percent of units remaining at end of 1990
1986	4	.01	.99	.99
1985	5	.05	.95	.94
1984	6	.10	.90	.85
1983	7	.25	.75	.63
1982	8	.50	.50	.32
1981	9	.80	.20	.06
1980	10	1.00	.00	.00

TABLE 5-4   ESTIMATING REPLACEMENT POTENTIAL

Year product was sold	Industry sales (in thousands)	Percentage left at start of 1991	Number left at start of 1991	Annual scrapping rate	1991 replacement potential
1987	14,000	1.00	14,000	.01	140
1986	13,500	.99	13,365	.05	668
1985	12,000	.94	11,280	.10	1128
1984	7,500	.85	6,375	.25	1594
1983	4,000	.63	2,520	.50	1260
1982	1,900	.32	608	.80	486
1981	1,300	.06	78	1.00	78

that 99 percent of the VCRs purchased in 1986 survived to the end of 1990. Of the VCRs purchased in 1985, 5 percent were scrapped in 1990. If we assume that the scrappage rate for four-year-old VCRs remained the same, 1 percent of the VCRs purchased in 1985 would have been scrapped during 1989. So, of the original units sold in 1985, the percent surviving to the end of 1990 would be calculated as follows:

Percent of units remaining after 4 years	.99
× survival rate during 5th year	× .95
Percent of units remaining after 5 years	.94

Once the scrappage and survival rates are calculated, future replacement potential can be estimated as long as prior industry sales data are available. Table 5-4 demonstrates how this estimate could be developed for 1991. Given that no units are scrapped until the fourth year we would begin with 1987 sales data. From Table 5-3 we project that 1 percent of these units will be scrapped. Of the 1986 sales, 1 percent were previously scrapped leaving 99 percent (13,365,000) still operating at the start of 1991. Of these (which are now 5 years old) we estimate from Table 5-3 that 5 percent will be scrapped. The total 1991 replacement potential is calculated by adding the number of units expected to be scrapped from each age group.

RELATIVE MARKET POTENTIAL

Relative market potential is simply the percentage distribution of market potential among different portions of a market (such as geographic areas or customer groups). Typically, measures of relative potential are used to help management efficiently allocate certain resources. In particular, there are three major uses of relative market potential:

1 *Allocating promotion expenditures:* A national marketer will generally want to allocate the sales promotion and advertising budget among different markets on the basis of the relative importance of each market. For instance, the rate of purchase of room air conditioners or snow tires will vary dramatically among television markets of equal population. By knowing the percentage distribution of potential between different television markets, management can allocate advertising expenditures in proportion to market potential.

2 *Allocating salespeople among territories:* Given a fixed number of salespeople, a manufacturer or wholesaler will want to assign them in the most efficient manner. Accordingly, if one territory has twice the sales potential of another, it should probably receive twice as many salespeople (assuming each member of the sales force is about equal to every other member in effectiveness).

3 *Locating facilities:* In order to minimize transportation costs and to maximize the ability to deliver products quickly, most organizations will attempt to locate facilities closer to markets of larger potential than to markets of lesser potential. Thus, in locating warehouses, production facilities, and district sales offices, the relative potential of the market being served is often a major input.

Measuring Relative Market Potential

When estimating relative potential, managers begin by identifying factors that are measurable and that are likely to be correlated with market potential. These measures, called *corollary factors,* can be used to represent market potential.

Single-Corollary Factor Approaches A manager in an industrial goods firm may know that market potential is directly related to a single, easily measured factor such as the number of production workers in the industries to which it sells or the total production value of shipments made by such industries.

Consider, for example, the following situation: Pitney Bowes' U.S. Business Systems Division makes postage meters and other mail handling equipment. Over the years, the division was plagued with sales force distribution problems: The number of salespeople in some territories was always too small while there would always be other territories with too many salespeople. In those territories with inadequate sales staff, potential sales force turnover was high because many salespeople could not earn adequate commissions. Finally, the division was able to project sales opportunities by developing a simple corollary with market potential: employment growth in each territory. The company buys data on employment trends from Data Resources Inc., a well-known consulting firm. Because employment growth results from new businesses being formed and existing businesses being expanded, the relative amount of growth in a territory is a good barometer of sales opportunity in that territory. As a result of using this approach to allocate salespeople, the company found that it could get by with 3 percent to 5 percent fewer people. Moreover, sales force turnover was expected to decline by 10 percent.[1]

---

[1]"And Now, the Home Brewed Forecast," *Fortune,* Jan. 20, 1986, p. 54.

For a consumer-goods firm, typical corollary factors include the number of housing units (for appliances), the number of single-family dwelling units (for home-repair items), disposable-income levels, the number of people in an age group, and several other possible buyer characteristics.

Multiple-Corollary Factor Indexes Managers can use more than one corollary factor in estimating relative market potential. In those cases, indexes will be developed to reflect the relative importance of the different factors.

For many frequently purchased consumer goods, a useful index is the Buying Power Index (BPI) provided by Sales and Marketing Management's *Survey of Industrial Buying Power*. A BPI is computed for each county to reflect the percentage of total United States buying power in that county. The index is compiled by weighing three individual factors (each of which is reported separately in the survey) as follows:

BPI = .5 × percent of effective buying income
   + .3 × percent of U.S. retail sales
   + .2 × percent of U.S. population

To illustrate one use of the BPI, consider the following example.

In 1990, a regional chain of department stores emphasizing middle-quality clothing and other "soft goods" began to look at several alternative new markets with an eye toward expanding the number of stores. Company officials knew that competition would have to be examined in each potential market, but before doing that, they wanted to know which markets had the greatest potential in the five-state market area the company currently served. On the basis of their knowledge of the size of the areas from which their stores drew, potential markets were defined in terms of the counties that would be included and data were obtained from the *Survey of Buying Power* for each market. Results from four of the markets in the state of Iowa are portrayed in the following table:

Metro area	Population	Effective buying income per capita	Retail sales per capita	BPI
Cedar Rapids	169,000	$12,759	$6600	.0693
Dubuque	90,800	10,010	6089	.0324
Iowa City	86,200	12,045	5425	.0324
Sioux City	115,600	10,263	6713	.0589

On the basis of the BPI data, Cedar Rapids was clearly the highest-potential market. Note that Dubuque and Iowa City had equivalent BPIs, as Dubuque's larger population and retail sales were offset by the greater level of income in Iowa City. Given these comparisons, the company was then able to concentrate its efforts on seeking out specific sites in those markets with the greater relative potential.

In practice, of course, management would also want to project population and buying power changes expected in the future in order to assess the long-run potential of each market.

Targeting High Potential Markets

In many cases, industry and company sales will vary quite sharply across geographic territories. In some territories, per capita purchases of a product (such as powdered lemonade mix) may be very high compared to other territories. This suggests that the primary demand gap is somewhat larger in the area with low per capita sales. Similarly, brand share differences often vary substantially across markets. Country Time lemonade may have a much larger selective demand gap in New Jersey than in Texas, for example.

Marketers frequently construct special indexes to portray these regionally-based gaps. A *category development index* (or CDI) is a measure that helps identify territories in which primary demand gaps are relatively large or small. A *brand development index* (or BDI) is a measure that can be used to assess selective demand gaps across territories.[2] The process of developing these indices is demonstrated in Table 5-5.

As Table 5-5 suggests, the same basic procedure is used to calculate a CDI or a BDI. Specifically for a CDI, within each territory the total sales for a product category (such as powdered lemonade) is divided by the number of households in that market. A BDI for Country Time would be calculated by dividing Country Time sales in that same market by the number of households.

Category and brand development indexes are useful as diagnostic tools to help managers identify the markets in which the largest primary demand or selective demand gaps exists. For example, the hypothetical indexes in Table 5-6 would enable managers to spot four kinds of variations from average market performance:

[2]F. Beaven Ennis, *Marketing Norms for Product Managers,* Association of National Advertisers, New York, 1985, pp. 26–31.

TABLE 5-5 CALCULATING A DEVELOPMENT INDEX

Area	Annual case sales (category or brand)	÷	Thousands of households	=	Sales per 1000 households	Index
Total	1,600,000		80,000		20	100
A	22,500		900		25	125
B	13,500		750		18	90
C	52,800		2,400		22	110

Total index = 100. Index for each territory is calculated as:

$$\text{Index} = \frac{\text{sales per 1000 households in territory}}{\text{sales per 1000 households total}} \times 100$$

TABLE 5-6 TYPICAL CATEGORY/BRAND DEVELOPMENT INDEXES

	CDI	BDI
Total U.S.	100	100
Eastern region		
Boston	144	239
New York	94	137
Baltimore	127	213
Southern region		
Atlanta	87	71
Memphis	74	58
Dallas	92	84
Central region		
Minneapolis	114	101
St. Louis	108	95
Denver	79	139
Western region		
Seattle	118	57
San Francisco	83	84
Los Angeles	73	70

Source: Adapted from: F. Beaven Ennis, *Marketing Norms for Product Managers,* Association of National Advertisers, New York, 1985, p. 27.

- High CDI/high BDI (Boston): In these markets, both brand and category consumption are very high. There is little need for additional development activity.
- High CDI/low BDI (Seattle): The brand needs support if it is to grow. Distribution and promotional support are probably inadequate.
- Low CDI/high BDI (Denver): Opportunities appear to exist to expand primary demand if management can identify why some people are not using the product.
- Low CDI/low BDI (Memphis): Neither the brand nor the category has widespread acceptance in this market.

ZIP Code-Based Indexes In recent years, marketers have gained access to new data bases for gaining a better understanding of relative potential and relative performance while at the same time enhancing their ability to target advertising and promotions. The best-known system for accomplishing this is PRIZM—Potential Rating Index by ZIP Markets. This index is based on the observation that demographically similar neighborhoods share the same consumer patterns regardless of the region of the country they are in. PRIZM assigns each United States ZIP Code into one of 40 ''ZIP quality'' clusters, each of which is internally similar on demographic and lifestyle grounds. Because so much consumer data is available on a ZIP Code basis (e.g., magazine subscription lists, warranty cards, auto ownership, and many consuming buying polls), PRIZM provides an array of useful data on media and purchasing patterns by which Zip Codes can be compared.[3]

Table 5-7 illustrates the kind of information available on PRIZM for two of the forty ZIP quality clusters. Note that these two clusters share common age ranges, but their consumption habits and media patterns are substantially different. Clearly, marketers interested in selling canned stews or foreign tour packages would not want to target their promotion efforts toward both clusters.

Summary

Market-potential measures can be of significant value to managers, as the examples in this chapter have indicated. However, because market potential is related to industry and company sales, the usefulness of the market-potential estimates can be enhanced by comparisons with sales forecasts.

SALES FORECASTING

Sales forecasts are estimates of future levels of demand. These market measurements can have a tremendous impact on all functional areas of an organization because they are used in making a number of different decisions. There are, however, important differences in the types of sales forecasts and in the methods of sales forecasting. Table 5-8 summarizes these distinctions which are discussed in the remainder of this chapter.

Basic Types of Sales Forecasts

The two major types of sales forecasts are industry sales forecasts and company sales forecasts. However, within these two classes, forecasts can be made at different levels of aggregation of sales.

Industry Sales Forecasts Managers may use an industry sales forecast to estimate the total sales that will be achieved by all suppliers in the relevant market. Depending on how the firm has defined the relevant market, industry sales can be measured for a product form or for a product class or for all competing classes satisfying the same generic need. Indeed, a manager may develop industry sales forecasts for more than one of these levels of aggregation, depending on how the forecast will be used.

There are four basic uses of industry sales forecasts. First, industry sales forecasts indicate the expected rates of growth of alternative markets. Therefore, they are useful elements in corporate marketing planning (as discussed in Chapter 2). Further, to the extent that industry sales forecasts indicate different rates of growth for various product forms or various product classes, decisions on the appropriate relevant market can be made. For example, if one product form (such as nutritional cereals) is growing faster than a competing form (such as presweetened cereals) then top management will probably provide greater marketing support to

[3]Michael J. Weiss, *The Clustering of America*, Harper & Row, New York, 1989, pp. 12–16.

brands in the product-form market with higher growth. Alternatively, if sales forecasts show that industry sales for either a product form or for a product class (such as cereals) are growing at a low rate, then strategies for stimulating sales of the product form or class may be examined.

Second, as we discussed in Chapter 4, the rate of industry sales growth is a major influence on competitive intensity. If management's forecast indicates a dramatic decline in the rate of industry sales growth, they will know that future company sales gains must come from increases in market share, a condition that often fosters heavy price and promotion competition.

Third, industry sales forecasts are also important to middle management. Knowing the future level of industry sales enables a firm to calculate the market share required to reach its sales goals. For example, given a sales objective for a product of one million units and an industry sales forecast of five million units, the managers can judge whether or not it is feasible to attain a 20 percent market share based on the company's planned level of marketing effort and on the product's current market-share positions. The relationship between industry sales forecasts and marketing budgets is discussed in detail in Chapter 6.

Finally, the rate of industry growth generally has a major influence on company sales growth. Accordingly, an industry sales forecast is often an important input to the company sales forecast.

TABLE 5-7   A COMPARISON OF TWO ZIP QUALITY CLUSTERS

ZQ 8: Young suburbia		**ZQ 16: Blue-collar nursery**	
5.3% of U.S. households		2.2% of U.S. households	
Primary age range:	25–44	Primary age range:	25–44
Median household income:	$38,582	Median household income:	$30,007
Median home value:	$93,281	Median home value:	$67,281
Thumbnail demographics		**Thumbnail demographics**	
Upper-middle-class outlying suburbs		Middle-class child-rearing towns	
Single-unit housing		Single-unit housing	
Predominantly white families		Predominantly white families	
College educations		High school educations	
White-collar jobs		Blue-collar jobs	
Politics		**Politics**	
Predominant ideology:	conservative	Predominant ideology:	conservative
1984 presidential vote:	Reagan (76%)	1984 presidential vote:	Reagan (74%)
Key issues: fiscal conservatism, trade protection		Key issues: fiscal conservatism, nuclear arms	
Sample neighborhoods		**Sample neighborhoods**	
Eagan, Minnesota (55124)		West Jordan, Utah (84084)	
Dale City, Virginia (22193)		Maryville, South Carolina (29440)	
Pleasanton, California (94566)		Princeton, Texas (75044)	
Smithtown, New York (11787)		Richmond, Michigan (48062)	
Ypsilanti, Michigan (48197)		Haysville, Kansas (67060)	
Lilburn, Georgia (30247)		Magnolia, Houston, Texas (77355)	

TABLE 5-7   A COMPARISON OF TWO ZIP QUALITY CLUSTERS (continued)

ZQ 8: Young suburbia				ZQ 16: Blue-collar nursery			
Lifestyle				**Lifestyle**			
High usage	Index	Low usage	Index	High usage	Index	Low usage	Index
$75,000 + life insurance	229	Theater	83	Campers	222	Downhill skiing	64
Swimming pools	228	Laxatives	81	Unions	192	Watch tennis	45
Health clubs	217	Convertibles	80	Watch pro wrestling	186	Foreign tour packages	45
Ice-skating	213	Malt liquor	78	Toy-sized dogs	175	Malt liquor	43
Lawn furniture	184	Civic clubs	65	Bowling	172	Money-market funds	41
Racquetball	179	Soul records/tapes	63	Hunting	171	Environmentalist organizations	38
Home computers	178	Watch pro wrestling	38	1960s rock records/	164	Travel by railroad	21
Foreign tour packages	158	Snuff	29	tapes	141	Slide projectors	16
				Tupperware			
Magazines/newspapers				**Magazines/newspapers**			
High usage	Index	Low usage	Index	High usage	Index	Low usage	Index
World Tennis	255	*National Enquirer*	76	*Lakeland Boating*	287	*Forum*	37
Business Week	190	*Esquire*	75	*Mother Earth News*	202	*Fortune*	35
Skiing	187	*True Story*	47	*Outdoor Life*	166	*Rolling Stone*	34
Golf	177	*Jet*	33	*American Photogra-*	165	*Atlantic Monthly*	12
				pher			
Cars				**Cars**			
High usage	Index	Low usage	Index	High usage	Index	Low usage	Index
Mitsubishi Galants	263	Plymouth Gran Furys	98	Ford EXPs	232	Jaguars	29
Ford EXPs	215	Chevrolet Impalas	97	Chevrolet Chevettes	208	BMWs	28
Toyota vans	209	Dodge Diplomats	97	Plymouth Turismos	196	Mitsubishi Galants	18
Nissan 300ZXs	208	Rolls Royce	39	Ford Escorts	188	Ferraris	18
				Chevrolet Cavaliers	184	Alfa Romeos	4
Food				**Food**			
High usage	Index	Low usage	Index	High usage	Index	Low usage	Index
Cheese spreads	138	Whole-wheat bread	95	Canned stews	141	Whole-wheat bread	85
Pretzels	134	TV dinners	94	Pretzels	119	Canned corned-beef hash	78
Frozen waffles	133	Canned stews	87	Children's vitamins	116	Canned orange juice	65
Children's vitamins	126	Powdered fruit drinks	76	Baked beans	115	Frozen corn-on-the- cob	56
Television				**Television**			
High usage	Index	Low usage	Index	High usage	Index	Low usage	Index
Cheers	130	*Knots Landing*	78	*Newhart*	132	*Miami Vice*	92
Night Court	123	*Highway to Heaven*	78	*Night Court*	127	*NBC Sports World*	80
Newhart	116	*The Young and the Rest-*	62	*Love Connection*	124	Sunday morning interview pro-	64
Family Ties	115	*less*		*Highway to Heaven*	117	gram	
		Friday Night Videos	61			*American Bandstand*	53

Source: Michael J. Weiss, *The Clustering of America*, Harper & Row, New York, 1989, pp. 292–293 and 316–317. An index of 100 would indicate usage at the national average.

TABLE 5-8   TYPES AND USES OF SALES FORECASTS

Uses of forecasts of industry sales
  Assess market growth for corporate marketing planning decisions
  Project the extent to which sales gains must come through market share gains
  Determine market share required to attain given sales goals
  Starting point for company sales forecast

Uses of forecasts of company sales
  Time-series forecasts
    Plan production schedules
    Estimate inventory requirements
    Establish sales quotas per territory
    Project cash flows
  Causal forecasts
    Determine marketing budget
    Set prices

Company Sales Forecast   Just as the industry sales forecast can be developed at any of three levels of aggregation, company sales forecasts can also be developed at more than one level. That is, a firm may wish to forecast company sales of a specific item (such as regular-size Tide), a brand (Tide), or a product line (Procter & Gamble detergents), or total company sales (all Procter & Gamble sales).

Forecasts at the *item* level are generally most useful for decisions related to production scheduling and to the transportation of goods to distributors. Forecasts at the highest level of aggregation, *company sales,* are most useful for overall company financial planning. From a marketing strategy and planning perspective, the most important forecasts are those which focus on *brand sales* or *product-line sales* because marketing decisions are most often designed to influence sales at these levels of aggregation. However, not all forecasting approaches are equally useful for marketing decision making. That is, even when brand or product-line sales are being forecasted, the managerial usefulness of the forecast will depend on the type of approach used to develop the forecast. As Table 5-8 suggests, when our concern is simply to get the best estimate of expected sales (which is usually the major concern of production and finance managers) time-series methods are generally used. However, causal forecasts are appropriate if we are concerned with understanding how our price and marketing budget might *influence* future sales.

Basic Forecasting Approaches

Although an extensive array of forecasting approaches exists, there are really three basic types of approaches: time-series models, causal models, and judgmental approaches. Any of these approaches can be employed in forecasting either industry or company sales.[4]

---

[4]See, for example, Spyros Makridakis and Steven Wheelwright, "Forecasting: Issues and Challenges for Marketing Management," *Journal of Marketing,* October 1977, pp.24–38; and David M. Georgoff and Robert G. Murdick, "Manager's Guide to Forecasting," *Harvard Business Review,* January–February 1986, pp. 110–120.

Time-Series Models   The basic assumption underlying time-series models is that sales can be forecast with acceptable accuracy by examining historical sales patterns. These models are relatively easy to use because the only data needed are past sales and because they can be implemented by means of easy-to-obtain "canned" computer programs. A further advantage of these models is that the probable range of the deviation of actual sales from forecasted sales (called the *forecasting error*) can be estimated statistically.

As a general rule, time-series models are most useful when market forces are relatively stable within the forecasting horizon. That is, if sales trends are not likely to change because of economic changes, marketing actions, or technology, these models are likely to be reasonably accurate. These conditions are often found when short-run forecast horizons (less than 1 year) are required. They may also be found over longer forecast periods in the case of markets that are technologically mature, are not very susceptible to the effects of economic fluctuations, and are expected to witness few major changes in marketing effort.

Even in the most stable markets, however, seasonal variations, changes in trends, and random fluctuations do occur. Accordingly, a variety of procedures have been developed for "smoothing out" random fluctuations by averaging recent sales levels, for giving weights to monthly sales levels to adjust for seasonality, and for increasing the importance of more recent sales data to reflect trends.

In cases where pronounced trends exist, where random fluctuations are not severe, and where manager wish to forecast several periods into the future, direct curve-fitting approaches are often employed to identify the sales time series. In this approach, a computer program is used to determine the equation of the "best-fitting" curve—the line or curve that most closely approximates the historical trend. This equation is then used to forecast future sales by projecting that same line or curve into the future.

Consider, for example, Figure 5-2. The dots in this figure portray annual sales

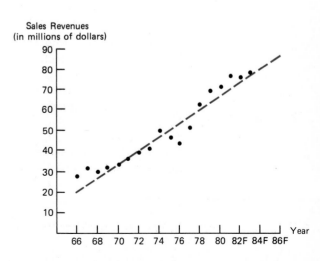

FIGURE 5-2   A time-series forecast for Tootsie Roll Inc. *(Developed from data presented in W. R. Dillon, T. J. Madden, and N. H. Firtle, Marketing Research in a Marketing Environment, St. Louis: Times Mirror, Mosby, 1987, pp. 705–706.)*

for the Tootsie Roll company from 1966 to 1983. As we can see, there is clearly an upward sales trend with modest fluctuations. The dashed line is the straight line that, according to a simple regression analysis between sales and time, best portrays the past trend. Sales forecasts for the subsequent years (1984 through 1986) can be made by simply extending the trend line.

Time-Series Diffusion Models   One special class of time-series model of particular interest to marketers is diffusion models, which are used to portray first-purchase, sales-growth patterns for new durable products or services. This class of model is somewhat different from conventional, simple time-series models in that it focuses on time series in which a turndown in actual sales can be expected as the industry approaches market potential.

The best-known of these models was developed by Frank Bass. In the 1960s, Bass used this model to correctly predict the sales peak for color television sets during the early years of that product in the life cycle. Since then, this model has been applied to a number of other new product-form or new product-class introductions.[5]

Basically, the model requires the manager to be able to make three estimates:

1 *m,* the number of potential buyers in the market
2 *p,* the coefficient of innovation (initial trial rate)
3 *q,* the coefficient of imitation (diffusion rate)

where *p* represents the probability of purchase (adoption) by individuals who are not influenced by other owners and *q* represents the effect of each adopter on each nonadopter.

The specific formula for this model is

$$S_t = pm + (q - p)Y_t - \frac{q}{m} Y_t^2$$

where S_t = number of sales during time period t
Y_t = cumulative number of previous sales up to time t

Essentially, the formula states that sales in the time period being studied (S_t) are determined by three factors. The first (*pm* in the equation) is the number of buyers who will try the new product on their own when it is introduced. The second factor represents buying by those who rely on word-of-mouth information from those who have already purchased. At any point in time, the number of these imitators will of course depend on the number of people or firms who have already bought (Y_t). The final factor reflects the fact that, ultimately, first-time sales will decline. As the number of previous buyers (Y_t) increases, the number of people left in the market who have never tried the product declines. At the start of the

[5]See Frank Bass, "A New Product Growth Model for Consumer Durables," *Management Science,* January 1969, pp. 215–227; and Vijay Mahajan and Eitan Muller, "Innovation Diffusion and New Product Growth Models in Marketing," *Journal of Marketing,* Fall 1979, pp. 55–68.

process there were m potential buyers. But at time t there are only $m - Y_t$ people or firms who have yet to buy.

Normally the p and q coefficients of this model are determined through statistical estimation procedures, and m is estimated using regular procedures for market potential estimation. Figure 5-3 portrays the kinds of results that can sometimes be obtained through the use of this model.

Even with more sophisticated time-series models, however, managers may find that a model fits historical data quite well, but fails to predict the future effectively.

This points out the basic limitation of time-series methods: They do not account for major changes in future sales that can occur because of changes in the economic or demographic environment, in marketing effort, or in competition. In general then, managers should exercise great care in using time-series forecasts. In particular, managers should answer the questions in Table 5-9 in order to evaluate the probable accuracy of such forecasts.

Causal Models   When environmental changes can be expected to create a shift in the historical pattern of sales, then time-series models are likely to prove unsatisfactory. In such situations, managers are more likely to seek to use fore-

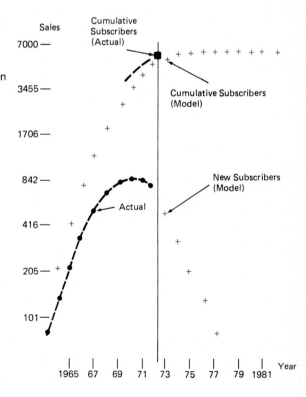

FIGURE 5-3   Projected new subscriptions and cumulative subscriptions of cable television based on 1963–1972 data. *Data are in millions; coefficients are m = 6,575,000 (based on market factors existing in 1972), p = 0.005447, q = .83687. (From Wellesley Dodds, "An Application of the Bass Model in Long-Term New Product Forecasting," Journal of Market Research, August 1973, p. 310. Reprinted by permission of The American Marketing Association.)*

TABLE 5-9 QUESTIONS FOR EVALUATING THE RELIABILITY OF TIME-SERIES FORECASTS

1. Do we have a long enough history of sales data to construct a reliable trend?
2. Can we expect industry growth trends to level off because industry sales are approaching market potential?
3. Is it likely that industry sales will shift because of economic, demographic, or technological factors?
4. Can new competition (including competition from other product forms or classes) be anticipated which will influence industry or company sales?
5. Can we expect major changes in the marketing activity of competitors?
6. Does the industry (company) have the production capacity to fulfill industry (company) sales forecasts?
7. Does our company plan any major changes in its marketing programs?

casting techniques that link sales to one or more factors that are thought to cause or influence sales.

The simplest type of causal model is the leading indicator forecast. Leading indicators are often used to forecast industry sales over a fairly short time horizon—usually 6 months or less. Specifically, some fairly broad economic changes in sales of business forms usually trail changes in sales of the nation's Gross National Product by 6 months, and the monthly consumer confidence index published by the Conference Board (a New York–based research group) predicts outboard motor sales with a lead time of 6 months.

Multiple-regression models are used when a number of factors have an impact on sales. These factors will include leading indicators, especially in *industry* sales forecasts. Additionally, however, multiple-regression forecasts also allow managers to incorporate the expected effects of any *controllable* marketing variables which are likely to be significant when forecasting *company* sales. That is, if historical data on price, advertising expenditures, or other marketing variables are available, managers can attempt to predict the different levels of sales which will occur for varying levels of price or advertising expenditures. Therefore, assuming that the relationship between sales and these controllable marketing variables can be clearly established, multiple regression provides a forecasting approach that can serve as a planning tool. (In contrast, time-series sales forecasts do not permit managers to examine the effects of changes in controllable marketing variables.)

Multiple-regression models, like time-series models, rely on historical data and are easily implemented through canned computer programs. However, they attempt to define equations that give the best historical statistical fit between sales (industry or company) and one or more causal (or *predictor*) variables.

For example, a company in the home-furnishings industry developed the following multiple-regression equation to forecast company sales.[6]

---

[6]George C. Parker and Edilberto L. Segura, "How to Get a Better Forecast," *Harvard Business Review,* March–April 1971, pp. 99–102.

$$
\begin{aligned}
\text{Annual sales (\$ millions)} = &- 33.51 \\
&+ \quad .373 \text{ (previous year's sales)} \\
&+ \quad .033 \text{ (previous year's housing starts,} \\
&\qquad\qquad \text{thousands)} \\
&+ \quad .672 \text{ (disposable personal income, \$ billions)} \\
&- 11.03 \quad \text{(time from beginning of data, yr)}
\end{aligned}
$$

Although it did not incorporate all the possible factors influencing sales, this equation explained 95 percent of the year-to-year variation in company sales over the previous 20 years. Additionally, as in any statistical forecast, the company was able to determine the standard error of the forecast—in this case $9.7 million. That is, there is always some imprecision in a statistical forecast. The standard error indicates the size of this imprecision in terms of past sales and past forecasts. Two-thirds of the time, the forecast estimate of sales will be within one standard error (in this case $9.7 million) of actual sales; 95 percent of the time, forecasted sales will be within two standard errors (in this case $19.4 million) of the actual sales.

While multiple-regression models do overcome many of the disadvantages of time-series models, they are never perfectly reliable. Several assumptions are made in the construction of regression models. Accordingly, managers should answer a number of important questions in order to assess the reliability of regression forecasts. The most important of these questions are presented in Table 5-10. If the answer to any of these questions is unfavorable, then the accuracy of the forecast result will be limited. More specifically:

• If important causal factors have been left out, sales may fluctuate for reasons not explained by the model. If these factors can have a major impact on sales, then the regression sales forecast should be adjusted judgmentally (if possible) to account for the other factors.

• If some causal factors cannot be accurately projected into the future, then management should develop a series of forecasts, each based on different assumptions about the future levels of these factors. For example, if average industry prices or competitors' prices are important but hard-to-predict factors, managers can make different estimates about future prices and see how each estimate changes the forecasted level of sales.

TABLE 5-10 QUESTIONS FOR EVALUATING THE RELIABILITY OF MULTIPLE-REGRESSION FORECASTS

---

1. Have any important factors that influence sales been ignored in testing the various equations?
2. Can the predictor variables that cause or influence sales be predicted or controlled?
3. Will some of the predictors change so dramatically in the future that their impact on sales will change?
4. Are the various predictor variables independent of one another, or do two or more of those variables really measure the same thing?

- If some of the predictors are expected to change dramatically, the historical relationship with sales may not hold up. For example, a dramatic rise in prices may increase buyers' sensitivity to price. If this happens, the relative importance of price in influencing sales will become greater than the regression equation suggests.
- If two predictors are highly correlated (for example, population and total household income), then the proportion of historical variation in sales explained by the equation will not be accurate. That is, our measures of the statistical error of the forecast will not be reliable.

While the last problem can be resolved by redefining the equation to eliminate one of the correlated predictors, the first three problems can be resolved only by the application of management judgment.

Judgmental Approaches Frequently it will not be possible to rely heavily on statistical approaches to forecasting. Time-series methods may be inappropriate because of wide fluctuations in sales or because of anticipated changes in trends. Regression methods may be infeasible because of a lack of historical data or because of management's inability to predict (or even identify) causal factors. The judgmental approach will be management's only possible avenue for forecasting in these situations.

Additionally, managers may use judgment to supplement statistical approaches for three reasons. First, even the most sophisticated statistical model cannot incorporate all of the potential influences (such as oil embargoes, strikes at major customers' manufacturing plants, or a major technological breakthrough in product or process design) on sales. Second, particularly in industrial markets, a small number of buyers may represent a large share of demand. Accordingly if management anticipates the loss or addition of a few major accounts this will usually have to be factored into a company sales forecast in a judgmental fashion. Third, a general rule of thumb is that statistical forecasts are more reliable for larger levels of aggregation. That is, it is more difficult to accurately forecast demand by sales territory than to forecast total national demand. Similarly, it is more difficult to forecast demand by detailed sizes and models than by brand or by product line. Consequently, managers must often employ judgment to develop the more detailed forecasts.

The sales force and distributors are usually the most expert at monitoring and assessing buying patterns and local competitive conditions. However, other management personnel may also be involved in the forecasting process. Particularly in the case of regression sales forecasting, the judgments of marketing and advertising research personnel or brand managers may be employed to estimate the impact of a change in marketing budgets or strategies on sales.

Interpreting the Forecast

In evaluating the managerial implications of a sales forecast, managers should be fully aware of: any *seasonality* patterns that exist; the *sensitivity* of forecast results to slight changes in forecast assumptions or techniques; and the costs of forecasting errors.

Seasonality   Seasonal variations exist in nearly all markets, usually because of variations in the frequency of usage occasions during the course of a year. Consequently, when marketing decisions are being made on a monthly or quarterly basis it is important to recognize seasonal sales patterns. (For example, advertising budgets might be increased during high-volume months or prices might be lowered in low-volume months.) Additionally, if monthly or quarterly sales data have been seasonally adjusted prior to use in a statistical forecasting model, time-series growth trends will be more noticeable and the impact of causal factors (in regression models) will be more accurately identified because seasonality may be a major cause of variation in sales that would not otherwise have been accounted for. Table 5-11 illustrates how seasonal indexes might be developed for data reported on a quarterly basis. Table 5-12 illustrates how the process of deseasonalizing can clarify an historical time-series trend.

Sensitivity Analysis   If several techniques give essentially the same results, the reliability of a forecast should be greater. Accordingly, some firms develop parallel forecasts based on alternative techniques. Similarly, several regression forecasts may be developed, each one based on different assumptions regarding causal factors. Knowing how different techniques or assumptions lead to alternative demand estimates enables a manager to determine how sensitive the forecast result is to a change in these factors. When forecasts are highly sensitive, managers should expect greater imprecision and should closely monitor the environment to find out which model and which assumptions most closely approximate reality.

TABLE 5-11   AIR PASSENGER ARRIVALS IN FLORIDA: CALCULATION OF SEASONAL INDEXES
(Passengers in thousands)

	Quarter			
Year	**1**	**2**	**3**	**4**
1981	3756	2660	2550	2496
1982	4251	2833	2425	2776
1983	4846	2932	2557	2881
1984	4562	3200	2715	3010
1985	4877	3280	2854	3305
5-year total	22,292	14,905	13,101	14,468
Quarterly mean				
for 5 years	4458.4	2981.0	2620.2	2893.6
÷ overall mean	÷	÷	÷	÷
for 20 quarters	3238.3	3238.3	3238.3	3238.3
Seasonal index	1.376	0.921	0.809	0.894

TABLE 5-12 CLARIFYING THE TREND OF AIR PASSENGER ARRIVALS IN FLORIDA BY SEASONAL ADJUSTMENT

Year/quarter	Actual arrivals (in thousands)	÷	Seasonal index	=	Seasonally adjusted arrivals (in thousands)
1981/1	3756		1.376		2729.7
2	2660		0.921		2888.2
3	2550		0.809		3152.0
4	2496		0.894		2791.9
1982/1	4251		1.376		3089.4
2	2833		0.921		3076.0
3	2425		0.809		2997.5
4	2776		0.894		3105.1
1983/1	4846		1.376		3521.8
2	2932		0.921		3183.5
3	2557		0.809		3160.7
4	2881		0.894		3222.6
1984/1	4562		1.376		3315.4
2	3200		0.921		3474.5
3	2715		0.809		3356.0
4	3010		0.894		3366.9
1985/1	4877		1.376		3544.3
2	3280		0.921		3561.3
3	2854		0.809		3527.8
4	3305		0.894		3696.9

The Costs of Forecast Errors If a sales forecast has a large standard error (a wide range of possible values), managers should consider the costs of overestimating and underestimating demand. To illustrate this point, assume that a manager has been given a company sales forecast of 200,000 units with a standard error of 10,000 units. In using this information, the manager may choose to plan around a level somewhat lower or higher than 200,000 depending on the firm's cost and competitive structure. A manager planning production and marketing budgets on the basis of exactly 200,000 units implicitly assumes that the costs of overestimation and underestimation are equal, but in most firms these costs are not equal.

As Table 5-13 indicates, there are different kinds of consequences associated with overestimating and underestimating *company sales.* For some firms, the cost of holding excess inventory may be extremely high (perhaps because the product is perishable) while the amount of sales lost because of delayed shipments is very low (perhaps because the company has loyal customers). Accordingly, if a firm is in that situation, management will be more willing to risk underestimation than overestimation. This is because the cost of excess inventory resulting from excess production will outweigh the lost revenue from an inadequate level of production. Because the costs of overestimation are greater for that firm, managers will probably want to plan decisions on a forecast that is more conservative than

TABLE 5-13   POSSIBLE RESULTS OF COMPANY SALES FORECAST ERRORS

Results of overestimation

Excess capacity leading to layoffs, loss of skilled labor
Price cuts or additional marketing expenses to move product
Distributor ill will because of excess distributor inventories
Inventory costs:
   Cash flow problems and cost of capital tied up in finished goods, components, raw materials
   Technical obsolescence or damage
   Storage or warehousing costs

Results of underestimation

Lost sales or customer goodwill
Overtime costs
Costs of expediting shipments
Reduced quality control due to reduced maintenance of machinery at full production capacity
Production bottlenecks due to lack of materials and parts

200,000 units. For example, statistical theory tells us that there is a 95 percent chance that the actual level of sales will be within two standard errors. Thus, with a standard error of 10,000, there is a 95 percent chance that sales will be within the range of 180,000 to 200,000 units. Further there is a 2½ percent chance that sales will be less than 180,000 and a 2½ percent chance that sales will exceed 200,000.

Additionally, errors in industry sales forecasts can also create problems for managers. The most significant of these problems is that a forecast error may lead to misclassifying a product in a firm's product mix plan. For example, if industry sales are *overestimated,* management may treat a cash cow as though it were a star; the result would be excessive marketing expenditures and lower profitability. On the other hand, if industry sales are *underestimated,* management may make the mistake of prematurely reducing marketing support in the belief that the market has matured and that less spending is necessary to maintain market share; the result in this case may well be a loss in market share because of inadequate spending relative to the competition.

In sum, managers must recognize that sales forecasts are only estimates and are based on certain assumptions. By being aware of these assumptions and the nature of the risks associated with forecast errors, managers should be able to make better judgments on how to use the forecast.

CONCLUSION

Market measurement is an activity of critical importance for a wide range of decisions. Market-potential estimates and industry and company sales forecasts are essential for the development of corporate marketing strategies and product objectives. Middle-management decisions regarding the size and allocation of marketing expenditures depend heavily on sales forecasts and on the relationship between forecasts and the factors to be considered in the next chapter.

In this chapter, we have examined the different kinds of market measurements, their uses, and the various ways in which they can be developed. By understanding the purpose and assumptions behind a given market measurement, it will be easier for a manager to specify the kind of information needed in a given situation and to understand the degree of reliability that should be placed on a given market-measurement estimate.

Additionally, managers should be aware of the available data sources that can be used for developing market measurement estimates. Some of these sources were mentioned in this chapter. However, a more complete listing and description of prominent sources of market information is contained in the appendix.

The various steps in market measurement and the relationships among these steps are portrayed in Figure 5-4. To gain a better understanding of some of these relationships, consider the market measurement challenges facing Algarve Tourism Research Associates.

FIGURE 5-4 Steps in market measurement and their relationship to other aspects of the situation analysis.

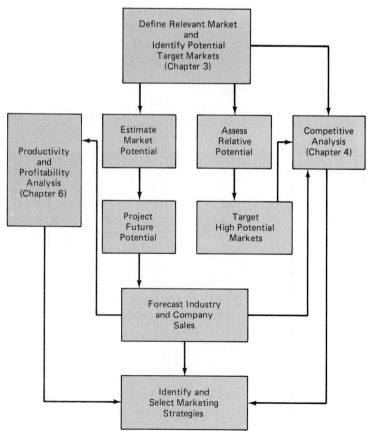

Algarve Tourism Research Associates

In the second half of the 1960s, Portugal began to actively promote tourism. Portugal's attractions lured a substantial number of foreign visitors and by 1989, it was estimated that tourism represented more than 8 percent of the nation's national income, with the main tourist destination being along the southern coast in the Algarve province.

In Portugal, tourism data are collected by the National Institute of Statistics. Tourism statistics include visitor arrivals, tourist arrivals, and excursionists. Both monthly and annual figures are provided and are broken down by nationality,' country of residence, mode of transportation, trip purpose, sex, and age. Other information available includes occupancy rates, average length of stay, and nights-in for accommodations with a breakdown by hotels, apartments, villas, and camping sites. In addition to locally collected data, Portugal shares data with other European nations and receives travel statistics and travel intentions data from the World Tourism Organization.

ATRA (Algarve Tourism Research Associates) performs market studies for a variety of tourism-related businesses and public agencies in the Algarve province. Early in 1989, ATRA was asked to forecast the number of hotel guest arrivals to the province for the four quarters of the coming year. ATRA had the following historical data on guest arrivals between 1979 and 1988.

Guest arrivals to the hotels and similar establishments*					
Year	**Quarter**	**In 1000s**	**Year**	**Quarter**	**In 1000s**
1979	1	55	1984	1	100
	2	158		2	223
	3	225		3	307
	4	96		4	149
1980	1	70	1985	1	150
	2	178		2	290
	3	245		3	360
	4	100		4	171
1981	1	69	1986	1	161
	2	177		2	306
	3	214		3	388
	4	104		4	181
1982	1	88	1987	1	132
	2	204		2	318
	3	244		3	412
	4	119		4	175
1983	1	101	1988	1	149
	2	209		2	312
	3	263		3	426
	4	119		4	193

*Includes self-catering villas and apartments.
Source: National Institute of Statistics (Portugal).

Using a trend forecasting model, ATRA's researchers developed the following forecast of guest arrivals:

1989	First quarter	165,652
1989	Second quarter	327,955
1989	Third quarter	441,596
1989	Fourth quarter	208,410

1 Calculate the seasonality indexes for each quarter for guest arrivals.
2 a For the first quarter of 1989, the standard error of the forecast is 17,080. If the users of this forecast want to take no more than a 2½ percent chance of underestimating guest arrivals for the first quarter of 1989, what level of demand should they plan around?
  b Do you think that users of these forecasts (such as hotels or car rental companies) should be more concerned about avoiding overestimation or underestimation? Explain.
3 How would you go about attempting to estimate market potential for the Algarve region? What factors determine the size of the gap between market potential and industry sales in this case?
4 Discuss the usefulness of knowing the seasonality indexes from a strategic point of view. If the company had comparable data from other locations in Portugal and in neighboring countries, what additional analyses might be done to identify demand gaps?

QUESTIONS AND SITUATIONS FOR DISCUSSION

1 As brand manager of Shulton Incorporated's Old Spice fragrance, you have been investigating the market potential for men's cologne. The Old Spice brand dominates all age categories of the men's cologne market but is strongest among male customers 35 years and older. You have recently come across the following population projections from the U.S. Bureau of the Census:

	Total U.S. population (in millions)	18–34 (in millions)	PCT	35–54 (in millions)	PCT	55–70 (in millions)	PCT
1991	252.5	69.3	27.4	65.4	25.9	31.5	12.5
1992	254.5	68.2	26.8	67.6	26.6	31.3	12.3
1993	256.4	67.2	26.2	69.6	27.1	31.3	12.2
1994	258.8	66.1	25.6	71.7	27.8	31.3	12.1
1995	260.1	65.2	25.1	73.6	28.3	31.4	12.1
1996	261.8	64.3	24.6	75.6	28.9	31.6	12.1

a How would this information be useful in estimating market potential for Old Spice? For men's cologne? What additional information would you like to have?

b How useful would this information be in comparison to the Sales and Marketing Management BPI?

2 Your company markets a line of clothing products for both secondary and university/college students. Your sweatshirts and T-shirts are embossed with the school's name and appropriate identifying symbols. How would you measure market potential to determine the different geographical territories you would assign to your salespersons? Would you measure potential differently if this was a new line for your company?

3 You have been given the assignment of determining relative market potential for each of the 50 states for (a) Morton salt, (b) Rolex watches, and (c) Motown compact disks. In each case, what are the most effective ways to complete this assignment?

4 Which of the following represent estimates of company potential and which represent estimates of market potential? Explain.

  a Potential demand for cellular phones facing a firm with a franchise to sell a specific brand in the state of Nebraska

  b Potential demand for graduation photographs of high school seniors within a single school district

  c Potential demand for a computer software sales forecasting package that runs only on color monitors and only on Apple computers

5 The U.S. Hispanic population has recently been increasing at four times the rate of the overall population growth. As a bottler of sugared colas, you know that the Hispanic market consumes 65 percent more colas per capita than the general population. How would this information be useful to you in determining the market potential for soft drinks? Would it affect your decision to use either time series or multiple regression in your sales forecast? Why?

6 Which of the following would linear trend extrapolation be more accurate for? (a) annual population for the twelve nations comprising the European Common Market, or (b) annual sales of cars produced in the common market by Fiat. Why?

7 If an industry sales forecast is needed for each of the following products, for which product will a time-series approach be the most appropriate?

  a Automobiles

  b Laundry detergent

  c Baby food

8 a For which of the following products would a diffusion forecasting model be most useful in 1989?

  1. Automatic bank tellers

  2. Compact disk players

  3. Home computers

  b For which of the products listed in *a*, above, do you think the coefficient of innovation is highest relative to the coefficient of imitation? (That is, in which case will sales to innovators be highest relative to sales to individuals who are influenced by previous adopters?)

9 General Foods quit advertising its Maxwell House coffee brand for 9 months. During this period Maxwell House lost several points of market share. Would this affect the basic approach(es) Maxwell House could use in forecasting sales?

10 In each of the following situations, would you tend to avoid overestimation or underestimation?

  a Your product has a large market share with loyal customers.

  b You compete in a market where technology changes and design changes are frequent.

    c You are a new competitor trying to build market share.

    d In order to maintain good employee relationships, your company wants to avoid layoffs.

    e Your product is not greatly differentiated from competitive products.

SUGGESTED ADDITIONAL READINGS

Bishop, William S., John L. Graham, and Michael H. Jones, "Volatility of Derived Demand in Industrial Markets and Its Management Implications," *Journal of Marketing,* Fall 1984, pp. 95–103.

Childress, Robert, "Optimal Planning: The Use of Sales Forecasts," *Decision Sciences,* July 1973, pp. 167–171.

Frisbie, Gilbert, and Vincent A. Mabert, "Crystal Ball vs. System: The Forecasting Dilemma," *Business Horizons,* September–October 1981, pp. 72–76.

Georgoff, David M., and Robert G. Murdick, "Manager's Guide to Forecasting," *Harvard Business Review,* January–February 1986, pp. 110–119.

Mahajan, Vijay, and Eitan Muller, "Innovation Diffusion and New Product Growth Models in Marketing," *Journal of Marketing,* Fall 1979, pp. 55–68.

Proctor, R. A., "A Different Approach to Sales Forecasting: Using a Spreadsheet," *European Management Journal,* Fall 1989, pp. 358–365.

Schnaars, Steven P., "Situational Factors Affecting Forecast Accuracy," *Journal of Marketing Research,* August 1984, pp. 290–297.

Sobek, Robert, "A Manager's Primer on Forecasting," *Harvard Business Review,* May–June 1973, pp. 6–15.

CHAPTER 6

PROFITABILITY AND PRODUCTIVITY ANALYSIS

OVERVIEW

In Chapters 3 and 4, we examined the importance of understanding buyers and competitors when framing marketing decisions. Additionally, in Chapter 5, we considered the relationships among market potential, industry sales, and company sales in the process of market measurement. As a result of performing the analyses in those chapters, managers should be in a position to identify market opportunities and strategies for taking advantage of such opportunities. Before embarking on a marketing strategy, however, middle managers will generally have to do a detailed analysis of what it will cost to implement a strategy and what the expected sales and profit consequences will be.

Productivity analysis is the assessment of the sales or market-share consequences of a marketing strategy. Specifically, a productivity analysis involves the estimation of relationships between price or one or more marketing expenditures (such as advertising budgets) and the sales volume or market share of a particular product or product line. As we show in this chapter, these estimates are generally developed based on insights obtained from market and competitive analyses and from market measurements.

Profitability analysis is the assessment of the impact of various marketing strategies and programs on the profit contribution that can be expected from a product or product line. In considering the role played by profitability analysis, managers should be aware that this analysis is important regardless of the kind of product objective that has been established. Certainly a manager would seldom significantly increase the marketing budget for a cash cow if the increase would not improve profitability. But even when the primary product objective is sales or market-share growth (rather than profitability), it is still important for a manager to know how much profitability must be sacrificed to achieve a given sales or market-share target.

For an overview of the concepts, tools, and approaches involved in analyzing the impact of marketing expenditures, consider the following situation. Oswald Optical is an eyewear business which sells prescription eyeglasses, contact lenses, and eyewear accessories (such as eyeglass holders and chains, clip-on sunglasses, and cleaning items). The company employs optometrists who provide examinations and write prescriptions. However, it also fills prescriptions written by other optometrists in the community. Because Oswald Optical has a machine to grind lenses and stocks a full range of contact lenses, it can usually provide 1-hour service in filling prescriptions.

Oswald has just finished its first year in business, during which it processed 7000 optometry patients, made 10,000 pairs of glasses, and sold 5000 sets of contact lenses. In preparing a budget for the second year, a major question faced by the owner is whether to increase the advertising budget for contact lenses. Specifically, an $18,000 increase is under consideration.

As Figure 6-1 indicates, Oswald's owner must consider four factors in making this decision:

1 The relative importance of market share and profitability as *product objectives* for contact lenses
2 The *industry sales forecast* for contact lenses
3 The anticipated *productivity* (that is, the effectiveness) of the increased advertising in increasing contact lens sales
4 The various types and levels of cost that determine the *profitability structure* of contact lenses

In the current chapter, we present procedures for measuring product profitability and for estimating the productivity of marketing expenditures. In addition, we illustrate how product objectives, sales forecasts, profitability, and productivity are related to marketing budgeting decisions, using the specific example of Oswald Optical.

FIGURE 6-1   Factors to be considered in making marketing expenditure decisions.

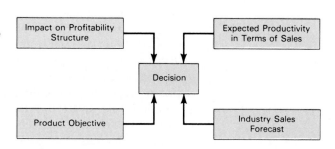

MEASURING PRODUCT PROFITABILITY

As most managers know, the income (profit-and-loss) statement is generally inadequate for analyzing product profitability. Consider the profit-and-loss statement for Oswald Optical given in Table 6-1.

If Oswald Optical were a single-product organization, the conventional profit-and-loss statement would provide a reasonably useful measure of product profitability. However, because the firm is a multiproduct organization, management will also be interested in the profitability of each of the various products. Moreover, the conventional profit-and-loss statement provides few clues to how profitability would be influenced by changes in those costs (such as advertising) that lead to changes in sales volume.

In order to examine these issues, we need to make two kinds of distinctions in types of costs. First, the distinction must be made between *fixed* and *variable* costs. Second, fixed costs should be separated into those which are *direct* or *traceable* to individual products and those which are *indirect* or *nontraceable*.

Variable Versus Fixed Costs

Variable costs are costs that vary with sales volume. Sales commissions, material, labor, and packaging are typically variable costs because they go up proportionately with sales. That is, each of these costs is incurred every time a product is produced and sold.

Nearly all other costs are *fixed*; that is, they remain essentially the same regardless of volume levels—at least as long as increases in the size of a production facility or in administrative and clerical staff are not required. Although some of these costs can be *changed* by management (such as advertising budgets and sales-force salaries), they do not vary *automatically* as sales change. For a manufacturer, the cost of goods sold (in the income statement) usually includes both fixed and variable elements. That is, each unit sold is assigned a share of the fixed

TABLE 6-1 OSWALD OPTICAL: PROFIT-AND-LOSS STATEMENT
(in thousands of dollars)

Sales		$1160
Less cost of goods sold		455
Gross profit margin		$ 705
Operating expenses:		
Advertising	$150	
Sales salaries	125	
Sales commission	45	
Optometrists' salaries	100	
Rent and utilities	120	
Other (general and administrative costs) .	150	
Total operating expense		690
Net operating profit (loss) before taxes		$ 15

costs to be added to its variable cost. For a retailer or wholesaler that only resells products made by other firms, the cost of goods sold is only a variable cost because it simply reflects the purchase price of items being resold.

Note that Oswald Optical is relatively unique because it is a manufacturer (of lenses), a retailer of goods (frames, lenses, and accessories), and a retailer of a service (optometry). The company's role as a manufacturer means that the labor costs involved in grinding lenses (machine technicians' salaries) are included in the cost of goods sold (shown in Table 6-1) but not in the *variable* cost of goods sold (shown in Table 6-2). Conversely, Oswald offers sales commissions of $3 per pair of glasses or per pair of contact lenses sold. These costs are variable costs (as seen in Table 6-2) but are not included in the cost of goods sold in Table 6-1.

By separating fixed costs from variable costs (as we have done in Table 6-2) the portion of cost that is sensitive to volume is identified. Out of every $1160 in retail sales, $450 (that is, $405 plus $45) is spent on the variable costs. The remaining $710 is the amount that is contributed to cover all fixed costs and profit after variable costs have been subtracted.

With costs separated in this way, managers can calculate a very useful measure: the *percentage-variable-contribution margin* (PVCM). This measure indicates the percentage of each additional sales dollar that will be available to help the firm cover its fixed costs and increase profits. The percentage-variable-contribution margin can be calculated in either of two ways:

$$PVCM = \frac{\text{unit price} - \text{unit variable cost}}{\text{unit price}}$$

or

$$PVCM = \frac{\text{variable contribution margin}}{\text{dollar sales}}$$

TABLE 6-2   OSWALD OPTICAL: CONTRIBUTION MARGIN STATEMENT
(in thousands of dollars)

Sales.		$1160
Less variable cost of goods sold (glass for lenses, frames, and accessories)		405
Gross profit margin		$ 755
Less other variable selling costs (sales commissions)		45
Variable contribution margin.		$ 710
Fixed costs:		
Advertising	$150	
Sales salaries	125	
Machine technicians' wages	50	
Optometrists' salaries.	100	
Rent and utilities	120	
General and administrative overhead.	150	
Total operating expense		695
Net operating profit before taxes		$ 15

In the case of Oswald Optical then,

$$PVCM = \frac{\$\,710}{\$1160} = 61.2\%$$

In order to fully appreciate the usefulness of this measure to a marketing manager, it is necessary to understand the distinction between direct fixed costs and indirect fixed costs.

Types of Fixed Costs

When fixed costs are incurred in a multiproduct firm, they are incurred either on behalf of the business as a whole or they are incurred on behalf of one or more specific products. For example, organizations may design advertisements to communicate a message about a particular product or product line, or they may use *institutional* advertising which presents a message about the company as a whole and may not even mention the specific products or services sold. Costs such as product-specific advertising that are incurred on behalf of a specific product or service are known as *direct fixed* costs. Costs such as institutional advertising that are incurred to support the total business are *indirect fixed* costs.

In practice, firms recognize that there are really two categories of indirect cost: traceable and nontraceable. *Traceable* costs are indirect costs that can be allocated to various products on some nonarbitrary basis. For example, if a common sales force is used to sell two or more products, the total selling cost is usually allocated between the two products on the basis of some factor such as the percentage of selling time devoted to each one.

The purpose of distinguishing the various types of fixed costs is to provide a basis for evaluating the contributions made by different products or services to the overall profitability of the firm. Thus, firms assign direct and traceable indirect costs to products in order to gauge the costs of supporting each product. But nontraceable indirect costs are not assigned.

Table 6-3 illustrates how the profitability of individual products and services can be measured once management has separated the fixed costs. The bottom line for the individual products and services is no longer net operating profit but *total contribution*. The total contribution is the amount that an individual product or service "contributes" to the coverage of nontraceable indirect costs and to profit. (From a portfolio perspective, large contributions would be expected from cash cows and small or even negative contributions would be expected from problem-child products.)

By examining Table 6-3, we can see that contact lenses generate the largest total contribution of the four products even though the dollar volume of eyeglass sales is twice as large. One reason for this is that contact lenses incur a much smaller level of direct and traceable costs than eyeglasses or optometry services. In this example, optometrists' salaries, machine technicians' salaries, and advertising are direct costs: These two salary categories clearly apply to only one prod-

TABLE 6-3   OSWALD OPTICAL: CONTRIBUTION BY PRODUCT LINE
(in thousands of dollars)

	Company total	Optometry services	Eyeglasses	Contact lenses	Accessories
Sales	$1160	$210	$600	$300	$50
Variable cost of goods sold	405	0	270	105	30
Gross profit margin	$ 755	$210	$330	$195	$20
Other variable costs	45	0	30	15	0
Variable contribution margin	$ 710	$210	$300	$180	$20
Direct, traceable fixed costs:					
Sales salaries	$ 125	$ 0	$ 90	$ 30	$ 5
Optometrists' salaries	100	100	0	0	0
Technicians' salaries	50	0	50	0	0
Advertising of specific product lines	75	10	50	15	0
Rent and utilities	120	40	60	16	4
Total	$ 470	$150	$250	$ 61	$ 9
Total contribution	$ 240	$ 60	$ 50	$119	$11
Indirect, nontraceable fixed costs:					
Institutional advertising	$ 75				
General and Administrative overhead	150				
Total	$ 225				
Net operating profit	$ 15				

uct and the product-specific advertising is self-explanatory. Sales salaries have been assigned on the basis of the estimated share of salesperson time devoted to the various lines. Rent and utilities have been allocated on the basis of the share of the store's total space that is used for each product or service. The data suggest that eyeglasses require more selling time than contact lenses (probably owing to the time associated with picking out a frame) and more space (since a large number of frames must be stocked).

The second factor influencing the relative profitability of the products and services is the percentage-variable-contribution margin. Table 6-4 summarizes the PVCM calculations and provides additional sales and average price data for the various lines. On a percentage basis, contact lenses are more profitable than eyeglasses. For each additional $1000 in sales of contact lenses, Oswald will retain $600 after variable costs are subtracted. For eyeglasses, $500 would be retained if sales rose by $1000.

IMPLICATIONS OF PROFITABILITY ANALYSIS

By identifying the fixed and variable components of cost and by distinguishing between direct and indirect costs, managers will be able to examine some of the profitability implications of pricing and marketing expenditure decisions. Specif-

TABLE 6-4   OSWALD OPTICAL: PERCENTAGE-VARIABLE-CONTRIBUTION MARGINS

	Optometry services	Eyeglasses	Contact lenses	Accessories
Number of customers	7,000	10,000	5,000	12,500
Average price paid	$30	$60	$60	$4
Variable cost per average customer	0	$30	$24	$2.40
Variable contribution margin per average customer	$30	$30	$36	$1.60
PVCM $\dfrac{(Price-VC)}{Price}$	100%	50%	60%	40%

ically, by understanding the profitability structure for a product, managers can identify *cost-volume-profit relationships* and *implications for marketing budgets*.

Cost-Volume-Profit Relationships

In many organizations, a large portion of the total operating cost is essentially fixed. In these situations, managers generally will pursue policies which take advantage of *economies of scale*. These economies will exist when a large change in volume leads to a significant change in the average cost of a product.

Consider, for example, Table 6-5. As sales volume doubles (from 10,000 to 20,000 units) total costs increase by a smaller percentage amount because a high proportion of total costs are fixed. Consequently, the average cost per unit is reduced from $55 to $42.50.

The existence of strong cost-volume-profit relationships means that managers should be more willing to increase marketing expenses or cut prices, if these actions will lead to significant increases in volume. Returning to Table 6-5, we can

TABLE 6-5   ECONOMIES OF SCALE FOR EYEGLASSES

	Annual sales volume	
	10,000 pair	20,000 pair
Unit variable cost	$30	$30
Multiplied by volume	10,000	20,000
Total variable cost	$300,000	$600,000
Total direct or traceable fixed cost	$250,000	$250,000
Plus total variable cost	300,000	600,000
Total direct cost	$550,000	$850,000
Divided by volume	10,000	20,000
Average unit cost	$55.00	$42.50

see that at a price of $55 per unit, the firm will just cover its average costs at a volume of 10,000 units. If, however, sales could be doubled by lowering prices, the firm could price the product as low as $43 per unit and still make a profit.

The advantages of employing economies of scale to be price-competitive are fundamental to the strategies of low-cost champions such as Heinz, Briggs & Stratton (small motors), and Kellogg.[1] Additionally, fixed costs are often extremely high in high technology businesses where expenditures on research and development are very large (such as in pharmaceuticals) and where manufacturing has become heavily automated. Particularly among global marketers, labor and material costs have declined relative to fixed costs, putting more pressure on firms to find ways for entering new markets to lower average costs.[2]

Managers must not only be aware of the opportunities associated with economies of scale, they also need to recognize the potential difficulties they create. As we saw in Chapter 4, when fixed costs are high and industry sales growth is low, intensive competition is usually the result. This can pose real difficulties for firms that lack established market positions as the following demonstrates:

In 1989, Miller Brewing withdrew its Matilda Bay wine coolers from the market. Matilda Bay had reached the number four position in the market, selling 5 million cases in 1988 following an introduction to the market in 1987. Miller entered the market believing industry sales forecasts that projected 20% annual sales growth. Instead the market declined by more than 20% between 1986 and 1989. Because of the high fixed costs of advertising (Miller spent $30 million to advertise Matilda Bay prior to 1989), the company needed a variable contribution margin of $5.85 per case just to cover those costs. But industry analysts estimated that with the discounts Miller had to offer to get retailers to stock up and promote the brand, the company was generating margin of less than $4 per case.[3]

Because of the potential negative consequences of economies of scale, many firms employ strategies that require minimal fixed costs. Specifically, some firms operate in market segments where the high fixed costs associated with advertising, selling, or high development costs are very low. Consider, for example, Rhino Records.

Rhino Records is a very small competitor in the U.S. record industry with less than 1% of total industry dollar sales in 1989. But the company has been quite profitable, focusing its efforts on repackaging 1960's rock 'n' roll albums. For example, the firm produced "best of" collections by Roy Orbison, the Turtles, and the Monkees, among others, and released one album containing ten renditions of "Louie, Louie" from artists ranging from the Kingsmen to the Rice University Marching Owl Band.

Rhino has no fixed artists' salaries or recording costs for developing an album: All songs are licensed from their owners for about $.10 to $.15 per album. With variable distributor commissions and minimal marketing, Rhino's total fixed costs may be as

[1]Bill Saporito, "Heinz Pushes to Be the Low Cost Producer," *Fortune*, June 24, 1985, pp. 44–54.
[2]Kenichi Ohmae, "The Global Logic of Strategic Alliances," *Harvard Business Review*, March–April 1989, pp. 145–146.
[3]Julia Flynn Siler, "How Miller Got Dunked in Matilda Bay," *Business Week*, Sept. 25, 1989, p. 54.

low as $30,000 per album. At a $8.98 retail price, unit variable contribution is around $3. As a result, all fixed costs are recovered once sales volume hits 10,000 records.[4]

Some firms have also found that variable costs may decline as volume increases. This phenomenon, known as the *experience-curve* effect, has been observed in companies such as Texas Instruments (consumer electronics), Black & Decker (power tools), and Du Pont (chemicals). Generally, these cost reductions occur as a firm becomes more experienced in producing a product for one or more of the following reasons:[5]

* The firm may design more efficient production equipment or processes.
* The firm may improve its ability to obtain discounts or to control inventories, leading to reduced costs for materials and components.
* Production workers may become more efficient (especially in assembly operations) as they become more familiar with the production process.

In sum, when average costs can be dramatically reduced because of economies of scale or experience curves, managers generally have a greater incentive to use competitive pricing or increased marketing expenditures in order to stimulate sales volume.

Special Profitability Issues for Retailers

In addition to evaluating the impact of margins and direct fixed costs on profitability, retailers must assess the amount of space (physical assets) or inventory investment (financial assets) that is appropriate for a given product, product line, or department. That is, since space and inventory dollars are really the most critical resources for most retailers, managers involved with retail decision making should also assess profitability in terms of these assets.

Whether profitability is being measured on a product, product-line, or departmental basis, four basic measures are typically used:

* Inventory turnover
* Sales per square foot
* Gross-margin return on inventory investment
* Gross-margin return per square foot

Inventory turnover is the ratio of a product's sales to the average dollar value of the inventory held for that product.

Sales per square foot is the ratio of a product's sales to the amount of selling space (measured in square feet) used for the product.

Gross-margin return on inventory investment measures the profit return rather

---

[4]Fleming Meeks, "The Gold in Oldies," *Forbes,* May 1, 1989, pp. 68–72.
[5]See George S. Day and David Montgomery, "Diagnosing the Experience Curve," *Journal of Marketing,* Spring 1983, pp. 44–58, for a thorough discussion.

than the sales return on inventory investment. This measure is calculated by multiplying inventory turnover by the percentage gross profit margin.

Gross-margin return per square foot is equivalent to sales per square foot multiplied by percentage gross profit margin.

Table 6-6 summarizes these four measures. In choosing one of these measures, managers should consider two issues. First, retailers may differ over whether inventory or space is the more critical resource. Some firms have adequate space but limited financial resources for purchasing inventory. Accordingly, these firms should use inventory turnover or gross-margin return on inventory investment because the most critical decisions will revolve around inventory allocation. However, if space is the scarcer resource, then sales per square foot or gross-margin return per square foot should be used.

A second consideration is whether to use sales or gross margin as a measure of return. Many retailers continue to use sales rather than gross margin because it is simpler to measure sales when product-line or departmental profitability is being measured. If departments or product lines vary significantly in gross margins, however, using sales as a measure of profitability will definitely be inadequate for comparing profitability.

Table 6-7 compares several of the product profitability measures for Oswald Optical. Contact lenses are more profitable than the other products for all three measures just as they were shown (Table 6-3) to be the most profitable in terms of total contribution. However, the relative profitability of accessories is heightened when we use these measures especially in comparison to optometry services. That is, on a per-square-foot basis, accessories are ranked as more profitable than optometry services on both of the asset profitability measures. This indicates that accessories represent a very good use of space.

Implications for Marketing Budgets

As we suggested at the beginning of the chapter, managers should have an understanding of the product objectives and an industry sales forecast in order to

TABLE 6-6   MEASURES OF PRODUCT PROFITABILITY FOR RETAILERS AND WHOLESALERS

Inventory turnover	=	$\dfrac{\text{sales}}{\text{average value of inventory}}$
Sales per square foot	=	$\dfrac{\text{sales}}{\text{square feet of selling space}}$
Gross-margin return on inventory investment	=	$\dfrac{\text{gross margin}}{\text{price}} \times \text{inventory turnover}$
Gross-margin return per square foot	=	$\dfrac{\text{gross margin}}{\text{price}} \times \text{sales per square foot}$

TABLE 6-7   OSWALD OPTICAL: MEASURING ASSET PROFITABILITY

	Optometry services	Eyeglasses	Contact lenses	Accessories
Sales	$210,000	$600,000	$300,000	$50,000
Square feet used	2,000	3,000	800	200
Gross profit margin percentage*	100%	55%	65%	40%
Total contribution	$ 60,000	$ 50,000	$119,000	$11,000
Sales per square foot	$ 105	$ 200	$ 375	$ 250
Gross margin per square foot	$ 105	$ 110	$ 243.75	$ 100

*Calculated from Table 6-3 as (sales − variable cost of goods sold) ÷ sales.

develop a budget. Further, managers must have some estimate of the productivity of a proposed price and marketing expenditure level in generating company sales (after taking the industry sales forecast into account). We will examine some procedures for developing these productivity estimates later in this chapter. However, assuming that management has developed these estimates of productivity, the budgeting process can proceed in either of two ways: the *direct* approach or the *indirect* approach.

The Direct Approach   In this approach, managers must make specific estimates of the sales that will result from a given price and marketing budget. (The steps in this approach are summarized in Table 6-8.) If data are available for developing industry sales forecasts, managers can obtain an estimate of company sales by estimating the market share they expect to obtain for a given price and marketing budget and then multiplying this market share by the industry sales forecast.

To illustrate, recall that Oswald Optical is considering an $18,000 increase in the advertising budget for contact lenses. Assuming that no changes occur in price or in other costs, the only elements in the profitability structure that will change are the advertising budget (which also leads to a change in total direct traceable fixed costs) and those costs which are variable. That is, if the increase in

TABLE 6-8   STEPS IN THE DIRECT APPROACH TO MARKETING BUDGETING

1. Develop an industry sales forecast (where feasible).
2. Estimate the market share that will result from a given price and marketing expenditure level. (If no industry sales are available, directly estimate company sales instead of market share.)
3. Calculate the expected company sales (market share × industry sales forecast).
4. Calculate variable contribution (company sales × PVCM).
5. Calculate total contribution (variable contribution margin less direct and traceable fixed costs included in proposed budget).
6. Determine whether the sales, market share, and total contribution levels are acceptable, given the product objectives.

advertising results in increases in sales volume, then *by definition* all variable costs will increase as well.

If total contact lens sales in Oswald Optical's market are expected to be 40,000 pair and if Oswald Optical's owner predicts the company's market share to be 15 percent, then projected company sales would be 6000 pair. Assuming the average retail selling price remains at $60, dollar sales would be $360,000. Recalling from Table 6-4 that PVCM for contact lenses is 60 percent of sales, Oswald's variable contribution margin will increase by $36 (60 percent × $60 selling price) for each additional pair sold. Table 6-9 summarizes the calculation of the projected profitability of contact lenses for the proposed budget.

The calculations suggest that the sales increase of $60,000 will result in an increase of $36,000 in the variable contribution margin (the remainder going to variable costs). Further breakdown of the $36,000 increase in variable contribution margin shows that $18,000 will be spent on the increase in advertising, leaving a net gain in total contribution of $18,000. The new total contribution of $137,000 must be evaluated (along with the projected market share) against the product objectives. If the projected share and total contribution are sufficiently high as to meet top-management expectations, the budget would be considered adequate. If not, then the manager must consider other possible budget levels.

The foregoing example is a rather simple illustration in that we have assumed only one change in projected expenditures. In a more typical case, managers would find that other changes would occur. Sales-force salaries might be increased, variable costs may change, or prices may rise or fall. If such changes are expected to occur they should be incorporated in the profitability projections. (Note that a change in price or variable cost will require a change in the PVCM and in the variable contribution margin per unit.)

Further, some degree of uncertainty usually exists in projecting sales and costs. Accordingly, managers who use the direct approach often must calculate several different estimates of total contribution to determine how much the total contribution figures would change if sales or various cost elements turn out somewhat

TABLE 6-9 OSWALD OPTICAL: PROJECTED PROFITABILITY FOR CONTACT LENSES
(in thousands of dollars)

	Current year	Projected
Sales	$300	$360
× PVCM	.60	.60
Variable contribution margin	$180	$216
Direct, traceable fixed costs		
Sales salaries	30	30
Advertising	15	33
Rent and utilities	16	16
Total direct, traceable	61	79
Total contribution	$119	$137

higher or lower. Fortunately, nearly all makers of large and small computers have developed so-called spreadsheet programs which allow managers to go through the many calculations required by this process very rapidly.

In most cases, the highest degree of uncertainty will rest with the productivity estimates. When managers are very uncertain about these estimates (a situation that is typical of relatively new products), it is often useful to employ the *indirect* approach.

The Indirect Approach   In the indirect approach (summarized in Table 6-10), an estimate of the sales productivity of a given price or budget is not required. Rather, managers are only required to estimate whether a benchmark level of sales can be achieved.

Specifically, managers who use this approach must first calculate the level of sales required to achieve the minimum acceptable target contribution for a given budget. This calculation requires three pieces of profitability information:

• The percentage-variable-contribution margin (or the variable contribution margin per unit) based on the expected prices and variable costs
• The total direct and traceable fixed costs to be incurred (including any expected changes in the marketing budget)
• The minimum target contribution that will be acceptable to top management

Given this information, the *required level of sales* can be calculated using the following formulas.

$$\text{Total dollar sales required} = \frac{(\text{target total contribution}) + (\text{total direct or traceable fixed costs})}{\text{PVCM}}$$

or

$$\text{Total unit sales required} = \frac{(\text{target total contribution}) + (\text{total direct or traceable fixed costs})}{\text{PVCM per unit}}$$

TABLE 6-10   STEPS IN THE INDIRECT APPROACH TO MARKETING BUDGETING

1. Establish the target level of total contribution.
2. Calculate the required level of sales to achieve target total contribution for a given price and marketing expenditure level: [(Proposed total direct and traceable fixed costs plus target total contribution) divided by PVCM].
3. Calculate the required market share: (Required level of sales divided by industry sales forecast).
4. Based on estimated productivity of the proposed price and marketing expenditures, determine whether the required sales and market share can be achieved.
5. Determine whether the required market share and required sales will be acceptable for the given product objectives. If not, determine whether the sales or market-share objectives can be reached with the proposed budget.

In the case of Oswald Optical, recall from Table 6-4 that the PVCM on contact lenses is 60 percent and that the variable contribution margin per set is $36. Given the proposed $18,000 increase in advertising, direct and traceable fixed costs will increase to $79,000 (as was shown in Table 6-9). If the owner is satisfied with the *current* total contribution of $119,000, then:

$$\text{Total dollar sales required} = \frac{(\$119,000) + (\$79,000)}{.60}$$
$$= \$330,000$$

$$\text{Total unit sales required} = \frac{(\$119,000) + (\$79,000)}{\$36}$$
$$= 5500 \text{ sets}$$

Note that if any changes in the target total contribution are made or if prices, variable costs, or other direct or traceable fixed costs are also changed, then the total sales required will change. For example, if Oswald's were to reduce prices so that the average price paid was reduced from $60 to $40, the PVCM would be reduced to 40 percent. That is, PVCM would be calculated as ($40 − $24/$40). Combining the proposed $18,000 increase in advertising with the reduction in price would result in the following calculations:

$$\text{Total dollar sales required} = \frac{(\$119,000) + (\$79,000)}{.40}$$
$$= \$495,000$$

$$\text{Total unit sales required} = \frac{(\$119,000) + (\$79,000)}{\$16}$$
$$= 12,375 \text{ sets}$$

The immediate task now facing the owner is to determine the market share that will be required. As suggested in the previous section, it is assumed that industry sales will climb to 40,000 units in the coming year. Based on the proposal of an $18,000 increase in advertising and a target total contribution of $119,000, the required level of sales was 5500 sets. Therefore,

$$\text{Required market share} = \frac{\text{required level of sales}}{\text{industry sales forecast}} = \frac{5500}{40,000} = 13.75\%$$

By determining the required market share, a manager develops a benchmark for evaluating the budget. That is, the owner can now evaluate the proposed budget by addressing the question "Will an $18,000 increase in advertising allow us to attain a 13.75 percent market share?" Although this question is not necessarily an easy one to answer, it is usually easier than developing a direct, specific estimate of the sales productivity of the marketing budget.

It should be noted, however, that the required market share calculated through the indirect approach only gives the minimum share needed in order to meet profitability requirements. In some cases, the product objective may call for market-share levels substantially higher than the share required to meet the target total contribution. In such cases, managers will also have to address the question of whether the proposed budget will be sufficiently productive to achieve the market-share objective.

PRODUCTIVITY ANALYSIS

Productivity analysis is the process of estimating the impact on sales of a change in price or in marketing expenditures. That is, the change in sales resulting from a given change in a marketing program indicates how productive that marketing program is. Frequently, the term *sales-response functions* is used to represent relationships between price or a marketing expenditure and sales.

Traditional Methods of Productivity Analysis

Most firms attempt to estimate productivity using one or more of the following approaches.

Analysis of Historical Relationships   Frequently, managers look to historical experience in estimating the responsiveness of sales to various expenditures. For instance, internal data may be available to estimate

• The average sales per retail outlet (when an organization is attempting to expand its market coverage)
• The sales increases that have resulted from increases in past advertising budgets
• The sales per sales call on new-prospect accounts
• Historical price elasticity

To the extent that these relationships are applicable to the current situation, they may provide some clues to the impact of proposed expenditures on sales. While management should not rely too heavily on such observed relationships unless they are supported by extensive sales data bases, more and more firms are developing computerized data bases tracking the purchases of customers. If data are also available on the prices buyers paid or on special promotions that buyers took advantage of, firms can begin to gauge the effectiveness of these tools. For example, American Express could examine customer account records to determine historically the sales response to direct mail promotions of a luggage product at various prices.

Competitive Parity Analysis   This approach also relies on historical experience but is designed to explicitly consider relative marketing effort. For example, when competing products are highly similar in product quality, a manager may find a very high correlation between a product's market share and

- Its share of industry advertising expenses
- The number of sales calls made relative to competitors' sales calls
- The relative number of retail accounts that carry the product
- The price of the product relative to the average industry price

To the extent that competitors' actions can be predicted, a competitive parity approach can provide clues to the likely impact of increased expenditures on market share. For example, it has been shown that successful new products maintain an advertising spending level over 2 years so that the brand's share of advertising is about *twice* the target share of market.[6]

Market Experiments In a market experiment, managers test a proposed policy (such as a price change, a sales-call policy, or an advertising theme) on some portion of the market and then observe the sales response. Often, marketers will attempt to test the effectiveness of a change in advertising or of a sales promotion plan by employing the plan in a designated market area. The observed sales will then be compared with the sales that would be expected in the absence of the change in marketing effort. In other cases, management may set different prices or different advertising weights (that is, different levels of spending) in two or more metropolitan areas and compare the sales results. Additionally, each of the syndicated marketing research firms SAMI/Burke, A. C. Nielsen, and Information Resources Inc. offers *electronic test markets* which work as follows:

- Different sales promotions (such as coupons) are targeted (via mail) or different advertising levels (in terms of number of advertisements) are targeted (via cable television) to distinct groups of households within a market.
- Each household has a special card which is scanned along with the household's purchases at supermarket checkout counters.
- Comparisons are made among the groups receiving each ad level or each type of direct mail promotion.

As a result of using electronic test markets, many consumer-goods firms have modified their marketing programs. For example, Nestle's found that sales of Quik chocolate drink responded very sharply to increases in newspaper ads that were combined with store displays.[7]

---

[6]See J. O. Peckham, *The Wheel of Marketing,* A. C. Nielsen, Northbrook, Ill., 1975; and Simon Broadbent, *The Advertiser's Handbook for Budget Determination,* Lexington Books, Lexington, Mass., 1988, pp. 131–132.

[7]Zachary Schiller, "Thanks to the Checkout Scanner Marketing Is Losing Some Mystery," *Business Week,* Aug. 28, 1989, p. 57.

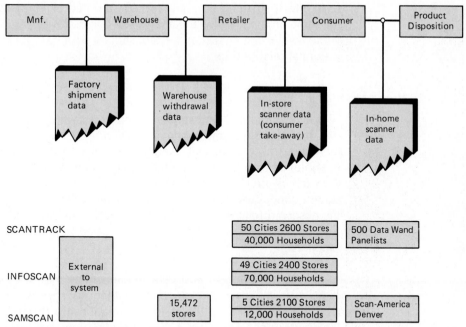

FIGURE 6-2   An overview of data collection in single-source systems. (*From David J. Curry, "Single-Source Systems Retail Management Present and Future," Journal of Retailing, Spring 1989, p. 4.*)

Single-Source Data

Each of the firms that offer electronic test market services has gradually been developing comprehensive systems of services to provide what has been termed *single-source data*. While their use is likely to be limited to manufacturers and retail firms marketing nondurable products, these systems promise to have a major impact on the ability to do productivity analyses.

Specifically, single-source systems will record each marketing signal (each price, each advertising message, each promotional action) that impacts a household either directly (at home) or indirectly via the retailer. The systems will trace each signal and link the content of each signal (for example, each price level) to household purchase behavior.[8]

Figure 6-2 provides an overview of the elements involved in the single-source systems offered by SAMI/Burke (SAMSCAN), Nielsen (SCANTRACK), and Information Resources Inc. (INFOSCAN). While factory shipment data will come from a firm's own sales data, the other data will be integrated. Electronic scanners in panel cities provide store-level sales of each product and household-level purchases. In-home meters monitor television viewing in panel households, with each service also auditing magazine and newspaper advertising in panel cities.

[8]David Curry, "Single Source Systems: Retail Management Present and Future," *Journal of Retailing,* Spring 1989, pp. 1–19.

In effect, single-source data provide a broad experimental capability while at the same time permitting the analysis of competitive parity (via price and *share of voice* advertising audits) and establishing a data base for conducting analyses of historical relationships.

Judgment-Based Productivity Estimates

Although traditional and single-source estimates can be useful, in many industries the data bases and syndication services necessary for effective use of these techniques may be absent. Additionally, experimentation is difficult (if not impossible) when a firm has a limited market and produces a very expensive product such as aircraft or mainframe computers. Finally, whether or not a firm uses some quantitative data obtained by these methods, it is not always certain that the observed relationship will hold up in the future. Specifically, managers must recognize several potential limitations when applying observed sales-response functions.

Interaction Effects   Historical relationships may not be valid when two or more major changes take place simultaneously. For example, a firm may have a good understanding of the historical relationship between advertising expenditures and sales. However, if that firm combines a change in advertising with a sharp change in price, the historical advertising-sales relationship may not continue. Unless a firm has an extensive history of combining advertising and price changes, it will be difficult to establish historical relationships among price, advertising, and sales.

Competition   When competitors modify their marketing policies as a reaction to competitive changes, the effectiveness of a given policy is often diminished. For example, a large increase in the advertising budget may lead competitors to respond by matching the increase, thus preventing any relative advantage from being gained.

Marketing Effectiveness and Efficiency   The effectiveness of marketing programs may improve over time and the efficiency with which expenditures are made and allocated may change. In both cases, improvements will mean that the same dollars will yield a larger sales payoff. Thus, advertisements which do a better job of communicating a product's benefits will be more productive on a per dollar basis than less effective advertisements. Similarly, improved selection of media may allow a firm to reach more potential buyers at the same cost. So to the extent that improvements in effectiveness and efficiency are forthcoming, a given marketing expenditure may be even more productive than would be projected from historical data.

Nonlinearity   Many marketing phenomena have a changing response function over time or over levels. For instance, promotional efforts may have a pattern

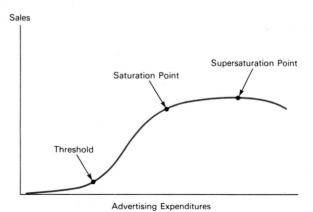

FIGURE 6-3 Hypothesized relationship between advertising expenditures and sales. (*Reprinted by permission from R. L. Ackoff and J. R. Emshoff, "Advertising Research at Anheuser-Busch," Sloan Management Review, Winter 1975, p. 4.*)

of sales effects similar to that presented in Figure 6-3. As this illustration demonstrates, the rate of sales response to an increase in marketing expenditures often changes over time, and thus the relationship is curvilinear. As the figure suggests, sales respond only minimally to low levels of advertising, but after a threshold level is reached, sales increase more rapidly with increases in advertising. Conceivably, at very high levels of advertising, a supersaturation point could be reached. Beyond this point, sales might actually decline if advertising expenditures were to increase further.

In judgment-based productivity estimation, managers use their knowledge of the factors influencing demand, competitors, potential environmental changes, and planned changes in marketing strategies and programs (that is, how marketing dollars will be spent) as supplements to (or even as substitutes for) the other three methods.

One of the most widely publicized approaches to judgment-based estimation is that developed by John D. C. Little.[9] In Little's approach, managers attempt to quantify their judgments about the relationship between each marketing variable and market share by answering four questions.

1 What level of expenditure is needed to maintain the current market share through the next budget period? (That is, what is the maintenance level of expenditures?)

2 What minimum level of market share will result in the next period if expenditures are reduced to zero?

3 What level of market share will result in the next period if expenditures are increased by 50 percent over the maintenance level?

---

[9]See John D. C. Little, "Models and Managers: The Concept of a Decision Calculus," *Management Science,* April 1970, pp. B-466 to B-485. An extended version of the model can be found in John D. C. Little, "Brandaid: A Marketing Mix Model," *Operations Research,* July–August 1975, pp. 628–673.

TABLE 6-11   FACTORS TO CONSIDER WHEN MAKING JUDGMENTAL ESTIMATES OF PRODUCTIVITY

1. Stage in product-form life cycle
2. Anticipated prices and expenditures by competitors
3. Likelihood of competitive retaliation if a major increase in expenditures or decrease in prices is made
4. Extent of distribution availability of the product
5. Major improvements in the efficiency with which dollars are spent
6. Major improvements in the effectiveness of strategies and programs which are expected to result in more favorable perceptions on determinant attributes
7. Extent of customer turnover
8. Degrees of customer awareness and preference for our product versus competing products or brands

4 What is the maximum market share that could be obtained in the next period if expenditures were unlimited?

In answering these questions, managers can use any information they might obtain from examining historical ratios, experiments, or competitive parity analysis. However, managers will also consider factors (such as those listed in Table 6-11) which are likely to influence the impact of changes in marketing expenditures or price on market share in the next period.

Given these four estimates, managers can develop a pictorial representation (that is, a *model*) of their productivity judgments. Consider, for example, a situation in which a manager is concerned with examining the impact of a change in advertising expenditures on market share. Depending on the answers to Little's four questions, the manager might portray the advertising–market-share relationship in a number of ways. One possible portrayal is presented in Figure 6-4. (This figure was developed by plotting the market shares at the zero, maintenance, and plus-fifty advertising levels, by identifying the maximum share, and by connecting these points with an approximately S-shaped curve to reflect the assumption that the relationship is nonlinear.)

In Figure 6-4, the estimates suggest that an increase in advertising from $1.5 to $2.0 million will be needed to simply maintain market share and that sharp increases or decreases in market share will result from major changes in the budget. These estimates might reflect judgments on several of the factors listed in Table 6-11. That is, market share may be highly sensitive to advertising expenditures if the brand is competing in the early stages of the product life cycle where neither brand awareness nor brand preferences have been strongly established or if the market is characterized by a high degree of customer turnover so that few previous buyers of a brand are still in the market.

Once a manager has developed a model of the productivity relationship, the effect of a proposed expenditure level can be incorporated into the budgeting process. Managers can use this model either to establish direct estimates of mar-

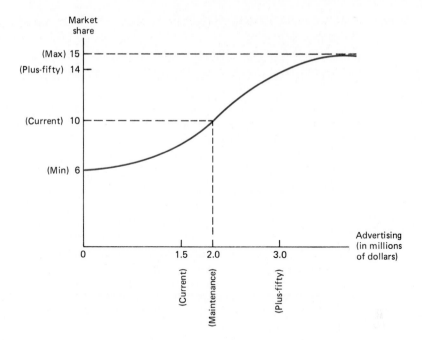

FIGURE 6-4

ket share or, if the indirect method is being used, to determine the likelihood of achieving a required level of market share.[10]

Cross-Elasticity Effects

Earlier we discussed the concept of indirect costs, indicating that these costs reflect the interdependencies in a multiproduct firm. However, products may also be interdependent in demand. Cross-elasticity effects reflect the interdependencies in demand across a set of products. These effects can be of two types: substitution effects and complementary effects.

Substitution effects take place when two or more products or services are used to perform the same generic function. Thus, eyeglasses and contact lenses are substitutes, and substitution effects will occur when one product receives a relative increase in marketing support: Increases in advertising for contact lenses are likely to have some negative impact on demand for eyeglasses.

[10]John D. C. Little provides a method for determining the equation for this curve based on the four estimates. With this equation, a manager can identify the market share that would result from any level of expenditure (assuming of course that the judgmental estimates are reliable). In order to determine the equation, managers must also estimate the long-run share that the brand will achieve with zero advertising.

Complementary products are those products (or services) that experience a sales *increase* when related products experience an increase in support. This relationship can occur for a number of reasons:[11]

• *Related use:* When two products are naturally used in conjunction with one another (as are men's suits and ties, or a mainframe computer and high-speed printers), the purchase of one product may lead to the purchase of the second. Consequently, many firms offer related products to more completely satisfy customer usage needs.

• *Enhanced value:* One product may enhance the value or increase the utilization of another. For example, a new camera attachment may make the camera easier or more interesting to use.

• *Quality supplements:* Products designed for repair, maintenance, or operating assistance may enable a customer to obtain or maintain a high level of quality performance. For this reason, many industrial and consumer firms today find that service contracts sold with electronics products and other durable goods are often very much in demand.

• *Convenience:* Products that may be totally unrelated in use may be complementary if they are bought from the same source because using a common source reduces buyers' search costs.

Thus, when contact lenses are promoted, not only do contact lens sales increase but sales of related-use cleaning solutions also increase. Moreover, promoting contact lenses will likely also lead to an increase in optometry appointments.

To the extent that managers can predict the cross-elasticity relationships among products and services, budgets should be adjusted to account for these effects. Consider, for example, the data in Table 6-12. This table is a simple extension of Table 6-9, which presented a hypothetical projected budget for contact lenses assuming an $18,000 increase in advertising resulted in a $60,000 increase in sales.

Given the average price of $60 per pair of contact lenses, the expected increase is 1000 units. Assume that Oswald Optical knows from its sales records that

• The average contact lens buyer purchases $3 worth of accessories.
• One-half of all contact lens buyers are new customers who also decide to be examined by an Oswald Optical optometrist at a charge of $30.
• Thirty percent of all contact lens buyers are substituting lenses for a pair of glasses (which normally cost $60).

Given these cross-elasticity estimates and the knowledge of percentage variable-contribution margins (from Table 6-4), the owner can estimate the net profitability impact of the budget change following the procedure presented in Table 6-12.

[11]For a more detailed treatment, see Alfred Oxenfeldt, "Product Line Pricing," *Harvard Business Review,* July–August 1966, pp. 137–144.

TABLE 6-12   OSWALD OPTICAL: PROJECTED BUDGET FOR CONTACT LENSES WITH CROSS-ELASTICITY EFFECTS

	Effect of new budget		
	Projected total		Projected change
Unit sales	6,000		+ 1,000
Dollar sales	$360,000		+ $6,000
Total contribution	$137,000		+$18,000
Plus complementary effects:			
Accessory sales		$ 3,000	
(1000 × $3)			
× PVCM		40%	+ $1,200
Optometry sales		$15,000	
(1000 × 50% × $30)			
× PVCM		100%	+$15,000
Minus substitution effects:			
Eyeglass sales		$18,000	
(1000 × 30% × $60)			
× PVCM		50%	− $9,000
Net change in total contribution from budget change			+$25,200

CONCLUSION

An understanding of the profitability structure of any product is essential in order to find ways of increasing or maintaining profitability. As we have seen in this chapter, marketing does cost money. In order to examine the desirability of maintaining, increasing, or decreasing the level of marketing expenses, the variable-contribution margin and other elements of the profitability structure for a product must be known. Moreover, some understanding of the responsiveness of sales to changes in marketing budgets is essential in the planning process. Productivity analysis is the process of determining what the likely sales response will be.

This chapter has examined the difficulties involved in productivity estimation. However, as we have demonstrated, by combining sales-forecast, market-share, productivity, and profitability information, a manager's ability to evaluate proposed expenditures will be improved.

The impact of marketing expenditures on sales and profitability cannot fully be examined by using the analytical tools presented in this chapter and summarized in Figure 6-5, however. Because these expenditures have some strategic purpose, expenditures must also be examined in the context of the marketing strategies and programs that managers design for a product. That is, these expenditures are more likely to achieve target sales and market-share levels if they are spent to support well-chosen strategies and programs.

The process of designing effective marketing strategies and programs is the subject of Part 3 of this book. Before continuing on to Part 3, however, consider once again the budgeting issue facing Oswald Optical.

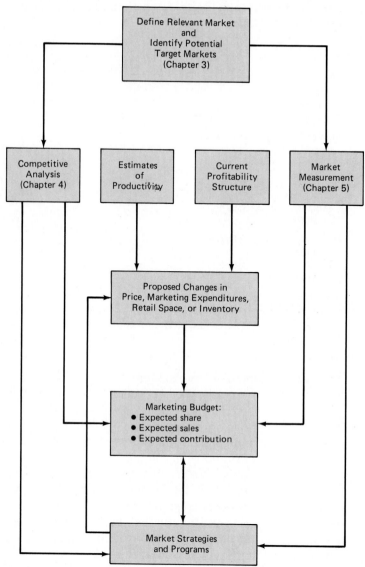

FIGURE 6-5   Steps in productivity and profitability analysis and their relationship to other aspects of the situation analysis.

Oswald Optical: Developing a Budget

Oswald Optical had just completed its first year in business in a Midwestern city of 300,000 people. Although the company had barely earned a profit, owner R. T. Oswald (who was also one of the two optometrists working at the store) felt that the results were reasonable for the first year. (Profitability results for the company and its various product lines are summarized in Tables 6-1 through 6-4.)

Although precise sales data were not available, Oswald estimated that eyeglass sales in the local market totaled 60,000 during the past year and would grow to 63,000 in the coming year. Oswald had two full-time optometrists and a 6000-square-foot store staffed with sales personnel. Its competition came primarily from four other well-established optical outlets. Each of these outlets was located in a different part of town but, like Oswald, emphasized quick service and low prices. Competing outlets averaged 4000 square feet in size, and each was staffed with only one optometrist. Eyeglasses could also be purchased from independent optometrists. However, these optometrists could not provide same-day delivery and were not price competitive with optical outlets. Together they accounted for only about 5 percent of all eyeglass sales.

Since the opening of Oswald Optical, R. T. Oswald had been careful to track the advertising of his major competitors. All competitors had large ads in the local telephone directory. All four competing outlets also used radio and local newspaper advertising. Like Oswald Optical, about half of all such advertising was institutional in nature. The four competitors averaged (according to R. T. Oswald's estimates) about $80,000 each in general advertising and about $55,000 each in advertising focusing on eyeglasses. With first-year sales of 10,000 pairs of glasses, Oswald's share of the market was 16.6 percent.

R. T. decided to focus next year's budget on building market share without sacrificing profitability. Before he established a budget, however, he wanted to examine the market-share and profit consequences of various budget levels. To do this in a thorough manner, he built a judgment-based model, establishing the following parameters for eyeglasses:

Maintenance advertising = $50,000
Maximum share   = 20 percent
Plus-fifty share   = 18 percent
Minimum share   = 5 percent

1 Discuss some of the specific factors that R. T. Oswald would have been able to use in making these estimates.

2 Based on Oswald's estimates, develop a graph portraying the relationship between Oswald's eyeglass advertising expenditures and market share. (Assume that the relationship is curvilinear, as is the case with Figure 6.4.)

3 Given your graph, estimate the market share that would result and calculate the profit consequences (using the *direct* approach) if the advertising budget is set

- At $65,000
- At $75,000

4 How would the market-share and profit estimates in Question 3 change if the industry sales forecast were changed

- To 60,000 units?
- To 68,000 units?

QUESTIONS AND SITUATIONS FOR DISCUSSION

1 In what situations would the indirect approach be more useful than the direct approach for evaluating a proposed change in marketing expenditures?

2 a Explain the importance of an accurate industry sales forecast to the budgeting process.

   b Can you think of any situations in which the industry sales forecast may change as a result of changes in the marketing budget? Explain your answer.

3 For which of the following companies would experience-curve effects likely be strongest? For which would economies of scale be greatest?

   a An aluminum can manufacturer

   b A garbage collection business

   c A firm that assembles VCRs

4 The Hudson Chemical Company manufactures and sells a complete line of insecticides and pesticides which are sold to homeowners and gardeners. As an addition to the product line, they began the manufacture of garden sprayers in the 1960s. The first sprayers were stainless steel, but since that time plastic containers have increased in importance. There has been little growth in the garden sprayer industry in the last few years because of the slowdown in new housing construction and the shift to multifamily and condominium living arrangements. Industry sales are expected to remain at the current level of 3 million units for 1992. Hudson has seen its market share decline to 10 percent and was considering a $200,000 increase in its advertising budget for 1992. Hudson sprayers are sold to wholesalers at an average price of $10 per unit. Wholesalers in turn sold the product to retailers for $12 per unit, and retailers priced the units at an average of $20 to consumers. The variable production costs were $5, and direct fixed costs for marketing, including advertising and sales, were about $1 million annually.

   a Calculate Hudson's current total contribution.

   b What level of market share will be required if Hudson is to maintain the product's current total contribution to indirect costs and profit?

   c What are some of the ways the marketing manager can determine if the market share is attainable?

5 The AM General Division of LTV Corporation is considering the production of a slightly altered version of its Hummer, a four-wheel-drive vehicle that has been replacing the Jeep as the U.S. military's all-purpose vehicle. The new version could be sold commercially to agencies or individuals in construction, farming, ranching, or forestry with modest changes to bring the vehicle into compliance with federal motor vehicle standards. In 1990, AM production of the Hummer was 45 vehicles per day at its Mishawaka, Indiana, plant where capacity was 260 vehicles per day. Assume the average cost of producing a vehicle is currently $20,000 with half of that cost going toward direct fixed costs, and that there is no change in variable cost required for the new model.

a Calculate the effects of increases of 20 and 45 units per day on costs.

b How would the economies of scale be different if fixed costs represent 25 percent of total costs at the 1990 volume?

c If the commercial version were to have a significantly different cost structure (perhaps because of additional options and the need for additional marketing expenses), how would this affect the way in which you would assess profitability?

6 Midwest Electronics was examining the profitability of two of its cellular phone products. Given below are the cost and revenue figures for 1990.

	Auto Deluxe	Micro Talk
Selling price	$550	$800
Unit sales	30,000	10,000
Total variable cost	$250	$300
Traceable promotion expenses	$1,500,000	$1,500,000

Assume that all other costs are indirect.

a Compare the current profitability of the two products.

b Given *only* the profitability data, if you had additional funds for promotion, which product should receive those funds?

c If the price of the Auto Deluxe was reduced by $50, what level of sales would be required to maintain the current level of total contribution?

7 You have just become director of marketing for the Irwin Memorial Blood Bank of the San Francisco Medical Society. The retail price of a unit of blood is $75. However, hospitals receive a $20 credit on a unit of blood if they convince a patient or someone designated by the patient to donate blood. This happens in approximately 60 percent of the cases. Irwin sells approximately 100,000 units of blood per year. The industry sells about 12.5 million units per year. Variable costs for producing a unit of blood are $22 per unit. Fixed manufacturing costs are $1 million. The marketing budget for blood products is $300,000. Donor recruitment salaries, including the manager's salary, constitute an expense of $175,000. Shipping costs, breakage, insurance, and so forth, are $2 per unit.

Irwin is contemplating lowering its prices for a unit of blood to $65 per unit in light of competitive pressure from hospitals to lower their costs. A second reason for considering a lower price is Irwin's concern over profit levels, and the effect that excessive profits might have on their tax classification as a not-for-profit organization.

a What is the unit variable-contribution margin for blood?

b What market share does Irwin need to cover all costs (that is, to break even)?

c If the price is lowered to $65, how many units will be needed to break even?

8 For each hypothetical situation given below, indicate what you think the best way of doing productivity analysis would be, and discuss the major problems a manager would face in doing an analysis in that situation.

a McDonald's wants to determine the best price for a new barbecue sandwich.

b IBM is considering whether to double advertising for its line of PS/2 personal computers.

c The brand manager for Wisk must decide on next year's advertising budget. Wisk has been on the market much longer than its major direct competitor, Liquid Tide. However Liquid Tide has a larger budget and has taken over from Wisk as the sales volume leader. In recent years, sales promotion has become increasingly important in this industry.

SUGGESTED ADDITIONAL READINGS

Alberts, William, "The Experience Curve Doctrine Revisited," *Journal of Marketing,* July 1989, pp. 36–49.

Ames, B. Charles, and James D. Hlavacek, "Vital Truths about Managing Your Costs," *Harvard Business Review,* January–February 1990, pp. 140–147.

Cook, Victor J., "The Net Present Value of Market Share," *Journal of Marketing,* Summer 1985, pp. 49–63.

Curry, David, "Single Source Systems: Retail Management Present and Future," *Journal of Retailing,* Spring 1989, pp. 1–19.

Hise, Richard T., Patrick J. Kelly, Myron Gable, and James B. McDonald, "Factors Affecting the Performance of Individual Chain Store Units: An Empirical Analysis," *Journal of Retailing,* Summer 1983, pp. 22–39.

Jones, John Philip, "Ad Spending: Maintaining Market Share," *Harvard Business Review,* January–February 1990, pp. 38–43.

Little, John D. C., "Decision Support Systems for Marketing Managers," *Journal of Marketing,* Summer 1979, pp. 9–27.

Piercy, Nigel, "The Marketing Budgeting Process: Marketing Management Implications," *Journal of Marketing,* October 1987, pp. 45–59.

Schroer, James, "Ad Spending: Growing Market Share," *Harvard Business Review,* January–February 1990, pp. 44–48.

MARKETING STRATEGIES AND PROGRAMS

The primary responsibilities of middle-level marketing managers are to develop and implement marketing strategies and programs for individual products or product lines. In Part 3, we examine concepts and procedures for selecting specific strategies and programs.

It is important to recognize that the concepts and procedures presented in the forthcoming chapters are not independent of those that we presented in previous chapters. Indeed, managers will not be able to make sound decisions on marketing strategies and programs without first having an understanding of:

- The product objectives to be achieved
- The factors that will influence the responsiveness of primary and selective demand to the marketing offer
- The potential market segments that might be served
- The extent, type, and sources of competition

• The size of various market opportunities, as indicated by market potential, industry sales, and company sales trends
• The profitability and productivity implications of making changes in prices or in marketing expenditures

Marketing programs are specific marketing decisions and actions that are the responsibility of middle managers. In Chapters 8 to 13, we examine the decision-making concepts, tools, and procedures for product development, pricing, advertising, sales promotion, and sales and distribution programs. In particular, we will underscore the importance of developing specific program objectives. These objectives can greatly simplify the process of selecting and designing the specific elements of the program. Additionally, we present procedures for understanding the specific budgetary consequences of each of these programs.

Although the development of effective programs is critical to success, different managers are often responsible for designing and executing different programs. Accordingly, some mechanism is necessary for assuring that the various programs are consistent and work in harmony to achieve the product objective. A *marketing strategy* can provide consistency of direction among programs by identifying the kind of total impact on demand that the overall marketing effort is designed to achieve. In Chapter 7, we will discuss the types of marketing strategies that can be employed, the relationship between strategies and programs, and considerations involved in selecting a marketing strategy for a product or for a line of products.

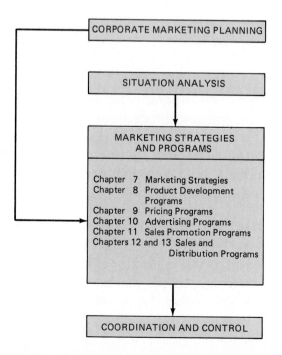

MARKETING
STRATEGIES

OVERVIEW

In Chapter 2, we presented the concept of a *corporate strategy:* a type of plan which outlines how a firm should use its resources to produce and market a specific array of products and services in order to achieve an overall *corporate objective.* In essence, the corporate strategy provided a *general* statement: It defined the products in which the organization would be involved but left open the details of how each product or product line would be marketed.

While the corporate strategy represents a plan developed by top management to guide the total organization, a marketing strategy is usually developed by a middle manager to guide a firm's activities for a product or a line of related products. More specifically, a marketing strategy is a plan which indicates how a manager deploys marketing resources on an individual product or product line in order to achieve a specified *product objective* (such as market-share growth or maximizing cash flow). Like the corporate strategy, a marketing strategy is a general statement: It defines the desired impact to be achieved on demand in a given target market but leaves open the fine print detailing how that impact is to be achieved. The detailed approaches for implementing these marketing strategies are determined through *marketing programs,* such as advertising programs, sales promotion programs, product-development programs, and sales and distribution programs.

To illustrate the distinction between a *strategy* and a *program,* consider the possible reasons that a manager might have for reducing the price of a product. Essentially there are four potential reasons for such actions. First, the manager may believe the lower price will lead some potential buyers to buy a product they otherwise would not. (Consider, for example, the tremendous increase in the

sales of personal computers as prices declined.) Second, the manager may believe the price decrease will result in increased rates of purchase of a product.
(For example, a decline in soft-drink prices may permit some buyers to consume
greater amounts of the product.) Third, prices may be cut to avoid losing existing
customers to competitors offering lower prices. Finally, the price cut may be an
attempt to lure customers from higher-priced competitors.

Note that price is used to influence demand in each of these four cases, but in
decidedly different ways. That is, each pricing program is designed to have a different *type* of impact on demand. In other words, in each case, price is being
used to implement a different type of marketing strategy, and consistent with our
pricing example, *marketing strategies* can be divided into *four* basic types:[1]

1 Stimulating primary demand by increasing the number of users
2 Stimulating primary demand by increasing the rate of purchase
3 Stimulating selective demand by retaining existing customers
4 Stimulating selective demand by acquiring new customers

In addition, because many firms offer arrays of related products, it is important
to consider two types of *product-line* marketing strategy. These are strategies
which will have one or more of the four types of impact on demand but do so by
virtue of relationships among products. For example, a lower price on a top-of-
the-line washing machine model may also increase sales of dryers or it may
cause some buyers to buy a more expensive model than they had originally contemplated. The types of product-line marketing strategy are:

1 Stimulating demand for substitutes
2 Stimulating demand for complements

Further, managers must direct their strategy toward specific *target markets*. In
selecting target markets, managers have two fundamental options. First, they can
attempt to market the product(s) to *all users* in the *relevant market* (usually all
potential users of the product form or class being sold). Second, they can focus
on one or a *limited number of market segments* where they believe a unique
competitive position or a higher degree of profitability can be developed. For instance, a firm often attempts to stimulate demand only in high-volume segments
or in those segments in which it will have a competitive advantage. Figure 7-1
portrays the basic elements involved in a marketing strategy.

In essence, a marketing strategy is the bridge between corporate strategy and
the situation analysis on the one hand and the action-oriented marketing programs on the other. Marketing programs should flow from and be consistent with
the marketing strategy. In turn, the selection of a marketing strategy should be
based on the results of the earlier steps in the planning process.

---

[1]The distinction between primary and selective demand strategies is examined in Derek Abell,
Competitive Market Strategies: Some Generalizations and Hypotheses, Marketing Science Institute report no. 75-10-7, Cambridge, Mass., April 1975.

Issue

Options

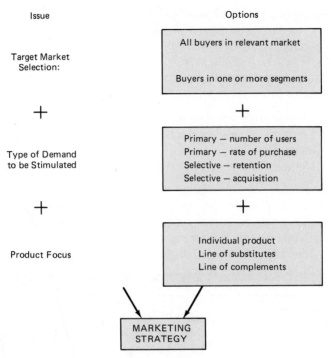

Target Market
Selection:

> All buyers in relevant market
>
> Buyers in one or more segments

+   +

Type of Demand
to be Stimulated

> Primary — number of users
> Primary — rate of purchase
> Selective — retention
> Selective — acquisition

+   +

Product Focus

> Individual product
> Line of substitutes
> Line of complements

MARKETING
STRATEGY

FIGURE 7-1   Basic elements of a marketing strategy.

In the remainder of this chapter, we examine the various *types* of marketing strategies that can be chosen, we present a *process* for selecting a marketing strategy, and we discuss some important *dynamic* aspects of marketing strategy.

PRIMARY-DEMAND STRATEGIES   INTRODUCTORY STAGE PLC

Primary-demand strategies are designed to increase the level of demand for a product form or class by current nonusers or by current users. Products in the introductory stage of the product-form life cycle (those having little or no competition) and products with large market shares are both likely to benefit from strategies designed to increase the number of product-form users. Similarly, a firm that attempts to increase the rate of sales to existing product-form buyers is employing a primary-demand strategy. There are, therefore, two fundamental strategic approaches for stimulating primary demand: increasing the number of users and increasing the rate of purchase.[2]

---

[2]Another perspective for assessing primary-demand growth opportunities is contained in John A. Weber, *Growth Opportunity Analysis,* Reston Publishing, Reston, Va., 1976, pp. 57–179.

Strategies for Increasing the Number of Users To increase the number of users, the firm must increase customers' willingness to buy or their ability to buy the product or service, or both.

Increasing the Willingness to Buy The willingness to buy may be increased by one of three approaches:

- Demonstrating the benefits already offered by a product form
- Developing new products with benefits that will be more appealing to certain segments
- Demonstrate or promote new benefits from existing products

A focus on demonstrating the basic product-form benefits is often necessary when a new product form is being marketed. For instance, Procter & Gamble had to demonstrate the convenience and performance of Pampers disposable diapers to a market in which washing cloth diapers was a time-honored behavior. Similarly, the popular Miller Lite beer advertisements successfully built the willingness of beer drinkers to try a new product form (light beer) by emphasizing the "tastes great, less filling" attributes. When new products yield significant additions to the benefits offered by existing product forms, the needs of some potential customers are more likely to be met.

For example, Carnival Cruise Lines had been leading renewed growth in the cruise business, largely by stimulating primary demand.

> Carnival's success can be traced to the day management stopped selling ocean voyages and began selling fun and entertainment to middle-income people. Recent industry surveys indicate there are 35 million first-cruise candidates, a group which represents Carnival's main target market. (Barely 5% of American vacationers have yet to take a cruise). To attract this group, Carnival turned its ships into floating resorts, offering a dazzling array of shows, sports activities, and games designed to offset potential customer's fears of boredom and confinement.[3]

The importance of this strategy type is paramount when a new product form or class is introduced because new products seldom sell themselves. Additionally, this strategy may not be important in advanced economies if a product is well-established but can be critical in bringing a product to a new market in a different culture. Thus, in the United States, Procter & Gamble must focus its marketing strategy for Pampers on acquiring potential customers from competitors, but in developing countries it will still be emphasizing the basic advantages of disposable diapers in order to stimulate primary demand.

Increasing the Ability to Buy The ability to buy can be improved by offering lower prices or credit or by providing greater availability (through having more distributors, more frequent delivery, or fewer stockouts). For example, reduced prices brought the cellular phone market rapid sales increases in the late 1980s.

[3]Mike Clary, "Carnival's Victory at Sea," *Adweek's Marketing Week,* July 17, 1989, pp. 18–25.

Prices of cellular phones averaged nearly $2,800 in 1983 but by 1988, Motorola and Satellite Technology Services were selling portable models for $700 and some discounters were offering a General Electric model for as little as $199 plus installation. Two critical considerations were involved in pricing. First, the market was clearly price-sensitive, with unit sales nearly tripling in 1988. Second, experience curve effects are widespread, with costs dropping 20% with each doubling of volume.[4]

Similarly, innovative financing plans can often help stimulate primary demand as the following example demonstrates.

The Artege Association of Dallas was founded by two entrepreneurs who were interested in art collecting but found it difficult to buy fine art. Their association offers a specialized credit card with credit limits of up to $5 million for the purchase of art, antiques and jewelry from any of more than 1,000 galleries. The major benefit of the card is its comparatively low 10.8% annual interest rate, which enhances affordability.[5]

Strategies for Increasing Rates of Purchase

When managers are concerned with gaining more rapid growth in a sluggish but mature market, the marketing strategy may be geared toward increasing the willingness to buy *more often* or in more volume, using one of the following approaches.

Broadening Usage   Buyers may expand usage if the variety of uses or use occasions can be expanded. In recent years, a number of advertising campaigns have been conducted to suggest broadened uses for products or services. For example A1 Sauce has been promoted for use on hamburgers, not just on steak, and Kraft has begun promoting Cheez Whiz for use as a cheese sauce for nachos.

Examples of attempts to broaden usage occasions include Coca-Cola's advertising campaign suggesting "Coke in the morning," American Express obtaining acceptance of its credit card in Exxon gas stations, and Pizza Hut's increased emphasis on developing its lunchtime business.

Increasing Product Consumption Levels   Lower prices or special-volume packaging may lead to higher average volumes and possibly to more rapid consumption for products such as soft drinks and snacks. Or, consumption levels may be stimulated if buyers' perceptions of the benefits of a product or service change. This reasoning underlies the efforts of the pork industry to stimulate consumption. A recent industry advertising campaign emphasized pork's similarity to chicken in terms of the health benefits received and in terms of being a white meat. Similarly, American Express expanded the benefits of its card to include automatic insurance of products that are purchased using the card.

[4]John J. Keller, "Will Cheaper Cellular Put a Phone in Every Pocket," *Business Week,* Dec. 5, 1988, p. 142.
[5]Marc Meyers, "A Credit Card That Will Cover Picasso," *Adweek's Marketing Week,* Oct. 16, 1989, p. 23.

Encouraging Replacement Product redesign may be thought of as a selective-demand strategy. It is, however, largely a primary-demand strategy in the fashion industry and in other durable-goods industries. Although a refrigerator may well last 20 years, many replacement sales will be made earlier if product convenience, space utilization, and operating cost can be improved.

In sum, primary-demand strategies may be implemented in a number of ways, as shown in Table 7-1. Although these strategies are generally less widely used than selective-demand strategies, they can be extremely useful if market measurements show large gaps between market potential and industry sales. Further, the analysis of the buying process may have identified the factors limiting the ability or willingness to buy or to adopt a product class or form. If so, managers should have some insights into the kinds of programs that can be used to stimulate primary demand.

SELECTIVE-DEMAND STRATEGIES

Selective-demand strategies are designed to improve the competitive position of a product, service, or business. The fundamental focus of these strategies is on market share, because sales gains are expected to come at the expense of product-form or product-class competitors. As suggested in Table 7-2, selective-demand strategies can be accomplished either by retaining existing customers or by acquiring new customers. In particular, if industry sales are growing slowly and yet are close to market potential, managers who want to build sales can only do so by acquiring competitors' customers. However, when the industry growth rate is high, sales and market share can also be increased by acquiring customers who have the ability and willingness to buy but who are just entering the market. For example, new mothers and persons moving into a new location may be new buyers for a diaper-rash product and a local bank, respectively.

Retention strategies, on the other hand, are more likely to be used by firms with a dominant share of the market and by small market-share firms with entrenched positions in particular segments. Moreover, both retention and acquisition can be segment-specific. Managers may decide to focus the marketing effort on one or on a limited number of target segments, even when a firm currently operates in several segments.

TABLE 7-1 PRIMARY-DEMAND MARKETING STRATEGIES

How demand is impacted	Basic strategies for influencing demand
1. Increase the number of users	Increase willingness to buy Increase ability to buy
2. Increase the rate of purchase	Broadening usage occasions for the product Increase level of consumption Increase rate of replacement

TABLE 7-2 SELECTIVE-DEMAND MARKETING STRATEGIES

How demand is impacted	Basic strategies for influencing demand
1. Retain current customers	Maintain satisfaction
	Meeting competition
	Relationship marketing
2. Acquire new customers	Head-to-head
	a. Market dominance
	b. price/cost leadership
	Differentiated positioning
	Niching

Retention Strategies

Increasingly, managers have begun to recognize that it can be more profitable to retain existing customers than to search for new ones. The Customer Service Institute, for example, estimates that it costs five times as much to acquire a new customer as it costs to service an existing one.[6]

In order to influence a customer to stay with a brand or supplier, marketers have three basic strategic options:

- Maintain a high level of customer satisfaction
- Meet competitors' offerings
- Establish a strong economic or interpersonal relationship with the customer

Maintain Satisfaction   Many well-established brands with dominant market shares focus their strategies and programs on maintaining customer beliefs regarding the superior quality of the product. Thus, managers of consumer brands such as Heinz, Budweiser, and Crest design advertisements that reassure customers of continued high quality. When successful, these efforts result in a positive psychological relationship between the consumer and the seller based on confidence in the brand. Satisfaction with product performance can also be enhanced if a firm provides additional information or services that will lead to proper and effective use of the product. Industrial marketers frequently offer maintenance, repair, and operating (MRO) services to enhance satisfaction, and many consumer-goods firms offer similar programs. For instance, music store retailers frequently offer a limited number of free piano lessons to new owners in the expectation that greater use may ultimately lead to the purchase of more expensive models.

The importance of product satisfaction has been argued as one of the reasons for the long-term market leadership of many brands (as displayed in Table 7-3). Research conducted by the Boston Consulting Group and *Advertising Age* magazine suggests that the loyalty achieved from *value-based* consumer brands is the most enduring of all competitive barriers.

[6]Joan C. Szabo, "Service = Survival," *Nation's Business,* March 1989, p. 17.

TABLE 7-3   THE LEADING BRANDS: 1925 and 1985

Product	Leading brand 1925	Current position 1985
Bacon	Swift	Leader
Batteries	Eveready	Leader
Biscuits	Nabisco	Leader
Breakfast cereal	Kellogg	Leader
Cameras	Kodak	Leader
Canned fruit	Del Monte	Leader
Chewing gum	Wrigley	Leader
Chocolates	Hershey	No. 2
Flour	Gold Medal	Leader
Mint candies	Life Savers	Leader
Paint	Sherwin-Williams	Leader
Pipe tobacco	Prince Albert	Leader
Razors	Gillette	Leader
Sewing machines	Singer	Leader
Shirts	Manhattan	No. 5
Shortening	Crisco	Leader
Soap	Ivory	Leader
Soft drinks	Coca-Cola	Leader
Soup	Campbell's	Leader
Tea	Lipton	Leader
Tires	Goodyear	Leader
Toothpaste	Colgate	No. 2

Source: Reprinted from *The Value Side of Productivity*, American Association of Advertising Agencies, New York, 1989, p. 18. This table was developed from *Advertising Age* and Boston Consulting Group analyses.

Meeting Competition   While maintaining satisfaction is always an important goal, competitors often are able to provide satisfactory products and services. And, they may offer more options and features, lower prices, and advertise heavily. Based on research conducted in several industries, the best defensive strategy to a competitive attack on product quality, price, or heavy advertising is to meet (or even surpass) the competition.[7] Often, especially in the international area, a firm must defend itself on several fronts as the following situation suggests.

> Caterpillar's dominance of the earth-moving market was threatened by Japanese attackers (especially Komatsu) in the early 1980's. At one point, Komatsu prices were 40% lower. But Caterpillar has managed to hold its position of leadership (although some market share was lost) by lowering prices while actually improving quality. Management accepted short-term profit reductions as the price needed to save market share while the company could revamp production operations to reduce costs.[8]

[7]John Hauser, *Theory and Application of Defensive Strategy*, Marketing Science Institute report no. 85-107, Cambridge, Mass., 1985.
[8]Ronald Henkoff, "This Cat Is Acting Like a Tiger," *Fortune,* Dec. 19, 1988, pp. 71–76.

Additionally, some firms often find they must match competitors in terms of the number of product-line options offered. This issue is discussed later in this chapter under product-line strategies.

Relationship Marketing A relationship marketing strategy is designed to enhance the chances of repeat business by developing formal interpersonal ties with the buyer. Long-term relationships are often established through contractual or membership arrangements with customers or distributors. Typically these arrangements are only successful because of some discount or an economic incentive associated with the cost of purchasing. For example, consumers who buy season tickets for a philharmonic orchestra series are essentially engaged in a membership relationship. Similarly, annual fees charged by health spas ensure at least a 1-year relationship. In industrial marketing, simplification may be achieved by programs such as long-term protection against price increases or inventory management assistance. Frequently these programs are so desirable to buyers or to distributors that they will commit themselves to use one supplier as the sole source of supply for a period of time. Another recent development involves the placement of computer terminals (and often, associated software) in customers' offices. These terminals are then hooked into the sellers' terminals, enabling customers to order products instantly (and thus better manage their inventories), check on the progress of deliveries, and obtain technical assistance. In recent years, firms that have experienced success with these systems include: Cigna Corp. (assistance on industrial customers' insurance problems), Inland Steel (ordering and checking on order delivery), and Benjamin Moore (analyzing color samples provided by paint stores to provide pigment prescriptions).[9]

Acquisition Strategies

A firm cannot acquire competitors' customers or new customers unless it is perceived by buyers as more effective in meeting customer needs. As we pointed out in Chapter 3, the choice process centers on a buyer's assessment of which brand or supplier has the best offer on the determinant attributes. Because choices will largely be based on these perceptions, customer acquisition strategies will essentially be based on how the product is to be positioned in the market. That is, a product's *position* represents how a product is perceived relative to the competition on the determinant attributes desired by each segment. From a managerial perspective, a firm can attempt to acquire customers in any of three ways: head-to-head strategy, differentiated positioning, or niching.

Head-to-Head Strategy In a head-to-head strategy, a firm offers basically the same benefits as the competition but tries to *outdo* the competition either by *market dominance* or by *price-cost leadership*. In market dominance, a firm can argue that it offers superior product quality. For example, Reynolds attempted to

---

[9]Peter Petre, "How to Keep Customers Happy Captives," *Fortune,* Sept. 2, 1985, pp. 42–46.

build market share in the reclosable plastic bag business by developing a triple-seal bag. In introducing the product, the company emphasized the superiority of the bag's strength compared to existing brands.

Alternatively, a firm can attempt to compete by out-spending the competition or by achieving better availability and distributor support or by lowering its price. Indeed in some markets, head-to-head competition involves multiple marketing programs.

> In an attempt to cut into AT&T's 80% share of the residential market for long distance telephone service, Sprint and MCI offer a variety of price discount programs. Price competition exists on the number of hours during which special rates apply, discounts for high-volume callers, and Sunday discount rates. At the same time, advertising is being used to enhance each firm's image of dependability and service in the business segment of the market.[10]

Although head-to-head competition cannot always be avoided, if the similarity among competitors' marketing strategies is very strong, several common marketing problems can result. First, if several brands have a common market offering, they are collectively more vulnerable to aggressive new entrants who offer a different benefit of equal value. Second, these commonly positioned brands usually must spend more to gain support from retailers or other distributors. Finally, because of the difficulty consumers may have in distinguishing such brands, increasing the advertising spending level seldom produces a comparable increase in sales.[11]

Differentiated Positioning   This is a strategic option in which head-to-head competition is avoided by offering unique benefits. Rather than offer the same features, price, convenience, or other attributes, a manager employing this marketing strategy offers one or more *different* benefits. A firm can employ a differentiated-positioning strategy by having a unique channel, performance characteristic, package, pricing method, set of related services, or promotional appeal. To the extent that a firm bases its marketing strategy on an attribute that is difficult or costly to duplicate, it is more likely to be successful in maintaining a differentiated position. As examples of differentiated positioning, consider the following.

> Mobil Corporation, the maker of Hefty Trash bags, began going after the wastebasket business in 1989, offering a line of five designs in a quest to challenge industry leader Rubbermaid. Hefty wastebaskets are priced above those of Rubbermaid, come in a wider variety of colors and sizes and offer distinctive new features such as a "retainer

[10]Warren Berger, "Upstart Phone Companies Intensify Efforts to Replace AT&T at Home," *Adweek's Marketing Week,* June 19, 1989, pp. 33–34.
[11]F. Beaven Ennis, *Marketing Norms for Product Managers,* Association of National Advertisers, New York, 1985, p. 41.

ring'' to prevent trash bags from slipping and at the same time eliminate ''ugly over-hang.'' They even offer attachments for storing replacement bags.[12]

Polaroid attempted a differentiation strategy when it entered the market for conventional 35mm film. Relying on research that indicated that 35% of amateur photographers don't know what film speed is, Polaroid offered a single all-purpose film for amateurs confused by having too many choices.[13]

In addition to offering something different, firms can also differentiate their product by offering *less*. Making products smaller (for example, Motorola's pocket-sized cellular phone or Oscar Mayer's microwavable line of minisnacks called Zappetites) can enhance versatility of use compared to competing products. Similarly, more simplified products (including disposables) are often promoted as easier to repair, clean, assemble, or install.[14]

Niching The third basic type of acquisition strategy, niching, represents any strategy in which a firm tries to isolate itself from major competitors by serving one or a limited number of special segments in a market. Often, niches are defined in terms of particular buyer characteristics. For example, Zenith first entered the personal computer market by focusing solely on government agencies and universities. However, niches can also reflect specialized buyer needs: Shouldice Hospital near Toronto, Canada, accepts only one type of patient—people with hernias. Finally, niching can be based on the development of a unique product personality or image.

Across the United States, new, local ''microbrewers'' are popping up and operating successfully. These brewers produce 10,000 barrels or less per year and together represent less than 1 percent of the total domestic beer market. These brewers keep costs down by doing little advertising and often by contracting with larger breweries for production, which reduces fixed overhead. However, they are still not cost-competitive and so rely on developing a distinctive local image and brewing a beer with unique tastes. Among the more successful of these beers are Anchor Steam (San Francisco), New Amsterdam Amber (New York), Boulder Extra Pale (Colorado), Dock Street (Philadelphia), and Eau Claire All Malt (Wisconsin).[15]

Niche marketing is also effective in overseas markets, even in Japan which has long been considered to be highly homogeneous. For example in the cigarette industry ''Lucky Strike'' and ''Dean'' are targeted to younger men, ''Kent'' to older men, ''Alex'' and ''Virginia Slims'' to young women.[16]

---

[12]Maria Mallory, ''Mobil Is Waging a Hefty War on'Wimpy' Wastebaskets,'' *Business Week,* May 29, 1989, p. 70.

[13]Lawrence Ingrassia, ''Polaroid Unveils Universal Film Aimed at Amateurs Confused by Market Variety,'' *The Wall Street Journal,* Apr. 6, 1989.

[14]Allan McGrath, ''Segmentation and Differentiation Positioning Strategies Are Timeless,'' *Marketing News,* Oct. 24, 1988, p. 6.

[15]''Specialized Suds: Labels for Locals,'' *Insight,* Sept. 1, 1986, pp. 46–47; and ''Small Time Brewers and Putting the Kick Back into Beer,'' *Business Week,* Jan. 20, 1986, pp. 90–91.

[16]Damon Darlin, ''Myth and Marketing in Japan,'' *The Wall Street Journal,* Apr. 6, 1989, p. B1.

PRODUCT-LINE MARKETING STRATEGIES

Most firms offer a line of products that are closely related because they serve similar needs, are used together, or are purchased together. Products that serve the same basic need are functional substitutes for one another. Thus, the various investment vehicles offered by a bank (savings accounts, money market accounts, certificates of deposit) are substitutes. Products that are used together or purchased together and serve related needs are complements. For a bank, checking accounts, savings accounts, and credit cards are all complementary.

Increasingly, firms are developing strategies that take these relationships into account. Developing a marketing strategy for each individual product without considering the impact of that strategy on substitutes or complements can lead to undesirable results. Table 7-4 lists the major kinds of product-line marketing strategies.

Strategies for Substitutes

There are two basic strategies for substitute products: line extensions and flanker brands.

Line Extensions A line extension is a variation of an existing product that retains the brand name while offering new or different features (such as sizes, colors, or forms). Often a line extension is used to retain customers who might otherwise be lured away by new competitive offerings. For example, Procter & Gamble launched Liquid Tide as a defense against the growth in demand for competing liquid detergents. On the other hand, the pioneer in a new category may be a line extension, even though this can lead to reduced sales of existing brands as the following example points out.

CPC International, maker of Hellmann's mayonnaise brought out Cholesterol-Free Light Hellmann's as an extension to Hellmann's and Hellmann's Light (which has about one-half the calories of regular mayonnaise) in 1989. At the time, mayonnaise annual sales growth was around 4%. The strategy was expected to stimulate primary demand for mayonnaise among cholesterol-conscious consumers as well as serve to

TABLE 7-4   PRODUCT-LINE MARKETING STRATEGIES

Type of relationship	Basic strategies
1. Substitutes	Line extensions
	Flankers
2. Complements	Leaders
	Bundling
	Systems selling

acquire competitors' customers. However, company officials also anticipated that the new product would draw up to 60% of the sales of Hellmann's Light.[17]

Clearly, the line extension is designed to capitalize on a firm's brand image or equity.[18] However, since that image is likely to be greatest among loyal brand buyers, the cannibalization of sales of existing products is more likely than is the case for a flanker strategy.

Flankers A flanker brand is a new brand designed to serve a new segment of the market. For example, American Express introduced the Optima card as an addition to its green and platinum cards which carry the American Express logo. Unlike its traditional cards, Optima is designed for use in obtaining a revolving line of credit, much the way VISA and MasterCard are used. While the use of multiple brands means that the company is not taking advantage of the equity it has built up in its brand name, many marketers expect that this will reduce the degree to which existing brands are cannibalized. Additionally, a flanker strategy will enable a firm to establish a new position or image which many be necessary to succeed in the new segment or to meet demand from "variety seekers."[19] Consider, for example, the experience of firms such as Hershey and Campbells.

> While the Hershey name has been used on some successful line extensions, generally the company has been more successful with flankers (Reese's Peanut Butter Cups, Kit Kat, and the newly acquired Mounds and Almond Joy brands) which cater better to variety seekers.[20]
>
> Campbell's Home Cookin', Chunky, Campbell Cup, and Golden Classics soups were all well-received line extensions, but their success came primarily from other Campbell products. Consequently the company has turned to using some other company-owned brands (Prego and Pepperidge Farm) for future soup products, recognizing a traditional rule-of-thumb in marketing that 40% appears to be the maximum share a single brand can achieve using line extensions.[21]

Strategies for Complements

These strategies are sometimes directed toward retaining customers in support of a relationship marketing strategy. By expanding the number of relationships, the supplier makes switching to an alternative supplier more expensive for the customer. For example, many financial institutions try to get checking account customers to use the institution as a source for their credit cards, loans, and savings accounts. In theory, as the consumer concentrates these accounts, he or she will be less likely to switch suppliers for any one product because it would sharply

[17]George Lazarus, "New Mayo Holds the Cholesterol," *Chicago Tribune*, Feb. 24, 1989, p. C4.

[18]John S. Blyth, "Underleveraged Brands Ripe for Takeover Attempts," *Marketing News*, June 19, 1989, p. 11.

[19]See also Barbara E. Kahn, Manohar U. Kalwani, and Donald G. Morrison, "Niching versus Change-of-Pace Brands: Using Purchase Frequencies and Penetration Rates to Infer Brand Positionings," *Journal of Marketing Research*, November 1988, pp. 384–390.

[20]Alix M. Freedman, "Mars Struggles to Reclaim Candy Crown," *The Wall Street Journal*, Mar. 29, 1981, p. B1.

[21]Bill Saporito, "The Fly in Campbell's Soup," *Fortune*, May 9, 1988, pp. 67–69.

reduce the convenience of *one-stop* banking. In other cases, these strategies may be designed to leverage a relationship on one product in order to acquire new customers on other goods and services. Three basic complementary strategies can be identified: leaders, bundling, and systems selling.

Leaders   In a leader strategy, a firm promotes or prices one particular product very aggressively in the expectation that buyers will also purchase complementary goods or services. For example, a low price on a major appliance may result not only in increased sales of that appliance but in more sales of service contracts as well.

Bundling   A bundling strategy involves the development of a specific combination of products sold together, usually at a price that is less than the sum of the prices if the products are sold separately. Thus, a bank may offer a credit card at no annual fee to bank customers who maintain large certificate of deposit accounts. This strategy can be effective when buyers have a very strong preference for the product being discounted and a need but no strong brand preference for the product purchased at full price. Additionally, bundling and leader strategies are effective when customers can save time by buying the set of products from a single source.

Systems Selling   In systems selling, a firm emphasizes the fact that individual products are designed to be highly compatible with one another. For example, a computer manufacturer may design personal computers that are very technically compatible with its mainframe computers. Thus, mainframe customers who want to purchase PCs that will be able to communicate with the mainframe (to form a system) will be more likely to buy the most compatible equipment.

It is important to recognize that product-line strategies are really special cases of the primary and selective demand strategies discussed earlier. That is, any product-line strategy is directed at influencing either primary or selective demand. However, this class of strategies can be used to impact different types of demand in different situations.

SELECTING A MARKETING STRATEGY

To choose the best marketing strategy, a manager must consider several kinds of information (see Figure 7-2). First, the marketing strategy must be consistent with the *product objective*. Second, the nature and size of the *market opportunity* should be clearly established based on the market analysis and market measurements. Finally, managers must have a sense of the *success requirements* in terms of the kinds of competitive advantages necessary and the level of marketing expenditures that will be necessary to meet profitability goals.

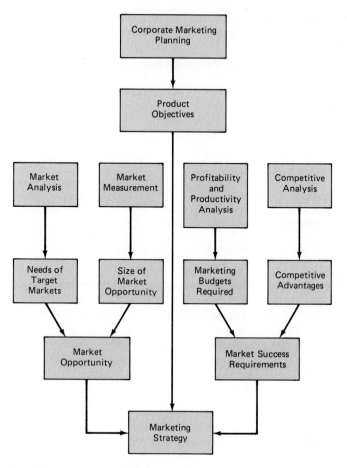

FIGURE 7-2   Selecting a marketing strategy.

The Role of Product Objectives

Product objectives help determine the necessary basic type of strategy. For example, if market-share objectives are important, managers will employ selective-demand strategies to retain or expand market share. Alternatively, the greater the importance of cash flow and profitability objectives, the more likely a manager will be to select retention strategies and strategies for increasing repurchase rates. That is, these strategies will, in *general,* be less costly than acquisition strategies or strategies aimed at increasing the number of users. (Put simply, it is usually easier to reach and persuade existing brand customers and existing product-form buyers than to convert competitors' customers and nonadopters.)

Table 7-5 summarizes the general types of marketing strategies that managers should typically use to achieve a given product objective. Managers can, however, use more than one strategy simultaneously if adequate resources exist. Of

TABLE 7-5 APPROPRIATE MARKETING STRATEGIES FOR VARIOUS PRODUCT OBJECTIVES

Product objective	Typical marketing strategy
1. To achieve viable level of sales (for new product form or class	1. *Primary:* Increase number of users
2. To achieve viable market share (for new brand)	2. *Selective:* Acquisition of customers
3. Market-share growth	3. *Selective:* Acquisition of customers
4. Market-share maintenance	4. *Selective:* Retention of customers, or *Selective:* Acquisition of customers new to the market
5. Cash flow maximization	5. *Selective:* Retention of customers, or *Primary:* Increase rate of purchase
6. Sustaining profitability	6. *Selective:* Retention of customers (in limited segments)
7. Harvesting	7. *Selective:* Retention of customers (with minimum effort)

course, in selecting a strategy, managers must also consider any impact the strategy may have on complementary or substitute products.

Additionally, the feasibility of a given strategy depends on the firm's ability to deal with the problems and opportunities identified in the situation analysis. If managers cannot identify a feasible marketing strategy for implementing the product objective, then the objective probably should be modified.

Implications from the Situation Analysis

Each of the issues addressed in the chapters on situation analysis (Part 2) has implications for the selection of marketing strategies and programs.

• Market analysis provides information on who buys (and who does not buy) the product form, the various situations in which the product is used (or not used), and the factors influencing the willingness and ability to buy. This information can help managers select strategies and programs for increasing either the number of users or the rate of use. By analyzing selective demand, managers should gain insights into the alternative segmentation opportunities that exist and the factors influencing buyer-choice processes.

• The competitive analysis enables a manager to determine who the competition will be, how intensive the competition will be, and what advantages must be developed in order to compete effectively either against direct brand competitors (in selective-demand strategies) or against indirect product-class competitors (in primary-demand strategies).

• Market measurements provide information on the size of the *primary-demand gap* between market potential and industry sales. As suggested in Chapter 5, the larger this gap, the greater the opportunity to expand primary demand for a product form or class. Further, the slower the industry sales growth, the more important it will be to find ways of expanding primary demand. Causal company sales forecasts can provide insights into the impact of various marketing programs on sales.

• By combining productivity estimates with profitability analysis, managers can determine the profit consequences of the strategies and programs required for achieving market-share objectives.

Maintaining a Customer-Driven Perspective

While the process of going through the situation analysis should help management define the marketing opportunity to be addressed by a marketing strategy, it is vitally important that the analysis not be so clinical that the customer's perspective of the product is lost.

Often, managers become so focused on the basic need they are trying to satisfy that they lose sight of the total customer-usage experience, especially if new products are involved. Consider, for example, Upjohn's recent difficulties with Rogaine.

In August of 1988, the Food and Drug Administration gave approval to Upjohn Company to market Rogaine, a product that stimulates hair growth. While the product does not work on all men or women, it can reverse a trend toward thinning hair for many users, especially among younger men. But in spite of this clear need and a large market (studies indicated a population of 33 million men between the ages of 18 and 45 have thinning hair) sales response has been slow. In part, the response has been ascribed to the fact that Rogaine is a prescription drug, so Upjohn's advertisements cannot directly promote the product to consumers, only the recommendation to see a doctor. But other difficulties have restricted consumer acceptance: a year's supply costs $600 with no guarantees and the product is a solution that is sticky, wipes off on pillows and gets in people's eyes. Finally, the heritage of false baldness-curing elixirs and a variety of competing products (all lacking FDA approval) has fomented doubt and confusion about the category. It seems likely that successful adoption will not occur until Upjohn is able to deal more effectively with these other problems and perceptions.[22]

At other times, management is successful with a strategy precisely because the strategy is customer driven, but then forgets the recipe for success, as the People Express experience demonstrates.

People Express Airline grew from a $38 million to a $1 billion business between 1981 and 1985. The firm's initial success was due to its focus on budget travelers, offering no frills service. There were no free meals, no advance ticketing, and a charge to check a bag if you didn't carry it on. Moreover, tight scheduling meant that flights were frequently late. This strategy worked well until People Express overexpanded and began to develop a large excess capacity on weekdays when budget travelers were outnumbered by business travelers. The airline then went after business travelers, initiating a first class service. But the inconveniences that budget travelers accepted were not ac-

---

[22]Michele Chandler, "Upjohn's Rogaine Off to a Thin Start," *Chicago Tribune,* June 5, 1989; and Gregory Witcher, "Slow Start for Upjohn's Baldness Drug," *The Wall Street Journal,* Apr. 5, 1989, p. B1.

ceptable to business travelers. And competitors began matching the cut-rate prices. People Express never filled the empty weekday seats and ultimately was taken over by Texas Air.[23]

The People Express story exemplifies the problem of a loss of focus. But it also reflects another strategic reality: the situation a firm faces regarding its markets, its costs, or its competition can change over time. Consequently, managers must consider the dynamic aspects of marketing strategy.

The Globalization Question

Because an increasing proportion of businesses operate across national boundaries, an important question is whether to offer a single standardized (and thus globalized) offering or to treat the various nations in the market as segments. If the latter (and more traditional) course of action is taken, the strategy is similar to a product-line flanker strategy. At the opposite extreme, a single brand is marketed with the same marketing programs in all nations.

The principle of selling the same product in essentially the same way everywhere in the world is not new. Exxon has been selling motor oil globally since 1911, and Caterpillar adopted a global approach to its marketing after World War II. Caterpillar organized an international network to sell spare parts and built a few large-scale efficient manufacturing plants in the United States to meet worldwide demand. The product was then assembled in regional markets with the addition of those features which were needed for local market conditions. The emergence of global markets has allowed corporations as diverse as Revlon (cosmetics), Sony (televisions), and Black & Decker to standardize manufacturing and distribution. Some concessions to cultural differences—such as producing cars with steering columns on the right or left side—are made, but this requires only minor modifications, and most other features of the product remain the same.

In the early 1980s, Professor Theodore Levitt of the Harvard Business School declared the global approach to be appropriate for all firms. He argued that advances in communication, transportation, and entertainment technology were bringing about more homogeneous world tastes and wants. Companies that failed to adopt a global strategy were seen as being vulnerable to global firms that could obtain savings from standardization.[24]

In reality few firms are totally globalized in terms of the full marketing mix. Even the largest multinationals with established worldwide images make some local adjustments. For example Coca-Cola introduced Diet Coke with a globalized name, concentrate formula, positioning, and advertising but varied the

---

[23]William H. Davidow and Bro Uttal, "Service Companies: Focus or Falter," *Harvard Business Review,* July–August 1989, pp. 77–87.

[24]Theodore Levitt, "The Globalization of Markets," *Harvard Business Review,* May–June 1983, pp. 92–96.

artificial sweetener and packaging across nations.[25] The basic strategic issue is how much customization is necessary and desirable.

Among the factors favoring globalization, four stand out as most significant.[26]

1 *Economies of scale exist:* The greater the economies of scale, the more advantageous a global strategy. The rapid increase in globalization for autos and construction vehicles reflects such economies.

2 *Product usage varies across cultures:* Some products (particularly those within the home) may not be consumed in comparable ways or rates by people in different cultures. For example, canned soup can be condensed for the North American market but is unacceptable in that form in Europe. In such cases, product or positioning variations are appropriate.

3 *The same competitors exist across markets:* To the extent competitors are global, a firm will likely have to compete in the same way in each market.

4 *Many of the firm's key customers operate globally:* Because so many large firms are multinational, the firms that sell to these multinational customers must offer the same basic strategy in each market. Thus IBM, Citicorp, and Nippon Steel are likely to be heavily globalized. To the extent that these conditions exist, globalization seems to be an appropriate strategic direction.

DYNAMIC ASPECTS OF MARKETING STRATEGY

A firm must usually change its strategy over time because the situation it faces will usually change. The product life cycle provides managers with guidance as to how the situation changes over time. These changes (which are summarized in Table 7-6) will impact both the choice of a type of strategy and the selection of marketing programs for implementing the strategy.

The Product Life Cycle and Strategy Selection

The most obvious impact of the product life cycle is the shift from a primary to a selective-demand strategy as the life cycle shifts from the introductory stage to the growth and maturity stages. As buyers become more knowledgeable about the product category and as the primary-demand gap declines, the need for and pay-off from primary-demand strategies declines.

A second consideration is that retention strategies should seldom be relied on, even by a market leader until the life cycle is well into maturity. As long as markets are growing rapidly, acquisition strategies are important.

Third, product-line extensions and flankers should be developed as soon as segmentation opportunities arise. While some marketing consultants argued that such products should be used to try to reinvigorate life cycles in maturity, the

---

[25]John Quelch and Edward Hoff, "Customizing Global Marketing," *Harvard Business Review,* May–June 1986, pp. 59–68.

[26]A more in-depth discussion is contained in Jean-Pierre Jeannet and Hubert D. Hennessey, *International Marketing Management,* Houghton Mifflin, Boston, 1986, chap. 8.

TABLE 7-6   HOW THE SITUATION ANALYSIS CHANGES OVER THE PRODUCT LIFE CYCLE

Market analysis
  Buyers become more knowledgeable about the product category and the alternatives
  Repeat purchases grow and first-time purchases decline
  Increased segmentation

Competitive analysis
  Innovators stimulate primary demand
  Early followers may imitate or leapfrog
  Only the strongest survive shakeout

Market measurement
  Primary-demand gap declines
  Industry growth rate declines
  Differences in penetration of geographic markets accelerate

Profitability/productivity
  Marketing costs rise, then level out
  Production costs decline with experience
  Selective-demand response to price, quality increases
  Selective-demand response to advertising, distribution decrease

conventional wisdom is now changing. Often line extensions are necessary to move a product through the growth stage because the variation in basic customer needs (for example, personal computers or microwave ovens) is very large. Additionally, market leaders who offer a full product line may preempt competitive opportunities from new entrants. Finally, committing extensive resources to an existing technology in maturity may be less effective than investing in new product forms or technologies.[27]

The Product Life Cycle and Marketing Programs

As we have suggested, a given type of marketing strategy may be achieved through two or more different marketing programs. For example, acquiring new customers through head-to-head positioning could imply direct competition on price, availability, quality, or brand awareness. However, over the course of the life cycle the productivity of different programs changes. Specifically, as the life cycle moves from introduction toward maturity and decline the following trends in the response of market share occur.[28]

    Price   The impact of price on primary demand is usually very high during introduction. But the impact of price on market share is relatively low at this stage

[27]Richard N. Foster, *Innovation: The Attacker's Advantage*, Summit Books, New York, 1986, pp. 134–135.

[28]This discussion is based largely on Gerard J. Tellis, "The Price Elasticity of Selective Demand: A Meta-Analysis of Econometric Models of Sales," *Journal of Marketing Research*, November 1988, pp. 331–341; and Leonard J. Parsons, "The Product Life Cycle and Time Varying Advertising Elasticities," *Journal of Marketing Research*, November 1975, pp. 476–480.

due to a lack of competitors. As the technology matures so that competing products become more alike and as buyers become aware of more alternatives, market share becomes *increasingly responsive to price.*

Product Quality As buyers gain more information from experience and from word-of-mouth communications they become more knowledgeable about the relative quality of various products. Thus, market share becomes *increasingly responsive to product quality.*

Advertising Over time, awareness of a brand and its attributes will grow with cumulative exposure to advertisements. As discussed in Chapter 6, saturation levels may ultimately be reached. In any event, diminishing returns will ultimately set in so market share will become *decreasingly responsive to awareness-oriented (as opposed to price-oriented) advertising.*

Distribution For consumer goods, the sales force usually focuses on obtaining distribution in large-volume stores initially and then on smaller, less important outlets. By maturity, only the marginal outlets are likely to not carry the product. Thus, money spent on additional salespeople, travel expense, or incentives to gain additional distribution will have diminishing returns. Market share will therefore become *decreasingly responsive to distribution expenditures.*

CONCLUSION

Although marketing strategies indicate the general approaches to be used in achieving product objectives, the implementation of these strategies through marketing programs is the most time-consuming part of marketing management.

Marketing programs (such as product-development programs, advertising and sales promotion programs, and sales and distribution programs) indicate the specific activities that will be necessary to implement a strategy. For instance, if a strategy requires the firm to achieve distributor cooperation, the details of *how* the sales force will achieve cooperation must be worked out in the sales and distribution program. No matter how appropriate a strategy might appear, it will fail if not properly implemented. Consequently, clear statements regarding target markets and marketing strategies are necessary to ensure that the correct programs will be developed.

As we have suggested in this chapter, then, a marketing strategy serves as the major link between corporate marketing planning and the situation analysis on the one hand and the development of specific programs on the other. Figure 7-3 portrays this relationship.

Perhaps the most important aspect of this relationship is the fact that marketing strategy should be viewed from a dynamic perspective: As the corporate strategy or the situation analysis changes over time, the marketing strategy should change. Consider, for example, the dynamics of marketing strategy at British Bakeries.

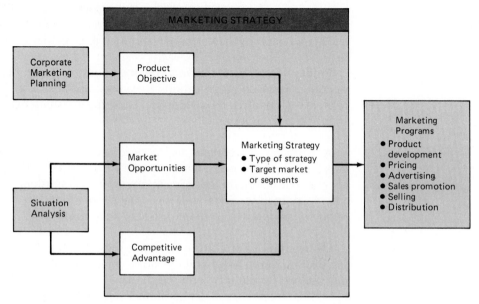

FIGURE 7-3 Relationship of marketing strategy to corporate marketing planning, situation analysis, and marketing programs.

British Bakeries: Changing Marketing Strategies for Hovis Bread*

In 1886, a new brown bread was introduced to the British market with the name *Richard Smith's Patent Germflower.* In an effort to find a more marketable name, a newspaper competition was held and the name "Hovis" (an adaptation of The Latin Hominis Vis—"The Strength of Man") was chosen. By the 1900s the Hovis brand was well established and only a few years later it was being claimed as "the world's best bread" by the parent company, British Bakeries.

Over the following seventy years, Hovis enjoyed sustained sales growth. A considerable level of marketing expenditures provided consistent support for the brand, emphasizing that it was still the same brown wheatgerm bread as was sold in 1900. Advertising and promotion were effective. It was not at all unusual to find the Hovis "V" sign on storefronts in the 1930s, and the phrase "Don't Say Brown Say Hovis" was popularized through TV commercials in the mid-1950s. However, even though the brand name was well recognized and memorable and consumers perceived the brand to be healthful and nutritious, sales stabilized and market share began to decline. By the end of the 1960s, Hovis had only a 30 percent share of the brown bread market which represented only 3 percent of total bread sales.

*Developed from Philip Rawstorne, "Born Again Products," *Financial Times,* Nov. 23, 1989, p. 11; and Philip Rawstorne, "How Hovis Used Its Loaf," *Financial Times,* Nov. 23, 1989, p. 11.

During the 1950s and 1960s, competition from softer, moister, white and brown bread had increased. In addition, slogans such as "Tea with Hovis" had positioned the brand as a special occasion product beginning in the 1930s. In an effort to regain market position, Hovis tried to reposition the product as a regular-use bread. However, despite the increased marketing support, sales-growth targets were not being met. Hovis had become less relevant and appealing to a substantial number of consumers and many persons in the company began to suspect the brand was in irrevocable decline.

Hovis's response was to modify its recipe and improve the texture of the loaf. In 1976, they introduced a softer wheatgerm product with new sizes and packaging. These changes better met the needs of supermarket operators who had traditionally been neglected by Hovis in favor of independent grocers. Although Hovis had responded slowly, the combination of a better product and the inherent strength of the brand resulted in a rapid increase in its market share of the wheatgerm sector to over 80 percent. However, Hovis was still a small factor in the total bread market having a small volume product with a very big name.

British Bakeries decided to enter the growing wholemeal bread market in 1981. Because it was felt that Hovis was associated with wheatgerm, a new brand "Windmill" was developed for this market. Windmill was positioned as the health-conscious family's wholemeal and Hovis was designated as a specialty niche brand. Demand for wholemeal bread increased as a result of the increase in marketing effort but the advertising effort needed to support two brands proved to be too costly.

An intensive research program was conducted in 1986 on Hovis customers and competitors. Research results showed Hovis to be the best-known name in brown bread. Consumers held a highly favorable opinion of its traditional values and baking skills. As a result, management perceived that the Hovis brand could be a major competitor in the standard wholemeal mass market.

British Bakeries quickly expanded its product line. In successive years Hovis Country Grain, Hovis Granary, Hovis Goldenbran, and Hovis Organic Wholemeal products were introduced. These new products were designed to ensure that the Hovis brand could be extended from wheatgerm. In September of 1989, Hovis Wholemeal was introduced as the ultimate combination—a mass market loaf from the United Kingdom's most famous bread brand.

1 Identify the various marketing strategies that have been used for Hovis over the past century.

2 In entering the wholemeal market, British Bakeries seemed to have fared better with a line extension strategy than with a flanker strategy. Based on the discussion in the text on these product-line marketing strategies, should this have been expected? Explain.

3 Consider British Bakeries' actions over the product life cycle for brown wheatgerm bread. With today's insights into marketing over the life cycle, what would you have done differently? Why?

QUESTIONS AND SITUATIONS FOR DISCUSSION

1 Explain how market potential and industry sales measures are important in the selection of a marketing strategy.

2 A leading cereal manufacturer recently mailed coupons to 10 million households. Two hundred fifty different coupon offers were tested depending on what particular brand of cereal shoppers purchased and on how much they bought. The firm's loyal customers received coupons ranging from 20 to 60 cents off the next purchase. Buyers of competing brands received offers ranging from 50 cents off to a free box of cereal. Explain the different offers in terms of underlying marketing strategies.

3 Toyota and Nissan both introduced new luxury upscale cars in 1989. The Toyota Lexus and Nissan Infiniti were designed to compete with BMW, Audi, and Mercedes and a separate dealer system was established for these models. What type of marketing strategy are Toyota and Nissan using? What factors do you think were most important in their selection of a strategy?

4 Each of the two leaders in a high-growth industry holds 20 percent market shares. One product has achieved its share by maintaining the lowest prices, the widest distribution, and the largest amount of advertising. The other product has been successful largely because a patented ingredient has enabled it to have a unique additional benefit. Which of the two products is most likely to be successful in acquiring competitors' customers? Explain your answer. What additional information would be useful in selecting a strategy for each product?

5 Heinz ketchup is able to charge a premium price for its product because of the texture and flavor perceived by customers. If you were Hunt's or Del Monte, what differentiated positioning strategy would you likely use in competing against Heinz?

6 Neutrogena Corp. is a small, Los Angeles-based business whose majority stockholders are members of the Cotsen family. The company was founded in the 1930s and for years relied on Neutrogena soap for the majority of revenues. Neutrogena soap was effectively positioned as a pure, safe, almost therapeutic product that was well worth its premium price. In the 1980s, this profitable market niche was invaded by Johnson & Johnson's line of Purpose soaps, Noxell's Clarion line, and new lines developed by Vidal Sassoon and Oil of Olay (both owned by Procter & Gamble). What marketing strategies should Neutrogena pursue at this point in time?

7 On June 21, 1989, the National Football League and card maker Pro-Set, Inc., announced the first official card of the NFL. These fourteen-card packs are targeted toward the 8- to 15-year-old consumer. Baseball cards are a $240 million a year market with five card makers whereas football card sales total $10 million annually with one company selling the large majority of them. Pro-Set and the NFL jointly developed a print and TV ad campaign using the slogan "Collect the Action." Is this a primary- or selective-demand strategy? Why?

8 Many firms rely on independent service organizations (called ISOs) to repair and sometimes rebuild office equipment such as high-speed copiers. ISOs normally purchase spare parts from manufacturers (such as Xerox) and, in effect, compete with these manufacturers in offering services.

In 1989, Xerox stiffened its policy on the sale of spare parts and technical documentation to ISOs. Those ISOs who were not end users of Xerox products were restricted from buying replacement parts for new Xerox products. In effect, this policy placed a ceiling on the ability of ISOs to compete with Xerox (which receives about 30 percent of its revenue from its service operation). Xerox was roundly criticized by ISO managers but defended its decision by arguing that customer attitudes about copiers are based on the quality of service and Xerox wanted to protect its service reputation.

What type of strategy is Xerox pursuing? Do you think the company's reasoning was valid?

9 In November of 1989, Procter & Gamble introduced a new powdered detergent called Cheer with Color Guard into selected U.S. markets. The new product was a super-concentrated detergent that required only a few spoonfuls per washload. Some resistance to the new product was expected because prior research showed that many consumers did not believe that such a small amount would be sufficient to clean the laundry. As a result, the small packages that contained the product looked very expensive.

Some observers suggested that Procter & Gamble's actions resulted from a lesson in Japan. In 1987, Japanese rival Kao introduced a concentrated detergent called Attack which quickly took 30 percent of the market—largely from P&G's brands. The company was able to regain part of its Japanese share when it responded with a Lemon Cheer superconcentrate in that country.

Superconcentrates have also hit the market in Britain where, as in Japan, the smaller box is appreciated because the average kitchen is much smaller. P&G's entry in the British market (where the P&G share is even greater than in the United States) is a brand called Ultra. Additionally, Ultra was marketed in a biodegradable package which P&G hoped would be well received by the environmentally sensitive Europeans.

a In marketing Cheer with Color Guard, will P&G need to develop a primary-demand strategy or a selective-demand strategy?

b Contrast the strategy and programs that would be most appropriate in Japan in 1989 with those that would be most appropriate in Britain.

c Do you agree with P&G's decision to use a line extension strategy in the U.S. market?

d Would you advocate a globalized marketing strategy for superconcentrated detergents? Explain.

SUGGESTED ADDITIONAL READINGS

Bloom, Paul, and Philip Kotler, "Strategies for High Market Share Companies," *Harvard Business Review,* November–December 1975, pp. 63–72.

Davidow, W. H., and Bro Uttal, "Service Companies: Focus or Falter," *Harvard Business Review,* July–August 1989, pp. 77–87.

DeBruicker, F. Stewart, and Gregory Summe, "Make Sure Your Customers Keep Coming Back," *Harvard Business Review,* January–February 1985, pp. 92–98.

Dickson, Peter, and James Ginter, "Market Segmentation, Product Differentiation, and Marketing Strategy," *Journal of Marketing,* April 1987, pp. 1–10.

Jain, Subhash, "Standardization of International Marketing Strategy: Some Research Hypotheses," *Journal of Marketing,* January 1989, pp. 70–79.

Kashani, Kamran, "Beware the Pitfalls of Global Marketing," *Harvard Business Review,* September–October 1989, pp. 91–98.

Lambkin, Mary, and George Day, "Evolutionary Processes in Competitive Markets: Beyond the Product Life Cycle," *Journal of Marketing,* July 1989, pp. 4–20.

Levy, Michael, John Webster, and Roger Kerin, "Formulating Push Marketing Strategies: A Method and Application," *Journal of Marketing,* Winter 1983, pp. 25–34.

Shostack, G. Lynn, "Service Positioning through Structural Change," *Journal of Marketing,* January 1987, pp. 34–43.

Woo, Carolyn, and Arnold Cooper, "The Surprising Case for Low Market Share," *Harvard Business Review,* November–December 1982, pp. 106–113.

CHAPTER 8

PRODUCT-DEVELOPMENT PROGRAMS

The process of developing and marketing new products is often critical to long-term success in business. As indicated in our discussion of corporate marketing planning (Chapter 2), new products may be essential in directing an organization's future growth and in maintaining a balanced portfolio of products. Moreover, product development is often the major ingredient of the marketing strategies discussed in Chapter 7. Consequently, it is not surprising to find that a large percentage of the sales of major firms come from new products.

However, product development is expensive, time-consuming, and risky. When RJR-Nabisco cancelled the introduction of its Premier "smokeless" cigarette in 1989 because of poor market test results, it was revealed that, in the brand's first year alone, capital expenditures for equipment would have been $80 million and operating losses $100 million. All in all the company had planned on spending $1 billion to develop and market the brand.[1] While few firms would incur an expense of this magnitude, managers should know that

- The costs of designing, producing, and marketing new products are increasing
- Most new products fail to achieve commercial success

This chapter covers four critical aspects of product-development program management. First, we classify the different *types of new products* and discuss the implications of the classifications for new-product management. Second, we present a *process for managing* product development that is designed to cope with the time, costs, and risks of development and commercialization. Third, we present several widely-used *analytical tools* and concepts that are used in the

---

[1]Peter Waldman and Betsy Morris, "RJR Nabisco Abandons 'Smokeless' Cigarette," *The Wall Street Journal*, Mar. 1, 1989, p. B1.

new-product management process. Finally, we discuss the relative merits of *acquisition and licensing* as alternatives to the internal development of new products.

TYPES OF NEW PRODUCTS

From a management perspective, new products are those which are new to the company and may include modifications of existing products, products acquired from other firms, or innovative original products. From a buyer's perspective, a new product is any addition to or change in the assortment of available choices. But clearly, not all new products are the same in terms of the degree of newness to the seller or the buyer. If IBM adds a new model to its line of PS/2 computers, that is substantially different from the introduction of a new "generation" supercomputer. In this section we examine the importance of understanding the degree of newness in assessing new-product risks and in managing the new product's development.

Newness to the Firm

The degree to which a new product is new to the firm depends on its role in corporate and marketing strategy. Table 8-1 summarizes the kinds of new products that would be pursued in implementing each type of corporate strategy.

Diversification   As we discussed in Chapter 2, diversification is a strategy in which the firm enters new markets with products that are functionally different from existing products. Often, diversification is achieved through acquisition. For example, Procter & Gamble entered the pharmaceutical market by acquiring two firms: Norwich-Eaton and Richardson-Vicks. Because diversification involves new products and new markets, it is the product-development avenue that is most "new" to the firm. Thus, the firm is usually less knowledgeable about buyers, distributors, production costs, and processes than for other product categories. This knowledge gap will be somewhat less of a problem if the diversification

TABLE 8-1   TYPES OF NEWNESS TO THE FIRM

Type of corporate strategy	Types of new product	Typical extent of newness
Diversification	• Completely new • Brand franchise extension	• New market • New technology probable
Market development	• Technical extension • Change in form	• New use • User-related technology
Product development	• Line extension • Flanker	• New segment • New technology possible
Market penetration	• Product modification (to meet or beat competition)	• No change in market • Small change in technology

focuses on products that are complementary to existing products. Thus, Gillette entered the shaving-cream market without much difficulty since the buyers and distributors were the same as for their line of razors.

In selecting new markets to enter, firms often try to capitalize on their existing brand equity. As we discussed in Chapter 4, brand equity is an important resource. If it is sufficiently strong, the firm may diversify through a *brand franchise extension*. In this strategy (also known as a "category" extension) a firm uses an established brand name on products that serve markets that are at least somewhat new to the firm. Some examples of successful franchise extensions include Jell-O Pudding Pops and Bic disposable lighters.

When successful, franchise extensions allow a firm to enter a new category at a lower promotional cost and, often, reduce the costs of gaining distribution. On the other hand, firms should avoid extensions that may negatively impact the equity. The success of a brand franchise extension will be greater to the extent that

• There is some link between the benefit offered by the parent brand and the leveraged brand. (For example Sunkist orange soda is logically linked to Sunkist oranges.)
• The products are complementary in usage. (Kodak batteries are widely used in cameras.)
• The brand name has not already been used on a very large number of products.
• The new product will meet or exceed the quality standard of the "parent" product and of competing brands in the marketplace.[2]

Market Development   Although there are several routes to market development, a very important one is to use a *technological extension* of an existing product to serve a new usage category and thus stimulate primary demand. For example, DuPont originally created materials such as rayon, teflon, and nylon for industrial users and subsequently introduced them into consumer products. Although the basic technology for these new products is usually well understood, the company must deal with new users and new distribution channels, which creates a fair amount of uncertainty over market acceptance.

Product Development   Basically a corporate product development strategy is implemented by a product line marketing strategy of either *flanker brands* or *line extensions* as we discussed in Chapter 7. Because the primary purpose of these strategies is to reach new segments of markets already being served, management should have a fair understanding of the buyer, established distribution channels, and (normally) will rely on known technology and production processes. The basic uncertainty revolves around how well the new product will be accepted com-

---

[2]This is based, in part, on Edward Tauber, "Brand Franchise Extension: New Product Benefits from Existing Product Names," *Business Horizons,* March–April 1981, pp. 36–41; and Peter Farquhar, "Managing Brand Equity," *Marketing Research,* September 1989, pp. 30–32.

pared to competing products and to what extent it will cannibalize sales of other product-line offerings.

Market Penetration   Minor product modifications are often used as part of a market penetration strategy. Specifically, a "new" or "improved" version or new "options" may be developed to retain customers being lured away by competitors or to increase market share by improving the benefits offered. For example, Procter & Gamble watched the market share of its Pampers drop from 60 percent in 1980 to 26 percent in 1989. In response, the company introduced a new Pampers with cuffs to block leakage around the leg openings.[3]

Of course, many large firms pursue multiple corporate and marketing strategies simultaneously.

> 3M Company was founded on sandpaper products and achieved rapid growth in the next several decades primarily through its tape products. By 1988 the company had 60,000 products with 32% of sales coming from products introduced since 1983. Newer products included diversifications (synthetic knee ligaments sold to orthopedic surgeons), technical extensions for market development (closure tapes sold to diaper-makers), product line extensions (new high-density floppy discs for personal computer users), and product modification (videotape with improved antistatic features).[4]

It is important to have a clear understanding of the firm's corporate and marketing strategy when examining new-product opportunities for two reasons. First, the purpose of a strategy is to provide direction. Any new-product idea should fit the company's primary corporate direction or a current need established by a marketing strategy. Thus, if a company is not immediately interested in diversification but wants to emphasize growth in current markets, new-product ideas should focus on product-line marketing strategy or selective-demand marketing strategy.

The second key reason for recognizing the type of newness of a product idea is to have an understanding of the type and extent of risk involved. Clearly diversifications and technical extensions are higher risk in that less is known about both production and demand than is the case with other types of new products and because major new marketing programs (for promotion and distribution) must be developed.

NEWNESS TO THE MARKET

When assessing any new-product idea, management must have some sense of how the market will respond to it. Specifically, managers will need to determine buying needs and preferences, the market's size and growth prospects, and the perceptions of the product relative to competitors. All of these issues have been discussed in earlier chapters. However, the uncertainty about market response is

---

[3]Alecia Swasy, "P&G Is Altering Pampers to Lift Drooping Sales," *The Wall Street Journal,* Aug. 9, 1989, p. B1.

[4]Russell Mitchell, "Masters of Innovation," *Business Week,* Apr. 10, 1989, pp. 58–63.

TABLE 8-2 TYPES OF NEWNESS TO MARKET

Type of innovation	Type of newness	Change required of buyers
Discontinuous	New-product class	Creates new consumption pattern (computer, radio)
Dynamically continuous	New-product form	Changes determinant benefits (personal computer, portable radio)
Continuous	New or improved model	Changes evaluation of brands but not determinant attributes (IBM-XT, Sony Walk-man)
Noninnovative	New brand	Changes set of alternatives within a product form (IBM computer clones, other pocket portable radios with earphones)

bound to be greater when a product has yet to reach the market. Uncertainty about market response can create two basic problems. First, uncertainty about the level of demand limits management's ability to determine whether the potential sales volume will be adequate. Second, the design and costs associated with promotion and distribution programs cannot be determined until market response is assessed.

In general, the degree of uncertainty will depend on the degree of newness of the product from the buyer's perspective. As Table 8-2 suggests there are four levels of newness which reflect the degree of innovativeness of the new-product idea.[5]

Discontinuous innovations are relatively rare. They represent products that create entire new-product classes usually as the result of a technological breakthrough. Because these products create entirely new demand categories, their ultimate size is very difficult to predict and the time and cost involved in building primary demand are usually substantial. Also, no matter how technologically exciting the idea, acceptance is not assured. Home banking by computer has never enjoyed the broad acceptance projected by several large banks and AT&T never really got to first base with its picturephone. Both of these cases are examples in which technology outpaced consumer needs.[6]

Dynamically continuous innovations are new products which reflect major but evolutionary improvements offered in the benefits available within a product class. In effect these are new-product forms which offer enhanced or different benefits from the existing forms. Acceptance is less uncertain since the product class already has been accepted. Rather, the concern is for the share of total product-class sales that will go to this form and for the amount of primary-demand stimulation necessary.

[5]See Thomas Robertson, "The Process of Innovation and the Diffusion of Innovation," *Journal of Marketing*, January 1967, p. 15 for a discussion of the three nonimitative types of innovation.
[6]Ronald Bailey, "Sweet Technology, Sour Marketing," *Forbes*, May 1, 1989, p. 140.

Continuous innovations are modest enhancements in performance within a product form. Most product-line extensions and product modifications will fall into this category, so the level of brand cannibalization is a matter of concern as is the impact of the change on the favorableness of buyers' ratings of the brand.

Imitations are not innovations at all, but attempts to capitalize on the success of a competing brand by offering a simple, stripped-down, or lower priced version.

The degree of newness to the buyer has important implications for the activities that management will take in the new-product development process. Clearly more time, effort, and funds will be devoted to develop an understanding of the market for products with higher degrees of newness. Not only is the level of market uncertainty greater for these products, but usually the amount of money at risk is larger because new-product forms and classes usually require more marketing expenditures and involve greater investments in technology.

Even for products with a modest degree of newness, however, new products often fail to achieve sales expectations. In Table 8-3, the major reasons for new-product failure are listed. This list is instructive for managers involved in new-product development because it identifies issues that should be addressed by the firm's formal new-product development and evaluation system.

THE NEW-PRODUCT DEVELOPMENT PROCESS

Because of the probability of new-product failure and since the consequences of new-product failure can be high, most organizations have developed some for-

TABLE 8-3 MAJOR REASONS FOR NEW-PRODUCT FAILURE*

1. Demand for the product form or class is overstated because management overestimates the ability or willingness to buy. (Examples: home banking, soft cookies, the supersonic aircraft Concord, low-alcohol beer.)
2. The product offers no new benefit or it does so only by eliminating an existing benefit. (Example: Premier smokeless cigarette was hard to light and had poor taste.)
3. Buyer needs or usage patterns are not fully recognized. (Example: IBM's PCjr for the home market had keys that were too small and limited memory.)
4. The product is not superior to or is easily matched by established competitors. (Example: Pillsbury's Gorilla Milk was designed to compete with Carnation Instant Breakfast but offered no advantage.)
5. Inadequate promotion or distribution effort. (Example: P&G Encapran aspirin was not effectively marketed to physicians.)
6. New technology makes a product obsolete quicker than expected. (Example: Philips initiated the VCR market but the Beta and VHS formats came along with superior technology.)
7. Company capabilities not well suited to this product. (Example: Gillette did not have the technological base needed to compete in the blank cassette-tape market.)

Source: This table was developed from Calvin Hoddock, "Rx for New Product Survival," *Marketing Communications*, February 1986, pp. 27–33; G. Urban, J. Hauser, and N. Dholakia, *Essentials of New Product Management*, Prentice-Hall, Englewood Cliffs, N.J., 1987, pp. 325–329; Ronald Bailey, "Sweet Technology, Sour Marketing," *Forbes*, May 1, 1989, p. 140; and E. Berkowitz, R. Kerin, and W. Rudeluis, *Marketing*, St. Louis Times: Mirror, Mosby, 1986, pp. 230–232.

malized system or structure for managing that new-product development process. In large companies that make complex products (such as advanced electrical or mechanical goods) this process may involve dozens of specific activities and reviews. In small firms with simple technologies (such as most service organizations) relatively few steps are involved. The *major types* of activities and analyses that are conducted, however, are similar in nearly all situations.

Phased versus Parallel Development

As portrayed in Figures 8-1 and 8-2, it is important to recognize that there are two basic approaches to the process: a *phased* development approach and a *parallel* development approach. In both cases, the activities that are conducted are essentially the same but the timing and organizational responsibility of the activities will differ.[7]

Phased development is more likely to be found in companies that operate in markets where the pace of technological change is slower and more predictable. In such businesses, development speed is less critical and the process is more orderly with individual managers able to focus on their own areas of expertise (be it manufacturing, R&D, or marketing research). The purpose of this process is to permit evaluations of a new idea at several points in time as additional information is developed about demand and costs of the new product. In the phased approach, the least attractive new-product ideas can be dropped from further consideration before extensive time and dollar commitments are made. For example, in the phased approach, R&D is less likely to become involved in the process (except in those cases where R&D generates the product concept) before the screening stage.

Parallel development has become the more widely accepted approach in high-technology industries such as computers, copiers, consumer electronics, and other product categories where the penalty for being late to market is severe and where new-product forms are generated fairly frequently. The enhanced development speed results from improved quality and decreased volume of communications and from the use of new-product teams of eight to twelve members. At 3M, for example, most new products come from someone in a technical area. That individual then forms an action team composed of technical people from other relevant R&D areas, manufacturing, marketing planning, sales, and perhaps finance. The team designs the product then develops the marketing and production plan.[8] The constant interaction among team members permits R&D, marketing, and manufacturing to proceed in parallel. Additionally, if new technology or marketing opportunities arise during development, adjustments can be accommodated much more quickly.

[7]This section was developed from Bro Uttal, "Speeding New Ideas to Market," *Fortune*, Mar. 2, 1987, p. 62; Hirotaka Takeuchi and Ikujiro Nonaka, "The New Product Development Game," *Harvard Business Review*, January–February 1986, pp. 137–146; and C. Merle Crawford, *New Products Management*, 2d ed., Irwin, Homewood, Ill., 1987, chap. 2.
[8]Russell Mitchell, "Masters of Innovation," *Business Week*, Apr. 10, 1989, p. 60.

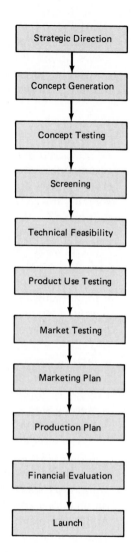

FIGURE 8-1   A phased new-product development process.

Regardless of which approach is utilized, the marketing tasks in the new-product development process remain essentially the same. Each of these tasks is discussed below.

Strategic Direction

It is useful for management to begin the development process by signaling a broad goal or strategic direction toward which marketing and research and de-

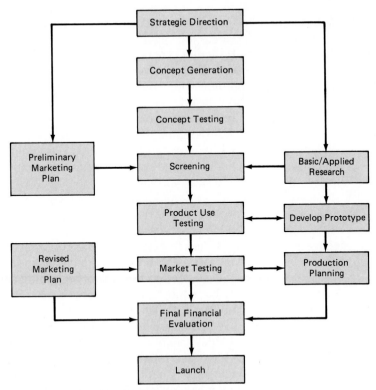

FIGURE 8-2   A parallel new-product development process.

velopment could think and work. Essentially, this is accomplished through the setting of corporate and marketing strategies. For example, if R&D and marketing managers know whether product-line extensions or diversifications are desired, they will be more likely to develop products that fit company needs while still returning a measure of freedom. For example Fuji-Xerox's top management stimulated development of its popular FX-3500 medium-sized copier by asking for a product-line extension that would sell at half the price of its high-end product.[9] Such a framework increases the likelihood that new-product concepts will be consistent with strategic needs.

Concept Generation

New-product ideas can come from a variety of sources. In addition to research and development personnel, useful ideas are often generated from dealers, com-

[9]Hirotaka Takeuchi and Ikujiro Nonaka, ''The New Product Development Game,'' *Harvard Business Review,* January–February 1986, p. 138.

petitors, salespersons, and other employees. But for most firms, customers remain the best source for new-product ideas or for modifications of existing products.

Often, however, *ideas* are vague, subjective, and provide little guidance to the process of actually designing a new product. Consequently, managers really need to generate *concepts*—a more complete specification of the idea that defines the *benefits* that the product will provide and the physical *attributes or technology* that will deliver those benefits. Clearly defined concepts will help management test the acceptability of a new-product idea as well as improve the chances that the product will be designed correctly to provide the specified benefits. Marketing's primary role in concept generation is to identify the benefits the potential new-product concept should offer. R&D or operations managers will then need to design the physical attributes or technology.

A variety of methods exist for identifying potential new concepts. For industrial products, an effective technique is *lead-user analysis*. Essentially this is an interviewing approach which focuses on identifying the anticipated future requirements of a company's "lead" customers—the customers who have the most to gain from product improvements and who are the technological leaders in an industry. Because lead users tend to be large or technologically advanced, it is expected that they will have the best ideas about the products and attributes that buyers in a given industrial market will need in the future. The effectiveness of lead-user analysis has been shown to be especially useful in technology-driven industrial markets such as computing and scientific instrumentation.[10]

For consumer products, a wider range of concept generation approaches is available. As we discussed in Chapter 4, new-product concepts may emerge from analyses of *perceptual maps*. By identifying "gaps" in a market—combinations of determinant attributes that are not offered by existing products—potential new-product opportunities can be identified. However, mapping techniques are limited in that many consumer usage problems may not be easily revealed simply by looking at perceptual maps. That is, with perceptual mapping we are assuming that the determinant attributes are already known. As a result, mapping techniques usually lead to continuous innovations and product-line extensions.

Problem analysis approaches are more likely to yield product concepts that provide new kinds of benefits because they focus on *usage problems and systems* not just the scanning of existing offerings.[11] In problem analysis, the firm conducts interviews with heavy users in the market for a product category to obtain a list of the problems consumers associate with a category. Users are then asked to rate each problem in terms of its frequency and the degree to which it is bothersome. Problems which are both frequent and bothersome are usually selected as the focus of new-product concept development. For example Table 8-4 gives the results of a problem analysis conducted in the pet products industry. Subsequently, managers initiate brainstorming or similar activities that are designed to devise potential solutions. Based on Table 8-4 we can see why pet products man-

[10]Eric von Hippel, *The Sources of Innovation*, Oxford University Press, New York, 1985, chap. 8.
[11]Claes Fornell and Robert D. Menko, "Problem Analysis—A Consumer-Based Methodology for the Discovery of New Ideas," *European Journal of Marketing*, 1981, pp. 61–72.

TABLE 8-4 MOST FREQUENTLY OCCURRING AND MOST BOTHERSOME PROBLEMS AMONG USERS OF PET PRODUCTS

Problems with pets	Problem occurs frequently		Problem is bothersome	
	%*	Rank	%*	Rank
Expensive to maintain	87	2	57	2
Mess up the yard	35	7	30	7
Annoy the neighbors	12	12	5	14
Chew up clothes and furniture	14	11	12	12
Get sick and require medical care	23	9	38	6
Need constant feeding	98	1	21	9
Get into fights with other animals	18	10	8	13
Need room to exercise them	31	8	18	10
Require babysitting	40	6	14	11
Die and cause family grief	2	14	95	1
Get fleas	78	3	53	3
Shed hairs	70	4	46	5
Make noise	66	5	25	8
Have unwanted babies	3	13	48	4

*The percent who cited the problem as occurring "often" or "sometimes" on a scale that also included "seldom" and "never."
†The percent who said the problem was "extremely" or "very" bothersome on a scale that also included "a little" and "not at all."
Source: Burton Marcus and Edward Tauber, *Marketing Analysis and Decision Making*, Little, Brown, Boston, 1979, p. 225.

ufacturers would want to develop a product that solves the flea problem. Similar techniques led to new products such as the Band Aid Sheer Strip from Johnson & Johnson and retractable seat belts from Borg-Warner.[12] In recent years, a variety of consultants has emerged to help firms respond to the problems uncovered in problem analysis by developing new methods for building innovation-oriented skills, often with unusual approaches. For example, Syntectics Inc. encouraged New York Telephone Company managers to link the problem of pay-phone vandalism to indestructible things in nature. When one manager thought of Mount Rushmore, the linkage inspired the company to build phones into the sides of buildings.[13]

The most widely used method for identifying problems in the problem-analysis approach and for identifying potential new determinant attributes is the *focus group*. These groups involve eight to ten people in discussions (led by trained moderators) about products, the needs they serve, perceived problems, and how the product is used. Focus groups can yield major insights or minor product modifications. For example, American Express modified the service provided by its

[12]C. Merle Crawford, *New Products Management*, 2d ed., Irwin, Homewood, Ill.,1987, p. 115.
[13]Daniel J. Wakin, "Product Consultants: Style Is Everything," *South Bend Tribune*, June 25, 1989.

TABLE 8-5   QUESTIONS AND TYPICAL METHODS FOR CONCEPT TESTING

Question	Method
1. How desirable is the concept to target customers?	1. Customers rate the concept on a series of dimensions such as uniqueness, problem-solving potential, believability.
2. What is the probability that the customer would try or use the product?	2. Customers are asked to rate the product on a scale from "would not try" to "definitely would try."
3. What is the relative utility for various attribute combinations?	3. (a) Customers rank-order their preferences for various combinations of all attributes (full-profile conjoint analysis). (b) Customers rank-order their preferences for various pairs of attributes.

credit card to include extended manufacturer warranties on products purchased with the card as the result of a focus group study.[14]

Concept Testing

The purpose of concept testing is to develop a more refined estimate of market acceptance for the new-product concept or to compare competing concepts to determine the most appealing one (or two). If a product prototype is already available, this step may often be excluded. But when a large number of possible concepts exist and the cost of building a prototype is large, concept testing may indicate a number of important aspects of market demand that should be considered before any prototypes are developed.

In particular, concept testing is designed to obtain the reactions of potential buyers to one or more hypothetical product concepts. Product features and benefits are presented in verbal form or explained through visual aids. Potential users are then interviewed to obtain comments about the merits and demerits of each concept or are asked to rate the products in various ways. Table 8-5 indicates some of the specific methods that can be used to help answer the questions management should ask in this step of the product-development process.

Consider, for example, the contents of Table 8-6. After presenting potential buyers with the product concept, the concept was evaluated through a series of questions that would tell management whether the product would likely enjoy a clear competitive advantage, what problems might be encountered in gaining market trial, and whether in general there was a positive reaction to the product. While the probability of trial that is recorded would certainly be a very rough estimate of acceptance, extremely favorable or unfavorable ratings on this ques-

[14]Jeffrey Trachtenberg, "Listening, the Old-Fashioned Way," *Forbes*, Oct. 5, 1987, pp. 202–203.

TABLE 8-6   EVALUATING A NEW CLEANING PRODUCT CONCEPT

Concept statement
A newly developed, nonabrasive, all-purpose cleaner which not only cleans, but inhibits dirt from adhering to the cleaned surface. By varying the strength of the product, the user can clean windows, vinyl, stainless steel, chrome, aluminum, tires, upholstery, carpet, bathroom fixtures, woodwork, appliances, kitchen cabinets, and counters.

Uniqueness: Which statement best describes this product?

_____ Sounds completely different from any other product now available.
_____ Very different from any other product now available.
_____ The same as some other product now available.

Competition: When people buy a new product, they usually buy it in place of some other product they had been buying. If you were to buy this new product, what item or items would it replace?

_____

Need: Does this product solve a problem or need that isn't being satisfied by products now on the market?

_____ Yes   What is the problem or need?_____
_____ No

Merits: What specific features do you find attractive about this new product? _____

_____

Limitations: What specific features do you find questionable about this new product? _____

_____

Believability: Are there any features or claims about this product that you find hard to believe?

_____

Probability of trial: How interested would you be in buying the product described above if it were available at your supermarket?

_____ I would definitely buy
_____ I would probably buy
_____ I might or might not buy
_____ I would probably not buy
_____ I would definitely not buy

tion are generally valuable in deciding whether continued research on the concept is warranted.

Concept testing is also especially useful for identifying potential cannibalization problems early in the process and for understanding how the various attributes of a concept contribute to preference. The highly popular methods of *conjoint analysis* are designed to show

• How people make trade-offs among various attributes (including brand name and price) of a product concept
• The share of preferences each product concept would enjoy when the buyer can choose among existing attribute combinations and the new concept

Such techniques, for example, allowed Buick to design its two-door, six-passenger Regal. Concept testing showed that (within the particular target market analyzed) the best attribute combination for a $14,000 vehicle included a "legit-

TABLE 8-7   AN EXAMPLE OF A CONJOINT ANALYSIS CONCEPT TEST

Please rank the nine combinations in order of your preference from 1 (most preferred) to 9 (least preferred).

Print Quality	Printer speed (characters per second)		
	180	240	300
Draft copy	$210	$290	$250
Near letter quality	$250	$210	$290
Letter quality	$290	$250	$210

imate back seat, at least 20 miles per gallon and 0 to 60 miles per hour acceler-
ation in 11 seconds or less" in addition to a stylish (yet not radical) look.[15]

These techniques assume that we know the determinant attributes for a new-
product concept. If these attributes are independent of one another, if the product
is not one that is highly subject to social influence, and if the customer can identify each attribute in a choice situation, the relative utility of each level of each
attribute can be assessed through a conjoint analysis. Essentially, this form of
concept testing helps managers identify the most preferred combinations of various attribute levels by forcing prospective buyers to rank their preferences for
different combinations. Even when the potential combinations are too numerous
to permit a rank ordering of the full set, the same result can be obtained by having customers rank a specific subset through a technique known as a fractional
factorial design.

Consider, for example, a concept test for a new lightweight printer that would
be compatible with any personal computer. Assume that the manufacturer is considering three levels of print quality, three levels of printer speed, and three levels
of price. Theoretically, there are twenty-seven possible attribute combinations
(that is, 3 speeds × 3 print quality levels × 3 prices = 27). Potential buyers
would have difficulty ranking twenty-seven combinations. But the same information about preferences could be elicited from the reduced array shown in Table
8-7. Now, only nine combinations need to be ranked. (Note that each speed appears once with each letter-quality level and once with each price; all two-way
combinations are thus represented in the reduced design.) Specifically, the
rankings that result will be adequate to determine how willing buyers are to trade
speed for quality, price for quality, and price for speed. The mechanics of the
statistical analyses involved are beyond the scope of this book. Additionally,
there are a number of variations of this methodology that could be chosen.[16]
However, the kind of output that is generated and its potential usefulness in new-
product development can be observed from Table 8-8. Based on the preferences
stated by a single customer, the relative utility of each possible attribute combi-

[15]Wakin, loc. cit.

[16]See Dick R. Wittink and Philippe Cattin, "Commercial Use of Conjoint Analysis: An Update,"
Journal of Marketing, July 1989, pp. 91–96 for a summary of current practices.

TABLE 8-8   RESULTS OF A CONJOINT ANALYSIS
ON ONE CUSTOMER'S PREFERENCES

Attribute	Utility
Print quality	
Draft copy	10
Near letter quality	33
Letter quality	45
Printer speed	
180	14
240	18
300	20
Price	
$210	40
$250	32
$290	18

nation can be calculated by adding the utilities for each component. For example, this customer's most preferred concept is the combination of letter quality, 300 characters per second speed, and a price of $210. The total utility for that concept is 45 plus 20 plus 40 equals 105. However, the data also show the trade-offs consumers are willing to make. A letter-quality printer and a $250 price are preferred to a near letter-quality printer at $210. (Add the utilities for these combinations to see why.) By performing the same analysis with other potential buyers, conjoint methods can yield estimated shares of preference for each potential concept within a set of possible competing concepts.

Screening

As the name of this step would suggest, this activity sifts out and eliminates more new-product ideas and concepts than any other step in the process. The purpose of this step is to rate the general desirability of the new-product concept to the firm. That is, even though the concept may be considered very marketable, it may be viewed as inappropriate for a firm that lacks the specific resources needed to produce and market it successfully. While the concept test provides useful information about potential market acceptance, this information must be interpreted in the context of a given firm and in the context of alternative new-product opportunities.

In evaluating new-product ideas at the screening stage, many firms use some type of scoring profile in which each concept is evaluated on the factors thought to be more important to long-term success.[17] Typical of such profiles is Figure 8-3.

---

[17]A useful discussion of the factors influencing new-product success is available in Roger Calantone and Robert Cooper, "New Product Scenarios: Prospects for Success," *Journal of Marketing,* Spring 1981, pp. 48–60.

Factors	Very poor 1	Poor 2	Score Average 3	Good 4	Excellent 5
1. Market size	—	—	—	—	—
2. Growth potential	—	—	—	—	—
3. Bought by customer we already know	—	—	—	—	—
4. Product has a competitive advantage	—	—	—	—	—
5. Intensity of competition	—	—	—	—	—
6. Uses existing sales force/channels	—	—	—	—	—
7. Uses existing production capacity	—	—	—	—	—
8. Financial requirements	—	—	—	—	—
9. Within scope of R&D capacity	—	—	—	—	—
10. Can use existing suppliers	—	—	—	—	—
11. Rate of technical change	—	—	—	—	—
12. Likelihood of new competition	—	—	—	—	—
13. Extent of government regulation	—	—	—	—	—
14. Marketing expenditures required	—	—	—	—	—
15. Fit with corporate, marketing strategy	—	—	—	—	—

FIGURE 8-3   A scoring profile for a new product.

In Figure 8-3, we can see that the major dimensions of a screening analysis include market factors, the degree to which the company can use existing resources, environmental constraints, and the strategic fit between this product concept and corporate and marketing strategies. Due to the variety of factors considered, screening must generally be carried out by a multifunctional group or committee so that appropriate inputs from production, finance, R&D, and marketing will be obtained.

Often, there will be disagreement among the evaluators regarding the relative importance of the various factors as well as on the ratings of an idea on each factor. This is part of the management process and should not be viewed as a negative feature of screening. Indeed, a key purpose of screening models is to force a dialogue among managers so that the thinking behind each evaluation is made explicit and managers can identify the specific items of additional information needed in subsequent steps.

Technical Feasibility

As a result of concept testing, only one or a very few concepts will usually be found worth pursuing. However, even those concepts that remain may not be carried to the prototype stage.

Technical-feasibility analysis is the process of determining the technical requirements for designing and producing the concept. The availability of technology and the time and cost required for development of the product will be considered at this point. Essentially, managers must resolve three issues in technical-feasibility analysis:

• Managers must determine if the firm can design a product that actually implements the concept.

• The investment that is required for development and production must be estimated.

• The unit cost of production (labor, materials, and packaging costs) must be estimated.

If technical feasibility is established, additional design considerations and technical evaluations must be made. In particular, the Consumer Product Safety Act of 1972 has had far-reaching implications for product development. The Consumer Product Safety Commission (CPSC) was created with powers to establish safety standards, inspect manufacturing facilities, ban products from the market, and engage in other actions that affect new-product development. Over 100,000 products fall within the jurisdiction of the CPSC. (Those product groups that are specifically exempted are still subject to safety regulations of other federal agencies.) The cost considerations of safety regulation and product liability are significant. For instance, Piper Aircraft Corporation's insurance amounts to more than $75,000 for every new plane built. This amount is more than the cost of manufacturing any of Piper's smaller planes.[18]

Additionally, technical testing is necessary to assess the performance of a product under different conditions and to develop information vital to the development of selling, advertising, and distribution programs. Specifically, technical testing can provide information on:

• Product shelf life
• Product wear-out rates
• Problems resulting from improper usage or consumption
• Potential defects that will require replacement
• Appropriate maintenance schedules

Each of these kinds of information may have cost consequences for the marketing of the product. Shelf-life estimates will influence the frequency (and cost) of delivery. Significant usage problems will mean that additional costs in providing advertising, labeling, or selling information will be required.

Product-Use Testing

Once a prototype of the product has been developed, performance should be assessed from the buyer's perspective. Product-use testing involves any test of the product by the consumer or industrial buyer. These tests may be done "blind" (where the brand or seller's identity are not disclosed).

One purpose of a product-use test is to gauge comparative advantage. To the extent that objective comparisons can be made with existing products on functional features, then significant advantages can be more effectively used in promotional programs. Comparisons on durability, speed, reliability, and other fea-

---

[18]Michael Brody, "When Products Turn into Liabilities," *Fortune*, Mar. 3, 1986, p. 23.

tures are increasingly being employed in promotions by consumer and industrial marketers based on product testing information.

However, buyers' perceptions of the product's performance must also be examined. And these perceptions may be influenced by how each customer uses the product. Consequently, buyer tests of product performance are usually a major part of product testing. These tests can be conducted in several ways. Two prominent approaches are as follows:

1 Consumers are asked to use a product (often unlabeled) in their homes, or industrial buyers are asked to try out a product in their business.

2 Comparison tests are performed. For example, potential buyers are asked to consume or use the test product and one or more competing products and then draw comparisons between them.

As Table 8-9 indicates, these tests can be used to answer a variety of questions. Product tests can provide a rough estimate of the achievable market share based solely on product performance. (That is, preferences are usually measured "blind" so that brand name, price, and advertising effects are excluded.) Additionally, the degree to which the new product is likely to acquire new customers rather than simply "cannibalize" the sales of any existing products can be established. Finally, consumer product testing can provide a check on whether or not the concept has been implemented. If consumer descriptions of the product do not match the intended concept, then reformulation may be necessary. Alternatively, consumers may not be using the product in the manner expected, causing the performance to differ from the concept. For example, it is often difficult to get all consumers to use detergents in the same way, and different washing techniques and equipment may cause deviations between the benefits that buyers receive and the benefits or attributes planned in the concept.

TABLE 8-9 QUESTIONS AND TYPICAL METHODS FOR CONSUMER PRODUCT-USE TESTS

Question	Method
1. Has the product concept been implemented?	1. Consumers rate products in terms of the degree to which each attribute in the concept exists in the product.
2. Is the product used in the manner expected?	2. Consumers list problems and specific usage situations for which product works best based on in-home trial.
3. Based solely on product features and performance, what market share could this product achieve?	3. Consumers make direct comparisons among alternatives (in-home or in-laboratory setting) and rate brands or rank-order their preferences.
4. Where will customers for this product come from (nonusers, users of the company's other brands, customers of specific competitors)?	4. Rank order preferences and ratings are examined relative to brand currently used.

Market Testing

While product-use tests can provide important information regarding the likely acceptance of a new product, they are limited in their usefulness for predicting sales response for two reasons. First, individuals in the sample may state preferences but do not have to make actual choices. Second, sales response is influenced by the firm's promotion, price, and distribution programs in addition to the product-use characteristics—especially in the case of consumer goods.

Market tests are essentially sales forecasts in which managers attempt to project sales or market-share growth patterns over a period of (typically) 1 year. These projections are made by developing estimates of selected components of sales or share based on observed or judged effects of the marketing programs.[19] Figure 8-4 portrays the relationships among the major elements of the marketing strategy and the components of sales response. Within the figure, the marketing program elements are portrayed along the left-hand side. These programs influence the consumer's awareness and access to the new product, the attractiveness of the product concept (as reflected in probability of trial), and the satisfaction with the product when purchased. The actual number who will try and repeat and the resulting sales volume are thus a function of how consumers respond to the programs. Typically, early sales are dominated by first-time triers. Then, as the maximum number of potential triers is gradually approached, fewer potential new triers remain and repeat sales to satisfied customers become the dominant portion of total sales. Figure 8-5 portrays typical growth patterns for sales to first-time and repeat buyers.

Market Testing through Test Markets

Test marketing has traditionally been the most effective way of market testing for consumer products. In test marketing, a firm offers a product for sale in a limited geographic area that is as representative as possible of the total market in which the product will eventually be sold. Test marketing has several distinguishing features relative to other research approaches (see Table 8-10):

• Test marketing lowers the risk of national failure, which could endanger channel relationships, reduce confidence and morale of employees, and have a negative impact upon present customers' images of a firm's other products.

• No special benefits are offered to induce purchasing other than those that would later be available on a national basis.

• The product competes with other competitive products in an authentic sales environment.

---

[19]The first major effort at developing such sales forecasting efforts is described in Henry Claycamp and Lucien Liddy, "Prediction of New Product Performance: An Analytical Approach," *Journal of Marketing Research,* November 1969, pp. 414–420. A more recent review that focuses on test-market models is Chakravarthi Narasimhan and Subrata Sen, "New Product Models for Test Market Data," *Journal of Marketing,* Winter 1983, pp. 11–24.

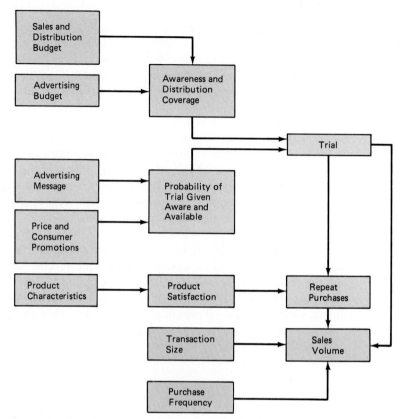

FIGURE 8-4   Determinants and components of first-year sales volume.

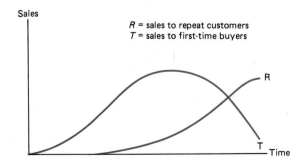

FIGURE 8-5   Typical first-year sales patterns:
trial and repeat.

TABLE 8-10   CONSIDERATIONS INVOLVED IN DECIDING WHETHER TO TEST-MARKET

Factors favoring test marketing
1. Acceptance of the product concept is very uncertain.
2. Sales potential is difficult to estimate.
3. Cost of developing consumer awareness and trial is difficult to estimate.
4. A major investment is required to produce the product at full scale (relative to the cost of test marketing).
5. Alternative prices, packages, or promotional appeals are under consideration.

Reasons for not test marketing
1. The risk of failure is low relative to test-marketing costs.
2. The product will have a brief life cycle.
3. Beating competition to the market is important because the product is easily imitated.
4. Basic price, package, promotional appeals are well established.

In a typical application, a firm selects two to four market areas which are thought to be "representative" demographically and which are sufficiently isolated that local television, radio, and newspapers can be used effectively to reach the market. Arrangements with retailers are made to assure complete distribution (in effect, eliminating lack of distribution as a potential cause of weak sales). The firm then applies its planned advertising, promotion, and pricing programs and observes sales response.

In the context of Figures 8-4 and 8-5, test markets enable the firm to track trial and repeat purchases by monitoring retail sales and using consumer panels (such as the scanner data discussed in Chapter 6) to separate trial from repeat and to identify purchase frequencies and sizes. As we discussed earlier, when single source data are used, the actual links between marketing programs and trial and repeat can also be studied. The importance of being able to do detailed trial and repeat analyses in test markets is exemplified by Ocean Spray's introduction of Mauna La'i Hawaiian Guava Drink.

> Because Guava is different from any other fruit drink in color, taste, and aroma Ocean Spray's marketing staff was very unsure of the product's ultimate acceptance. Using a Behavior Scan electronic test market [as discussed in Chapter 6], the company tracked trial and repeat rates and the identity of the buyers. Initially, the company was disappointed in the repeat rate. But more detailed analyses showed that while the percent of triers who repeated was below expectations, those who did repeat were purchasing at a much higher frequency than anticipated. Moreover, this niche was largely composed of upscale buyers. By refocusing the advertising media used before the national launch, Ocean Spray was able to substantially enhance trial and repeat within this new segment.[20]

Test markets can also be used to improve the productivity of the marketing mix. For example, Kraft tested Bulls-Eye barbecue sauce in two of IRI's Behavior

[20]Leslie Brennan, "Test Marketing Put to the Test," *Sales & Marketing Management,* March 1987, p. 68.

Scan test markets. In one market, advertising was equivalent in scope to that which would result from a $9 million budget while in the other market, a $5 million equivalent level was used. Within each market, prices of $1.79 and $1.59 were tested. Based on the results, Kraft learned it could reach its 5 percent market-share goal with the lower ad budget and the higher price.[21]

Although the appeal of test marketing is great, most marketers believe that it takes at least 10 months to evaluate test-market results, with more conservative companies testing for 1 year or even 2 years. Indeed, test markets for grocery products can easily result in expenditures of $1 million or more. At the same time, test-market results may prove meaningless if competitors disrupt the test by lowering their prices or increasing advertising within these markets. Finally, by test marketing, a firm alerts its competitors about its new products and gives them time to develop matching new products or to design defensive strategies for established products.

Market Testing through Simulated Test Markets

Simulated test markets were designed to be used prior to test marketing but, in practice, are often used in place of test markets. Also called *laboratory test markets* or *pretest market models,* this class of techniques is available from a number of market research service organizations, each of which has developed a variation with its own name. Among the most popular suppliers are Information Resources Inc. (ASSESSOR), SAMI/Burke (BASES), A. C. Nielsen (TESTSIGHT), and Yankelovich, Clancy, Shulman (LTM).

While each model differs slightly the general process for these models incorporates the following steps:[22]

1 Interviews (usually intercepting shoppers in a mall) are conducted with roughly 300 consumers who use the product category. Each consumer lists the brands they are aware of and brand attitudes and preferences are measured.

2 Consumers are then asked to view a series of concept boards or commercials which include ads for the product being tested.

3 Consumers are brought into a mock (laboratory) store, given cash, and offered the opportunity to purchase a product from the product category being studied.

4 People who do not select the test product in step 3 are given a sample of the test product as a gift.

5 After a period of time sufficient for product trial, telephone interviews are conducted to assess any changes in preference, attitudes toward the new brand, and intentions to repurchase. In some cases, respondents are given repeated options to repurchase the product through phone orders.

---

[21]Leslie Brennan, "Quick Study," *Sales & Marketing Management,* March 1988, p. 51.
[22]Allan Shocker and William Hall, "Pretest Market Models: A Critical Evaluation," *Journal of Product Innovation Management,* Fall 1986, pp. 87–88.

Essentially, the research is designed to provide estimates of

- Probability of trial given awareness and availability (step 3)
- Percent of triers who will repeat purchase (step 5)

Most firms will reduce the trial estimate by some "fudge factor" such as 20 percent because experience shows that this trial measure is probably inflated. Additionally, the models use perceptual mapping and preference analysis techniques to develop parallel estimates of the product's likely market share.

Referring back to Figure 8-4, we can see that trial and repeat are critical elements in projecting first-year sales. Users of the simulated test market also input their judgmental estimates of the percentage of awareness that will be achieved from the proposed advertising budget and the percentage of all outlets that will carry the product based on the sales and distribution program. Combining these estimates with expected purchase size and frequency will yield a sales forecast.

Simulated test markets are based on numerous assumptions. While the details are beyond the scope of this book, it is certainly clear that assumptions about the quality of the judgments made by management and about the realism of the laboratory setting are critical. Additionally, experience with these techniques is limited to products which do *not* represent new forms or classes. Finally, while some models allow for the testing of durable goods, these methods have typically been used for nondurable food and drug products.[23]

On the other hand, simulated test markets can be conducted for a fraction of the cost of a test market (roughly $60,000 to $70,000). Moreover, while the overall rate of *success* of new products in test markets is 40 percent, that percentage doubles among products that have first reached target sales or share levels in simulated test markets.[24] Thus, simulated test markets can serve as a screening device to eliminate questionable new products prior to test market. Additionally, while simulated test markets are far from perfect substitutes for test markets, extremely positive results in a simulated test market may lead a firm to skip the test market, particularly if the costs of failure are low and the risks of competitive imitation are high.

Financial Evaluation

In Chapter 6, the elements involved in product-profitability analysis were examined and the basic criteria for measuring profitability were provided. In the case of new products, the issue of profitability is slightly more complex, for four reasons.

First, sales forecasts are inherently more uncertain for new products. However, the results of product testing can provide rough estimates of the number of potential buyers for a product, and market tests can further improve the accuracy of sales estimates.

[23]Shocker and Hall, op. cit., p. 92.
[24]Glen Urban and Gerald Katz, "Pretest Market Models: Validation and Managerial Implications," *Journal of Marketing Research,* August 1983, pp. 221–234.

Second, the pattern of sales and costs for a new product will vary by a greater extent over time. New products are seldom adopted immediately, and the cost of marketing will often be very high in the first year because of the need to provide awareness of the product and incentives for product trial. In general, first-year earnings will understate long-term profitability. If a significant additional investment in production facilities is required, projected profitability should be measured over a longer period of time (anywhere from 3 to 10 years, depending on the expected duration of sales and on the life of the facilities).

Third, if the new product will be a potential substitute for existing products or will share production or marketing resources with existing products, only the incremental effect of the new product on profits should be evaluated. That is, if the new item is expected to cannibalize sales, managers should consider the net sales gain in evaluating the profitability of the product. Similarly, management should include only those increases in cost that are directly attributable to the new product. When excess capacity exists, the new product is often charged with a share of indirect costs. But if those indirect costs would be incurred even if the new product were not added, then they would not be incremental costs. By including them, a firm is penalizing a product for helping the firm operate more efficiently.

Finally, new products may require an additional investment in facilities or equipment. Investments are not costs, because they are one-time outlays rather than recurring expenditures. However, because alternative opportunities for capital investment exist and because different products require different amounts of investment, managers must take the size of the initial investment into account in measuring the profitability of new products.

The data presented in Table 8-11 illustrate one kind of analysis that might be used in assessing new-product profitability. In this example, based on market testing, a product-line extension is expected to achieve sales of 500,000 units. However, based on concept tests, of the 500,000 units 100,000 are expected to result

TABLE 8-11 FINANCIAL ANALYSIS FOR A NEW PRODUCT

	New product projections	Incremental analysis
Sales forecast	500,000	400,000
Unit price	$22	$22
Total revenue	$11,000,000	$8,800,000
Variable expense (30% of sales)	−3,300,000	−2,640,000
Advertising and promotion expense	−1,000,000	−1,000,000
Allocated share of sales force expense	−1,200,000	0
Other fixed-expense	−1,950,000	−300,000
Depreciation	−1,000,000	−1,000,000
Net profit before tax	$2,550,000	$3,860,000
Investment	$10,000,000	$10,000,000
Return on investment (ROI)	25.5%	38.6%

from cannibalization of the existing brand's sales. Thus, the net gain to the firm is 400,000 units. Projected sales and distribution expenses (from the marketing plan) and estimated production expenses (from technical feasibility studies and production planning) provide the data on variable and direct costs. Of these costs, some (such as the new product's allocated share of sales-force costs and a portion of the fixed expenses) are not really incremental. The investment in additional plant and equipment for the new product is $10,000,000 to be depreciated over 10 years.

The analysis shows that the projected first-year return on investment is substantially higher when the project is evaluated on an incremental basis. This kind of assessment is important because most firms will evaluate the new product's financial prospects relative to the return on investment from other new-product opportunities and relative to lower risk investment opportunities. Indeed, most firms establish minimum returns in the range of 20 to 30 percent in order to take inflation and risk into account. Additionally, if the firm attempts to project profitability over a number of years managers will generally calculate the cash flow (which is equal to net profit after taxes plus depreciation) for each future year and then discount these future cash flows to assess their *net present value*.[25]

Launch

Some firms spend so much time and effort in the development of a product that they overlook the planning required to effectively bring the product to market. A number of key decisions are necessary to the development of a launch plan.

First, the timing of the introduction should be carefully evaluated. In particular, it is generally more appropriate to introduce the product during peak periods if demand is highly seasonal. This will permit the firm to obtain a higher level of sales from new-product trial, thus helping to offset large initial advertising and sales promotional expenditures. The introduction should also be timed to assure that distributors will have high levels of inventory by the time the advertising and promotion program kicks off.

Additionally, no attempt at launch should be made until the firm is satisfied that it has done the best job possible in designing the advertising, sales promotion, and sales and distribution programs, and in selecting the best price. These programs are examined in detail in subsequent chapters. However, it is important to note that the first few months of a new product's existence are critical to long-term success. Distributors usually have little patience carrying new products that do not show early prospects for success.

---

[25]The present value of future cash flow is calculated as follows:

$$\text{Present value of cash inflow in year } i = \frac{\text{cash flow in year } i}{(1 + d)^i}$$

where d = discount rate (desired percentage return)
i = year in the planning-period sequence

ALTERNATIVES TO INTERNAL DEVELOPMENT

Internal product development is only one way to expand the product line. Firms can also expand their product lines by acquiring the products of other companies. Additionally, firms can acquire a license to market products that are developed and manufactured by other firms. These approaches are more likely to be employed when the product-development objective is diversification, or when a lack of time, skills, or financial resources would limit the effectiveness of any internal efforts.

Advantages of Acquisitions and Licensing

There are three major advantages of licensing and acquisitions. First, licensing and acquisitions save a company time. In advanced-technology industries, the time it takes to do the research, as well as the time it takes to build and operate production facilities, often precludes successful market entry. If timeliness is a key factor, licensing or acquisition of the resources of another company may be the only viable alternative.

Second, if a firm is unfamiliar with the management, technology, or production skills needed to enter a market, the chances for success may be improved by acquiring those skills.

Third, acquisitions or licensing may be less costly to the firm than internal expansion. The acquisition of companies by direct purchase or by exchanging securities may appear costly until compared with the future cost of bringing a new production facility on stream during a period of inflation. Further, the cost of building market share may be much greater than the cost of acquiring brands that already enjoy established positions in the market. As we discussed in Chapter 2 this is especially true when high technology or extensive government regulation (as occurs in the pharmaceutical industry) create long development lead times.

Establishing Acquisition and Licensing Criteria

In planning for new products through the acquisition or licensing route, management should have clearly established guidelines for evaluating and selecting candidates. Essentially this means that, at a minimum, the steps of establishing strategic direction, screening, and financial evaluation should be followed. Specifically, acquisitions are usually expected to fit the company's corporate strategy and resources and to achieve some target level of return on investment. Other standards that are often established include

- Having a leading position in a market
- Meeting some minimum sales volume levels
- Showing a likelihood of satisfying high-growth rate goals

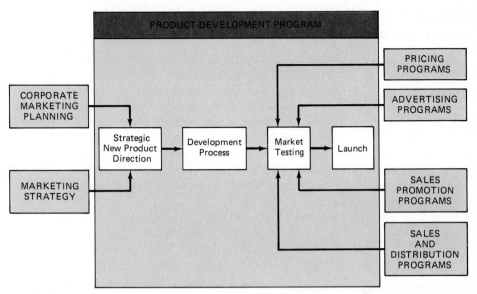

FIGURE 8-6   Relationship among corporate marketing planning, marketing strategy, product-development programs, and other marketing programs.

CONCLUSION

With rapid changes in technology and markets, a firm's product mix must be dynamic. New products play an important role in corporate and marketing strategy, and the development of these products should involve all elements of the business. Because of the high rate of failure for new products, it is important that firms develop appropriate product-development objectives to guide the product-development process. Additionally, product-development costs can be high, even for new products that never reach the market. Accordingly, it is imperative that firms develop systematic procedures for identifying and screening new-product ideas, for testing concepts and prototypes, and for examining profitability.

In this chapter we have presented a comprehensive approach for guiding the product-development process, and we have examined some specific procedures for projecting the market acceptance and profitability of new products. Clearly, the product-development process will not really be complete until advertising, pricing, and other marketing programs are established. The relationship between product-development programs and other marketing programs is portrayed in Figure 8-6. This figure also illustrates how corporate marketing planning and marketing strategy should influence the selection of a new-product direction. To gain a better understanding of how the product-development process is linked to corporate and marketing strategy and to these other programs, consider Gillette's recent introduction of the Sensor.

Gillette Introduces the Sensor Razor*

The first safety razor was invented by King C. Gillette in 1895. Since that time, the Gillette Co. has continued to develop and market products designed for an easier, safer, and more comfortable shave. The average man in Europe and North America has 30,000 whiskers on his face which grow at the rate of one-half inch per month. Because the average male spends 3 to 4 minutes each day or 140 days during his lifetime in the act of shaving, these products have become a major business for many companies, with North American and European men using 5.5 billion blades a year. Gillette has a 60 percent share of the $2.4 billion worldwide market. (Over 50 percent of Gillette revenues come from the European market.)

In the 1970s and early 1980s, total industry sales in dollars declined. During this period, most companies focused their marketing emphasis on low-priced disposable razors rather than on more expensive cartridge razor systems. However, improvements in cartridge razor systems were made and new products were introduced. As a result, between 1986 and 1989 the market grew by 2.6 percent in units but by 26.7 percent in dollar sales. By late 1989, disposable razors accounted for 63 percent of the units sold but only 42 percent of dollar sales. At the same time, the cartridge system's segment increased its unit share from 23.8 percent of the units sold to 28.7 percent and its dollar share from 43 percent to 51 percent of the total razor market.

In an attempt to further the growth of cartridge systems and continue its position as the market leader, Gillette spent over $150 million developing a new razor, the Sensor, over a 10-year period. The prototype was produced at their Reading, United Kingdom, research facility and was based on engineering and manufacturing processes that were developed and perfected in Boston. The Sensor razor consisted of laser-welded, narrow twin blades that were chromium/platinum-hardened, and independently mounted on springs. The Sensor also featured a spring-mounted metal spring guard and pivot head which enabled the razor to adjust automatically to the individual contours of each man's face. Alan Boath, Gillette's General Manager for Northern Europe, described this razor as "the first and only personalized shaving system." Product-use tests showed that the Sensor provided a closer more comfortable shave and that its cartridges were easier to clean and change.

Gillette anticipated that the Sensor would achieve a 5 percent market share by the end of 1990, its first year on the market. It was expected that most of this share would be obtained from other razors in the Gillette product line. However, Gillette executives anticipated approximately one-third of Sensor's sales would come from competitors' disposable razors. For every 1 percent of market share obtained from the competition, Gillette would gain $20 million in pretax profit.

*Developed from Martha T. Moore, "Gillette Arms Itself with Sensor Razor," *USA Today: International Edition,* Oct. 5, 1989, p. 19; and Philip Rawstone, "Gillette Hones Its Competitive Edge," *Financial Times,* Oct. 5, 1989, p. 12.

For every 1 percent it took from another Gillette product, pretax profits were expected to increase by $10 million.

The marketing budget for Sensor's introduction in North America and Europe was $175 million. The $110 million advertising campaign supported a single Gillette product for the first time. The theme "Gillette: The Best a Man Can Get" was consistent along with the brand name, packaging, and advertising in the United States, Canada, United Kingdom, and sixteen other European countries. Gillette hoped to increase both the total dollar value of the North American and European wet-shave market and Gillette's market share.

The Sensor system was introduced at a price 25 percent more than Gillette's top-of-the-line Contour Plus razor. It was estimated that the average consumer's annual cost based on eight shaves per blade would be $28.74 for the Sensor. This compared to an annual cost of $15.99 for Gillette's ATRA and $12.75 for Bic disposables. The system was introduced with sample offers and point-of-sale promotions. In an attempt to get disposable users to switch, even buyers of Gillette's Good News disposable were given a coupon worth $1 off the price of Sensor.

1 What marketing strategy(s) does Gillette seem to be following with the development and introduction of the Sensor razor?

2 Do you think a phased or a parallel development approach would be most appropriate for this new product? Explain.

3 Explain how Gillette could have used concept testing in developing this razor. Design a specific concept test that would be useful.

4 What purposes would product-use testing play in the development of this razor? In conducting product-use tests, what difficulties might Gillette encounter in designing a valid use test?

5 What type of market testing would you advocate for Sensor? Explain.

QUESTIONS AND SITUATIONS FOR DISCUSSION

1 Kraft Cheez-Whiz, Phillips Milk of Magnesia, Barbasol shaving cream, Aqua-Velva after-shave lotion, Brylcreem hair styling products, and Geritol are all products that had declining sales and were considered for elimination from their company's product lines. However, by repositioning these brands and investing heavily in marketing, these aging products have been rejuvenated. Are there any limits to a company's ability to revive once popular brands that are in the mature or declining stage of their life cycle? When would a company want to develop new products rather than try to rejuvenate aging once popular brands?

2 In 1989, Hershey Foods Co. bought Peter Paul Almond Joy, Mounds, and York Peppermint Patties from Cadbury Schweppes. At about this same time the CEO of Hershey indicated that new products were Hershey's lifeblood and their objective was to develop at least one new "hot" product a year. What could explain Hershey's decision to acquire these existing brands from Cadbury-Schweppes while at the same time it was developing new products from within the company?

3 Abbott Laboratories Diagnostic Division introduced 107 new products in 1988. What limits the number of new products that a business could introduce and market in a given time period?

4 Emerson Electric spends only 0.1 percent of sales on research and development. Emerson very seldom is the first company to introduce a new product. Instead they let competitors do expensive market testing and pioneering of the market. Emerson may then enter the market with less expensive imitation products. What are the advantages/disadvantages of such a new-product policy?

5 Timberland Company became immensely successful in the 1970s with the sales of its comfortable, rugged, and water-resistant boots. In the late 1970s and early 1980s, the company added a line of handsewn leather moccasins similar to the popular Topsider "deck shoe." Identify some other possible brand extensions for the Timberland brand name. What specific criteria would be used in selecting brand extension candidates.

6 Outline the concept testing procedure you would suggest for (a) a car powered by solar energy and (b) a new at-home personal banking and shopping system using a personal computer. Is there any difference in concept testing for products as compared to services?

7 Test marketing and consumer-use testing are two approaches used to assess the potential success of a new product. Based on the strengths and weaknesses of each approach, which method would you suggest for each of the following items (a) a new improved detergent, (b) high-definition, flat-screen television, and (c) a new Nintendo computer children's game.

8 An advertising agency conducted a conjoint analysis to determine how consumers traded off among brand name, price, and various features for airline flights. The results indicated that a typical consumer had relative utilities for each attribute as listed below:

Airline	
American	29
Continental	17
Delta	20
TWA	23
United	28
Round-trip fare	
$199	69
$249	45
$299	26
$349	1
Flight plan	
Nonstop	42
One-stop	21
Change planes	2
Smoking	
None	33
Only if flight is over 2 hours	30
Yes	19

Source: Betsy Sharkey, "The People's Choice," *Adweek's Marketing Week,* Nov. 27, 1989 (Special section: Marketer's Report Card 1989, p. 7).

a What inferences would you draw from such data about brand equity in this industry?

b If an airline was considering offering a new no smoking, one-stop flight at a price of $249 to compete in a market with a $299, nonstop flight which permitted smoking because the flight was over 2 hours what do the conjoint analysis results suggest the *typical* consumer will do?

8 In the late 1970s, Coca-Cola Company found its Coke brand falling behind Pepsi Cola in supermarket sales. Coca-Cola felt that taste was a major problem in this loss of share and began to develop new slightly sweeter formulas. By 1984, they had developed a new taste which they proceeded to test in over 30 cities. Forty thousand consumers participated in these tests, which was eight times the number Coke usually sampled to test a new product.

In blind taste tests, 55 percent chose the new Coke over the old and 52 percent chose it over Pepsi. When the drink was identified as Coke, but not as a new formulation, Coke and Pepsi tied. When participants learned they were drinking a new Coke, they chose it over Pepsi by 8 percentage points. The $4 million spent on research was the largest amount spent on any new product in Coca-Cola's history.

New Coke was introduced in April 1985. Before May 30, 53 percent of shoppers said they liked the new Coke. By June, more than one-half of those surveyed indicated they didn't care for the new Coke. By the time Coca-Cola decided it had made a mistake in this introduction, only 30 percent of 900 consumers surveyed every week said they liked the new Coke. Donald R. Keough, Coke's president and chief operating officer, stated that "All of the time and money and skill poured into consumer research on the new Coca-Cola could not measure or reveal the deep and abiding emotional attachment to the original Coca-Cola."

a Should a company even consider extensive product research when its existing brand(s) have high brand loyalty?

b What would be the advantages, if any, of Coca-Cola's extensive reliance on research prior to this new-product introduction?

c What suggestions would you make for improving on the research approach taken by Coca-Cola?

SUGGESTED ADDITIONAL READINGS

Aaker, David, and Kevin Keller, "Consumer Evaluations of Brand Extensions," *Journal of Marketing,* January 1990, pp. 27–41.

Crawford, C. Merle, "Evaluating New Products: A System, Not an Act," *Business Horizons,* November–December 1986, pp. 48–55.

de Brentani, Ulrike, "Success and Failure in New Industrial Services," *Journal of Product Innovation Management,* December 1989, pp. 239–258.

Gupta, Ashok, S. P. Raj, and David Wilemon, "A Model for Studying R&D Marketing Interface in the Product Innovation Process," *Journal of Marketing,* April 1986, pp. 7–18.

Kerin, Roger A., Michael G. Harvey, and James T. Rothe, "Cannibalism and New Product Development," *Business Horizons,* October 1978, pp. 25–31.

McIntyre, Shelby H., and Meir Statman, "Managing the Risk of New Product Development," *Business Horizons,* May–June 1982, pp. 51–55.

Shocker, Allan, and William Hall, "Pretest Market Models: A Critical Evaluation," *Journal of Product Innovation Management,* Fall 1986, pp. 86–107.

Takeuchi, Hirotaka, and Ikujiro Nonaka, "The New Product Development Game," *Harvard Business Review,* January–February 1986, pp. 137–146.

Von Hippel, Eric, "Get New Products from Customers," *Harvard Business Review,* March–April 1982, pp. 117–122.

Wheelwright, Steven C., and W. Earl Sasser, "The New Product Development Map," *Harvard Business Review,* May–June 1989, pp. 112–127.

CHAPTER 9

PRICING
PROGRAMS

Price is typically one of the most important factors influencing demand for a good or a service. Additionally, a firm's prices (and those of competitors) can usually be changed more frequently than advertising themes, product features, sales campaigns, or other marketing programs. Because of the importance of pricing decisions and the fact that these decisions may be made on a frequent basis, managers need to have a clear and workable framework for selecting pricing programs.

A *pricing program* is a plan that indicates how a firm will set the basic list price (that is, the price that is asked of the buyer). Note that a pricing program does not have the selection of some "optimal" price as a goal. Rather, a pricing program provides some general guidelines as to what level of price should be charged relative to competitors or to other products in the firm's product line in order to be consistent with the marketing strategy.

Of course, if a firm uses wholesalers or retailers to distribute its products, the final list price may not be the manufacturer's suggested price: wholesalers and retailers can modify that price to fit their own strategic needs. Additionally, initial price levels may be modified by sales promotions (such as coupons and cents-off specials) and by sales and distribution arrangements in which negotiated prices, cash or quantity discounts, or long-term contracts are employed. Although these programs may lead to changes in the actual price paid, they will be treated in greater detail in later chapters.

In order to establish an effective pricing program, managers must first establish a pricing objective and obtain an understanding of the price-elasticity of demand for the product. These are the first two topics we examine in this chapter. Subsequently, we examine the pricing implications of the competitive analyses and the profitability analyses discussed in Chapters 4 and 6. We then show how managers can integrate these analyses in developing pricing programs. Finally, we examine some special international and legal considerations in pricing.

PRICING OBJECTIVES

The purpose of any pricing program is to support the marketing strategy that has been developed for the product or product line. Pricing objectives specify how price is expected to help implement the marketing strategy. Table 9-1 lists the major types of marketing strategies discussed in Chapter 7 and some pricing objectives that would typically be associated with each strategy type.

Primary-demand-based objectives are selected if the firm believes that price can be used to increase either the number of users or the rate of purchase. Especially in the introductory or growth stages of a product life cycle, lower prices may reduce the buyer's perceived risk of trial. Or, lowering a price may enhance the relative value of one product form versus another. For example, lower prices for compact disc players have not only reduced the risks of trial, but they have also made the product relatively more attractive compared with conventional record players. Alternatively, lower prices could be designed to enhance the rate of purchase either by increasing consumption frequency (as when the prices of high-quality cuts of beef are reduced) or by broadening the number of usage situations to include lower priority uses. For example, lower long-distance telephone rates may lead people to make phone calls to friends they normally would write to.

Selective-demand-based objectives are those designed to support either a retention strategy or an acquisition strategy. Generally speaking pricing designed to

TABLE 9-1   MARKETING STRATEGIES AND POSSIBLE PRICING OBJECTIVES

Marketing strategies	Pricing objectives
Primary-demand strategies	
• Increase number of users	• Reduce economic risk of trial
	• Offer better value than competing product forms/classes
• Increase rate of purchase	• Enhance frequency of consumption
	• Enable use in wider range of situations
Selective-demand strategies	
• Retention	• Meet competition (establish price parity)
• Acquisition	• Undercut competition on price
	• Use price to signal premium quality
Product-line strategies	
• Substitutes	• Get buyers to "trade-up"
	• Distinguish product-line alternatives on value/features
• Complements	• Expand range of products bought by existing customers
	• Attract new customers on superior value of a system or package of products

meet the competition will be used if a firm's primary concern is to retain the existing customer base. When the strategy is acquisition-oriented the pricing objective may be to become the low-price alternative or to underscore a quality-based differentiation. It should be noted, however, that meeting the competition is not necessarily an inappropriate objective for an acquisition strategy. A firm may want to compete on non-price factors and thus decides to match competitors' prices in an effort to remove price as a consideration in making a choice.

Finally, product-line-based objectives are those which guide the pricing of a line of substitutes or of a product that has many complements. For substitutes, the objective will be either to encourage some buyers to consider more expensive models within a line (an important issue in pricing a line of automobiles) or to make quality distinctions very clear. For example, most banks offer different prices to distinguish checking account plans that have different balance requirements or check writing limits. For complements, the primary objective may be to expand the range of products purchased by existing customers (as when a bank offers a no-annual-fee credit card to its existing checking account customers). Alternatively, the objective may be to attract new customers through offering superior value on a system or package of new products. Thus, an appliance dealer may offer a free extended warranty on a new television set.

As we shall see later in this chapter, pricing objectives provide substantial guidance for pricing programs. However managers should recognize that pricing objectives cannot be simply established from knowing the marketing strategy. It may turn out that price will not be useful in implementing a marketing strategy because customers are not sensitive to price, because competitors offset the price programs by the price actions they take in response, or because the profitability consequences of a pricing program are unacceptable.

However, the purpose of setting a pricing objective is to identify the specific kind of impact on demand that management wants to achieve through pricing. After a manager has calculated a price level that will achieve the pricing objective, the profitability consequences can be evaluated by using the procedures we discussed in Chapter 6. That is, the pricing program should result in a price level that will achieve the price objective (and thus help implement the marketing strategy) and at the same time ensure that the product's target contribution will be achieved.

More fundamentally, managers cannot establish meaningful pricing objectives unless they believe that demand will be responsive to price. That is, managers cannot determine how price may contribute to a marketing strategy unless they have analyzed the price-elasticity of demand.

PRICE-ELASTICITY OF DEMAND

Because the effectiveness of any pricing program depends on the impact of a price change on demand, it is necessary to understand the extent to which unit sales change in response to a change in price. However, unlike other productivity relationships a change in price has a two fold effect on a firm's sales revenue: a change in the units sold and a change in revenue per unit. Thus, managers should not be merely concerned with the price-sensitivity of the market, they must also be concerned about the impact of the change on total dollar revenue.

The term "price-elasticity of demand" explicitly takes this into account. That is, price-elasticity is not simply another way of saying price-sensitivity. If a change in price causes a change in *units sold,* we can say that demand is somewhat price-sensitive. But when we use the term "price-elasticity," we are examining the impact of a price change on *total revenue.*

More specifically, *price-elasticity of demand* is measured by the percentage change in quantity divided by the percentage change in price. Given an initial price P_1 and an initial quantity Q_1, the elasticity of a change in price from P_1 to P_2 is calculated by:

$$e = \frac{Q_2 - Q_1/\frac{1}{2}(Q_2 + Q_1)}{P_2 - P_1/\frac{1}{2}(P_2 + P_1)}$$

If the elasticity measure e can be calculated, then management can predict the impact of the price change on revenue, as Table 9-2 indicates.

Note that the important number to keep in mind is -1. If elasticity is -1 or smaller (such as -2 or -3), then demand is very sensitive to price and the change in revenue will be in the opposite direction from the direction (increase or decrease) of the price change. Similarly, if elasticity is greater than -1 (such as $-\frac{1}{2}$ or $+1$), then demand is not very price-sensitive and an increase (decrease) in price will result in an increase (decrease) in revenue. This point is significant because, in practice, it is difficult for managers to develop a precise, reliable estimate of elasticity. But simply being able to determine whether e is greater than -1 or less than -1 will enable managers to understand the general profit impact of a change in price on revenue.

However, in attempting to develop an estimate of elasticity, managers should recognize that there are really two kinds of price-elasticity: elasticity of *market demand* and elasticity of *company* (or brand) *demand.*

TABLE 9-2 EFFECTS OF DIFFERENT TYPES OF ELASTICITY

Value of e	Type of elasticity	Effect on total revenue of:	
		Price increase	Price decrease
$e > -1$	Inelastic	Increase	Decrease
$e = -1$	Unitary elastic	No change	No change
$e < -1$	Elastic	Decrease	Increase

Market versus Company Elasticity

Market elasticity indicates how total primary demand responds to a change in the average prices of all competitors. Company elasticity indicates the willingness of customers to shift brands or suppliers (or of new customers to choose a supplier) on the basis of price. For a product that offers an example of the significance of this distinction, economists often point to table salt. The market demand for table salt is inelastic, because people cannot consume much more even if all prices are lowered. However, if one producer lowers its price, that producer is likely to gain market share. So although market demand may be inelastic, at the same time company demand can be elastic because buyers may be very sensitive to competitive price differences.

For example, consider the industry demand schedule presented in Table 9-3 and portrayed in the industry demand curve of Figure 9-1. (These data are an approximation of average industry retail prices and industry sales in the blank videocassette tape market during the mid-1980s.) As indicated in Table 9-3, when industry prices fell from $12 to $6, demand increased substantially from 65 million units to 95 million units. However, while industry sales grew, total revenue declined: The decrease in price more than offset the gain in volume. Therefore, demand in the range from $12 to $6 is inelastic. However, in the $6 to $5 range, demand is elastic as the additional $1 reduction in price results in an increase in total revenue.

However, this information gives only *market* elasticity information. Even during elastic demand periods (such as that which occurred when prices dropped from $6 to $5), some products could have experienced inelastic *company* demand if they were clearly differentiated with respect to quality. Similarly, during market-inelastic periods (such as the one that existed between $12 and $6), company demand could be elastic if price were important to consumers in selecting a specific brand.

Managers should note that the distinction between market elasticity and company elasticity is directly related to the two major types of marketing strategies discussed in Chapter 7 and to the pricing objectives discussed earlier in this chapter. Specifically, if a manager's pricing objective is to increase rates of purchase for the product form or to increase demand among users (both of which reflect *primary-demand* strategies), then the manager should determine whether *market demand* is inelastic. On the other hand, if the pricing objectives reflect *selective-demand* strategies (such as the retention or acquisition of customers), then managers should be concerned about the elasticity of *company demand*.

TABLE 9-3   ILLUSTRATION OF A DEMAND SCHEDULE

Price	Quantity demanded	Total revenue
$12	65 million units	$780 million
$ 6	95 million units	$570 million
$ 5	180 million units	$900 million

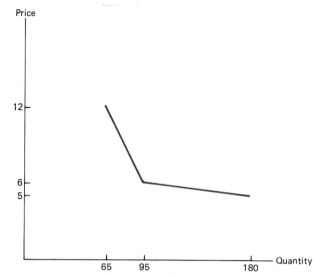

FIGURE 9-1 Illustration of a demand curve: quantity sold as industry prices decline.

However, it is *not* necessary that demand be elastic in order to achieve a pricing objective. Managers may be very committed to retaining customers or to acquiring new customers when the product objective is to maintain share or to increase market share. Often this commitment is so strong that managers will be willing to risk some reduction in total revenue in order to maintain (or in order to establish) a strong position in a market.

To illustrate, consider the company demand schedule in Table 9-4. Demand is inelastic because total revenue declines as the price is reduced from $2.00. However, buyers are still *sensitive* to price: Volume does increase as price declines. Consequently, if the impact of higher volume on total revenue and profitability is acceptable (given the product objective and target total contribution), then a manager may well decide to lower the price, sacrificing some degree of profitability for market share and sales-volume gains.

ESTIMATING PRICE-ELASTICITY

As we have shown in the previous section, managers should have some estimate of the degree of price-elasticity that exists in order to predict the unit sales vol-

TABLE 9-4 ILLUSTRATION OF A COMPANY DEMAND SCHEDULE

Price	Demand	Total revenue
$2.00	500,000	$1,000,000
$1.50	600,000	$ 900,000
$1.00	750,000	$ 750,000

ume and total revenues that will result at various price levels. In order to develop this estimate, managers can employ several alternative procedures.

Historical Ratios

In Chapter 6, we indicated that historical ratios may exist that will indicate the past effect of changes in a marketing variable (such as price) on sales. Multiple-regression sales forecasting models are often employed to develop the historical relationship between price and sales volume.

When using this approach, managers must have historical data not only on company sales and prices but also on industry sales and competitive prices. That is, to estimate market elasticity, managers need to determine the historical relationship between *industry* sales and some average of *industry* prices. However, both pieces of information are also needed to estimate company elasticity. That is, the effect of a company's price on selective demand will really depend on how much the company's price differs from the prices of direct competitors. (For example, if, in the past, a firm has consistently raised its price without any loss in sales, management cannot necessarily infer that company demand is inelastic because competitors may also have been raising prices.) Further, estimates of company elasticity cannot be made without considering changes in industry sales. That is, an increase in company sales may reflect an increase in market share or an increase in industry sales. (In fact, price cutting frequently leads to increases in both primary and selective demand.) Accordingly, managers should examine the historical relationship between a company's relative price (that is, relative to competitors' prices) and market share when attempting to assess company elasticity.

Managers must remember that historical ratios do not necessarily reveal price-elasticity levels if changes in other marketing variables have taken place. Returning to our example of videocassette tapes (Table 9-2 and Figure 9-1), the change in tape sales could not realistically be attributed solely to lower prices. Rather, growth in industry tape sales reflects increases in VCR ownership, in advertising, and perhaps in other factors, as well as decreases in average industry prices. Because it is often difficult to separate these various effects on sales and because historical relationships may change (as Figure 9-1 above demonstrates), historical ratios can seldom be effective as the sole basis for predicting the degree of elasticity.

Experimentation

Field experiments (including the electronic scanner experiments discussed in Chapter 6) in which actual retail prices are manipulated while other factors (advertising, packaging, shelf space) are held constant are often employed by consumer-goods marketers to examine the impact of price changes on sales. This method can be useful but is typically costly and time-consuming. Another disadvantage is that competitors who are aware of the experiment can confuse the findings through the use of short-term "specials" or other actions in the experimental areas. Finally, distributors are often unwilling to cooperate in such experiments. Since they have legal control over retail prices, distributors may block the experiment effort unless they can see a direct financial benefit to themselves.

Experiments done in a *laboratory setting* can also provide useful information regarding price-elasticity. By simulating a shopping situation and by varying prices, it is possible to generate estimates of elasticity. This approach generally permits more control over price, because competitors' prices can be manipulated as well as the price of a company's own product. However, the lack of a realistic setting raises questions about the reliability of any precise elasticity estimates derived in this manner.[1]

Survey Methods

When new products are being priced, the historical ratio method cannot be of any real help since no historical data exist. If experimentation is also judged to be impractical or if managers wish to reduce the number of possible price levels for subsequent experimentation, then various survey methods may be useful.

In the *direct questioning* approach, a product concept is described and customers are asked what is the most they would be willing to pay and what is the least they would be willing to pay and still trust the quality of the product. While the precise number who actually would buy at a given price cannot be realistically projected from these results, managers can use these data to gain insight about consumer perceptions of the appropriate *range* in which the price should fall. Generally speaking, this range will reflect consumer perceptions about which other products are most comparable to the product that is being priced.[2]

A variant of this direct questioning approach is the *buy-response survey*. In this method, consumers are given a product or product concept at a preselected price and asked if they would purchase at that price. Because this form of questioning is structured more like an actual purchase decision, responses are thought to be somewhat realistic. Moreover, by aggregating the responses of various consumers, a buy-response curve like that pictured in Figure 9-2 can be generated. The buy-response curve shows the percentage of consumers asked who answered "yes" at each price. The major use of this data is to identify price levels at which substantial changes in price-sensitivity can be anticipated. For example, consumers seem to be very sensitive to a price increase from $1.69 to $1.79.[3]

Finally, *conjoint analysis,* a technique we discussed in Chapter 8, is widely considered to be the preferred survey method for identifying the effect of price on demand. Specifically, conjoint analysis allows managers to isolate the differential

---

[1]See John R. Nevin, "Laboratory Experiments for Estimating Consumer Demand: A Validation Study," *Journal of Marketing Research*, August 1974, pp. 261–268.

[2]Andre Gabor and Clive Granger, "The Pricing of New Products," *Scientific Business*, August 1965, pp. 141–150.

[3]Thomas T. Nagle, *The Strategy and Tactics of Pricing*, Prentice-Hall, Englewood Cliffs, N.J., 1987, p. 280.

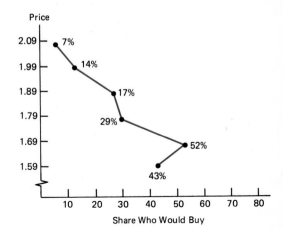

FIGURE 9-2 A buy-response curve from willingness-to-buy data. (*From Thomas T. Nagle, The Strategy and Tactics of Pricing, Prentice-Hall, Englewood Cliffs, N.J., 1987, p. 280.*)

effect of price on brand preferences given various combinations of product features.

Judgmental Estimates

In Chapter 6, we suggested that some judgmental inputs are usually necessary in estimating productivity, and we illustrated an approach for making judgmental estimates of the productivity of advertising expenditures. Judgmental estimates are also often appropriate for estimating the anticipated productivity (that is, the elasticity) of price changes. (In fact, the same approach discussed in the context of advertising expenditures in Chapter 6 can be employed.)

Managers can gain many insights into the elasticity of market and company demand by examining the diagnostic questions that were discussed in Chapter 3. For example, Table 9-5 indicates some of the buying-process factors that would suggest that market demand is likely to be elastic. To the extent that an industrywide price decline results in an increase in the willingness or ability to buy, the gap between market potential and industry sales becomes smaller. For

TABLE 9-5   FACTORS SUGGESTING ELASTIC MARKET DEMAND

1. Many alternative product forms or classes exist for which the product can be substituted.
2. Only a small percentage of potential buyers currently purchase or own the product because of the price and because the product represents a discretionary purchase.
3. The product represents a relatively high percentage of buyer income or purchases so that low price is a very important benefit.
4. The rate of consumption or the rate of replacement can be increased through lower prices.
5. Demand for the (industrial) buyer's product is price-elastic, so that if the company lowers prices, the buyer can lower prices on the final product and demand will increase.

TABLE 9-6   FACTORS SUGGESTING ELASTIC COMPANY DEMAND

1. Buyers have and are aware of a large number of alternatives.
2. Buyers can compare alternative brands/suppliers on the determinant attributes/benefits through observation.
3. Brands are not perceived as being highly differentiated.
4. The perceived economic risk is high relative to other perceived risks.
5. The supplier or brand can be changed easily and with minimal costs.

example, price will have an impact on demand for one product form (aluminum) if competing product forms (such as steel) have similar performance characteristics so that the forms may be substituted for one another on a price basis. Similarly, if the number of potential buyers is far above the number who currently buy the product form, lower prices may be one mechanism to gain new buyers.

Table 9-6 presents some of the buying-process factors that would suggest that company or brand demand is elastic. Economic theory suggests that the greater the number of alternatives about which a buyer is informed, the greater the price-elasticity of demand. Additionally, elasticity will be greater if buyers can rely on observation through their search efforts to make comparisons. Thus, airline competition is price-elastic because the primary non-price determinant attributes (departure times, flight time) are readily observed. Further, if quality differences are perceived to be minimal, demand will be more elastic. Additionally, in some situations, perceived differences in quality will not exist and the perceived economic risk will be high relative to performance, convenience, or other forms of risk. In those situations, price is likely to be a determinant attribute. Finally, if the cost of searching out new alternatives is relatively low, demand will more likely be elastic. For example, the time and effort involved in shifting a person's banking relationship is much greater than the time and effort involved in selecting a different brand of canned peas. Accordingly, a much larger change in price will generally be required to induce customers to switch banks than to switch brands of canned peas.

Managers should recognize that, in most markets, demand will be elastic in some segments and inelastic in others. For example, it has been observed that relatively few banks use price as a competitive device in marketing bank credit cards such as VISA and MasterCard even though each issuing bank can set its own annual fees and interest rates. One reason for this behavior is that many customers want credit cards only for convenience. They plan to pay off their balances each month rather than borrowing so they are not attracted by lower rates. Those who do plan to borrow are more rate sensitive.[4]

Additionally, recent research findings are available that provide other useful insights into the judgmental assessment of price-elasticity. These findings result in the following generalizations:

[4]Alan Blinder, "Plastic Puzzle: Why Rates for Credit Cards Don't Go Down," *Business Week*, Aug. 7, 1989, p.14.

1 A price change will have no effect on demand unless it is large enough to be noticeable, and (all other things being equal) the higher the price, the larger the price change must be to be noticed.[5]

2 The further a brand's price is from the average price for the product category, the more distinct it is from the competition and the less the price-elasticity is.[6]

3 The lower a brand's market share, the greater the price-elasticity (because a small change in units sold translates into a larger percentage change than is the case for large market-share brands or firms).[7]

4 Market elasticity of demand is generally highest in the early stages of the product life cycle and company or brand elasticity is generally highest in the later stages of the product life cycle (when technological differences are minimal).[8]

COMPETITIVE FACTORS

Whether a manager is concerned with market or company elasticity, competitors' reactions to a price change must be considered. After all, if the change in price is matched by all competitors, then no change in market share should result. In that event, the price cut will have no effect on selective demand. Accordingly, managers should attempt to determine what competitors' pricing reactions will be.

Usually, it will be useful to examine historical patterns of competitive behavior in projecting price reactions. Some competitors may price their products primarily on the basis of costs. These firms often do not shift their pricing policies over time; instead, they either price very competitively (if they are trying to take advantage of experience curves or economies of scale) or attempt to maintain consistent contribution margins and thus avoid direct price competition. Additionally, by analyzing competitors' historical pricing behavior, managers may obtain insights into the likely customer reaction to a price change. Specifically, if an industry has historically been characterized by extensive price cutting, buyers will more likely be price-sensitive because they will have come to expect price differences.

Managers can also use their knowledge of competitive strengths and weaknesses and of the degree of competitive intensity in an industry (as discussed in Chapter 4) in predicting competitors' responses. However, even when price is the decision issue at hand, managers should assess non-price reactions as well as direct price reactions in a market because competitors' non-price actions may influence price-elasticity. Consider, for example, the relationship between adver-

[5]See Kent B. Monroe, *Pricing: Making Profitable Decisions,* McGraw-Hill, New York, 1978, pp. 40–49 for a discussion of these research findings.

[6]William T. Moran, "Insights from Pricing Research," in E. L. Bailey (ed.), *Pricing Practices and Strategies,* The Conference Board Inc., New York, 1978, p. 9.

[7]Thomas T. Nagle, *The Strategy and Tactics of Pricing,* Prentice-Hall, Englewood Cliffs, N.J., 1987, p. 79.

[8]Gerard Tellis, "The Price Elasticity of Selective Demand: A Meta-Analysis of Econometric Models of Sales," *Journal of Marketing Research,* November 1988, pp. 339–340.

tising expenditures and price-elasticity.[9] One theory about this relationship contends that advertising reduces brand/company price-elasticity by building brand loyalty. An alternative view is that advertising broadens the number of alternatives about which consumers are informed which should increase brand/company price-elasticity. More recent evidence suggests that the effect of advertising on price-sensitivity depends on competitors' reactions to a change in advertising: If competitors react by increasing their own advertising, brand comparisons are encouraged so price-sensitivity should increase, but price-sensitivity is reduced if competitors do not react because the brand experiencing higher advertising will be more widely remembered.[10] Additionally, the type of advertising that characterizes a market also appears to be a factor. Specifically, if the advertising focuses on building *awareness* then the number of brands a consumer will consider tends to increase so price-elasticity will increase. However, if the emphasis is on *positioning-oriented* advertising, the effect will normally be to differentiate the various brands, resulting in more inelastic demand.[11]

COST FACTORS

In Chapter 6 we discussed the pricing implications associated with economies of scale. Specifically, we discussed how lower prices also resulted in lower average costs if they led to significant increases in volume: As volume increases, fixed costs are spread over more units. Therefore, the gains from economies of scale are greatest when fixed cost represents a very high proportion of total cost. (Of course, if a firm is already producing close to its capacity, the economies of scale are already fully realized; so such firms have little to gain from reducing prices.)

In many firms, current or anticipated average costs serve as the primary basis for pricing. Specifically, many firms use the *cost-plus* approach, in which the price is determined by taking the cost per unit and then adding a dollar or percentage-target-contribution margin.

To illustrate one version of the cost-plus approach, consider the data in Table 9-7 which presents the cost structure for a case of a liquid dishwashing detergent brand. In arriving at the manufacturer's price (the price per case paid by the retailer), a firm using cost-plus would usually take the variable costs of producing the detergent and then add on an estimate of each case's share of fixed overhead costs and of estimated advertising and selling costs. Note that in order to estimate the fixed cost per case, the company must have some estimate of the number of cases that will be sold because

$$\text{Fixed cost per case} = \frac{\text{total fixed cost}}{\text{number of cases sold}}$$

[9]See Hubert Gatignon, "Competition as a Moderator of the Effect of Advertising on Sales," *Journal of Marketing Research*, November 1984, pp. 387–398 for a succinct overview of these issues.

[10]Ibid.

[11]John Hauser and Birger Wernerfelt, "The Competitive Implications of Relevant-Set/Response Analysis," *Journal of Marketing Research*, November 1989, pp. 391–405.

TABLE 9-7 AN ILLUSTRATION OF COST-PLUS PRICING FOR A LIQUID
DISHWASHING DETERGENT

Variable costs per case (materials, packaging)	$ 6.80
Plus allocated share of manufacturing overhead	1.70
Plus allocated share of advertising	6.50
Total unit cost	$15.00
Plus target profit per case	2.00
Manufacturer's selling price to retailer	$17.00

Subsequently, a target profit (usually expressed as a percentage of total costs) is added on—hence the name "cost-plus."

A key issue in using the cost-plus method is the determination of the true unit cost. In many cases, some costs are allocated arbitrarily. For example, fixed costs (such as those shown in Table 9-7) will often include direct fixed costs plus some contribution to company overhead. Additionally, since the amount of fixed costs must be based on some estimate of the number of units sold, the company is (implicitly at least) assuming that demand will not vary dramatically with any change in the factory price. For example, assume that total annual advertising and selling expenses are expected to be $26 million. In order to determine the share of these costs to assign to each case sold, a manager must have some estimate of the expected sales volume, even though the total cost (and thus the final price) has yet to be determined. In our Table 9-7 example, the $6.50 allocation per unit must mean that sales are expected to be 4 million cases. That is,

$$\$6.50 = \frac{\$26 \text{ million}}{4 \text{ million cases}}$$

Marketers should recognize, however, that there are two alternative approaches to cost-plus pricing. The previous example illustrated the use of a full-cost approach. (That is, all costs are considered in setting the minimum price.) Alternatively, our detergent manufacturer could also consider a variable-cost pricing approach. As we discussed in Chapter 6, a firm operating in a price-elastic market at less than full capacity may be able to improve total profitability through pricing below the average unit cost. That is, as long as the company is pricing the product above variable costs, each unit sold makes some contribution to fixed costs. Accordingly, if sales stagnate below the expected volume (that is, the volume used to compute average fixed costs), the detergent maker will be better off to lower the manufacturer's price (assuming demand is elastic) below $17 as long as the price exceeds $6.80 per case (the variable cost). However, if managers assume that demand is inelastic, they are not likely to pursue this course of action.

INTERNATIONAL CONSIDERATIONS

The firm's competitive situation and cost structure must also be evaluated in the context of several special international considerations. Even if the firm has no overseas business, foreign firms are likely to be competing in the domestic market, and the ability to compete with foreign-based firms on price is often influenced by nation-specific cultural, political, and economic factors.

Differences in the *cost of funds* are especially important in pricing products that require a large financial investment in plant and equipment such as new automobile models or new semiconductor products. In such cases, companies must price their products to recover the interest on borrowed funds. But these costs have been much lower in Japan, for example, than in the United States because the national savings rate (which is ultimately the main source of loaned funds) is much higher in Japan. In 1988, the after-tax cost of funds was 6 percent in the United States versus 1.5 percent in Japan. The result is that U.S. firms must set higher prices to get the same profit return as their Japanese competitors.[12]

Of course, tariffs and other trade barriers can have a direct effect on price competitiveness. Japan levies a 27 percent tariff on leather shoes. But the tariff jumps to 60 percent once total imports reach 3 million pair in a given year. By contrast, the United States (which imports 900 million pair of shoes per year) has an average shoe tariff of 9 percent.[13] Consequently, price competition is much more extensive in the United States in this category.

Finally, *currency exchange rates* must be considered in pricing decisions. Because the exchange rates for currency among nations are subject to fluctuations because of market forces, price flexibility is critical. For example, a Waterford crystal wine decanter sold in the United States in 1985 for $150 which brought the Irish company 148 Irish pounds at the then-current exchange rate. By 1986, $150 was worth only 106 Irish pounds due to the declining value of the dollar. The choice for Waterford was either to raise U.S. prices or accept a large profit squeeze.[14]

TYPES OF PRICING PROGRAMS

Managers can select a pricing program once they have established the pricing objective and the elasticity of demand and once they have assessed their competitive cost and the multinational situation. Essentially, there are three basic types of programs for pricing individual products: penetration, parity, and premium. (Later in this chapter we will give example programs for product-line pricing.)

Penetration Pricing

A pricing program designed to use low price as the major basis for stimulating demand is a penetration pricing program. When using these programs, firms are

---

[12]Christopher Farrell, "Why Junk in the First Place? Skimpy Savings," *Business Week,* Sept. 11, 1989, p. 92.

[13]Rick Reiff, "Party Crusher," *Forbes,* June 12, 1989, pp. 128–129.

[14]Richard Stern, "Dangerous Fun and Games in the Foreign Exchange Market," *Forbes,* Aug. 22, 1988, pp. 69–70.

TABLE 9-8 CONDITIONS FAVORING A PENETRATION PRICING PROGRAM

1. Market demand is elastic.
2. Company demand is elastic and competitors cannot match our price because of cost disadvantages.
3. The firm also sells higher margin complementary products.
4. A large number of strong potential competitors exist.
5. Extensive economies of scale exist so that the variable-cost approach can be used to set the minimum price.
6. The pricing objective is to accomplish either of the following:
   - Build primary demand
   - Acquire new customers by undercutting competition

attempting to increase their product's degree of penetration in the market either by stimulating primary demand or by increasing market share. Accordingly, penetration pricing is generally applicable when price is being used to stimulate primary demand or to acquire new customers on price.

The success of a penetration pricing program requires that either market demand or company demand must be elastic. If market demand is elastic, then primary demand is elastic, and therefore, primary demand should be stimulated by the lower price. Even if competitors match the lower price, market demand should grow so that all firms are better off. If economies of scale exist or if the product has many complements, the benefits of the increased volume are even greater.

If market demand is inelastic, then penetration pricing can make sense only if company demand is elastic (so buyers will change suppliers on the basis of price) and if competitors cannot or will not match the lower price. The failure of competitors to match the lower price could reflect a lack of competitiveness on costs or a willingness to concede market share (at least for a while) in exchange for higher profits or because the low price appeals to a minor segment of the market. Consider, for instance, the case of Emerson Radio Corporation.

> Emerson has effectively competed in the electronics industry with its televisions, VCRs, radios, and stereos by pricing its line about 10% below Sony and Panasonic. The Emerson brand has retained a high degree of consumer recognition in spite of the fact that it is no longer heavily advertised. More importantly, by designing its products to achieve a cost that will facilitate penetration pricing and contracting out its manufacturing to low cost foreign sources to assure that cost targets are met, Emerson has been able to maintain this price differential.[15]

Table 9-8 summarizes the conditions favoring a penetration pricing program. Generally, these conditions will reflect the kinds of industry situations we discussed in Chapter 4 in the section on competitive intensity. Illustrative of many such markets is the situation in the semiconductor industry.

> Manufacturers of microchips used for computer memories face a constant emphasis on penetration pricing, especially from Japanese competitors. For example, during the mid-1980s, prices for E-PROM chips dropped from $17 to $4.

[15]Laura Walbert, "Copycat," *Forbes*, May 18, 1987, p. 92.

TABLE 9-9 CONDITIONS FAVORING A PARITY PRICING PROGRAM

1. Market demand is inelastic and company demand is elastic.
2. The firm has no cost advantages over competitors.
3. There are no expected gains from economies of scale so that the price floor is based on fully allocated costs.
4. The pricing objective is to meet the competition.

E-PROM's (erasable, programmable, read-only memories) are a type of computer chip used to store software programs. Part of the reason for penetration pricing is that tremendous economies of scale and experience curve effects exist in this industry. Additionally, both company and market demand are elastic: It's very difficult to differentiate chips made by different firms, and the products that use chips face elastic demand curves. Indeed, leading Japanese chipmakers are also vertically integrated, using their own chips in producing other computer-based products.[16]

Parity Pricing

Parity pricing means setting a price at or near competitive levels and not "rocking the boat." In effect, parity pricing programs attempt to downplay the role of price so that other marketing programs are primarily responsible for implementing the marketing strategy.

Frequently, this approach will be selected when company demand is elastic, industry demand is inelastic, and most competitors are willing and able to match any price cut. In such situations, managers should avoid penetration pricing because any price cuts will be offset by competitive retaliation (precluding any market share gains). The resulting lower industry prices will not yield a significant gain in industry sales, and so total revenues and profit margins will decline. Table 9-9 summarizes the conditions that generally favor a parity pricing program.

It should be noted that parity pricing is highly compatible with the practice of cost-plus pricing, especially when average costs are based on the full-cost approach. In many industries, cost structures will be very similar for the various competitors, especially when similar labor contracts, raw materials, production technologies, and distribution channels are used. In such situations, firms who perceive that market demand is inelastic and that competitors' costs are comparable are hardly likely to anticipate major volume gains from penetration pricing because they expect competitors to retaliate. Thus, the potential gains of any economies of scale would go unrealized, meaning that a variable-cost price floor is impractical.

As long as these demand and cost conditions remain, parity pricing remains a practical policy. However, these conditions may change over time resulting in a shift to intensive competition.

[16]Bro Uttal, "Who Will Survive the Microchip Shakeout?" *Fortune,* Jan. 6, 1986, pp. 82–85.

TABLE 9-10   CONDITIONS FAVORING A PREMIUM PRICING PROGRAM

1. Company demand is inelastic.
2. The firm has no excess capacity.
3. There are very strong barriers to entry.
4. Gains from economies of scale are relatively minor so that
   the full-cost method is used to determine the minimum price.
5. The pricing objective is to attract new customers on quality.

Parity pricing was the dominant pricing method in the passenger airline industry for many years because fares were regulated and because costs were comparable across competitors. Following the deregulation of airline fares in the early 1980s, new competitors with nonunionized work forces entered the market with discounted fares, especially on high-volume routes. Because company demand is elastic in this industry, the newcomers (such as New York Air and People Express) rapidly gained market share. Ultimately, however, the older, established airlines were able to bring costs in line with the new competitors. For example, United Airlines established two-tier wage scales that paid new workers less than those previously hired. At United, this policy was expected to lower average pilot costs by 30 percent. Meanwhile, the costs of the discount air carriers began to rise as their work forces got older and they bought costly new aircraft. Operating costs at the very aggressive East Coast carrier People Express rose 9.6 percent in one year. Soon the largest airlines began slashing prices to match or undercut the newcomers' prices. As price parity was re-established, non-price attributes (such as reliability, flight frequency, and amenities such as in-flight meals) once again became the focal point of competition.[17]

Premium Pricing

Premium pricing involves setting a price above competitive levels. (In the case of a new-product form or class where there are no direct competitors, premium pricing involves setting a price at a level that is high relative to competing product forms.) This approach will be successful if a firm is able to differentiate its product in terms of higher quality, superior features, or special services, thereby establishing an inelastic company-demand curve—at least within one or more target segments. Firms which are successful in implementing this approach will generate higher contribution margins and, at the same time, insulate themselves from price competition. However, even if this effort is initially successful, managers should continue to monitor the marketplace to determine whether a differential advantage is being maintained and whether the importance of price (relative to quality or special services) remains unchanged in the target segments. Table 9-10 summarizes the conditions that usually favor a premium pricing program.

Importantly, premium pricing can be implemented even in markets that would

[17]John A. Byrne, "Donald Burr May Be Ready to Take to the Skies Again," *Business Week,* Jan. 16, 1989, pp. 74–75.

appear to be very price-driven if special services can be added that provide demonstrated added value.

> Consolidated Freightways Inc., one of the nation's largest trucking companies has successfully charged premium rates for its trucking services even in a deregulated environment that has driven industry prices downward. Consolidated specializes in less-than-truckload shipments and has been a technological leader with its sophisticated computer systems. Such technology allows Consolidated's terminal managers to know three days in advance how much freight is coming in and allows customers to closely monitor each shipment from pickup to delivery.[18]

PRICING PROGRAMS FOR A LINE OF SUBSTITUTES

When a firm markets a line of products which essentially serve the same needs, an increase (decrease) in price for one member of the line will result in an increase (decrease) in demand for the other products in the line. In such cases the *cross-elasticity of demand is said to be positive.* Basically, there are two kinds of situations in which positive cross-elasticities can exist.

In some situations, the various products serve different segments that are clearly demarcated in terms of major differences in the product's function or benefits. In such cases, the primary pricing objective is to distinguish the product from the rest of the line and focus on competing within that segment. Generally, this will result in major price differentials within the product line and differences in brand name or distribution to match. Thus, Marriott prices its full-service hotels at $80 to $120 per night and its Fairfield Inns (with smaller rooms and fewer amenities) at $35 per night or less.[19] Entrepreneur Donald Hoffman pursues a similar program in his swing-set business.

> Donald Hoffman, a former Sears merchandising manager bought the Creative Playthings division of CBS and used the brand name on a new line of well-finished swing sets that sell for $799 to $999 in specialty stores. Hoffman also offers a Swing Design line (priced at $500 to $549 and made of thinner wood) through mass merchandisers, and an Original Jungle Gym line (which is totally unfinished and unassembled) at $200 to $399 through home-improvement stores.[20]

Alternatively, in some product lines, the various members may be much more similar, differing from one another on a single dimension. A typical L. L. Bean catalog, for example, offers three "grades" of men's chino pants, and a line of rider mowers may vary primarily in terms of horsepower. In such cases, a primary objective of pricing is usually to encourage demand for the higher priced product. Consider, for example, the successful strategy of Amoco.

> Chicago-based Amoco is one of the most profitable of the major oil companies because of its success in marketing its 93-octane Amoco Ultimate and it 89-octane Amoco Sil-

---

[18]Marc Beauchamp, "Skillful Driving," *Forbes,* Aug. 22, 1988 p. 98.
[19]Jeffrey Trachtenberg, "When Cheap Gets Chic," *Forbes,* June 13, 1988, pp. 108–109.
[20]"Donald Hoffman: A Swing Set for Every Pocketbook," *Business Week,* Aug. 8, 1988, p. 73.

ver gasolines. Compared to 87-octane Amoco regular these higher octane lines cost only two to five cents per gallon more to produce but are priced five to twenty cents more per gallon.[21]

Because of this difference in pricing objectives, managers need to have some understanding of the impact that variations in price differentials will have on demand. In developing this understanding two key psychological concepts must be considered: The concept of anchoring and the concept of subjective price scales.

Anchoring is the effect that a price stimulus has on the reference points that buyers use to assess prices. Specifically, buyers evaluate a price in the context of the entire range of prices with which they are confronted. Thus, adding a product at a new price at either the high or low ends of a market will change the standards by which customers evaluate each item in a line. For example, if a catalog retailer offers a line of men's chino pants at prices of $20, $28, and $36, the addition of a new pant priced at $45 will raise the price standard by which other pants are judged: The perceived quality of the lowest priced pants will be somewhat diminished and some customers will trade up to the $36 pant as well as to the new pant. Similarly, the introduction of a new item at the low end will enhance the quality image of the products that formerly were at the low end of the line.[22]

Subjective price scales are the psychological scales on which buyers code price information. Because this scale resembles a logarithmic scale rather than a natural arithmetic scale, equal price differentials are not perceived as being equal. Rather, price differentials should reflect *relative* rather than absolute differences among prices. For example, in our earlier example, the $28 pant is priced 40 percent above the $20 pant, but the $36 pant is priced only 28 percent above the $28 pant. Research on price perceptions suggests that, assuming the difference in quality between the top- and middle-priced pants is *equal* to the difference in quality between the low- and middle-priced pants, the higher priced pant should also be priced at a 40 percent differential, yielding a price of $39.20.[23]

PRICING PROGRAMS FOR A SET OF COMPLEMENTS

As we indicated in Chapter 6, complementary products are those products (or services) that experience a sales increase when related products experience a price decrease. Thus, as prices are reduced on compact disc players, not only do compact disc player sales grow but sales of discs (a complement to disc players) grow as well. In such cases, there is a negative cross-elasticity between the products.

Analyzing the effect that a price change on one product has on the sales of complementary products can often be difficult. However, managers can attempt

---

[21]James Cook, "First-Rate Company," *Forbes*, May 1, 1989, p. 84.

[22]Nagle, op. cit., p. 187.

[23]Kent B. Monroe and Albert Della Bitta, "Models for Pricing Decisions," *Journal of Marketing Research*, August 1978, pp. 413–428.

TABLE 9-11   CHARACTERISTICS OF A GOOD PRICE LEADER

1. The product is widely used by individual buyers in the target market.
2. The product's prevailing market price is well-known.
3. The product has a high degree of price-elasticity.
4. The product has many complements which enhance the value of the leader or which are convenient to purchase when buying the leader.
5. The product has few or no substitutes.
6. The product is not usually bought in large quantities and stored.

Source: Adapted from J. Barry Mason and Hazel F. Ezell, *Marketing: Principles and Strategy,* Business Publications, Plano, Texas, 1987, p. 392.

to take advantage of complementary relationships through either of two special product-line pricing programs: leader pricing or price bundling.

Leader Pricing   If the demand for a product is elastic and if that product has a number of complements either that enhance its value or that can be purchased more conveniently by buying from the same source, that product may then be used as a leader. Leader pricing simply involves setting a penetration price on the leader and promoting the special price. The expectation is that sales of complements to new customers will increase sufficiently to more than offset the reduced profit on the leader.

Table 9-11 lists the major characteristics that make for a good leader product. Note that in selecting a leader, managers are generally advised to avoid products which customers are likely to stock during the special prices or where strong substitution effects will lead to a simple shift in sales from high-margin to low-margin products.

Price Bundling   Price bundling is the practice of marketing two or more products or services together for a special price.[24] Technically, most firms employ mixed price bundling: Buyers are given the choice of buying two products in a package or buying the products individually. Buyers who place a low value on one of the two products will avoid the bundle. However, the economic incentive of a lower price on one item will lead to additional sales of both products to some buyers who otherwise would buy only one. When complementary relationships are very strong, the effects of the special price are even greater.

Mixed price bundling can be accomplished through either of two approaches. In the *mixed leader* form, the price of a lead product is discounted on the condition that a second product be purchased. In *mixed joint* bundling, two or more products or services are offered for a single "package" price. For example, assume a bank offers a VISA credit card at an annual fee of $15 and a safe deposit box for $25 per year. A mixed leader bundling option would be to discount the VISA to $5 per year on the condition that a customer also rented a safe deposit

[24]This section draws heavily on Joseph Guiltinan, "The Price Bundling of Services: A Normative Framework," *Journal of Marketing,* April 1987, pp. 74–85.

box at the regular price. The comparable mixed joint bundling option would be "a VISA card and safe deposit box for $30 per year."

Both forms of bundling could be used to achieve the objective of expanding the range of products bought by existing customers. For our bank, the mixed leader option would then make sense if we have a large VISA base and a small safe deposit box base: The discounted VISA serves as an incentive for buying the safe deposit box. The mixed joint option would be more useful if our customers tend to buy either one or the other product. Safe deposit box holders would then have an incentive to buy a VISA and vice versa.

If bundling is to be used to attract new customers, both approaches are feasible. In making a choice between mixed leader and mixed joint bundling, managers should consider the demand-elasticity and complementarity characteristics listed in Table 9-12. In general, the characteristics leading to successful mixed leader bundling are similar to the characteristics leading to successful leader pricing policies. However, mixed joint bundling may be used when there is no natural sales-volume leader and when two or more products or services have a mutually reinforcing complementarity. Illustrative of such situations are home entertainment centers (packaging electronic audio and video products into a total system) or vacation packages (incorporating airline, car rental, and hotel arrangements).

ADDITIONAL PRICING CONSIDERATIONS

Price Elements of Other Marketing Programs

As we have frequently suggested in this book, the various marketing programs are usually interrelated. In the case of price, these interrelationships will often be very strong. This chapter has focused on the basic list-price strategy. In subse-

---

TABLE 9-12   CHARACTERISTICS OF SUCCESSFUL MIXED PRICE BUNDLING PROGRAMS

Mixed leader programs
1. Demand for the lead product should be price-elastic.
2. Complementarity is based on the leader being enhanced by the other product(s) or on convenience.
3. If the objective is to cross-sell complements to regular customers,
   - The leader is the lower margin product (so that the lost profit from the price reduction is minimized).
   - Sales volume for the leader exceeds that of other products.

Mixed joint programs
1. Demand for the total package is price-elastic.
2. Complementarity is bidirectional (each product in the bundle enhances the value of the others) or is based on convenience.
3. If the objective is to cross-sell complements to regular customers, the various products in the bundle are approximately equal in volume and in profit margins so that sales gains from regular purchasers of any product are about equal.

---

quent chapters, other programs relating directly or indirectly to price will be addressed. These programs are summarized in Table 9-13.

Although these programs involve modifications of the list price, managers usually employ them to achieve different kinds of program objectives. Decisions regarding the use of these elements are usually made by different managers. Accordingly, they will be treated in subsequent chapters.

Legal Considerations

Managers involved in the pricing process have a considerable number of options in developing a pricing program. Legal limitations, however, do exist on the pricing process. Many of these limitations are industry-specific: Public utilities, banks, oil companies, distillers, and firms in other industries have, to varying degrees, had their pricing flexibility limited by state and federal regulations.

Some regulations are designed to preserve competition and apply to virtually all industries. Federal regulations limit pricing behavior in two ways based on the Sherman Antitrust Act, the Federal Trade Commission Act (Section 5), and the Robinson-Patman Act. Collusive behavior (agreements among competitors) is the most fundamental unlawful action in pricing. All the collusive practices listed in Table 9-14 are automatically illegal. Companies that distribute through retailers and wholesalers should be aware of the issue of price discrimination if different prices are charged to different resellers. Price discrimination is not automatically illegal. However, it will be illegal if these price differences fail to pass at least one of the criteria given in Table 9-15.

CONCLUSION

Management's recognition of the importance of price decisions has increased in recent years. Deregulation, greater international competition, changes in technology, and occasionally, inflation have all created changes in the patterns of price competition in one industry or another.

However, the process of developing a basic pricing program and arriving at a specific price remains a difficult one. As we have indicated in this chapter, there are no simple rules of thumb that managers can use to guarantee a "correct"

TABLE 9-13   PRICE ELEMENTS OF OTHER MARKETING PROGRAMS

Sales promotion programs	Sales and distribution programs
Coupons	Quantity discounts
Cents-off deals	Cash discounts
Promotion allowances	Credit or financing assistance
Rebates	Long-term contracts
	Negotiated pricing

TABLE 9-14   EXAMPLES OF COLLUSIVE PRICING PRACTICES

1. Agreement to reduce prices in order to injure competitors
2. Agreement on selling prices, bids, discounts, or credit policies
3. Agreement upon and enforcement of resale prices
4. Agreement to fix price differentials, discounts, or important terms of sale to designated groups of customers
5. Agreement to rotate bids among competitors

TABLE 9-15   SITUATIONS IN WHICH DIFFERENT PRICES MAY LEGALLY BE OFFERED TO DIFFERENT RESELLERS

1. The products sold are not of "like grade and quality" in technical content and features.
2. Price differences do not result in injury to competition.
3. Price differences can be justified by differences in the cost of serving the different customers.
4. Price differences are made in good faith to meet equally low prices of competitors in retaining customers and where the competitor's price is not discriminatory.
5. Discounts and allowances are offered on proportionately equal terms to all competing resellers.

price. However, by employing the process that this chapter has suggested, managers should be able to devise a pricing program that is consistent with the marketing strategy. While the pricing program may be modified by sales-promotion programs and by sales and distribution programs, the basic role that pricing will play in implementing a marketing strategy should be determined by (1) establishing clear pricing objectives, (2) analyzing price-elasticity, competition, and costs, (3) identifying international constraints and opportunities, and (4) taking into account legal constraints. Figure 9-3 summarizes these steps and provides an overview of the relationships among them. Some of these relationships can be observed by considering the pricing issues confronting Volkswagen AG.

Volkswagen AG: Pricing Programs for 1990[25]

Volkswagen AG is the number one carmaker in Europe and the fourth largest automobile manufacturer in the world. The first two Volkswagen cars were imported into the United States in 1949 and by 1970 Volkswagen's U.S. sales had reached 569,182 units (or 7 percent of the market). Volkswagen always had been an innovator in the industry, having developed the first popular minivan and a diesel engine that was much more efficient than those made by U.S. automakers. Volkswagen built a strong reputation for quality engineering. Rather than adapt-

[25]*Source:* "Mercedes, BMW Join Price War," *USA Today: International Edition,* Oct. 7, 1989, p. 20; "Volkswagen Changes Gears," *USA Today: International Edition,* Oct. 5, 1989, pp. 20–21; and Volkswagen AG.

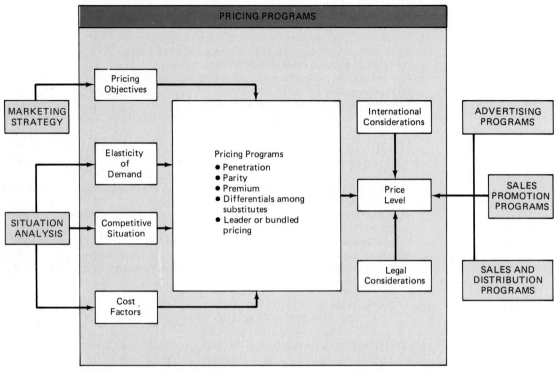

FIGURE 9-3   Relationship of pricing programs to the situation analysis, marketing strategy, and other marketing programs.

ing their cars to the current styles preferred by U.S. car buyers, the company kept changes to a minimum and offered few options.

By 1989, U.S. sales of Volkswagens were down to approximately 150,000 units (a 1.3 percent share of the U.S. market). Where VW had at one time been the largest seller of imported cars in the United States, they had dropped to seventh by the end of 1989. In addition, Volkswagen's Audi Division was the subject of a 1986 *60 Minutes* television report suggesting that Audi 5000s tended to accelerate suddenly without warning, resulting in several fatalities. Although safety experts later cleared Audi, annual sales of Audi models dropped by 69 percent (from more than 73,000 to 23,000) between 1985 and 1988.

In late 1989, VW announced its prices for U.S. 1990 models. Nearly all 1990 model prices reflected reductions from 1989 prices. In addition, the 1990 models included more standard equipment. For instance, the Golf and Jetta models included as standard equipment radios that formerly had cost an additional $265. Volkswagen's newest models, the Corrado sports car and the Passat sedan, were introduced with lower than expected prices. The company introduced the 1990 prices with an advertising campaign that featured the slogan "It's Time to Look at Volkswagen Again."

Volkswagen models	1989 base plus options price	1990 base price
Fox	$ 7225	$ 7225
Golf GL-20R	$ 9435	$ 8695*
Jetta GL-40R	$11,385	$10,295*
Cabriolet Deluxe	$16,335	$15,485†
Vanagon GL	$19,770	$16,490‡

*Includes $265 radio as standard equipment.
†Includes driver's side airbag and height adjustable seats worth $865 as standard equipment.
‡Includes $2700 worth of new standard equipment.

Audi models	1989 base plus options price	1990 base price
Audi 80	$20,885	$18,900*
Audi 90	$25,430	$23,990†
Audi 100	$29,520	$26,900‡
Audi 200	$35,875	$33,405§

*Includes driver's airbag, radio, and other equipment worth $1535.
†Includes new standard equipment worth $680.
‡Includes automatic transmission, driver's airbag, and other standard equipment worth $1770.
§Includes automatic transmission, leather interior, and other.

At the same time that Volkswagen was reducing prices, most other automobile manufacturers announced higher prices on their 1990 models. For instance Ford Motor Company car price increases averaged 4.9 percent. However, BMW cut prices on four high performance models and kept the same prices on all others. Mercedes-Benz's 1990 price increases averaged 2.2 percent.

1 What did Volkswagen's marketing strategy appear to be? Do you think this pricing program effectively supports that strategy?
2 What (apparently) were VW's views about elasticity of company demand?
3 Do you think that company demand is elastic? Explain.
4 Discuss the impact of international considerations on this market. How would Volkswagen's pricing process differ depending on where they elect to manufacture their products?
5 Contrast the product-line marketing strategy and pricing program for Audi with that for Volkswagen.

QUESTIONS AND SITUATIONS FOR DISCUSSION

1 A marketing manager for a consumer electronics company is considering a reduction in the price of one of its VCRs from $220 to $199.99. Currently, sales of this model are averaging 15,000 units per month.

    a If sales increase to 17,000 units per month, would this imply that demand is inelastic or elastic?

    b What other factors must the manager consider in determining whether the change in demand truly reflects the degree of price-elasticity?

2 Would the *market* demand for each of the following products be elastic or inelastic with respect to price? Why?

    a Open heart surgery

    b Airline tickets for a vacation

    c A yacht

    d Gasoline

3 For each of the following producers, do you think *company* demand would typically be elastic or inelastic with respect to price? Can there be exceptions to your answer for any of these producers?

    a A paint manufacturer

    b A hairstylist

    c A manufacturer of electric razors

4 In which of the following situations would historical ratios be most useful in estimating price-elasticity of company demand? Why?

    a Ticket prices for a professional baseball team

    b Setting prices on a new brand of beer

    c Pricing blank videocassette tapes

5 When Toyota priced its luxury *Lexus* model LS400 at $35,000 to $43,400, competitors stated they had "low-balled" the price given the advanced multivalve V-8 engine and other technical features. If this were true, what pricing strategy does Toyota appear to be following?

6 Under what conditions would you recommend that a manufacturer of a new flat-screen television set adopt a skimming price approach? A penetration approach?

7 In each of the following situations, what type of pricing program would typically be appropriate?

    a Market demand is inelastic and company demand is elastic.

    b A firm has a distinct quality advantage.

    c A firm is not producing at full capacity and company demand is elastic.

8 For each of the following situations, discuss the kinds of product-line issues that should be considered in making pricing decisions.

    a A publisher offers a book in both hardcover and softcover versions and must set a price on each one.

    b A bank introduces a NOW account (a checking account that pays interest) as an alternative to other checking accounts and must determine the level of service charges (if any) on this type of account.

    c A camera manufacturer also produces and sells the film for its cameras, and is considering a reduction in the price of its lowest priced model.

9 TWA offers a "get-away" vacation package that includes airfare, lodging, and side-trips to historical sites in Europe. IBM sells personal computers, software, and maintenance contracts in one package. What demand-oriented pricing practice are TWA and IBM practicing? What are the benefits to consumers? To the companies?

10 One approach to pricing for overseas markets is to establish the foreign list price by adding international customer costs and a gross margin to domestic manufacturing costs. The final cost to the customer includes administrative and R&D overhead costs, transportation, insurance, packaging, marketing, documentation, and customs charges as well as profit margins for distributor and manufacturer. What are the advantages and disadvantages of such a pricing approach?

SUGGESTED ADDITIONAL READINGS

Cavusgil, S. Tamer, "Unraveling the Mystery of Export Pricing," *Business Horizons,* May–June 1988, pp. 54–63.

Curry, David J., and Peter Riesz, "Prices and Price/Quality Relationships: A Longitudinal Analysis," *Journal of Marketing,* January 1988, pp. 36–51.

Dolan, Robert, and Abel Jeuland, "Experience Curves and Dynamic Demand Models: Implications for Optimal Pricing Strategies," *Journal of Marketing,* Winter 1981, pp. 52–73.

Farley, John U., James M. Hulbert, and David Weinstein, "Price Setting and Volume Planning by Two European Industrial Companies: A Study and Comparison of Decision Processes," *Journal of Marketing,* Winter 1980, pp. 46–54.

Guiltinan, Joseph, "The Price Bundling of Services: A Normative Framework," *Journal of Marketing,* April 1987, pp. 74–85.

Monroe, Kent B., and Andris Zoltners, "Pricing the Product Line during Periods of Scarcity," *Journal of Marketing,* Summer 1979, pp. 49–59.

Nagle, Thomas, "Pricing as Creative Marketing," *Business Horizons,* July–August 1983, pp. 14–19.

Tellis, Gerard J., "Beyond the Many Faces of Price: An Integration of Pricing Strategies," *Journal of Marketing,* October 1986, pp. 145–160.

Wilcox, James B., Roy D. Howell, Paul Kuzdrall, and Robert Britney, "Price Quantity Discounts: Some Implications for Buyers and Sellers," *Journal of Marketing,* July 1987, pp. 60–70.

Wind, Jerry, "Getting a Read on Market-Defined Value," *Journal of Pricing Management,* Winter 1990, pp. 5–14.

CHAPTER 10

ADVERTISING PROGRAMS

OVERVIEW

As seen in previous chapters, marketing management entails developing the appropriate products and services for the target markets at the right price and making them readily available. However, in order to persuade consumers to buy the product or service it is necessary to communicate a considerable amount of information about the company, its products, and the price structure and distribution to a variety of audiences. Included among these audiences are consumers, distributors, and the media. Effective communication is often a prerequisite for successful marketing and can offer a significant advantage that may distinguish the product or service from that of the competition.

The term *promotion* is often used to summarize the various activities that are associated with marketing communications. Promotion strategy has been described as a "controlled, integrated program of communication methods and materials designed to present an organization and its products to prospective customers; to communicate need-satisfying attributes of products to facilitate sales and thus contribute to long-run profit performance."[1] For management to develop an effective promotional strategy, it is necessary that they have an understanding of the buying process, competition, market segments, and product positioning.

Of the various promotion activities, advertising is clearly the most visible. Indeed, many consumers tend to equate advertising with the term *marketing*. This is partially explained by the large amount of dollars spent on advertising by both profit and not-for-profit organizations. For instance, in 1988, advertising expenditures exceeded 118 billion dollars.

[1]James F. Engel, Martin R. Warshaw, and Thomas L. Kennew, *Promotional Strategy*, Irwin, Homewood, Ill., 1987, p. 6.

TABLE 10-1 EFFECTS OF COMMUNICATIONS AT VARIOUS STAGES OF RESPONSE

Stages	Specific Effects
1. Cognitive stage	Exposure to message Message recall Awareness of product Knowledge of product attributes and uses
2. Affective stage	Willingness to seek more information Interest in product Favorable evaluation of product or brand attributes Intention to try or buy
3. Behavioral stage	Product trial Product purchase

Unfortunately, this preoccupation with advertising sometimes leads people to ascribe a level of effectiveness to advertising that may far exceed the level actually achieved. Probably the most important facets of advertising planning are the development of a clear understanding of what the impact of advertising might be on a specific product or service, and a clear statement of what the advertising objective should be. Put another way, advertising programs should be developed not only in the context of a clear marketing strategy but also in the context of the plans and expectations for the other communications-oriented programs: sales promotion and personal selling.

Generally, communications programs can achieve one or more of the types of effects listed in Table 10-1. Advertising and communications theorists have developed a number of frameworks for discussing the relationships among these effects.[2] However, a generally agreed-on grouping (as Table 10-1 suggests) classifies these effects into three levels:

1 Cognitive responses—those which indicate that the message has been received

2 Affective responses—those which indicate the development of attitudes (liking or disliking) regarding the product or company

3 Behavioral responses—actual actions taken by the members of the target audience

As we shall see, each type of communications program has unique characteristics, and managers must consider these characteristics as well as the types of effects they hope to achieve when designing each program. In this chapter, we will examine the first of these communications programs. In subsequent chapters, sales promotion and personal selling will be discussed.

---

[2]For a discussion of these effects and the theoretical relationships among them, see Robert J. Lavidge and Gary A Steiner, "A Model for Predictive Measurements of Advertising Effectiveness," *Journal of Marketing*, October 1961, pp. 59–62.

Advertising consists of paid messages designed to inform or persuade buyers or users about a product, service, belief, or action. The purpose of this chapter is to present some concepts and procedures that managers can use in developing (or in coordinating the development of) advertising programs (also called advertising campaigns) in order to implement the marketing strategy. In particular, we will examine (1) the process of setting advertising objectives, (2) procedures for developing advertising budgets, (3) the important considerations involved in devising a message and a media plan, and (4) various approaches for evaluating the effectiveness of a program.

It is important to note that the process of managing the advertising program can be exceedingly complex because of the number of individuals that may be involved. Much of the work of advertising is performed by outside organizations (such as advertising agencies). In addition, different kinds of managers are responsible for advertising programs in different firms. Accordingly, we will begin our discussion by examining the kinds of decisions involved in advertising programs and the ways of organizing advertising decision making.

ADVERTISING PROGRAMS: DECISIONS AND ORGANIZATION

Decisions regarding the advertising message (what is to be said and how to say it) and the media (where the message is to be presented and how many times) are fundamental to advertising programs. These decisions generally require highly specialized creative and technical skills and yet are made relatively infrequently. As a result, most organizations find that it is uneconomical to perform this work internally. Instead, these organizations often purchase the skills of independent specialists who perform tasks such as

- Developing creative copy ideas
- Artwork and photoengraving
- Testing copy for consumer reactions
- Buying media time
- Audience research on readership or viewing habits

Advertising agencies may also be used to perform several or all of these tasks.

Although outside specialists or agencies can provide the needed skills economically, certain problems can result from using them. First, these specialists may not have a great deal of knowledge about the product's market potential, about the buying process, or about the various segments that exist. Further, they may not have knowledge of the profitability of the product to be advertised or of the product objectives and marketing strategy. Even when an in-house advertising agency exists, the number of products being advertised is usually so large that technical specialists will have little knowledge of the situation analysis and marketing strategy for each product. Additionally, advertising programs must be coordinated closely with other marketing programs and with pricing, sales, and sales promotion, as well as manufacturing capabilities. If not closely coordinated with other activities this can drastically effect profit performance. For example,

Klondike chocolate-covered vanilla ice-cream bars initiated an expensive summer advertising campaign on national TV. The extensive advertising resulted in "overselling" the product. Even though Klondike's three manufacturing facilities produced 56,000 bars an hour, 21 hours a day, 7 days a week, the company ran out of product just as the combination of heavy advertising and hot weather were stimulating consumer demand.[3] Accordingly, message and media decisions can be made most effectively when advertising agencies, specialists, and in-house departments have some guidance on

• How the advertising program is expected to contribute to the marketing strategy and relate to other programs
• What level of advertising expenditures will be consistent with the firm's product mix allocation plan and with product profitability

This means that clearly specified advertising objectives are necessary to provide guidance on message and media decisions. These objectives should be developed by the managers who are responsible for developing and implementing the overall marketing strategy.

Responsibility for Advertising Programs

Organizations differ on the question of who should serve as the coordinator or liaison with the agency or with other advertising specialists. Because the primary purpose of this chapter is to provide insights and procedures for managing advertising programs (rather than for developing the creative and technical elements of advertisements), it is important to briefly identify the marketing positions and organizational approaches involved in advertising management.

The position of *advertising manager or advertising director* often exists in firms that are organized on a functional basis. In industrial firms, this individual may report to the sales manager, because advertising is often a small portion of the marketing effort and because its primary role is to support the sales function. Otherwise the advertising manager will typically report to a senior marketing manager.

The *product or brand manager* will be involved in advertising in firms that are organized on a product basis. When there are a large number of products in a firm, these managers tend to take on more of the responsibility for market analysis, short-run planning, and coordination with the other functions (such as sales and marketing research).

Although advertising managers and product managers work most closely with outside agencies and specialists, their role in advertising management is often shared with the chief marketing executive or the divisional manager. There are two reasons why top management may become involved in these programs rather than delegate all responsibility to middle managers. First, advertising managers are staff personnel. Although they have expertise in selecting the advertising message and media, they are not directly responsible for sales or profits. Second,

---

[3]Kerry Hannon, "Meltdown," *Forbes,* Aug. 7, 1989, pp. 130–131.

FIGURE 10-1   Basic elements of an advertising
program.

product or brand managers usually have sales or profit responsibility but are often
seeking increases in advertising budgets—especially if they are responsible for
sales volume but not profitability. However, this will vary company by company.
For instance, Procter and Gamble has 90 brands and relationships with 16 advertising agencies. In 1987 P&G eliminated the position of ad manager for most
of its brands in an attempt to more effectively coordinate activities of brands that
were in the same product category. In 1989, they restored the ad manager position because they discovered that those brands that kept their ad managers out-
performed those that didn't. At P&G, brand managers usually maintain close contact with the ad agencies whereas ad managers help set overall product-line
strategy and approve all advertising and promotions.[4]

Consequently, in order to control the allocation of resources in accordance
with product objectives, top management may make the major decisions regarding advertising expenditures, creative policy, or media plans (with the technical
support of staff advertising specialists).[5]

Elements of the Advertising Program

As we suggested in the preceding section, message development and media
scheduling are not the only elements involved in advertising programs. In fact, as
Figure 10-1 indicates, there are a number of decisions to be made in managing
the advertising program. Although advertising agencies and other specialists are

[4]Laurie Freeman, "P&G Keen Again on Ad Managers," *Advertising Age,* Sept. 25, 1989, p. 6.
[5]Victor Buell, "The Changing Role of the Product Manager," *Journal of Marketing,* July 1975, pp.
3–11.

primarily involved in message design and media decisions, marketing managers in the firm doing the advertising must be somewhat involved in every step of the process.

Given the situation analysis and marketing strategy, these company managers are responsible for defining the objectives of the advertising program and for determining the budget. Subsequently, the advertising agency or outside specialists can develop message and media decisions that are consistent with the objectives and the budget. Additionally, managers should be responsible for examining the proposed message and media plan for consistency with the marketing strategy and the product objectives. Finally, managers should evaluate the program to see if objectives are being attained and to determine whether any elements of the program should be revised.

ADVERTISING OBJECTIVES

There are two basic reasons for establishing objectives for advertising programs. First, as suggested already, the advertising objectives can provide guidance for the development of message and media decisions. Second, advertising objectives serve as standards for evaluating the performance of the advertising program. Unless managers have defined what the advertising effort is designed to achieve, there will be no fair way of evaluating the results.

Of course, over the long run, firms would not spend money on advertising unless they expected that their expenditures would help to achieve sales, market-share, and profitability objectives. But sales and profits are generally inappropriate objectives for advertising programs for several reasons. First, sales generally respond rather slowly to advertising. This is especially true for products that are infrequently purchased. But it is also true for frequently purchased products, because most advertisements must be seen more than once before the message is received and acted on. Second, changes in sales and market share are often influenced by environmental factors and competitive actions. An advertising message may be very effective in communicating a particular product benefit about an automobile, but if interest rates rise or if unemployment rises, industry sales and company sales may decline in spite of the advertising effort. Finally, advertising is only one of the marketing programs that may influence sales. Price, sales promotions, and other programs can also influence sales, and it is often difficult to determine the relative impact of different programs on sales changes.

Additionally, sales and market-share objectives provide very little direction for developing messages and selecting media. Indeed, as we suggested at the outset of this chapter, motivating an action (such as purchase) is only one of the possible types of effects of communications programs.

What advertising can do, however, is to help implement the marketing strategy for a product or service. That is, managers can establish other types of advertising objectives which can guide the selection of messages and media, permit program performance to be evaluated, and make a specific contribution to achieving the marketing strategy.

Types of Advertising Objectives

Although no single typology of advertising objectives is considered to be a "standard" set, we can identify seven basic types of advertising objectives.[6]

However, it is possible to achieve more than one objective during a given campaign, although this can be very difficult and costly. Moreover, each objective is generally most useful for implementing a particular type of marketing strategy. For instance, for the same product, there may be different advertising objectives for different customer groups. Obtaining trial of a particular product or brand may be the objective for nonusers and/or new entrants into the market. However, for present users, the objective may be to obtain preference or loyalty for the product or brand. In addition, the promotion objective might be to stimulate demand for the entire product class, for example, electric shavers, and for a particular brand, for example, Braun electric shavers. Consequently, if more than one objective is employed, it is important to make sure that the various objectives are compatible with the marketing strategy.

The basic types of objectives include

1 Awareness
2 Reminder to use
3 Changing attitudes about the use of the product form
4 Changing perceptions about the importance of brand attributes
5 Changing beliefs about brands
6 Attitude reinforcement
7 Corporate and product-line image building

Awareness Very frequently the primary advertising objective is simply to generate or increase recognition of a brand name, a product concept, or information regarding where or how to buy a product. This can be an important objective in several different situations.

First, when a brand enters the market it will often be difficult for buyers to develop an attitude if the brand and its basic product concept are not known. That is, awareness of the product and comprehension of its basic concept must exist before favorable attitudes toward the brand can be developed.

Second, managers should also employ awareness objectives when customers need information about how to buy or how to get more information about a product. Managers of consumer products with highly selective distribution systems may need to emphasize this objective, especially if competing brands have more intensive distribution. Advertisements for Curtis-Mathes televisions, John Deere lawn mowers, and many other brands usually identify local dealers at the end of the commercials. Similarly, industrial marketers—especially those with small sales forces—may include inquiry slips or toll-free phone numbers in their adver-

---

[6]For additional background on these objectives, see Harper Boyd, Michael Ray, and Edward C. Strong, "An Attitudinal Framework for Advertising Strategy," *Journal of Marketing*, April 1972, pp. 27–33; and Kenneth A. Longman, *Advertising*, Harcourt, Brace, Jovanovich, New York, 1974.

tisements to enable interested potential customers to obtain more detailed information, thus providing potential prospects for the sales force.

Finally, awareness and brand-name recognition are usually essential objectives in marketing low perceived-risk products when little deliberation or search is involved. In these situations, buyers will make brand selections largely on the basis of brand familiarity. That is, the brands that are most widely recognized will tend to have the largest market shares.

Reminder to Use   For discretionary items with irregular usage patterns, an appropriate marketing strategy may be to stimulate primary demand by increasing the rate of usage. The primary role of advertising in implementing this strategy is to remind buyers to use the product or to restock the product. That is, purchases may decline because the product is highly discretionary and consumers have no remaining stock to remind them to use it. For example, H. J. Heinz's Ore-Ida division designed an advertising program to build frequency of usage for french fries by showing that the product fits in with a fast-moving, contemporary everyday family lifestyle. Research had indicated that even though the quality of Ore-Ida was good, consumers didn't see french fries as a regular part of their contemporary lifestyle.[7]

Changing Attitudes about the Use of the Product Form   This objective is designed to support primary-demand strategies for attracting new users or for increasing the number of uses. Advertising programs to implement these strategies usually take one of two basic forms. First, advertising campaigns may demonstrate new ways to use the product or new usage occasions. Thus, Arm & Hammer has used advertisements showing the use of baking soda to eliminate refrigerator odors, and A-1 Steak Sauce has been promoted as an alternative to ketchup for use on hamburgers. Second, some advertising campaigns have been designed to overcome negative perceptions about product categories.

Oldsmobile, realizing that its customer base was getting smaller and older, decided to directly attack Oldsmobile's fuddy-duddy image with its "New Generation" advertising campaign. The "New Generation" ads featured celebrities of the 1950s and 1960s and their children in a series of playful vignettes with Oldsmobile cars. Surveys indicated positive responses to the campaign among consumers aged 35 to 44 which was the target audience Olds desired. Although there was not a measurable sales increase after the first year, Oldsmobile marketing executives contend that this is because it takes about 3 years for an advertising theme to work its way down to sales. Nevertheless, Cutlass Supreme buyers who were 50 years old when the car was introduced in 1987 now average 45

[7]Warren Berger, "The Big Freeze at Heinz," *Adweek's Marketing Week,* Aug. 21, 1989, pp. 20–25.

years old. In addition, dealers report more younger people coming into the showrooms.[8]

Changing Perceptions about the Importance of Brand Attributes An effective way of acquiring new customers through differentiated positioning is to advertise a "unique selling proposition." As suggested earlier, for an attribute to be determinant in the buyer's choice process, the attribute must be important and buyers must perceive that alternatives differ in the degree to which they possess the attribute. Therefore, if a brand or supplier has a unique attribute, advertising may be used to stress the importance of the attribute in order to make it determinant. For example, Kentucky Fried Chicken has attempted to distinguish its product from the chicken items offered by fast-food hamburger restaurants by stressing the fact that, unlike "those hamburger places," KFC concentrates strictly on chicken.

Changing Beliefs about Brands If an attribute (or benefit) is already considered important, buyers will examine the degree to which each alternative product or brand possesses that attribute or provides that benefit. Accordingly, the advertising objective may be to improve buyers' ratings of a brand on important attributes or to change the relative ratings of competing brands on the attribute. Because the attribute is not unique to a brand, advertising that is designed to demonstrate this relative superiority would be supporting a marketing strategy of head-to-head competition. For example, Con Agra introduced its *Healthy Choice* dinners and entrees illustrating the superiority of its products by attacking the nutritional merits of competitors' frozen dinners. In a $15 million advertising campaign the company showed that *Healthy Choice* was healthier in terms of sodium, fat, and cholesterol. Sales of *Healthy Choice* were $150 million in the first year with more than 55 percent of initial purchasers buying the product again. In addition, on average consumers purchase three boxes of *Healthy Choice* compared to 1.5 boxes of most frozen meals.[9]

Attitude Reinforcement Brands or suppliers with a strong market position and with no major competitive weaknesses are more likely to be concerned with customer-retention strategies. By reassuring customers that the brand or supplier continues to offer the greatest level of satisfaction on the most important benefits, advertising can reinforce attitudes and thus maintain brand preferences and "loyalty." Accordingly, to achieve this kind of objective, Heinz displays the continued high level of thickness and quality of its ketchup by advertising the product's slow-pouring quality, and Budweiser reminds customers of its use of "beechwood aging" to maintain high quality.

---

[8]Joanne Lipman, "New Olds Ad Campaign Updates the Old," *The Wall Street Journal,* Aug. 23, 1989, p. 5; Raymond Serafin, "Olds Keeps the Faith," *Advertising Age,* Aug. 25, 1989, p. 50; and Joseph B. White, "New Ads Give a Boost to the Olds Image but Don't Help the Old Sales Woes Much," *The Wall Street Journal,* June 19, 1989, p. B-1.

[9]Steve Weiner, "How Josie's Chili Won the Day," *Forbes,* Feb. 5, 1990, pp. 57, 60, 62, 63.

Corporate and Product-Line Image Building   Frequently, advertising is used to establish or change perceptions of organizations or broad product lines but without focusing on specific product attributes or benefits. General corporate advertising usually is designed to enhance a corporation's public image, ostensibly to make it more attractive to prospective stockholders. For example, Dow Chemical ran an extensive advertising campaign telling why Dow is a great place for young people to work and emphasizing the corporation's efforts to improve the quality of life. It is possible that such advertising may increase awareness about certain corporate attributes, but many experts question its actual effectiveness and value.[10] However, Metropolitan Life Insurance's research suggested that insurance companies were measured by their trademark images. Accordingly, they licensed *Peanuts* cartoon characters from their creator. Met Life's campaign is intended to position them as a nonthreatening insurance company with a human side, while at the same time improving the awareness factor that gets agents in the door of prospective customers.[11]

On the other hand, product-line image building is frequently very effective. This type of objective usually becomes important when a firm offers a line of related products that have a complex set of benefits. In automobiles, computers, most consumer electronics products, and many other categories, many products (each with distinct features and positioning strategies) share a common brand name and a common distribution system. Product-line image advertising is used to provide an umbrella image for the specific attributes and benefits of each item in the line. Thus, in the automobile business, General Motors' Pontiac automobiles have been marketed under the "We Build Excitement" image, while Chevrolets were linked together by "The Heartbeat of America" theme. The Chevrolet program was designed to target the product line toward the middle of the market: Reasonably priced cars and trucks satisfying the "secret desires harbored in the Middle American heart."[12] Advertising designed to build product-line perceptions will then be augmented by advertising designed to build brand beliefs or attribute importance for individual products and models within the line.

Stating the Objective

Once management has determined the most appropriate type of advertising objective, a specific and measurable statement of objectives should be made. Additionally, the target audience should be clearly defined in this statement.

For example, an awareness objective might be stated as follows: "Increase the percentage of males aged 25 to 44 who are aware of our brand from 30 to 50 percent." By stating the objective in this manner, management is accomplishing two things. First, the target audience is identified, enabling managers to select appropriate media. Second, the objective is stated in specific terms (50 percent).

---

[10]Anne B. Fisher, "Spiffing Up the Corporate Image," *Fortune*, July 21, 1986, pp. 68–70.
[11]Dan Koeppel, "What Have Snoopy and Gang Done for Met Life Lately?" *Adweek's Marketing Week*, Nov. 13, 1989, pp. 2–3.
[12]"Those Heartbeat Ads Are a Hit in the Heartland," *Business Week*, Feb. 23, 1987, p. 107.

This will enable management to evaluate the degree to which the communications objective is being achieved if measures of awareness are conducted during and after the advertising campaign.

THE BUDGETING PROCESS

Establishing the advertising budget is one of the more difficult tasks facing marketing managers. As we suggested in our discussion of productivity analysis (in Chapter 6), it is extremely difficult to predict the impact of a given level of advertising expenditures on sales for several reasons: The relationship between advertising and sales is not likely to be a direct, linear relationship; competitive actions or environmental factors may offset the effectiveness of advertising efforts; and advertising effects are sometimes offset by changes in price, selling effort, or other marketing programs. An additional problem is that advertising effects tend to be cumulative. That is, expenditures in one year will have some immediate impact on sales, but they will also have a longer term impact on sales in subsequent periods as seen in the case of Oldsmobile's campaign. Buyers who have been influenced to buy the product (or at least to become aware of it or develop favorable attitudes toward it) because of the first-year's advertising effort will often make purchases in subsequent years. A final difficulty revolves around the issue of efficiency. Increased advertising expenditures can never guarantee increased sales; that is, the additional money may be ineffectively spent because of a poor message design or inefficient media scheduling.

In spite of these difficulties, it is important to establish a tentative budget in order to provide some guidance for message designers and media planners. These tasks cost money, and it is essential to have some feeling for the resources that will be available before reasonable message and media alternatives can be identified. (Figure 10-2 explores the development of a tentative advertising budget.)

Although the specifics of the advertising budgeting process will vary among companies, managers can use a general approach that includes the following steps:

1 Establish a baseline budget.

2 Based on the advertising objectives, estimate the message design and media cost required.

3 If time and resources permit, run experiments to obtain a rough estimate of the impact of the proposed program.

4 Revise the budget (or objectives) as necessary on the basis of the costs of the tasks, the results of any experiments, and the costs and expected impact of other marketing programs.

In making these revisions, managers may find it useful to employ judgment-based models, as discussed in Chapter 6.

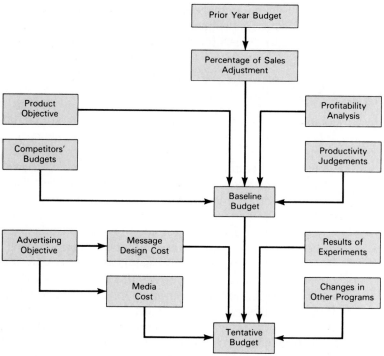

FIGURE 10-2   Developing a tentative advertising budget.

Establishing Baseline Budgets

In most organizations, the total advertising budget does not vary greatly from year to year, and so a possible baseline is to use the previous year's budget. More realistically, managers will adjust budgets each year because of a number of factors.

1 *Product objectives* (based on the product portfolio analysis) determine which products should receive increased, sustaining, or reduced support. Accordingly, managers may modify budgets to reflect any changes in product objectives, with problem children receiving increased amounts, for example, and dogs receiving declining amounts.

2 *Product profitability* should be a major consideration in budgeting. The greater the contribution margin, the smaller the increase in sales that will be needed to cover the costs of increased advertising budgets.

3 *Productivity judgments* (especially when combined with profitability analyses) can be useful in determining the effects of changes in budgets. As discussed in Chapter 6, managers may decide that the level of advertising needs to be increased just to maintain the market share at the current level. Many advertisers believe that it is necessary to keep their advertising budgets (or share of voice) at a consistent ratio of expenditures with the total advertising expenditure of the product category if they are to maintain their market share. This type of competitive parity approach would require the necessity to increase their "share of voice" to the same percentage level as the desired market share. Firms such as Procter and Gamble, McDonald's, and Wendy's have been reported to use such an approach.[13] This form of budgeting may be misleading for two reasons. First, it ignores the possibility that there may be limits to the market share that is attainable. For example, a brand with a 10 percent share could not reasonably be expected to increase its market share to 50 percent simply by spending 50 percent of the category's advertising dollars. Second, this approach to budgeting doesn't take into consideration the many other buying behavior factors influencing the brand's sales response function that we discussed in Chapter 6.

Message-Design and Media Costs

Given an advertising objective, a manager can estimate message-development costs (for production costs, technical fees, royalties to participants) and media costs (of print space, radio, or television time) fairly quickly. Generally, message-development costs will be a minor proportion of total cost, with media costs constituting the major component. As discussed in detail later in this chapter, media costs are influenced by the size of the target market, the size or length of the advertisement, the number of times the advertisement is presented, and the specific costs of each media vehicle.

Experimentation and Revisions

When feasible, the proposed advertising program should be tested in a limited market area to determine whether the advertising objectives are being achieved and to estimate the sales response. These tests can provide insights into whether historical advertising effects on sales are optimistic or pessimistic relative to the present program. But experiments usually indicate only the short-run effects of a program because the length of the experiment is usually limited. However, experiments can be particularly useful in determining the effect of alternative copy and media schedules. If different media or different numbers of advertisements are used in different markets, the value of each medium and of different levels of audience exposure to a message can be measured. These measures may enable managers to adjust budgets to obtain the most efficient media schedules.

Revisions may also be necessary because of the impact of other programs. To some degree advertising competes with sales, sales promotion, and product development for funds. Further, price changes will lead to changing contribution margins. Accordingly, changes in the budgets for other programs may force managers to modify the advertising budget to stay within the resources available for a product.

[13]M. L. King, "Wendy's New Management Cooks Up Plans for Growth and Diversification," *The Wall Street Journal*, Mar. 27, 1981, p. 34.

MESSAGE DESIGN

An increasing number of advertising researchers seem to believe that the creative component (the message design) of advertising is far more important than the rate or pattern of advertising expenditures.[14]

The advertising message includes two basic elements: the appeals (or copy claims) that represent the central idea of the message and the method of presentation (or execution style) that is used to present the copy claims. Although message design is primarily the responsibility of the advertising agency or of other creative specialists, the advertising director or product managers can provide significant input to see that the message design is appropriate for the marketing strategy and advertising objectives. In particular, information regarding the demographic and lifestyle characteristics of the target audience is useful in deciding what kinds of individuals might be portrayed in the advertisement. Product usage situations and usage problems can be used to establish a setting or context in which the advertisement takes place. Factors limiting the willingness to buy can be considered by message designers, and the advertisement can be structured so that the existence or significance of these factors can be reduced. In addition, a knowledge of buyer perceptions of competing alternatives and of objective differences among alternatives will be useful.

Requirements of an Effective Message

Information on the buying process can help the agency or specialists to deal with the three major requirements of an effective message: desirability, exclusiveness, and believability.[15] The use of desirability and exclusiveness criteria is simply a way of saying that a firm should try to emphasize those determinant attributes on which it has an advantage. If desirability is a problem, the usefulness of the product in solving a usage problem might be portrayed. Exclusiveness may be demonstrated through comparisons (direct or indirect) once the real and perceived product differences are known. Believability will become important in those situations where the product benefit or attribute is difficult to demonstrate or is highly subjective, or where it requires a major change in usage patterns. For example, Del Monte Foods scrapped a new shelf-stable yogurt, Little Lunch, after consumer research revealed that yogurt buyers refused to accept the idea that yogurt could be kept unrefrigerated. Early research indicated that the concept was viewed as desirable and unique, but the cost of achieving believability was finally judged too high after lengthy test marketing with various types of messages.[16]

[14]Joseph Eastlack and Ambar Rao, "Modeling Response to Advertising and Pricing Changes for V-8 Cocktail Vegetable Juice," *Marketing Science,* Summer 1986, pp. 245–259.

[15]Dik Warren Twedt, "How to Plan New Products, Improve Old Ones and Create Better Advertising," *Journal of Marketing,* January 1969, pp. 53–57.

[16]Sally Scanlon, "Calling the Shots More Closely," 1978 Sales and Marketing Plans (Sales and Marketing Management), 1979, p. 90.

Copy-Claim Alternatives

The copy claims (or basic appeals of the message) are the motivational arguments or descriptive statements contained in the message. These claims can be of three types:

- Claims that describe the *physical* attributes of the product
- Claims that describe the *functional* benefits that can be obtained from the product
- Claims that *characterize* the product in terms of the types of people who use it, the results of obtaining the functional benefits or moods

In choosing the type of copy claim to use for a given advertising program creative specialists should first of all be guided by the statement of the firm's advertising objective. That is, the advertising objective should clearly state the specific features that buyers are to be made aware of or the specific attributes or benefits on which perceptions are to be changed or reinforced. In addition, some advertising objectives may focus on exclusiveness, while others may emphasize the desirability (importance) of an attribute. Given the advertising objective, creative specialists can then select a copy approach that will support the desirability, exclusiveness, or believability (or any combination of these) of the attribute or benefit being featured. For instance, Compaq has set its worldwide objective as consistently ranking number two for business personal computers. Advertising's role in attaining the objective is to make Compaq's leadership believable. To accomplish this, Compaq has planned its ads around its fast growth.[17]

In developing the copy, creative specialists must also consider the type of brand concept involved. Products can be classified as relating to one of the following types of needs.[18]

1 *Functional needs.* Products which resolve consumption-related problems that are brought on by the individual's environment (lawn mowers, for example)

2 *Symbolic needs.* Products which fulfill internally generated needs, such as self-enhancement or ego identification (automobiles, for example)

3 *Experiential needs.* Products which provide sensory pleasure, variety, or other kinds of stimulation (such as food or entertainment)

Clearly, characterization becomes a more important element of the copy when symbolic or experiential needs are involved. In addition, the type of need is often a significant influence in selecting an execution style.

---

[17]Richard I. Kirkland, Jr., "Europe Goes Wild for Yankee PCs," *Fortune,* June 5, 1989, pp. 257–260; and Jennifer Lawrence, "Compaq Prepares for European Push," *Advertising Age,* June 12, 1989, p. 38.

[18]C. Whan Park, Bernard Jaworski, and Deborah MacInnis, "Strategic Brand Concept-Image Management," *Journal of Marketing,* October 1986, pp. 135–145.

Execution Style

The execution style is the specific method of presenting the copy claim that is used to provide an environment for enhancing the copy. Although the details of the selection of execution style are beyond the scope of this book, an array of options and their uses can be examined.[19]

Humor may be used to draw attention to the message. However, to be effective, the basis for the humor should be related to the product's benefits. Humor also appears to have negative effects when applied to "serious" products or problems, and it may obscure the basic message. Further, humorous ads tend to lose their effect more quickly than other types. Similarly, exaggeration attracts attention and increases the memorability of advertising content.

Symbolic associations may provide a means of dramatizing intangible attributes or benefits by associating the product or service with a certain type of individual (usually the case in automobile advertisements) or a tangible object. (Note the symbols of assurance used by insurance companies: sentries, shields, the rock of Gibraltar, and so forth.)

Functional benefits can be communicated in a variety of ways. *Testimonials* are employed to support the believability of benefits by using celebrities with some tie to the product category (in vocation or reputation) or with some special credibility with the target segment. *Product demonstrations* or recipes are used to show how a particular buyer problem can be solved to enhance desirability. *"Slice of life"* sequences portraying buyers in problem-solving situations are similar to demonstrations that provide a vehicle for showing product benefits. *Case histories* documenting the benefits of a product (such as flashlight batteries that burn all night) provide both credibility and a demonstration of product benefits.

If the copy claims focus on product attributes, *documentation* of the product's attributes (by presumably unbiased organizations) may be employed. More recently, *comparison advertising* formats (in which two or more brands are compared on one or more attributes) have enjoyed wider utilization as a means of demonstrating the uniqueness or believability of a product-attribute claim. For instance, Subaru uses test demonstrations against other cars such as Mercedes-Benz and Volvo. Subaru hopes to establish definitive differences of importance and value by running comparative advertising.[20]

As the preceding discussion has indicated, a great many options are available to creative specialists. However, they are more likely to select effective copy and execution styles if they understand the advertising objective and if they understand the buying process. Accordingly, it is important for managers to state these objectives and to provide these specialists with the insights gained in buyer analysis.

---

[19]An extended discussion is available in David W. Nylen, *Advertising: Planning, Implementation and Control,* South-Western, Cincinnati, 1975, pp. 386–398.
[20]"Subaru Takes Comparative Angle," *Advertising Age,* Nov. 27, 1989, p. 33.

MEDIA SCHEDULING

Media scheduling decisions are extremely important for two reasons. First, purchases of radio and television time and of newspaper and magazine space represent the largest element of cost in the advertising budget. Second, the success of an advertisement in achieving the advertising objectives largely depends upon how well each show or magazine reaches buyers in the target market segment.

Because the cost and the audience size and characteristics of each media alternative are generally known, managers can employ some quantitative tools in media scheduling. However, as we will demonstrate, managers must also employ judgment in media scheduling decisions because some of the attributes of media are not easily measured.

In this section, we will present the major steps that are involved in developing the media schedule. In particular, we examine each of the following kinds of decisions:

- Selecting the type of medium to use
- Selecting specific vehicles for consideration
- Determining the size, length, and position of an advertisement
- Determining the desired reach and frequency distribution of messages

After these decisions have been made, one or more media schedules can be developed. Managers should then examine the media schedule to determine if it will be adequate for achieving the objective and if revisions in the tentative budget will be needed.

As in the case of message design, advertising managers and product managers may not make each of the detailed decisions involved in this process. However, these managers should review and analyze those decisions to be sure that they are consistent with the type of advertising objective and that they will be appropriate for the target market and the message design. We provide some guidelines for making these reviews and evaluations in this section of the chapter.[21]

Selecting the Type of Medium

Each medium (TV, radio, newspaper, magazine) has its unique characteristics that may or may not be appropriate for the kind of message to be presented and for the kind of target segment to be reached. For instance, when using direct mail advertising, a firm usually relies on a mailing list containing the names of individuals with some common characteristic such as age (for example, senior citizens), occupation (student or doctor, for example), geographical area (such as suburban locations), or product ownership (such as homeowners). Because the audience is narrowed down, this tends to be an economical way of reaching specific target segments with complex messages. Alternatively, managers may use

---

[21]Dennis Gensch, "Media Factors: A Review Article," *Journal of Marketing Research,* May 1970, pp. 216–225; and Leo Bogart, "Mass Advertising: The Message, Not the Measure," *Harvard Business Review,* September–October 1976, pp. 107–116.

media such as billboards, posters, and advertising on mass-transit vehicles when short, clear messages are presented to a (typically) nonselect audience.

Selecting Possible Vehicles

A *vehicle* is a specific magazine, newspaper, or radio or television program. In selecting a specific set of vehicles, managers should understand each vehicle's ability to reach the target market segments. Rating services and special research provided by the vehicles or by advertising agencies provide information on the audience size and demographics for each vehicle. Additionally, some magazines provide separate editions for reaching specific demographic groups. For example, *Time* magazine provides separate editions containing special advertising for doctors, educators, business executives, and students.

Additionally, vehicles should be evaluated on their likely effectiveness for the specific product and message. For instance, the editorial climate of a respected vehicle (such as *Time* or *Newsweek*) may enhance the credibility of an appeal because the vehicle is perceived as trustworthy. Similarly, a vehicle that is recognized for its prestige or expertise on a given subject may be an excellent choice for certain products (for example, *Sports Illustrated* for athletic equipment). Or the technical ability to adequately deliver the message (because of its use of color, available page size, or amount of commercial clutter in the program) may influence the selection of a specific vehicle.

Media availability and conflicting national regulations vary dramatically around the world. For instance in certain countries commercial television and radio are not available, or are limited in use. Print media accounts for 100 percent of advertising expenditures in Oman and 97 percent in Norway.[22] In addition, there are conflicting national regulations which may include limits on the amount of time available from advertisements on television ranging from complete prohibition (Sweden) to 15 to 20 minutes a day in blocks of 3 to 5 minutes (West Germany). In some cases it may be necessary for companies to wait up to 18 months for allocation of airtime in those countries where the percentage of revenues that state monopoly systems can derive from advertising is limited (France and Italy). In addition, different nations have varying restrictions on comparative claims and gender stereotypes and many of these regulations may be standardized by the European Economic Community in the near future.

By examining audience characteristics and effectiveness, managers can reduce the number of potential vehicles to a more manageable number for subsequent analyses. In addition, the cost per insertion in various media can be obtained from direct contact with media personnel, from media buying specialists (who are often able to obtain discounts on these rates), and from Standard Rate and Data Service publications.

Cost will be an important consideration in the final media scheduling deci-

[22]Lena Vanier, "U.S. Ad Spending Double All Other Nations Combined," *Advertising Age*, May 16, 1988, p. 36.

sion. However, except in the case of vehicles that are unusually costly relative to the size of the advertising budget, managers will not generally eliminate specific vehicles from further consideration at this point. Additionally, the actual cost per insertion will depend on the size, length, and position of the advertisement.

Determining Size, Length, and Position

In general, the probability that an advertisement will be seen varies with the size and length of a commercial or with different positions in a magazine (such as the back cover or inside the front cover). Additionally, these differences can influence recall. For instance, a 30-second commercial has about 60 to 75 percent of the recall value of a 60-second commercial.[23] However, these effects vary among types of products. That is, size, length, and position effects will be more important for low perceived-risk products because buyers are less active in searching for information and less quick to notice advertisements for those kinds of products.

The cost of an insertion is also influenced by the size, length, and position of the advertisement. After a particular size, length, and position decision has been made, managers will calculate the cost of each vehicle relative to the size of the audience reached. The typical measure used is cost per thousand (called CPM). Assuming that the firm has data on the demographic makeup of the audience, the CPM for one insertion in a magazine or broadcast program is calculated as

$$CPM = \frac{\text{cost of a single insertion}}{\text{number of target market members in the audience (in thousands)}}$$

(In cases where only the total size of the vehicle's audience is known, the same formula is used, except that the total circulation—of a magazine—or the total number of households reached—by broadcast—is substituted in the denominator.)

Determining the Desired Distribution of Messages

For a given planning period, advertising expenditures can be distributed in different ways: according to the timing of the expenditures or according to reach and frequency.

Timing of Expenditures   Timing reflects the manner in which expenditures are distributed over the course of the planning period. Many products and services have highly seasonal sales patterns. Toy sales peak in November and December, cold tablet sales in winter, greeting card sales before major holidays. To the extent that seasonal patterns are known, managers can schedule advertising

[23]Jack Z. Sissors and E. R. Petray, *Advertising Media Planning*, Crain Books, Chicago, 1976, p. 185.

so that the bulk of the dollar expenditures coincides with (or slightly leads) the peak sales period.

An additional timing consideration (especially for smaller advertisers) is the idea of *flighting*. When the total number of dollars available for advertising is very limited, some firms believe that these funds should be spent in lump sums that are adequate to generate sufficient impact. That is, if a small budget is spread evenly over the planning period, the weekly or monthly level of advertising might be too low to be noticed. By placing larger chunks of advertising intermittently, many managers believe that the visibility of the advertising will be greater than if the same dollars are spent in smaller but more frequent amounts. For instance, Porsche Cars North America scheduled virtually its entire $5 million fall ad budget behind two 2-minute commercials and a 20-page insert in selected magazines. Because Porsche couldn't match competitors' total spending levels they attempted to create impact and memorability through this concentrated burst of effort.[24]

Measuring Reach and Frequency   Managers must also determine how to distribute expenditures among members of the target audience according to reach and frequency. *Reach* represents either the number or the percentage of target audience members who will be exposed to a message. *Frequency* represents the average number of times a member of the target audience is exposed to the message.

Reach and frequency measures are based on estimates of the size of an audience as calculated by independent rating services. When possible, these measures should be calculated in terms of the target audience rather than in terms of the total audience.

For example, assume that a magazine has a circulation of 1 million, of which 800,000 subscribers are in a target audience defined as females aged 15 to 24. Defined in terms of the target audience, the reach of one insertion in that magazine would be 800,000. If an advertiser made one insertion in that magazine in each of 4 weeks, the total reach would be 4 × 800,000 or 3.2 million. Advertisers use the term *gross impressions* to indicate the number of target audience members reached by a given advertising plan. Therefore 3.2 million can be referred to as the number of gross impressions resulting from four insertions in this magazine.

However, reach can also be calculated in terms of the percentage of the target audience. If the total target audience consists of 20 million females, each issue of this magazine reaches 800,000 out of the 20 million, or 4 percent of the target audience. Advertisers use the term *gross rating points* (or GRPs) to indicate the reach in percentage terms. Therefore, if a firm advertised in four issues of this magazine, the number of GRPs would be calculated as 4 percent per issue multiplied by four issues, or 16 gross rating points.[25]

[24]Raymond Serafin, "Porsche Ads Go for High Impact," *Advertising Age,* Sept. 11, 1989, p. 25.
[25]This section is based on Sissors and Petray, op. cit., pp. 97–118; and Grossman, *The Marketers Guide to Media Vehicles, Methods and Options,* Euorum Books, Westport, Conn., 1987, chap. 1.

Both of these measures can be used to describe the total reach of a combination of media as well as of a single vehicle. However, there will be some overlap in media usage among target audience members. That is, some readers of *Time* magazine also read *Newsweek*. Therefore, in determining the total number of individuals reached one or more times by these magazines, some measure of the duplication in audience coverage is needed. The terms *net coverage* and *combined coverage* indicate the total reach of a combination of vehicles after adjustments for overlapping coverage.[26]

Once the net coverage (the total number of audience members reached at least once) is known, the frequency can be calculated as follows:

$$\text{Frequency} = \frac{\text{gross impressions}}{\text{net coverage}}$$

Using Reach and Frequency Managers often use measures such as gross impressions and gross rating points in order to rank alternative vehicles or combinations of vehicles by their coverage of the audience. However, many advertisers and agencies believe that some vehicles are more effective than others in gaining actual audience perception—for the reasons cited earlier. Thus, these vehicles may receive more positive consideration even if they generate a slightly lower number of gross impressions than other vehicles.

Reach is, of course, desirable because the advertiser would prefer to reach as many individuals in the target audience as possible. In general, broader net coverage can be achieved by using a number of different vehicles, since different vehicles are likely to reach different members of the target audience.

On the other hand, it is generally recognized that some level of repeated exposure to a message is necessary before the message has any impact. And in general, repetition of the same advertisement in the same vehicle will tend to reach the same audience members. Therefore, by using only a limited number of vehicles, an advertiser may reduce net coverage but increase frequency.

Further, average frequency figures may be misleading. In reality some audience members are heavier readers of viewers than others, and so the distribution of frequency of potential exposure is usually unbalanced. Consider for example Figure 10-3. In this example, the average frequency of exposure is 1.67 times. But nearly a third of those reached were exposed (potentially) only once.

The critical question regarding frequency is, "How much is enough?" It can usually be established that, up to a point, repeated exposures increase brand awareness and foster favorable attitudes (assuming appropriate copy exists).[27] On the other hand, excessive repetition can lead to the phenomenon of wear-out.

---

[26]Some procedures for measuring duplication are discussed in David B. Montgomery and Glen L. Urban, *Management Science in Marketing,* 1969 Prentice-Hall, Englewood Cliffs, N.J., pp. 98–100.

[27]See David Aaker, "ADMOD: An Advertising Decision Model," *Journal of Marketing Research,* February 1975, pp. 37–45; and Michael Ray and Alan Sawyer, "Repetition in Media Models: A Laboratory Technique," *Journal of Marketing Research,* February 1971, pp. 14–20.

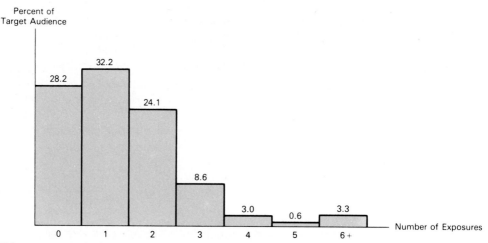

FIGURE 10-3   Example of a distribution of frequency of exposure.

That is, continued repetition of an advertisement may not only be a waste of money but may actually lead to a decline in awareness or positive attitudes toward the product.[28]

Developing the Media Schedule

As indicated in Figure 10-4, the preceding steps provide the basic management inputs to the media scheduling decision. Computer routines, based on budget limitations, the target audience for the commercial, the desired frequency and reach, the cost per insertion for a given length and position, and the audience size and demographics for each acceptable vehicle, are typically used to allocate the budget among the acceptable vehicles. Generally, these routines will yield a set of media schedules that provide the largest number of gross impressions for the given budget, with slight variations in reach and with frequency trade-offs among the alternative media schedules.

Table 10-2 provides an example of a media schedule for a product that is a frequent gift item for men. In examining the table, we can see that advertising tends to be heaviest during the Easter, graduation, and Christmas periods. Reach (as measured by gross rating points) and frequency levels are provided for each month. (The specific magazines and television programs selected were examined for consistency with the product.) The resulting schedule was then determined by examining the budget constraint and the cost per insertion using a computerized scheduling model.

[28]See, for example, C. Samuel Craig, Brian Sternthal, and Clark Leavitt, "Advertising Wearout: An Experimental Analysis," Journal of Marketing Research, November 1976, pp. 365–372.

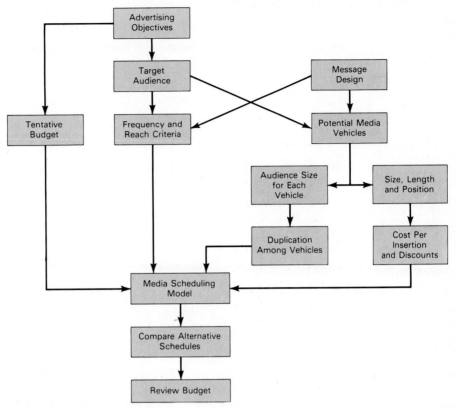

FIGURE 10-4   Developing the media schedule.

Although a number of media scheduling models have been developed by using a variety of mathematical procedures,[29] it is important to recognize that the use of such models does not serve as a substitute for managerial judgment. Rather, these models merely serve to display the best schedules based on the budget and on prior management decisions regarding message and objectives and size, length, and position. In fact, even the most sophisticated models available to advertisers require very extensive inputs by advertising or product managers.[30]

EVALUATING EFFECTIVENESS

Advertising frequently consumes a large proportion of the marketing budget and is often a critical ingredient in the success of a product. Accordingly, managers

[29]An excellent overview of alternative approaches is contained in Dennis Gensch, *Advertising Planning: Mathematical Models in Advertising Media Planning,* Elsevier Scientific, Amsterdam, 1973.
[30]John D. C. Little and Leonard M. Lodish, "A Media Planning Calculus," *Operations Research,* January–February 1969, pp. 1–35.

TABLE 10-2 MEDIA PLAN FOR A MEN'S GIFT PRODUCT

Month	Medium	Men 25–49	
		Reach	Frequency
March	Televison	78	3.1
	Magazines	69	2.1
	Combined	93	2.4
April	Television	78	3.1
	Magazines	33	1.3
	Combined	84	3.4
May	Magazines	34	1.3
June	Magazines	34	1.3
	Rado	38	5.3
	Combined	59	4.1
July	Radio	38	5.3
September	Magazines	35	1.3
October	Magazines	59	1.7
November and December	Television	81	3.5
	Magazines	32	1.2
	Radio	38	5.3
	Combined	92	5.7

should attempt to evaluate the effectiveness of advertising to determine whether advertising expenditures are being well utilized. In particular, they should evaluate the effectiveness of individual messages (before or during the implementation of the program) and the effectiveness of the overall advertising program in achieving advertising objectives.

The role of advertising managers and product managers in the evaluation process is critical—especially in regard to monitoring the achievement of objectives. Advertising agencies and creative specialists are likely to be more skilled and very objective in evaluating individual messages to determine the most effective copy. But advertising managers, product managers, and top-level marketing managers should attempt to determine whether the message will create the desired effect on awareness or attitudes. Advertisements well liked by the ad industry and recalled by viewers do not necessarily move product. Gallo's Bartles & Jaymes wine cooler's folksy ads featuring a pair of likable country "rubes" promoting a sweet drink were popular and award winning. However, at the same time, Seagrams Golden used Bruce Willis as a spokesperson and ran ads that were less memorable with a smaller ad budget and took over the number one position in this market.[31] Further, advertising and product managers should be primarily responsible for evaluating the effectiveness of the total program, for two reasons.

[31]Jeffrey A. Trachtenberg, "Terrific! I Hate It," *Forbes,* June 27, 1988, pp. 130–132.

First it will be nearly impossible for agencies to be perfectly objective. Second, even when clearly specified communications-oriented objectives have been established, awareness and attitude results may still be influenced partly by other factors (such as changes in distribution availability, prices, and competitors' actions). Only the marketing managers in the firm doing the advertising can properly assess the impact of those factors.

One other point regarding evaluation is important. When possible, evaluation should be diagnostic. That is, it should not merely indicate which of two alternative messages is superior or how well the advertising objective is being achieved, but it should also provide insights into the specific remedial actions needed.

Procedures

As indicated in Table 10-3, a number of alternative procedures for evaluating advertising effectiveness are available.[32] Some of these procedures must be implemented by the advertiser or its agency, while others are available from syndicated research services such as those indicated in the table. Advertising effectiveness techniques used in international markets do not differ from those used domestically. However, costs of advertising research are usually higher because syndicate services may not be available, and audience measurement technologies and analyses may vary from country to country.[33]

It is important to recognize that different procedures are used for different kinds of evaluations. In particular, three kinds of effectiveness evaluations can be made:

• Evaluating individual advertising messages (copy and format) in order to choose the best of two or more alternatives or to measure the degree to which the message is being received by the audience
• Evaluating the achievement of awareness and attitude objectives
• Evaluating the motivational impact of the advertising program as reflected in sales or intentions to buy

Note that when measuring awareness, attitudes, intentions to buy, and sales, managers should make these measurements before a campaign begins and again at intervals of time during the campaign. This procedure will enable management to catch problems and think of possible modifications in message design or media scheduling at as early a time as possible. Further, managers should note that those tests which provide diagnostic information are generally most useful in de-

[32]For a thorough comparison of methods see Lee Adler, Allan Greenberg, and Darrel B. Lucas, "What Big Agency Men Think of Copy Testing Methods," *Journal of Marketing Research*, November 1965, pp. 339–345; D. Dalbey et al., *Advertising Measurement and Decision-Making*, Allyn and Bacon, Boston, 1968; and David W. Nylen, *Advertising: Planning, Implementation and Control*, South-Western, Cincinnati, 1975, pp. 517–545.

[33]Joseph T. Plummer, "The Role of Copy Research in Multinational Advertising," *Journal of Advertising Research*, October–November 1986, pp. 11–15.

TABLE 10-3   PROCEDURES FOR EVALUATING ADVERTISING PROGRAMS

Procedures for evaluating specific advertisements

---

1. Recognition tests:
   Estimate the percentage of people claiming to have read a magazine who recognize the ad when it is shown to them (e.g., Starch Message Report Service).

2. Recall tests:
   Estimate the percentage of people claiming to have read a magazine who can (unaided) recall the ad and its contents (e.g., Gallup and Robinson Impact Service; various services for TV ads as well).

3. Opinion tests:
   Potential audience members are asked to rank alternative advertisements as most interesting, most believable, best liked.

4. Theater tests:
   Theater audience is asked for brand preferences before and after an ad is shown in context of a TV show (e.g., Schwerin TV Testing Service).

Procedures for evaluating specific advertising objectives

---

1. Awareness:
   Potential buyers are asked to indicate brands that come to mind in a product category. A message used in ad campaign is given, and buyers are asked to identify brand that was advertised using that message.

2. Attitude:
   Potential buyers are asked to rate competing or individual brands on determinant attributes, benefits, characterizations using rating scales.

Procedures for evaluating motivational impact

---

1. Intentions to buy:
   Potential buyers are asked to indicate likelihood they will buy a brand (on a scale from "definitely will not" to "definitely will").

2. Market test:
   Sales changes in different markets are monitored to compare effects of different messages, budget levels.

---

termining what specific modifications are necessary. For example, recall tests help to diagnose weaknesses in a message by indicating which copy claims are not recalled. Additionally, differences in recall between vehicles can reveal differences in the effectiveness of vehicles (or in the effects of size, length, and position factors, if these differ). Similarly, attitude tests can serve to tell whether the copy is effective in changing perceptions and whether unintended changes in perception have resulted from the copy.

GLOBALIZATION

The global approach has received considerable attention; it views the world as one market rather than as a collection of many national or regional markets.[34] This orientation employs a uniform marketing approach and standardized products. The advantages of this highly standardized approach include lower production costs, higher quality products, a consistent worldwide image, and more efficient marketing. As previously discussed in Chapter 7, it has been argued that advances in communication, transportation, and entertainment technology have brought about more homogeneous world tastes and wants. The biggest hindrance to global marketing may still be cultural differences. There is little evidence to support the contention that world consumers are becoming more alike. In fact, as people become more affluent and better educated, their tastes diverge, and it may become necessary to make greater adjustments for local culture and conditions. The Grey Advertising Agency has identified three questions that companies should ask when selling products in foreign markets. A negative answer to any one of these would suggest that a global marketing strategy is not appropriate.[35]

• Are consumer targets similar in different nations? For instance, Kentucky Fried Chicken may be viewed as an ordinary meal in the United States while considered a treat in Japan.

• Do consumers share the same wants and needs around the world? General Foods successfully positioned Tang as a substitute for orange juice at breakfast but found that in France people drank little orange juice and almost none at breakfast.

• Has the market developed in the same way from country to country? For instance, Kellogg's Pop-Tarts failed in the United Kingdom because toasters were not widely used, whereas a toaster is a common household appliance in the United States.

The most visible of the firm's marketing activities in international markets may be its advertising effort. The same advertising may be used in different countries or country-to-country variations may be made. For example, Gillette Company used one ad campaign to support the new Sensor shaving system.[36] Gillette felt the product category enabled it to market across multinational boundaries as if they were one country. Previously, Gillette had introduced Contour Plus (called Atra Plus in North America) in fifteen European nations with identical commercials in each country. The European commercial differs from the North American execution only in that it used the Contour Plus name and featured sports footage that better reflected European culture. However, in the majority of cases, differences among countries require that the promotional effort be tailored to reflect

[34]Robert D. Buzzell, "Can You Standardize Multinational Marketing?" *Harvard Business Review,* November–December 1968, p. 102. Professor Buzzell was one of the first persons to raise the question of how much multinational marketing could be standardized. Theodore Levitt, "The Globalization of Markets," *Harvard Business Review,* May–June 1983, pp. 92–96, declared the approach appropriate for all firms. Also see "Differences, Confusion Slow Global Marketing Bandwagon," *Marketing News,* Jan. 16, 1987, p. 1. In a study of 100 advertisers selling products overseas, only 9 percent used a global marketing approach.

[35]Ronald Alsop, "Efficacy of Global Ad Projects Is Questioned in Firm's Survey," *The Wall Street Journal,* Sept. 13, 1984, p. 1.

[36]Allison Fahey, "International Ad Effort to Back Gillette Sensor," *Advertising Age,* Oct. 16, 1989, p. 34.

local considerations. In Gillette's case this meant using a different brand name. Similarly, Sara Lee's best selling herbal bath soaps in Great Britain is Radox. However, many Europeans confuse this name with Raid, the bug killer, and Radox comes across as being unsuitable as a product to put on your skin. In place of Radox, Sara Lee promotes Sanex, a Spanish soap that is seen by Europeans as a brand that lathers nicely and kills germs. However, in the big British market it sounds like "sanitary" and has the wrong connotations. Other names such as L'eggs do not translate for many European markets. For instance the word for L'eggs in France would have to be Les Oeufs (the eggs).[37]

CONCLUSION

Although the process of developing and implementing advertisements is often the primary responsibility of an advertising agency, it is critical that advertising managers, product managers, and top-level marketing management personnel take an active part in this process. In particular, it is essential that managers set advertising objectives that are (1) consistent with the marketing strategy, (2) specific enough to provide guidance to the copy and media people, and (3) measurable so managers can effectively evaluate the program's effectiveness.

The importance of taking an active role in the development of an advertising program seems obvious. But far too many firms, especially smaller ones, allow their agencies too much freedom in developing the program. In effect, creative concerns often receive more attention than managerial concerns. Of course, agencies or other specialists are essential to the advertising process. But by taking an active role in specifying the marketing strategy, the target market, the advertising objectives, and the basis for evaluating effectiveness, managers can assure that advertising programs are viewed as part of the marketing effort (rather than vice versa) by the agency.

In this chapter, we have presented several guidelines and procedures for developing effective advertising programs. Additionally, we have presented a process within which these guidelines and procedures can be most effectively used. Figure 10-5 summarizes this process and indicates the relationship between advertising programs and the other elements of the planning process. As this figure indicates, advertising programs are closely related to the other kinds of marketing programs. Sales-promotion programs must often be communicated through advertising. Further, sales promotions and advertising should be closely coordinated, for reasons discussed in Chapter 11. Additionally, advertising and personal selling efforts should be coordinated as well, because advertising is often a means of paving the way for the sales force. This relationship will be discussed in greater detail in Chapter 12.

[37]Steve Weiner, "How Do You Say L'eggs in French?" *Forbes*, Nov. 27, 1989, pp. 73–77.

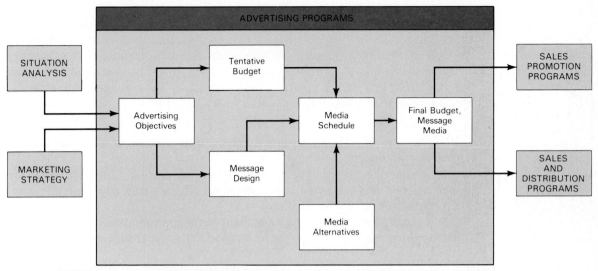

FIGURE 10-5 Relationship of advertising programs to situation analysis, marketing strategy, and other marketing programs.

Braun: Establishing a Global Advertising Campaign[38]

Braun, the West German manufacturer and marketer of shavers and coffee makers, spends about $60 million annually advertising its products in 100 different countries. Historically, Braun's ads have differed from country to country. In some cases, these advertisements were so different they gave the appearance that they were for totally unrelated products. After reviewing previous advertising campaigns, Braun executives concluded they wanted to present Braun and their product line in a more uniform manner.

Lowe Marschalk (Braun's advertising agency) has created a uniform campaign for Braun that will be translated into native languages in Europe and other countries. A series of advertisements were developed that reflect the product rather than the culture. For instance, a print ad for a Braun coffee maker shows a coffee cup filled with orange juice and a glass filled with coffee beneath the headline, "Life is complicated enough at 7 a.m." With the lowering of European trade barriers in 1992, Braun and its ad agency feel that such a campaign will present a more uniform and a truer reflection of the company and its products.

Many global campaigns have encountered difficulty because they were imposed by headquarters on local managers. Braun intends to avoid this problem by letting managers run other ads if local market conditions are unique enough to preclude the use of the overall creative campaign. Local ad agencies will still be

[38]This case was developed from Joanne Lipman, "Lowe Marschalk Takes Braun World-Wide," *The Wall Street Journal*, Feb. 10, 1989, p. 12.

used to buy media and to create local ad campaigns if necessary. However, the flexibility given local managers is intended to result in less resentment and ensure that Braun's ads make sense in each country. Because local managers have the option not to run the campaign, this could result in uniform ads in some countries and contradictory ads in others. Braun's strategy might be described as tailored global advertising. In this approach there is one plan but managers can tailor it to their market if they feel this is necessary.

1 What are the advantages and disadvantages to Braun of a modified global marketing approach?

2 Considering the varying elements of an advertising campaign, what are some reasons why it may be inappropriate to offer a single advertising program that is uniform across many nations?

3 Are globalized advertising campaigns more appropriate for industrial products or for consumer products such as coffee makers and shavers?

QUESTIONS AND SITUATIONS FOR DISCUSSION

1 Do you think advertising is more effective at the cognitive stage or at the affective stage? Explain.

2 In which of the following cases would it be most reasonable to use sales volume as a primary advertising objective?

   a A small software firm is planning an advertising program in leading business magazines.

   b Kellogg's is introducing a new anticholesterol cereal product to the market.

   c Marshall Fields is advertising its private-label line of men's sports coats.

3 Upjohn Company has taken a low-key approach to advertise its hair-loss remedy, Rogaine. The advertisements do not mention either Rogaine or Minoxidil, its active ingredient. The U.S. Food and Drug Administration prohibits the mention of drugs in advertisements unless there is full disclosure of any warnings and side effects. The ads appear in male-oriented magazines such as *Golf Digest, Sports Illustrated,* and *Gentlemen's Quarterly.* In addition to not using the name, the treatment in the ad isn't even referred to as a drug. The result is that the audience does not know if the treatment is a hair weave, a transplant, or a drug. The message is "if you're concerned about hair loss you should see your doctor." What are the advertising objectives Upjohn seems to have for their campaign for Rogaine? What are the advantages of advertising in magazines as opposed to broadcast media for a high-involvement product such as Rogaine?

4 What effect does the product life cycle have on the advertising a company employs?

5 Coca-Cola beat out PepsiCo. to become the exclusive soft-drink sponsor for the 1992 Universal Exhibition in Seville, Spain. Coca-Cola paid $8.4 million to be the official sponsor and another $5.3 million to be a "collaborating company," financing certain facilities and services. In addition, Coca-Cola paid $650,000 to be able to sell soft drinks on the fairgrounds. In exchange, Coca-Cola can use the exposition's official logo and Curro mascot (a bird with crest of rainbow colors) on promotions of products approved by the exposition. Coca-Cola's communications director said the "only reason we are taking part in Expo is to impede competitors from getting the upper hand." Does this appear to be a reasonable objective for Coca-Cola?

6 Since 15-second commercials were first introduced in 1986, they have increased to where they now account for 41 percent of all daytime television spots. How would you expect the shift from 30- to 15-second spots to influence the design of messages? Studies have shown that 15-second ads are generally 70 percent as effective as longer ads. Would this have any implications on establishing the baseline advertising budget?

7 What is the difference between gross impressions and gross rating points? What are the limitations of using these measures in estimating the reach of an advertising program?

8 Abacus, Inc., had been formed by three recent MIT graduates who had developed a quiet and powerful disk-drive system. This disk system was 100 percent compatible with the Apple II and Apple IIe personal computers. The Abacus system had a 5-year electromechanical design life with a full, 1-year parts-and-labor warranty. In addition, standard equipment included three software programs and a handsome portable carrying case.

In developing their marketing program for this system, the founders had chosen to utilize some print media. Faced with a limited budget, they were trying to choose between two magazines. Magazine *Alpha* had 1 million readers and charged $200 for a full-page ad, while magazine *Beta* had 1.5 million readers and charged $2500 for the full-page ad. In addition, they knew that *Alpha* readership consisted of 10,000 personal computer owners and that *Beta* readership included 15,000 personal computer owners.

a If you had to choose between *Alpha* and *Beta,* which would you use, given the above information?

b What additional information would you feel necessary prior to making such a decision?

SUGGESTED ADDITIONAL READINGS

Aaker, David, "ADMOD: An Advertising Decision Model," *Journal of Marketing Research,* February 1975, pp. 37–45.

Hanssens, Dominique, and Barton Weitz, "The Effectiveness of Industrial Print Advertisements across Product Categories," *Journal of Marketing Research,* August 1980, pp. 294–306.

Hite, Robert E., and Cynthia Fraser, "International Advertising Strategies of Multinational Corporations," *Journal of Advertising Research,* August–September 1988, pp. 9–17.

Kashani, Kamran, "Beware the Pitfalls of Global Marketing," *Harvard Business Review,* September–October 1989, pp. 91–98.

Leckenby, John, and Shizue Kishi, "Performance of Four Exposure Distribution Models," *Journal of Advertising Research,* April–May 1982, pp. 35–46.

McMeekin, Gordon C., "How to Set Up an Advertising Budget," *Journal of Business Forecasting,* Winter 1988–1989, pp. 22–26.

Ogilvy, David, and Joel Raphaelson, "Research on Advertising Techniques That Work— and Don't Work," *Harvard Business Review,* July–August 1982, pp. 14–18.

Plummer, Joseph T., "The Role of Copy Research in Multinational Advertising," *Journal of Advertising Research,* October–November 1986, pp. 11–15.

Rice, Marshall D., "Estimating the Reach and Frequency of Mixed Media Advertising Schedules," *Journal of the Market Research Society,* October 1988, pp. 439–451.

Schroer, James C., "Ad Spending: Growing Market Shares," *Harvard Business Review,* January–February 1990, pp. 44–48.

Zaltman, Gerald, and Christine Moorman, "The Management and Use of Advertising Research," *Journal of Advertising Research,* December 1988–January 1989, pp. 11–18.

CHAPTER 11

SALES-PROMOTION PROGRAMS

OVERVIEW

Sales promotions include all *short-term* offers (or incentives) directed at buyers, retailers, or wholesalers and designed to achieve a *specific, immediate response*. The incentives directed at consumers include coupons, premiums, free samples, and special exhibits. *Trade promotions,* which are directed toward retailers and wholesalers, include cash and merchandise allowances, equipment, and awards to such firms or to their personnel.

Sales promotions, especially those that are directed toward consumers, are often communicated through or coordinated with an advertising program. Consequently, these programs may contribute to the building of brand awareness, to the development of more favorable attitudes, or to some other advertising objective. However, because the primary function of sales promotion is to create immediate and specific *behavioral* responses by buyers or resellers, sales-promotion programs do serve different objectives.

In recent years, the rate of growth in sales-promotion expenditures has greatly exceeded the rate of growth in advertising. This shift has been attributed to five basic forces:[1]

- Slow population growth has intensified the competition for market share in packaged goods industries where promotions are most widely used.
- Increased audience segmentation and media costs have made advertising less cost-effective.
- As more products reach the maturity stage of the life cycle, opportunities for differentiation decrease and price becomes more important.

[1]Paul Farris and John Quelch, "In Defense of Price Promotion," *Sloan Management Review,* Fall 1987, p. 63.

- Retailers and wholesalers are placing increasing demands on manufacturers for promotions.
- Price promotions are usually more reliable than advertising for boosting short-term earnings, which is appealing to firms whose stock prices are under pressure to show such bottom-line results.

In this chapter, we will examine the ways in which managers can use sales-promotion programs to implement a marketing strategy. In particular, we will examine (1) the objectives that various kinds of sales-promotion programs can achieve, (2) the factors that should be considered in selecting a specific sales-promotion alternative, and (3) procedures for developing the sales-promotion budget.

SALES-PROMOTION OBJECTIVES

The array of specific sales-promotion ideas, tactics, and activities that have been used is enormous, and it seems to grow weekly as creative marketing minds generate still more new promotions. As was the case with advertising programs, however, a sales-promotion program should not be designed until the objective is clearly understood. Moreover, the sales-promotion objective should be consistent with the marketing strategy.

Although the number of possible specific sales-promotion objectives is very large, there are a limited number of basic types of objectives that may be established.[2] Tables 11-1 and 11-2 list these types of objectives and indicate some typical programs that can be used to achieve each objective.

Objectives Directed at Final Buyers

There are five basic types of buyer actions that can be stimulated by sales promotions: inquiries, product trial, repurchase, traffic building, and increasing the rate of purchase.

Stimulating Inquiries   Inquiries can include returning a form requesting additional information about a product or service or visiting an exhibit at a trade association meeting. Managers can generate inquiries by offering such things as a free catalog or some premium or prize. (Often, the incentive is offered in the context of some advertising message designed to introduce the product benefits. Accordingly, such promotions must be closely coordinated with advertising programs.) A manager will often select this objective when attempting to identify and attract new prospects for a product or service. This objective is especially important when clients or customers must be periodically replenished (a problem facing colleges and the military). In addition, it is often important to attract only

---

[2]See, for example, Ovid Rose (ed.), *The Darnell Sales Promotion Handbook,* 6th ed., Dartnell Corp., Chicago, p. 128; and William H. Lembeck, "Selecting the Right Strategy for a Successful Promotion," *Marketing and Sales Promotion: A Special Report,* Bill Publications, New York, 1978, pp. 2–4.

TABLE 11-1   SALES-PROMOTION OBJECTIVES AND ALTERNATE PROGRAM
DIRECTED AT FINAL BUYERS

Objective	Alternate programs
Inquiries	Free gifts Mail-in coupons for information Catalog offer Exhibits
Product trial • New products • Related products • Brand switchers	Coupons Cents-off specials Free samples Contests Premiums Demonstrations
Repurchase	On-pack coupons Mail-in coupons for rebate Continuity premiums
Traffic building	Special sales Weekly specials Entertainment events Retailer coupons Premiums
Increased rate of purchase • Inventory building • Increased usage rate	Multipacks Special prices on twos Information on new usage situations

TABLE 11-2   SALES PROMOTION OBJECTIVES AND ALTERNATE PROGRAMS
DIRECTED AT THE TRADE

Objective	Alternate programs
Inventory-building • New-product acceptance • Increased space allotment	Returns allowances Merchandise allowances Slotting allowances
Promotional support • Local ad feature • Displays • Price special	Promotional allowances Cooperative promotions Reusable display cases Sales contests Merchandise allowances

high-interest prospects, especially when the potential buyers are few and hard to identify. In these cases, firms that are effective in stimulating inquiries will be able to focus their follow-up sales and other marketing activities on high-interest prospects. Further, when new models or versions of a product or service are being offered, sales promotions may be designed to stimulate inquiries from past customers in order to maintain contact with prospects.

Generating Product Trial   A product trial objective is certainly appropriate in marketing new products. Free samples and coupons are usually useful in stimulating trial for low perceived-risk products because they generate a low-cost usage experience which may lead to favorable attitudes faster than advertising. For more complex, higher priced products (such as durable goods or many services) in-store demonstrations appear to be most useful. For houseware items, demonstrations have been known to increase sales by 80 to 300 percent during the week of the demonstration.[3]

Generating product trial is also an important objective for problem-child products hoping to convert competitors' customers who may be price-sensitive. Moreover, the increasing sophistication of marketing data bases is making it more economical to focus incentives at this group.

> Seagrams offered 500,000 drinkers of Johnnie Walker, Cutty Sark, Dewars, or J&B scotches their choice of a calculator, a set of old-fashioned glasses, or a $5 rebate if they would purchase the company's Glenlivet brand. The promotion resulted in 10,000 new Glenlivet buyers. The source of the 500,000 names was a company-developed list of 5 million Scotch drinkers generated from responses to a series of surveys on consumption habits developed by a company such as Donnelley Marketing or Computerized Marketing Technologies that develops such data bases using a variety of free samples to generate consumer data.[4]

Additionally, firms which market a number of different products (such as franchise extensions or complements) may use techniques such as cross-couponing to build trial for these other products. Thus, a package of Gillette razor blades might contain a coupon for a new Gillette Foamy shaving cream line extension.

Encouraging Repurchase   To the extent that habit building will lead to brand loyalty (especially for low perceived-risk products), promotional incentives that "tie" a buyer to a seller may be desired. For example, the use of coupons contained in the package that can be redeemed on the next purchase occasion can have this type of impact and will be especially valuable in implementing retention strategies. Similarly, retailers may encourage store loyalty (or at least continued visits to the store) through special sales offered to charge-account customers or through continuity promotions. *Continuity promotions* include trading stamps, games, and contests that run over a period of weeks, or gifts distributed in increments over time (such as encyclopedias or sets of dishes). These promotions stimulate repurchase from a retail store because customers must continue to return to the store to obtain the full value of the program. Additionally, "frequent patron" programs (such as frequent shopper or frequent flyer programs) are a form of continuity promotion.

Frequent buyer programs have become noticeably more widespread and more sophisticated in recent years. The growth of data bases from mailing lists (such as

---

[3]Elaine Appleton "Houseware Companies Are Convinced That Seeing Is Believing," *Adweek's Marketing Week,* Oct. 9, 1989, pp. 20–21.

[4]Joshua Levine, "Stealing the Right Shoppers," *Forbes,* July 10, 1989, pp. 104–105.

the Seagram's data base discussed earlier in this chapter) and other services have made these kinds of programs much more cost-effective, often because several manufacturers share the costs. Consider, for example, the Frequent Shoppers Advantage Club.

> The Frequent Shoppers Advantage Club was launched in 1988 to provide a vehicle for targeting continuity programs. More than 100 brands participate in the club in which consumers clip codes from the products of participating brands and redeem them for points that can be used for catalog merchandise. Firms participating in the plan include Frito-Lay, Nestlé Foods, General Foods, Lever Brothers, and Ralston-Purina.[5]

Traffic Building   Retailers employ sales promotions as vehicles for stimulating more store traffic from new buyers as well as for the repurchase objectives already cited. Special entertainment events (such as having authors autograph copies of their books) and special attractions placed in shopping malls may attract customers, who will then make some purchases. Additionally, by establishing price specials on so-called *leader* products, retailers may draw customers who buy the leader plus other items at nonsale prices.

Increase Rates of Purchase   Often the major desired effect of a promotion is to get more purchases from existing buyers. But there are two alternative strategic purposes underlying this objective: consumer loading and increased consumption rate. *Consumer loading* reflects a retention-oriented marketing strategy in which the main goal is to get buyers to stock up on the product. A buyer who is carrying above-normal stocks of a product is not likely to buy competing products. Thus, multipacks and similar promotions may be used just before new competing products are introduced or in anticipation of increased competitor promotional activity. Alternatively, the promotion may stimulate primary demand if the lower prices encourage a higher rate of consumption (often the case with products such as soft drinks or some meat products). Additionally, if the promotion includes information pertaining to new ways of using the product or new usage situations, this can complement and reinforce the price incentive to use more of the product.

> Quaker and Nestlé generated incremental sales increases of 38% and 23%, respectively, on oatmeal and hot chocolate in the winter of 1989 through a joint promotional effort. Consumers were offered a free box of Nestlé Quik with the purchase of two boxes of instant oatmeal. The promotion was backed by store displays containing the product as a visual showing both products being conveniently prepared together in a microwave.[6]

While the Quaker-Nestlé "tie-in" promotion was successful, it is important to recognize that this promotion was not automatically supported. The companies

[5]Laurie Petersen, "Frequent Buyer Mania," *Adweek's Marketing Week,* July 10, 1989, special "Promote" supplement, pp. P.8–P.10.

[6]"Breakfast Summit: Anatomy of a Tie-In," *Adweek's Marketing Week,* Aug. 7, 1989, special "Promote" supplement, pp. P.14–P.20.

needed to generate the support of supermarkets (that is, the "trade") to ensure that displays were put up and that sufficient additional inventory was available. This required some form of trade promotion.

Trade-Promotion Objectives

The fundamental purposes of trade promotions are to *push* the product through the marketing channel by getting resellers (retailers and wholesalers) to aggressively market the product or to help ensure the success of consumer promotions designed to *pull* the product through the channel. These two purposes are reflected in two types of sales-promotion objectives.

Encouraging Trade Inventory Building   Marketers who are developing extensive consumer-oriented promotions will nearly always want to pursue this objective simultaneously. If the consumer promotion is expected to build short-run demand, retail stockouts must be avoided. Thus, manufacturers may offer special margins or extra merchandise at no extra cost to induce an increase in retailer or wholesaler inventories. In addition, special returns allowances—higher-than-usual prices paid to retailers who want to return unsold goods—may also be used to encourage retailers to risk higher inventories.

With respect to building acceptance for new products, manufacturers have increasingly encountered retailer demands for so-called slotting allowances. These allowances are either straight cash payments or free cases of the product which are given to retailers in exchange for stocking a new product for a specified period of time. According to one source, it can easily cost $70,000 to get a truckload's worth of a new product line accepted into a chain with 50 stores. The cause of the rise in slotting allowance is the proliferation of new grocery products. In a typical supermarket the number of items carried grew from 13,000 in 1979 to 26,000 by 1989. Because most products fail and because many new products cannibalize sales of products the retailer already sells, the risks of adding new products are substantial.[7]

Obtaining Distributor Promotional Assistance   The objective of obtaining distributor promotional assistance must usually be achieved by coordinating sales promotion with personal selling. However, it is often the purpose of sales promotions offered to distributors. Sales contests and special cash or merchandise allowances may be offered in return for distributor agreements to provide special display space or to provide additional selling or advertising effort. If successful, these programs may help to ensure the success of a consumer promotion. For example, the Quaker-Nestlé tie-in promotion (discussed earlier in this chapter) was accompanied by a strong trade-promotion effort. Retailers that accepted the display (containing nine cases of Quik and thirty-six cases of Quaker Oatmeal)

---

[7]Lois Therrien, "Want Shelf Space at the Supermarket? Ante Up," *Business Week,* Aug. 7, 1989, pp. 60–61.

received the nine cases of hot chocolate mix for free. As a result, the promotion received participation from retailers who represented 60 percent of all-commodity-volume (ACV) of retail sales in the nation.[8]

Relationship of Sales-Promotion Objectives to Marketing Strategy

As we have indicated, different types of sales promotions serve different sales-promotion objectives. In turn, each of the sales-promotion objectives is more appropriate for some marketing strategies than for others.

With respect to promotions directed toward final buyers, inquiries and product trial are generally more appropriate when the marketing strategy is either to increase the number of product-form users or to acquire new customers. Repurchase-oriented promotions support a retention strategy. Promotions for increasing the rate of purchase may support a primary-demand strategy (through increasing the rate of usage) or a retention strategy, as we discussed above. Traffic building is a broad objective and may serve any of the basic strategies, depending on the specific nature of the promotion: Weekly specials tend to stimulate retention while unique exhibits may attract new customers. Finally, trade promotions must be viewed as a means rather than an end. The basic purposes of trade promotion are to support advertising or consumer sales promotions. Thus, the different trade-promotion objectives may ultimately serve any of the marketing strategies.[9]

SELECTING A SPECIFIC SALES PROMOTION

As we suggested in the previous section, managers should establish the sales-promotion objective before selecting a specific type of sales-promotion incentive. Further, the sales-promotion objective should support the marketing strategy for the product.

However, a number of alternative types of incentives may be used to try to achieve the sales-promotion objective. In selecting a specific sales-promotion program, it is essential that managers examine the buying process in order to understand the likelihood of response to a type of incentive. In this section, we will examine some of the most important buying process factors that managers should consider in developing consumer promotions, promotions to distributors, and promotions directed at organizational buyers.

Consumer Promotions

Although the amount of research that has been reported on consumer responses to specific types of promotions is still relatively small, managers should closely

---

[8]Same reference as footnote 6.
[9]Kenneth Hardy, "Key Success Factors for Manufacturers' Sales Promotions in Package Goods," *Journal of Marketing*, July 1986, pp. 13–23.

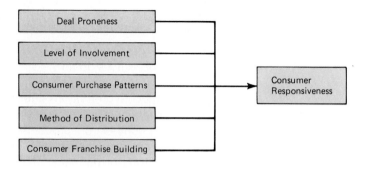

FIGURE 11-1   Factors influencing consumer
response to sales promotion.

examine three facets of the consumer decision process (deal proneness, level of
involvement, and purchase patterns) and two basic aspects of the promotion
(method of distribution and extent of consumer franchise building) as presented
in Figure 11-1.

Deal Proneness   Markets can frequently be segmented in terms of *deal proneness*—the degree to which consumers are likely to search out and respond to
sales-promotion incentives or "deals." Few generalities can be stated about consumer responses to sales promotions. In particular, prior research is unclear about
who deal-prone consumers really are. However, most recent studies suggest that
affluence is correlated with deal-proneness. For example, 38 percent of households with incomes over $40,000 are heavy coupon users compared to 19 and
24 percent of households in the "under $10,000" and "$10,000 to $15,000" in-
come categories respectively.[10] Accordingly, a number of consumer-goods firms
have used manufacturers' coupons designed and promoted by Donnelley Marketing, Inc. Donnelley uses a mailing list of persons selected for "upscale demographic qualities" who tend to be heavy users of mass-distribution goods.
    Additionally, coupon-prone consumers have been shown to be younger and
less store loyal and brand loyal, and are more likely to live in urban areas.[11]

[10]"How Consumers Use Coupons," *Adweek's Marketing Week,* Sept. 25, 1989, special "Pro-
mote" supplement, p. 20. See also Robert Blattberg et al., "Identifying the Deal-Prone Segment,"
Journal of Marketing Research, August 1978, pp. 369–377.
    [11]Kapil Bawa and Robert Shoemaker, "The Coupon-Prone Consumer: Some Findings Based on
Purchase Behavior across Product Classes," *Journal of Marketing,* October 1987, pp. 99–110.

Level of Involvement   The consumer's level of involvement in the search process will have some impact on the kind of response that management can anticipate. Recent research evidence suggests that the degree to which product trial leads to changing preferences depends on the type of promotion. For example, one recent study suggests that sustained loyalty to a brand that is first purchased during a sales promotion will be greater where the effort involved in trying the brand is *high* relative to the economic value obtained. This suggests that coupons requiring some consumer effort to cut out, save, and redeem may be more effective in the long run than simple on-package or on-shelf price deals because they may increase the likelihood of conversion to the new brand.[12]

Additionally, when consumer involvement is low, behavioral learning theory suggests that, in general, reinforcers (such as coupons and premiums) work best when they are immediate rather than delayed. This implies that mail incentives will be weaker than in-package, on-package, or cents-off incentives when involvement is low.[13]

Consumer Purchase Patterns   Frequently, the effectiveness and efficiency of a program can be increased by knowing buyer purchase rates. That is, incentives should be available long enough to allow all heavy buyers an opportunity to respond during their normal purchase cycles. However, if the program lasts too long, all potential new buyers will have had an opportunity to buy. As a result, most sales in the later stages of the program will come from regular buyers who are simply stocking up on the product while the lower price (or other incentive) is available. (One advantage of using coupons instead of simply offering a lower sales price is that the number of coupons distributed is the upper limit on the quantity that can be purchased at sale prices, and so stocking up is more difficult.) Similarly, size loyalty may exist in some product categories, so that a promotion on one size may not attract competitors' customers who prefer other sizes. This would imply that if size loyalty exists, a firm should offer the incentive on the size in which it has the *lowest* market share if the purpose of the promotion is to induce trial. By focusing on its lowest market-share size, the firm will reduce the proportion of coupons used by its regular customers and will be more likely to attract competitors' customers.[14]

Method of Distribution   Consumer response to sales promotions will, in large part, depend on the amount and type of search effort required of the consumer. For example, in-pack or on-pack coupons generally have the highest redemption rate because regular users do not have to exert much effort to acquire these coupons and because these customers are already favorably disposed to the product.

---

[12]Joe Dodson, Alice Tybout, and Brian Sternthal, "Impact of Deals and Deal Retraction on Brand Switching," *Journal of Marketing Research,* February 1978, pp. 72–81.

[13]Michael Rothschild and William Gaidis, "Behavioral Learning Theory: Its Relevance to Marketing and Promotions," *Journal of Marketing,* Spring 1981, pp. 70–78.

[14]P. J. Robinson et al., *Promotional Decisions Using Mathematical Models,* Allyn and Bacon, Boston, 1967, pp. 79–81.

TABLE 11-3   AVERAGE COUPON REDEMPTION RATES
FOR ALTERNATIVE DISTRIBUTION METHODS

Distribution method	Average redemption rates
Newspaper	2.8%– 3.3%
Sunday supplement	2.1%– 2.4%
Free-standing insert	5.0%– 5.3%
Magazine, on page	2.5%– 3.0%
Magazine, pop-up	4.8%– 5.4%
Direct mail	10.2%–11.6%
On package	13.3%–14.8%
In package	18.4%–22.2%

Source: Developed from David J. Reibstein and Phyllis A. Traver, "Factors Affecting Coupon Redemption Rates," *Journal of Marketing,* Fall 1982, p. 105; and Don Schultz and William Robinson, *Sales Promotion Essentials,* Crain Books, Chicago, 1982, p. 22.

However, when the objective is to attract new users, direct mail usually generates the most response (all other aspects of the coupon being equal) because such coupons require little effort to obtain. Additionally, direct mail coupons are more likely to be noticed than coupons surrounded by newspaper and magazine content. Consequently, they appear to be superior in generating brand awareness among new buyers.[15] Table 11-3 summarizes how redemption rates vary depending on the method of distribution.

Consumer Franchise Building   A major distinction among sales promotions directed at buyers is the degree to which the promotion is supportive of brand attributes, benefits, or characterization—*consumer-franchise-building* (CFB) promotion—as opposed to being a straight economic incentive (non-CFB promotion). CFB promotions are free samples, premiums, demonstrations, or coupons that are presented through an effective sales message that reinforces the brand image. For example, General Foods offered a free stoneware mug as a mail-in premium in a promotion in which its Maxim brand (a freeze-dried instant coffee) was described as "the spoonful rich enough for a mug full." A more complex example is offered by Rainbow Foods.

Rainbow, the leading grocery chain in Minnesota's Twin Cities area, became a sponsor of U.S. Olympic Festival-90 by becoming the official pin collection center for the event. A set of forty-seven sports-related images were represented on pins and each was made available for 49¢ with the purchase of specific products on a rotating basis. (The pins could be purchased separately for $4.95.) The promotion provided Rainbow with traffic building and continuity potential. Importantly, however, the premium was believed to reflect "value"—a key dimension of Rainbow's image—because pin trad-

[15]K. C. Blair, "Coupon Design, Delivery Vehicle, Target Market Affect Conversion Rate," *Marketing News,* May 28, 1982, p. 1.

ing has become a widespread hobby. (The pin industry is estimated to be worth $100 million per year.) Rainbow featured the pins and related products in its "Wall of Values" the dominant store display area.[16]

The use of CFB-type promotions is often viewed as a way to maintain a brand's image and to reduce the chances of building a high degree of *price-sensitivity* among consumers. This is an especially important consideration for products in the growth and maturity stages, because as consumers become more familiar with alternative brands and as products become more technologically mature, price may come to be a primary factor in the choice process. Even those brands with strong quality images may suffer losses in sales if extensive non-CFB promotions are used, unless they have been clearly differentiated on a product attribute or unless they have vastly superior distribution.[17]

Promotions to Resellers

As discussed earlier, trade promotions (those which are directed at retailers or wholesalers) are designed either to achieve inventory building or promotional support. Indeed, it may be necessary to achieve both of these sales-promotion objectives to ensure the success of consumer promotions.

Unfortunately, many trade promotions are not achieving these objectives. Specifically, there is evidence of three major problems with trade sales promotions.[18]

1 Many trade buyers respond to promotions by purchasing for normal inventory. In some cases, buyers buy in large volume during deals to avoid buying at normal prices.

2 Trade buyers often accept the incentive but fail to perform the promotional requirements expected.

3 Some retailers make purchases beyond their own requirements during price "deals" and then resell the discounted merchandise to other retailers at a profit.

Although these problems are not easily resolved, managers can take several steps to reduce the severity of them.[19]

First, managers must understand the distributor's needs with respect to the product category. Some understanding can be gained by knowing the kinds of pricing programs that the distributor uses. For example, price-oriented promotions (such as merchandise allowances) may be more effective in gaining support from retailers who are volume-oriented. Similarly, promotions that help to build a retailer's image on quality may be more important for margin-oriented retailers.

[16]Amy Gross, "Rainbow Pinpoints Olympic Event," *Adweek's Marketing Week,* Jan. 8, 1990, special "Promote" supplement, p. P.12.

[17]Roger Strang, *The Relationship between Advertising and Promotion in Brand Strategy,* Marketing Science Institute, Boston, 1975, pp. 79–82.

[18]John Quelch, "It's Time to Make Trade Promotion More Productive," *Harvard Business Review,* May–June 1983, pp. 130–136.

[19]A useful discussion of these steps is in Rockney Walters, "An Empirical Investigation into Retailer Responses to Manufacturer Trade Promotions," *Journal of Retailing,* Summer 1989, pp. 253–272.

In the latter case, cooperative advertising programs may be more effective because these promotions are similar to consumer franchise building. Indeed one recent study suggests that retailers are more likely to use trade allowances for advertising than for deep price cuts or for display.[20]

Managers should also recognize the profit impact of a sales promotion on a dealer's space and inventory constraints and on the retailer's assortment of products. For example, many manufacturers may attempt to run promotions simultaneously. When a large number of products in a similar category are promoted at the same time, distributor attention, space, and inventory investment will all be divided. Accordingly, off-season promotions are more likely to generate distributor support. Because resellers are likely to vary along these and other dimensions, most experts now believe that greater flexibility should be provided in defining the promotional performance requirements expected of retailers. Thus, firms such as Procter & Gamble often allow retailers to decide whether to support a product through cooperative advertising or special displays or by means of some other mechanism, depending on which will best fit that retailer's needs.

The advent of electronic scanning has certainly affected the ability of firms to assess the impact of consumer promotions on retailer performance as well as on the performance of the brand. Thus, managers are increasingly aware of which kinds of trade efforts will pay off. If manufacturers can show how a given promotion affects *total* sales for a given retailer it will be easier to gain trade acceptance. For example, Procter & Gamble salespeople were able to gain extensive support for featuring Liquid Tide when they presented scanner results showing that the product attracted shoppers who spent more on that shopping trip.[21]

International Considerations

In many cases, managers will find that sales-promotion programs will be more difficult to globalize than other programs. Specifically, there are three fundamental reasons why promotions tend to be localized: cultural differences in product usage and perceptions; large variations in retailing and distribution structures and practices; and inconsistent legal treatment of promotions. To illustrate the impact of these factors, consider the following examples and facts confronting consumer packaged-goods marketers in the European Common Market.

Cultural differences. Countries differ in terms of the degree to which price promotions would hurt a brand's quality image. For example, in Spain beer is simply a refreshing beverage but in northern Europe, beer is a part of the national heritage.

Distribution structure and practices. In France, retailing is heavily concentrated in large-sized "hypermarket" stores that carry everything from auto parts to

---

[20]Ibid.
[21]Laurie Petersen, "Getting Smart," *Adweek's Marketing Week,* Jan. 8, 1990, special "Promote" supplement, p. P.8.

clothing to groceries but in Spain most of the population lives and shops in small rural stores where sales-promotion activity is modest.

Legal restrictions. While there are virtually no restrictions on sales-promotion practices in Great Britain, Germany has extensive legal barriers. Additionally, differences exist in the application of ''value-added'' (sales) taxes. A recent Italian law was designed to place a 45 percent tax levy on premiums, for instance. Presently, there is little uniformity governing the application of these taxes which vary across nations on regular sales as well.[22]

SALES-PROMOTION BUDGETS

The answer to the question, ''How much should be spent on sales promotion?'' is an elusive one. Just as in the case of advertising, the sales results of a given level of expenditure are difficult to predict. In fact, managers often find it difficult to estimate the costs that will be incurred by a sales-promotion program. However, it is both necessary and possible to analyze the profitability impact of a sales promotion in order to establish a sales-promotion budget.

In this section, we will review the basic elements that should be considered in the budgeting process. These elements are depicted in Figure 11-2. Additionally, we illustrate the approaches that can be used in developing the budget. Because consumer promotions are the most widely used types of promotions, and because they are generally the most complex from a budgeting perspective, our discussion will focus on the budgeting process for those types of promotions.

The Relationship of Advertising to Sales Promotion

As indicated earlier, advertising and sales-promotion decisions should be closely coordinated in order to achieve the right balance between consumer-franchise-building and non-CFB efforts. Further, both programs may be managed by the same individual (usually a product manager or advertising manager) in the organization. Consequently, a major decision in setting a budget is the determination of the appropriate balance between advertising expenditures and sales-promotion expenditures.

To a large extent this balance will be influenced by competitive activity and distributor pressures. That is, sales promotion must receive more attention if competitors are heavy users of promotion and if distributors are active in seeking sales promotions in a product category. Additionally, there are a number of other factors that will cause a firm to place different emphasis on advertising and sales promotion, as indicated in Table 11-4.

---

[22]Laurie Petersen, ''1992 and Promotion,'' *Adweek's Marketing Week,* Nov. 6, 1989, special ''Promote'' supplement, pp. P.6–P.9.

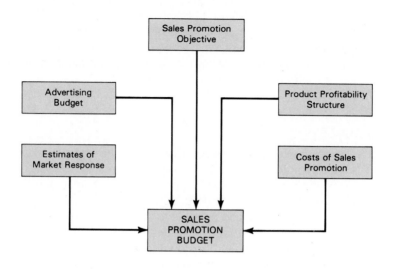

FIGURE 11-2 Factors to be considered in developing the sales-promotion budget.

Determining Costs

Most promotions will incur direct fixed costs and variable costs. Among the direct fixed costs are the costs of physically distributing samples, mailing coupons, and advertisements carrying coupons, inquiry slips, and premium offers. Additionally, contribution margins may be reduced, because the value of the coupon or cents-off special is effectively a price reduction. Further, when coupons are used, retailers must be remunerated for each coupon redeemed (usually at the rate of 7 cents each), and this represents an increase in the variable cost per unit.

One key problem in estimating costs is that contribution margins are reduced only on those items actually purchased at promotional prices. Therefore, some estimate of sales response will be necessary to determine the actual reduction in contribution margins.

Additionally, when coupons are used, some retailers will redeem coupons even when the product is not actually purchased and then redeem the face value of the coupon, as well as receiving the 7-cent handling charge. While this procedure (called *misredemption*) is a fraud, it is believed to be very extensive and is highly costly to manufacturers. Thus, some provision for estimating the level of misredemptions should be considered in projecting costs.

TABLE 11-4   REASONS FOR DIFFERENCES IN RELATIVE ADVERTISING AND
SALES-PROMOTION EXPENDITURES

Lower levels of promotion relative to advertising are associated with brands that:

1. Have a profit-contribution rate above the company average
2. Have a high level of brand loyalty
3. Have a strong competitive differentiation
4. Have a high degree of perceived risk associated with purchase
5. Are in the growth and maturity stages of their life cycle
6. Have a large market share

Higher levels of promotion relative to advertising are associated with brands that:

1. Have a profit-contribution rate below the company average
2. Have little brand loyalty
3. Have little competitive differentiation
4. Are directed to children
5. Are purchased with little planning
6. Are at the introductory or decline stage of their life cycle
7. Have a marked seasonal sales pattern
8. Have a small market share
9. Face promotion-oriented competitors
10. Are in a market where private labels are important

Source: Roger Strang, *The Relationship between Advertising and Promotion in Brand Strategy*, Marketing Science Institute paper 75–119, Boston, p. 13. Reprinted by permission.

Estimating Market Response

In Chapter 10, we suggested that managers must have some estimate of sales response in order to set the tentative advertising budget. These estimates are even more critical in sales-promotion budgeting, for two reasons. First, as noted already, some costs cannot be estimated without estimates of sales response. Second, unlike advertising objectives, sales objectives generally have a very direct link to sales volume. Product-trial, repurchase, increasing the rate of purchase, and traffic-building objectives are specifically sales-oriented. Promotional support and inquiries can be expected to result in increased sales with a small time lag. Consequently, the ability to predict response will enable the manager to assess not only the profitability consequences but also the degree to which the program objective will be achieved.

In developing estimates of market response, managers generally will rely on judgment. These judgments should reflect a manager's understanding of the buying process (as discussed earlier in this chapter) and the firm's past experience in promoting the product (or in promoting similar products). Additionally, managers may use experiments to estimate market response. This approach is especially useful for organizations that have limited experience in sales promotion and for comparing two or more alternative incentives. In particular, electronic scanner data results (as discussed in Chapter 6) are extremely useful for both experiments and for extracting historical ratios. As the promotion services manager of Kimberly-Clark put it:

Before it was more of a guess, a gut feeling. Traditional wisdom entered into the decision-making process. Now we have hard data supporting our planning process. We can accurately predict coupon liability even before the coupon drops.[23]

Specifically, there are six types of market response which managers should examine: (1) redemption rates, (2) displacement rates, (3) acquisition rates, (4) stock-up rates, (5) conversion rates, and (6) product-line effects.

Redemption Rates   This measure indicates the total number (or percentage) of buyers responding to the incentive. As suggested earlier in the chapter, the percentage of coupons that will be redeemed is largely a function of how they are distributed. However, there are a number of other factors which will determine the percentage of coupons redeemed or the number of buyers responding to other kinds of incentives (such as games, premiums, or cents-off deals). Specifically, redemption rates will be higher when[24]

• The product or brand is well established so that the value of the incentive is well understood.
• The product is widely distributed or easy to obtain so that coupon redemption is easy or there is a low effort required to acquire the incentive.
• The product form is used by a large percentage of households or organizations.
• The frequency of purchase of the product form is high.
• The value of the incentive is high (although coupon users will buy their regular brand using 25-cent coupons, the average face value necessary to obtain trial for a new brand is 58 cents according to one recent study).[25]

Additionally, it appears as though the impact of the value of the incentive depends upon the brand and the product category. That is, recent research on price promotions suggests that[26]

• High market-share brands are more inelastic with respect to a brand price promotion than low-share brands.
• A brand's sales are more inelastic with respect to a price promotion if the brand or category is one that receives frequent store display.
• A brand's sales are more elastic with respect to a price promotion if the brand or category is frequently featured in local newspaper ads.

Displacement Rates   Some of the sales made during a promotion will simply displace sales that would otherwise have been made to regular buyers at the nor-

---

[23]Amy Gross, "Kimberly-Clark Masters the Science of Couponing," *Adweek's Marketing Week,* Jan. 8, 1990, special "Promote" supplement, p. P.9.
[24]For additional discussion see Don E. Schultz and William A. Robinson, *Sales Promotion Essentials,* Crain Books, Chicago, 1982, pp. 29–31.
[25]"How Consumers Use Coupons," *Adweek's Marketing Week,* Sept. 25, 1989, special "Promote" supplement, pp. P.20–P.21.
[26]Ruth Bolton, "The Relationship between Market Characteristics and Promotional Price Elasticities," *Marketing Science,* Spring 1989, pp. 153–169.

mal price. In fact, studies show that 75 percent of coupons are redeemed by consumers who already use the couponed brand.[27] Accordingly, managers must determine the amount of the lost contribution margin that results from selling to regular buyers at discounted prices. In general, regular buyers of a brand will be more likely to take advantage of coupons or cents-off specials than will nonregular buyers. Consequently, the redemption rate will typically be a percentage which is somewhat greater than the product's market share. Additionally, the displacement rate will depend on the method of coupon distribution or the method by which potential buyers are made aware of a promotion. For example, in-pack coupons "good on next purchase," and incentives handed out or mailed out to regular customers are likely to create very large displacement rates (perhaps intentionally if the objective is simply to build repurchase rates).

Acquisition Rates   Some of the buyers purchasing during a sales promotion will be nonregular buyers who purchase the specific brand or product because of the incentive. Note that this group can include buyers who usually purchase another brand and buyers who previously were nonusers of the product form. The percentage of "redeemers" who are not regular buyers will normally be greater when[28]

- Average purchase quantity is high.
- Perceived risks and prices are generally low for the product form.
- The incentive is directed toward demographic groups or geographic areas in which the product or firm's market share is relatively low.
- Direct mail is used to distribute coupons or other information about a promotion (as mentioned earlier in this chapter).

Managers should note that the displacement rate and the acquisition rate may not add up to 100 percent of the number of redemptions. That is, there is one more category of response that managers must consider when identifying redeemers—stock-up effects.

Stock-Up Rates   If an incentive is sufficiently large, some of the sales made during a promotion period will reflect "borrowed" sales from future sales periods, as buyers stock up on the product while special prices are in effect. Although this effect may be desirable when the sales-promotion objective is to build buyer inventories, managers should recognize that this will result in some reduction in sales in the postpromotion period. Additionally, the borrowed sales are made at a lower contribution margin than would be obtained if the stock-up did not occur. Consequently, as in the case of displaced sales, managers should determine the reduction in total contribution resulting from these sales. In attempting to es-

---

[27]Liz Murphy, "Redemption Isn't Always Salvation in Couponing," *Sales and Marketing Management,* Jan. 13, 1986, p. 46.

[28]Some findings that support these conditions are available in Karl Irons, John D. C. Little, and Robert L. Klein, "Determinants of Coupon Effectiveness," in "Advances and Practices of Marketing Science," *Proceedings of the 1983 ORSA/TIMS Marketing Science Conference,* pp. 157–164.

timate the magnitude of stock-up effects, managers should recognize that stock-up effects will be greater when

- Buyers are reasonably sure that they will use the extra amounts purchased in the future.
  - Buyers will not have a large amount of space or money tied up in inventory.
  - The risk of spoilage or obsolescence is low.
  - Promotions are directed toward regular buyers or large market-share territories.
  - No limits on volume (such as two to a customer) are established.

Importantly, coupons and in-store price promotions have been shown to result in large differences in stock-up rates. A price promotion is only temporary and usually applies to multiple purchases, so stock-up effects are generally high. By contrast, coupons (usually) do not have short-term expiration dates and are only good for one purchase, so the incentive to stock up is less.[29]

Conversion Rates   When the marketing strategy is to build market share, the role of sales promotion is normally to build a larger customer base. Additionally, even large market-share firms may find that market share can be improved among certain demographic groups or geographic areas in which the firm's market share is somewhat lower than the overall market share. In these cases, the primary objective of sales promotion is to build product trial in order to convert nonregular buyers into regular buyers in the future. Indeed, the primary justification for sales promotion in this case is to gain converts for a product or brand. Accordingly, managers should attempt to estimate the level of postpromotion sales that will come from customers acquired during the promotion period. (As suggested earlier in this chapter, conversion rates appear to be higher when the promotion requires high degrees of customer effort relative to the value of the incentive in order to take advantage of the promotional offer. However, conversion rates are very difficult to estimate without some base of historical experience to draw upon.)

Most of the results from research on the effects of couponing, however, suggest that brand switching consumers generally revert to their own brands after making a coupon redemption or a promotion purchase.[30] Thus, managers would appear to be wise to make very conservative assumptions about conversion rates when attempting to project the outcome of a given price promotion.

Product-Line Effects   Managers should recognize that sales promotions are very similar to price cuts. Consequently, cross-elasticities of demand may exist between the promoted product and complementary or substitute products. Retailers and other firms which offer many complementary products should, there-

---

[29]See Robert Blattberg, Gary Eppen, and Joshua Lieberman, "A Theoretical and Empirical Evaluation of Price Deals for Consumer Nondurables," *Journal of Marketing,* Winter 1981, pp. 116–129.

[30]Kapil Bawa and Robert Shoemaker, "The Effects of a Direct Mail Coupon on Brand Choice Behavior," *Journal of Marketing Research,* November 1987, pp. 370–376.

fore, attempt to identify increases in sales of these products (that is, drag-along sales) due to increased sales in the promoted "leader" product. Similarly, if the promotion creates sales shifts among different sizes or models of a product, such "cannibalized" sales should be considered in evaluating the total impact of the promotion.

Figure 11-3 summarizes the relationship among these six response estimates.

Assessing Profitability Implications

Assuming that managers can identify the direct costs associated with a sales promotion and can develop some rough estimates of market response, the profitability implications of a given promotion can be assessed by comparing the "normal" contribution over the period of the promotion with the expected promotional contribution. As Figure 11-4 indicates, there are three steps involved in assessing profitability implications: (1) Estimate the reduced contribution from displaced and stock-up sales; (2) estimate the increased contribution from incremental sales to new buyers; (3) subtract the direct costs of the sales promotion. These steps are illustrated in the following example.

FIGURE 11-3   Relationship among types of market responses to sales promotions.

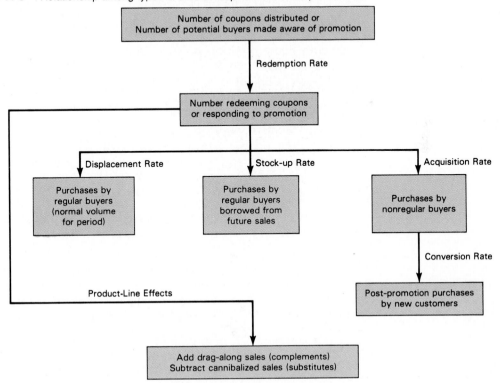

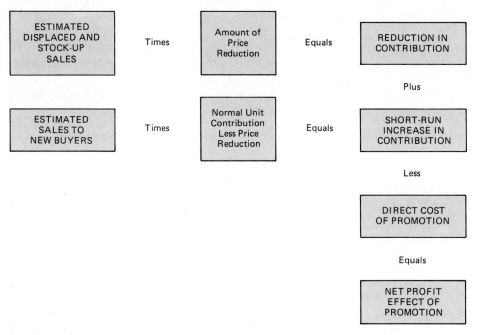

FIGURE 11-4 Assessing the profitability of a sales promotion.

Monterrey Foods produces a variety of frozen dinner entrees. The firm is contemplating a 1-month coupon promotion (during March) that is designed to attract buyers to its line of Mexican dinners. Specifically, the company is planning to distribute 10 million coupons (good on any Monterrey Mexican dinner entree) by direct mail at a cost of $200,000.

Currently, Monterrey sells its Mexican dinners to retailers at an average manufacturer's selling price of $16.08 per case (with each case containing six units). Monterrey's variable costs are $9.00 per case. Consequently, the current variable-contribution margin (VCM) per case is

$$\text{VCM per case} = \text{price per case} - \text{variable cost per case}$$
$$= \$16.08 - \$9.00$$
$$= \$7.08 \text{ per case}$$

Under the terms of the coupon offer, Monterrey will reimburse retailers for the consumers' savings at the rate of 60 cents per unit (or $3.60 per case) and for retailers' redemption charges of 8 cents per unit (or 48 cents per case). So Monterrey's VCM per case on coupon sales will be

$$\text{VCM per case} = \$7.08 - \$3.60 - \$0.48$$
$$= \$3.00 \text{ per case}$$

Based on previous company and industry experience, Monterrey managers expect 6 percent of the coupons to be redeemed. Additionally, based on the company's market share and the fact that direct mail is to be used, about 20 percent of the redeemed coupons are expected to be displaced sales. (Because most consumers have a limited amount of freezer space, Monterrey's managers do not expect any significant stock-up effects due to the promotion.) Given these estimates, then, the estimated total sales resulting from coupon redemption will be

Number of coupons distributed times redemption rate = number redeemed

or

$$10 \text{ million} \times 6\% = 600,000$$

At six items per case, the 600,000 items purchased with coupons will be equivalent to 100,000 cases. Of these, 20 percent (20,000 cases) represent displaced sales. The remainder (80,000 cases) represent sales to nonregular buyers because Monterrey has assumed zero stock-up sales.

The profitability consequences of the promotion (based on the estimate of response) can be identified in Table 11-5. Note that the increase in variable contribution that results from sales to nonregular buyers is outweighed by the combination of the direct costs of the promotion (the cost of distributing the coupons) and the reduction in variable contribution on displaced sales.

TABLE 11-5 DETERMINING THE IMPACT ON PROFIT CONTRIBUTION
OF MONTERREY'S COUPON PROMOTION

Increases in contribution due to sales to new buyers
equals coupon sales to new buyers times contribution on coupon sales

$$= 80,000 \times \$3.00$$
$$= \underline{\$240,000}$$

Lost contribution on displaced sales and stock-up sales equals coupon sales to regular buyers times reduction in variable contribution margin due to promotion

$$= 20,000 \times (\$7.08 - \$3.00)$$
$$= 20,000 \times \$4.08$$
$$= \underline{\$81,600}$$

Increases in direct costs due to promotion
$$= \underline{\$200,000}$$
Net impact on total contribution
$$= 240,000 - 81,600 - \$200,000$$
$$= -\$41,600$$

In examining the profitability impact, several other points should be considered. First, the reduced profitability may well be acceptable to management if the promotion has achieved its primary objective of acquiring new customers. In this particular case, nonregular buyers are expected to purchase 80,000 cases of the product during the promotion. Second, the analysis in Table 11-5 does not account for future gains in contribution from the new customers. Third, managers should examine their prior experience and the buying process to determine whether the promotion will cannibalize sales of other products or create any drag-along sales from complementary products.

In sum, the Monterrey example indicates several of the problems faced by sales-promotion managers. Although the profitability consequences of sales-promotion programs can be calculated, they will often be based on very rough estimates of market response. Firms that use a given sales-promotion device frequently, and that carefully monitor the results in terms of these types of market response, will be able to develop a fairly high degree of accuracy in projecting the effects of the sales promotion. Firms with limited experience can use management's knowledge of market share and of the buying process factors in order to project displacement, conversion, and stocking-up effects. All firms can also use the experience of sales-promotion specialists in estimating coupon-redemption rates.

But no matter how extensive a firm's experience, managers should determine how sensitive the profitability results will be if slight errors in estimation are made. That is, a series of profitability analyses should be conducted to determine the profit impact of lower redemption and conversion rates or of higher displacement rates. For example, Monterrey might examine the profitability of the proposed program at a redemption rate of 10 percent instead of 6 percent, or at a displacement rate of 50 percent rather than 20 percent. This procedure will provide managers with greater understanding of the profitability risks involved in the program.

Testing and Monitoring the Program

In addition to using experience and judgment, managers can use test-marketing experiments to predict the kind of market response that will occur—at least in terms of total sales and in terms of coupon redemptions.

In order to obtain precise information on displacement and conversion rates, however, managers should supplement test marketing by employing other research techniques. For example, panels of consumers may be employed. By monitoring specially selected households' purchasing patterns over time, brand-switching behavior and changes in purchase rates can be measured to estimate conversion and displacement effects. Additionally, when industry sales data are known, changes in competitors' retail sales and market shares can be measured by using syndicated services such as A. C. Nielsen. Increasingly, however, large packaged goods firms are relying on electronic test markets (discussed in Chapter

6) for detailed tracking of sales promotion because such services provide the most comprehensive information.

Additionally, managers are finding that the effectiveness of sales promotions for a given product may vary substantially across geographic areas. As we saw in Chapter 5, product consumption rates can vary dramatically across ZIP Code clusters. Thus it is generally wise to test different versions of promotions (when feasible) in different markets and to measure performance in a way that allows management to observe any geographical differences in response.

CONCLUSION

The recent rate of growth in sales-promotion activity appears to reflect the effectiveness of this marketing tool in influencing demand. However, several cautionary notes are in order to users of sales promotions.

First, the long-term impact of sales promotions on brand equity is not certain. Some feel that promotion can damage the brand image especially if it is not combined with consumer-franchise-building activity. A judicious mix of advertising and sales promotion would generally be advisable. This means that management should stimulate closer coordination between advertising and sales-promotion programs and should involve advertising agencies in the sales-promotion decision process.

Second, managers have much to learn about the ways in which buyers and distributors respond to promotions. For a given objective, a number of sales-promotion alternatives are usually available. In order to make intelligent choices among these options, more research is needed to determine the relative effectiveness of various programs.

Third, sales promotions must be coordinated with advertising programs (to communicate the special offer) and with sales programs (to follow up on customers' inquiries and trade support). This means that clearly defined objectives and logically developed programs will be essential if these programs are to work in a synchronized way to implement the marketing strategy.

In this chapter we have presented several concepts and tools managers can use to develop effective sales promotions. In addition, we have described a process for combining various kinds of information in order to select programs that will be consistent with the marketing strategy and with a product's profitability requirements. This process is summarized in Figure 11-5.

To review some of these elements and their relationships to one another, consider the following sales-promotion program.

McDonald's: The Big Mac Birthday Promotion

McDonald's is one of the leading practitioners of sales promotion in the world. Not only are national promotions such as games, contests, and special meal combinations offered frequently, but individual stores and regions offer a wide array

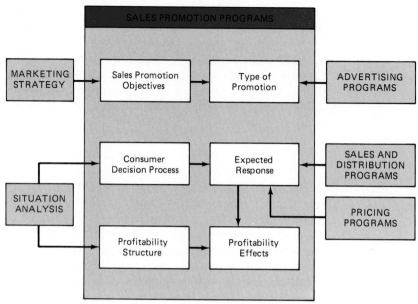

FIGURE 11-5 Relationship of sales promotion to marketing strategy, situation analyses, and other marketing programs.

of local promotions such as special celebrity appearances and tie-in's with local charities. When combined with extensive advertising these programs create a high level of awareness of the company and its products. Nevertheless, eating at McDonald's is a discretionary activity and the competition in the restaurant business is intense. Thus, most promotions are designed to do more than build awareness.

In January 1989, McDonald's implemented a "$.99 Big Mac" promotion to celebrate the twentieth anniversary of that sandwich. National television and radio ads ran for the first 2 weeks of the 3-week promotion period. The ad campaign was funded out of the cooperative advertising funds provided by franchisees. (The actual promotion lasted for 3 weeks.) Local stores were responsible for buying in-store displays and point-of-purchase materials to remind customers of the promotion. Additionally, each store was responsible for adding the extra labor help required because of the increased business such promotions generate. In a typical store this might amount to $2000 for a 3-week promotion of this sort.

The results of the Big Mac promotion in one Florida outlet are given below. The sales data contrast the 3 weeks prior to the promotion with the promotion period's sales. Both of these periods are normally high-volume periods for the company.

1 What were the probable sales-promotion objectives of this promotion?

2 Why would McDonald's run a promotion of this magnitude during what is normally a high-volume period?

3 How would the various issues discussed under "Selecting a Specific Sales Promotion" in this chapter have been useful in considering the design of the Big Mac promotion?

4 Outline, in an expanded version of Table 11-5, the various categories of sales and costs that would need to be considered in evaluating the profitability of the Big Mac promotion. (Put in the numbers that are available, and identify the additional data needed for a complete evaluation.)

	3 weeks prior	Promotion period
Sales	$27,285	$33,184
Transactions	8692	10,745
Average check	$ 3.15	$ 3.09
Big Mac	1191	4221
Quarter Pounder	1033	800
McDLT	310	219
Nuggets	554	578
Salads	449	434
Filet	790	705
Regular fry	2322	2876
Medium fry	406	597
Large fry	1479	2084
Regular drink	1118	1304
Medium drink	1549	1731
Large drink	1047	1161
32 oz. drink	258	256

QUESTIONS AND SITUATIONS FOR DISCUSSION

1 What sales-promotion objective and program would be most appropriate for each of the following? Why?
a A leading brand of spaghetti
b A new substance-abuse health care facility
c A lawn care company
d A sports magazine
2 About 60 percent of all manufacturers' sales are accompanied by trade deals which reduce prices to distributors by an average of 12 percent. Why wouldn't manufacturers just reduce the regular price of their products by an equivalent amount?
3 Two banks (in different markets) are offering a set of silverware as a premium. One bank is offering the premium at no charge to customers who deposit $500 in an account. The other bank is offering the premium for $5 plus a deposit of $500. Taking into account the buying process factors discussed in this chapter, are there any reasons why the $5 offer may be as effective as (or even more effective than) the no-charge premium offer in generating a response?

4 For which of the following brands would the level of promotion be lowest relative to the level of advertising expenditure? Explain your answer.
  a Sears-brand paint
  b Jello pudding
  c Minute Maid frozen orange juice

5 In general, which of the following kinds of sales responses do you think would be most *difficult* to predict for a firm with extensive experience in sales promotion?
  a Displacement rates
  b Conversion rates
  c Coupon redemption rates

6 In 1989, Donald Trump acquired the Eastern Shuttle which flies to Boston, New York, and Washington. At the time of the acquisition, competitor Pan Am held an 80 percent share of the shuttle market versus 20 percent for Eastern. Once it became known that Trump would acquire (and rename) the shuttle, Pan Am initiated a promotion called the "Corporate Jet Game," a scratch-off card that made passengers eligible to win free miles or a trip to Bermuda. A follow-up frequent flyer promotion offered a chance to earn free tickets to other destinations. Trump countered with 500,000 direct mail coupons containing bonus miles to former Eastern frequent fliers followed by a "Be My Guest" promotion in which Trump Shuttle passengers received $25 certificates good at selected quality restaurants.

   Discuss the sales-promotion objectives of each airline as reflected in these promotional events. In your opinion, is the apparent high level of sales-promotion expenditures surprising? Explain.

7 General Foods has begun to more carefully consider regional differences in brand sales before embarking on sales promotions. For example, Country Time Drink Mix was experiencing a declining share of market nationally but was sufficiently strong in certain regions to warrant continued support. Accordingly, promotions were developed at a regional level in order to appeal to consumers and to retail buyers more effectively. For example in Dallas, the company ran a picnic to accompany a Willie Nelson concert. The firm offered 40-cent coupons on Country Time products in a print ad describing Nelson's July Fourth picnic. Additionally, a local country music station promoted a contest in which anyone at the picnic spotted with any Country Time label would win $25 in groceries at selected supermarkets. To participate, supermarkets had to meet certain product display requirements. The promotion boosted sales volume by 65 percent.

   Discuss the facets of this program that helped make it successful in terms of short-run sales. Are there any features of the program that would also lead to enhanced long-term sales?

8 In the fall of 1990, Quaker Oats Company launched Quaker Direct, a system that delivers coupons for Quaker products to households that are individually targeted based on a promotional data base run by Computerized Marketing Technologies of New York. Thus, only households with dogs will receive coupons for Gaines Burgers. Moreover, coupon values will vary by household. Finally, because each coupon is coded, Quaker can track redemptions by households. The system also permits Quaker to design surveys to detect changing customer needs. To attract and retain these households, Quaker will also run sweepstakes and contests for participants.

   The cost of Quaker Direct is about $27.50 per 1000 households reached. This is double the rate of independent targeted-household services and four times the cost of distributing free-standing inserts. Given this higher cost, what offsetting benefits might Quaker receive that relate to enhanced future sales-promotion opportunities?

SUGGESTED ADDITIONAL READINGS

Bawa, Kapil, and Robert Shoemaker, "Analyzing Incremental Sales from a Direct Mail Coupon Promotion," *Journal of Marketing,* July 1989, pp. 66–78.

Blattberg, Robert, Thomas Buesing, Peter Peacock, and Subrata Sen, "Identifying the Deal-Prone Segment," *Journal of Marketing Research,* August 1978, pp. 369–377.

Bolton, Ruth, "The Relationship between Market Characteristics and Promotional Price Elasticities," *Marketing Science,* Spring 1989, pp. 153–169.

Buzzell, Robert, John A. Quelch, and Walter Salmon, "The Costly Bargain of Trade Promotion," *Harvard Business Review,* March–April 1990, pp. 141–149.

Farris, Paul, and John A. Quelch, "In Defense of Price Promotion," *Sloan Management Review,* Fall 1987, pp. 63–69.

Hardy, Kenneth, "Key Success Factors for Manufacturers' Sales Promotions in Package Goods," *Journal of Marketing,* July 1986, pp. 13–23.

Quelch, John A., "It's Time to Make Trade Promotion More Productive," *Harvard Business Review,* May–June 1983, pp. 130–139.

Reibstein, David J., and Phyllis A. Traver, "Factors Affecting Coupon Redemption Rates," *Journal of Marketing,* Fall 1982, pp. 102–113.

Varadarajan, P. Rajan, "Cooperative Sales Promotion: An Idea Whose Time Has Come," *Journal of Consumer Marketing,* Winter 1986, pp. 15–33.

Walters, Rockney, "An Empirical Investigation into Retailer Response to Manufacturer Trade Promotions," *Journal of Retailing,* Summer 1989, pp. 253–272.

CHAPTER 12

SALES AND DISTRIBUTION PROGRAMS: ESTABLISHING OBJECTIVES AND APPEALS

OVERVIEW

Sales and distribution programs include all activities that involve direct personal contact with final buyers or with wholesale or retail distributors. Principally, these activities focus on three functions:

- Communicating individually-tailored sales messages
- Providing customer service—information or assistance regarding product features, order status, or complaints for individual customers
- Coordinating the scheduling and methods of product delivery

These activities are of paramount importance in executing a marketing strategy when individual buyers or distributors have highly complex and varied needs and wants. In such circumstances, personal interaction is critical to properly understand and respond to each customer's buying situation or problem.

Although the range of activities involved in sales and distribution programs seems rather broad, in reality these activities are all a part of the sales function in a typical organization. Indeed individual salespeople often spend more time on the many customer service activities than on *selling* per se. Additionally, as we discuss later in this chapter, salespeople may find that the various terms associated with the frequency and size of product shipments are often as important as product quality or list price in making a sale.

These same basic activities take place whether a firm is selling direct to final buyers or to distributors or both. In smaller industrial firms in particular, the same salespeople or sales managers may have responsibility for both direct sales to buyers and for working with distributors.

Because the topics of personal selling, customer service, distribution-channel relationships, and physical distribution policy are so highly integrated, they must be viewed as parts of comprehensive sales and distribution programs. In this chapter and the next, we examine the process for developing and evaluating these programs. Four major steps are required in this process:

1 Defining sales and distribution *objectives* designed to implement the firm's marketing strategy

2 Identifying the most appropriate sales *appeals* to be used in accomplishing objectives

3 Determining and assigning the human and financial *resources* required for the program

4 Evaluating program *performance* to adjust the program as necessary

The first two of these steps are examined in this chapter. In particular, we will present the kinds of objectives that can be used to guide the sales and distribution effort and the kinds of appeals the firms can employ. Subsequently, we will discuss the factors to be considered in selecting the best appeal and the best approaches that the sales force can use in presenting and gaining acceptance of the sales appeal. Finally, we will examine some of the unique considerations involved in selling through distributors.

Before examining sales and distribution objectives, however, it is important to understand the basic types of *sales and distribution systems* which can be employed by organizations. An understanding of these types of systems is important because the specific role of the sales force in implementing a marketing strategy will vary across these types of systems. (Figure 12-1 shows the main elements of a sales and distribution program.)

TYPES OF SALES AND DISTRIBUTION SYSTEMS

As summarized in Table 12-1, marketers can employ four basic types of sales and distribution systems, each of which differs in terms of the role played by personal selling.

Direct Response Systems Direct response systems are essentially hybrid pro-

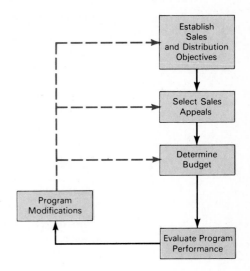

FIGURE 12-1   Elements of a sales and distribution program.

grams which may combine advertising, personal selling, and sales-promotion programs. However, because of their rapid growth and because they possess some special characteristics, they deserve to be viewed as sales and distribution systems. Specifically, direct response systems are characterized by the following:

• Unlike mass advertising, sales messages are directed to individually targeted customers, usually through telephone calls or direct mail.
• Customers are preselected from lists of individuals whose characteristics presumably indicate that they are good prospects. (For example, a mailing list of travel-card holders might be considered a good prospect list for luggage or vacation travel products.)
• Products are delivered directly to the final buyer.

Direct response marketing has grown dramatically in recent years. In large part, this growth is attributable to the fact that sales and distribution costs are substantially lower in such systems. Therefore, if only a small fraction of targeted customers responds with an order, direct response sales programs can be successful. For example,

> Paris-based Hermés, a retailer of exclusive women's fashions, has recently opened several stores in the United States and developed a mail-order catalog operation. Hermés sends out 300,000 catalogs to get around 4600 orders. But these orders generate $1.7 million in sales (about $375 per order), while the catalogs cost only $1.10 apiece.[1]

While historically, direct response systems have been viewed by the general public to be very consumer goods-oriented, the use of direct response (especially telephone selling) has also grown rapidly in the industrial sector. Well over $100

[1]Phyllis Berman, "Mass Production? Yech!" *Forbes,* Sept. 22, 1986, pp. 182–183.

TABLE 12-1   TYPES OF SALES AND DISTRIBUTION SYSTEMS

Types	Key characteristics
Direct systems	
1. Direct response systems	• Products distributed directly to final buyer • Sales message delivered to individual buyers by telephone or direct mail • Primary function is to obtain orders
2. Direct personal selling systems	• Products distributed directly to final buyer • Sales message delivered to individual buyers by face-to-face contact (Telephone selling may be used for order taking) • Primary functions are to provide product information, technical advice, customer service, identify changing customer needs
Indirect systems	
1. Trade selling systems	• Products distributed through wholesalers or retailers who usually buy for resale to final buyers • Sales message delivered by face-to-face contact (Telephone selling may be used for order taking) • Primary functions are to obtain distributor support, provide product information, provide sales training and assistance to distributors
2. Missionary selling systems	• Products distributed through wholesalers or retailers who usually buy for resale to final buyers. • Sales message delivered by face-to-face contact • Primary function is to provide product information and customer service directly to final buyer or to those who influence buyers

billion worth of industrial products are sold by telephone each year with no clear limits on the kinds of products that can be effectively sold in this way, as General Electric's experience shows.

> General Electric's telemarketing operation grew to 45 telemarketing centers employing 2,000 employees under the management of Richard Huether. GE sells everything from medical accessories to hi-tech energy systems by telephone and, as Huether suggests, "We don't see this as some kind of special selling function reserved for certain products."[2]

As is the case with consumer goods, economics has an important part to play in the growth of direct response in the industrial sector. Put simply, telemarketing is a more efficient way of contacting small-volume accounts than direct personal selling. Additionally, however, many firms (such as GE) have found that once telemarketing relationships are established, the amount of business generated from smaller customers often grows dramatically. Usually this occurs because customers begin to use the *inbound* telemarketing network to call for technical advice or order information. In effect the system empowers customers to obtain

[2]Bill Kelley, "Is There Anything That Can't Be Sold by Phone?" *Sales and Marketing Management,* April 1989, pp. 60–64.

some control over the business relationship in terms of determining the information they want at a time they select.

Direct Personal Selling Systems   As with direct response systems, products are shipped direct to the customer. However, unlike direct response systems most sales messages are delivered face to face. Note that this direct selling may be performed by a manufacturer's own sales force or by commissioned sales representatives. Technically, such representatives are wholesale distributors, but they perform only selling activities, so if they call only on final buyers they function as a direct sales force. Direct personal selling is used when the role of the sales force is more complex than the presentation of a simple sales message and asking for the order. Specifically, these salespeople focus their efforts on helping customers solve specific purchasing problems by demonstrating how a product (or service) can be used or adapted to fit customer needs. Additionally, they may also be responsible for identifying new products that might be developed to satisfy these needs. Finally, they may also perform *customer service* activities such as following up on customer complaints; providing maintenance, repair, and operating (MRO) services; assuring reliable delivery; providing information on inventories and order processing; and assisting customers in managing spare parts inventories.

Trade Selling Systems   When organizations employ wholesalers and/or retailers to physically distribute products to final customers, a major role for the sales force is to assure that distributors are willing and able to support the marketing strategy. Accordingly, the sales force is usually called on to demonstrate to distributors how they can benefit from following specific policies which also enhance a manufacturer's sales. These policies can include promotion, service, space allocation, inventory, and production-assortment decisions. Additionally, this sales force may be responsible for providing distributors with the same kinds of customer service support that the direct sales force provides for the final buyer.

Missionary Selling Systems   Missionary selling also involves activities that enhance distributors' sales. However, these activities are primarily directed toward final buyers or toward individuals who influence the buying decision rather than toward distributors. For instance, a hospital-equipment manufacturer may use a wholesaler but will rely on its own missionary sales force to provide product information to key hospital personnel. Similarly, publishers use their own sales force to call on college professors, who influence students' purchases of textbooks, even though a local bookstore is used to distribute the product. These kinds of sales forces are employed when distributors' salespeople are inadequately trained or insufficient in number to provide the technical information required. Additionally, when distributors carry extremely wide and diverse product lines and when new products are developed at a high rate (as happens in the pharmaceutical industry), the missionary sales force will be especially useful.

The foregoing characterization suggests that there are significant differences in the role of the sales force across sales and distribution systems. However, there are also many differences in the role of the sales force *within* each type of system, as each selling organization has different products, customers, competitors, and strategies. Moreover, some organizations will employ more than one type of system. For example, IBM uses both direct response and direct personal selling systems in marketing typewriters and employs a trade selling system as well as direct personal selling for personal computers. Finally, when selling through distributors, the type of system used will have a bearing on the design of sales and distribution programs. We examine some distribution channel alternatives in the next section of this chapter.

DISTRIBUTION CHANNEL STRUCTURE

A *distribution channel* is a set of organizational units (such as manufacturers, wholesalers, and retailers) that performs all the functions required to get a product from a seller to the final buyer. The structure of the channel is determined by three elements: the *tasks* and activities to be performed by intermediaries, the *type* of distributor to be used, and the *number* of each type of distributor.[3]

Tasks   Firms use distributors to perform those marketing tasks that a supplier cannot perform as effectively or efficiently. The most widely performed distributor tasks include maintaining availability through local delivery or by having the product at locations convenient to the customer, providing customer financing and maintenance or repair services, and local selling and advertising of the product's benefits. These tasks are most likely to be performed by distributors rather than by suppliers when

• There are large numbers of buyers, each of whom purchases in small dollar amounts so that the cost of making personal sales calls on each one would be very high if performed by a manufacturer.
• A detailed knowledge of local market conditions and buyer needs is important because customers vary dramatically in their needs.
• Special emergency service is important.
• Competitors provide a high level of availability, and therefore convenience or speed of delivery are necessary to be competitive.
• Buyers purchase a wide assortment of related products in small volumes while the manufacturer provides only a narrow assortment and thus cannot meet the buyer's full range of needs.

In other words, the tasks which distributors must perform will depend on what is needed to competitively meet customer needs and on the relative economic efficiency of performing or delegating the task.

---

[3]For a comprehensive examination of distribution channels, see Louis Stern, Adel El-Ansary, and James Brown, *Management in Marketing Channels,* Prentice-Hall, Englewood Cliffs, N.J., 1989.

Type of Wholesale-Level Distributor   A manufacturer considering the use of wholesale-level distributors has a variety of options. As indicated in Figure 12-2, the major differences among types of wholesalers are in the type and number of functions they perform. While all wholesale-level distributors provide a selling function, only merchant wholesalers assume the risk associated with taking title to goods as they move toward the final buyer. Not surprisingly, these wholesalers also receive the largest margins on the sales they make—as high as 25 percent compared to 3 to 7 percent for most agents and brokers. This distinction in functions between merchant wholesalers and agents (or brokers) is the reason why merchant wholesalers are part of a trade selling system while agents are basically just substitutes for a manufacturer's sales force. Thus, when agents call on other

FIGURE 12-2   Characteristics of major types of wholesalers.

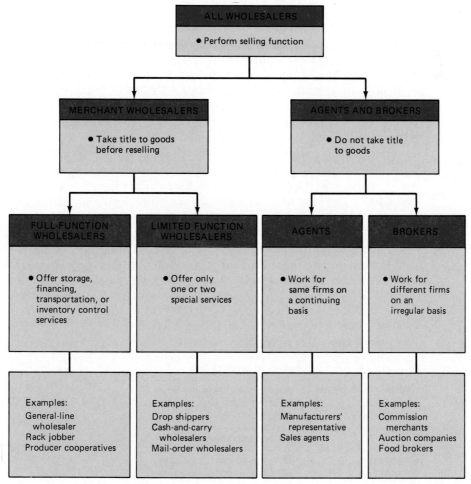

distributors (as is the case with food brokers) they are part of a trade selling system. If they call on final buyers, they are part of a direct selling system.

Type of Retailer   Retailers differ in terms of two major factors: the extent of the product lines they carry and the type of consumer search effort they cater to. Table 12-2 summarizes these distinctions.

The type of retail intermediary employed will depend upon the firm's target markets. For example, in catering to a price-oriented market, stores that are classified as shopping goods-oriented are more likely to be chosen. In attempting to reach a market that is concerned with personal service and an image of quality, specialty stores are generally more appropriate.

At both the wholesale and the retail level, sales managers should target their efforts toward distributors who will perform the required tasks and who are of the type desired to reach the target market.

Number of Distributors   Channels may have an *intensive* pattern of distribution (in which a relatively large number of distributors exist for a given area) or a *selective* pattern of distribution (in which only a few distributors exist for a given area). At the extreme, a distributor may be designated the *exclusive* representative in an area. In general, the more functions a distributor is expected to perform, the more likely an exclusive or selective pattern of distribution will be necessary as a protective measure to provide the incentive for holding large inventories, for offering service, and for aggressive promotion. Selective distribution has other advantages for a supplier as well. When a firm has fewer distributors, the selling costs, delivery costs, and cost of monitoring distributor performance are usually lower. These advantages exist because fewer sales personnel are needed and because fewer points of delivery (normally with more economically sized loads) are required. On the other hand, to the extent that convenience in buying is very important to the buyer (especially for low-involvement consumer goods), then more intensive distribution will be required. Accordingly, managers should be sure that the desired number of accounts in each market is considered before stating the specific number of new accounts to be developed.

TABLE 12-2   WAYS OF CLASSIFYING RETAILERS

Extent of product line	
General merchandise	(Department, discount)
Limited line	(Women's clothing)
Specialty store	(Jeans)

Extent of search effort	
Convenience	(Emphasize location, hours)
Shopping	(Emphasize price, assortment)
Specialty	(Emphasize unique brands, personal service)

Vertical Marketing Systems

The increased recognition of the importance of selling *through and not just to* the distributor had led many firms to develop highly coordinated channels. The term *vertical marketing system* is generally used to describe types of channels in which distributor actions are very highly coordinated with the manufacturer's marketing strategy because a strong, continuing, formal relationship has been established. These systems can be of three types: corporate, contractual, and administered systems.

Corporate systems are channels in which some degree of vertical integration has taken place. That is, if a retailer is owned by a supplier (or vice versa) then a corporate system exists. Today, many oil companies, tire companies, and clothing companies own at least some of their retail outlets. Although the cost of owning distribution outlets may be great, the sales representatives are generally assured that the distribution outlets will fully support the marketing strategy.

Contractual systems include franchising programs and voluntary associations in which legally binding contracts are established that specify the tasks which each party will perform. Specifically, *franchise* programs are contractual arrangements between a manufacturer and a retail- or wholesale-level distributor that specify what assistance suppliers will provide as well as the obligations of distributors. In recent years, these programs have been dominant in such retail businesses as automobile sales, fast-food restaurants, automotive supplies and services, and in some wholesaling businesses (including soft-drink bottling). These lines of trade are similar in several respects: distributors rely primarily on one supplier, extensive capital investment is required of the distributor, and maintenance of quality service standards is important. Because of these features, suppliers and distributors are highly dependent on each other. This means that a relatively high level of distributor support can generally be achieved. *Voluntary associations,* on the other hand, are contractual systems organized by wholesalers to provide comprehensive merchandising and promotional programs to independent retailers. These programs are primarily designed to assist wholesalers' customers in maintaining a competitive posture with respect to franchised or vertically integrated chain retailers. IGA food stores, and Western Auto stores are among the organizations falling into this category.

Administered systems are channels in which distributors have no contractual or ownership dependency on a supplier. Essentially, these manufacturers provide a wide range of incentives in exchange for extensive promotional support and for carrying large inventories and a full line of products. These systems are employed by firms such as O. M. Scott and Sons (lawn and garden products) and Kraft (food products) to provide distributors with comprehensive merchandising advice, protective provisions (such as exclusive distributorships), and direct financial assistance.

SALES AND DISTRIBUTION OBJECTIVES

Given a marketing strategy, managers can define one or more basic objectives for the sales and distribution program. Further, these objectives should be defined in specific terms in order to provide direction to the sales force and establish a basis for evaluating program success.

Of course the most specific kind of objective that can be set and the easiest to measure is a dollar or unit-sales objective. And indeed, sales volume is an important program objective and a widely used basis for evaluating salesperson, sales-territory, and program performance. However, in most cases, sales volume will not be adequate as a program objective, for several reasons.

First, sales and distribution programs cost money, and efforts designed to increase sales may not lead to increased profitability, for reasons discussed in Chapter 13. Accordingly, a sales objective may not be consistent with a product objective of increased profitability. Second, sales results are often determined by competitors' actions, environmental forces, or other marketing programs outside the control of the sales force. Third, the primary role of a marketing program is to implement a marketing strategy. Because the marketing strategy defines target markets and the kind of impact on demand to be achieved, program objectives should reflect the marketing strategy, and simply establishing a sales or profit objective will not reflect the strategy very precisely. Fourth, and finally, a sales objective does not provide the sales force with any guidance on *how* to increase (or maintain) sales volume. Managers should be responsible for providing direction to the sales force by helping to identify the best opportunities for sales development.

In sum, although sales-volume objectives are useful—especially when a direct response system is employed—managers should also establish sales and distribution objectives that

- Reflect the marketing strategy
- Provide a focus for sales-force activities
- Can be used to evaluate sales-force efforts as well as results
- Identify the targets from which future sales volume will come

In general, four kinds of sales and distribution objectives can be employed (each of which should be stated in specific terms): account development, distributor support, account maintenance, and account penetration.

1 *Account-development* objectives are designed to emphasize the acquisition of new distributors or customers. Preferably, managers should identify specific targets for new accounts depending on the marketing strategy. For example, managers might identify: specific user groups or industries in a direct selling system; organizations of a specific size or consumers with special characteristics in a direct response system; specific types of retail outlets in a trade selling system.

2 *Distributor-support* objectives apply to trade selling and are designed to gain the cooperation of retail or wholesale distributors in implementing the marketing strategy. Specifically, manufacturers may seek a variety of types of support, such as distributor participation in cooperative advertising or special sales promotions, aggressive selling of the product, or providing extensive customer service. Distributor support is generally viewed as essential in indirect systems because the distributor is a key partner in the marketing effort. Indeed, when products are in the mature stage of the product life cycle, distributor support may well be the major marketing element in sales successes because technically similar products may be broadly available.

3 *Account-maintenance* objectives typically take up the bulk of a salesperson's time in direct personal selling systems and in trade selling systems. These objectives are emphasized when management is concerned with maintaining an effective selling position through regular sales calls designed to provide information about new products, acquire information on changing customer or distributor needs, and perform customer service activities.

4 *Account-penetration* objectives are designed to increase total sales volume or to increase the sales of more profitable products or complementary products to existing distributors or buyers. For example, direct response marketers often focus their selling efforts on offering different products to customers who have been good respondents in the past. Similarly, industrial firms often share the business of some customers with one or more competitors. (For instance, some automobile manufacturers will purchase tires from two or three suppliers.) An attempt by such firms to increase their share of a buyer's purchase volume reflects an account-penetration objective. Finally, firms which are attempting to get distributors to carry more inventory or allocate more selling space to a product are also pursuing account penetration.

Selecting an Objective

Managers should select a sales and distribution objective that is based on the marketing strategy for each product or product line, because the purpose of sales and distribution programs is to help implement these strategies. This means that managers should identify the needs of the target buyers or distributors and the marketing strategies to be implemented when selecting sales and distribution objectives.

Note that being able to "type" a product according to a portfolio model will not alone enable a manager to select a sales and distribution objective. Although account development is typically an important objective for new products and problem-child products, account penetration may also be employed in those cases. Similarly, reseller support may be an objective sought by managers of any of these types of products. Table 12-3 summarizes the marketing strategies that are typically associated with the various sales and distribution objectives.

Once the program objective has been established, management can then turn its attention to the question of how to achieve the objective. Specifically, managers must identify the kinds of appeals that will be most effective in stimulating the desired buyer or distributor response.

SALES APPEALS

Sales appeals are the basic elements of the marketing offer that the sales force will communicate. That is, appeals reflect the benefits that a seller will offer in order to obtain the type of customer or distributor response stated in the program

TABLE 12-3   SALES AND DISTRIBUTION OBJECTIVES AND RELATED
MARKETING STRATEGIES

Sales and distribution objectives	How they implement marketing strategies
1. Account development	Increasing availability relative to competitors Gaining access to new segments Increasing ability to buy
2. Distributor support	Increasing availability (inventory) Increasing consumption rate Reducing competitive opportunities Increasing promotional support relative to competition
3. Account maintenance	Assuring user satisfaction Reducing competitive opportunities
4. Account penetration	Simplification Increasing consumption rate and purchase volume Increasing ability to buy Head-to-head competition Complementary product sales

objective. Because the sales force communicates directly with final buyers and distributors, it is possible to particularize the appeal to a much greater degree than is possible with advertising. This attribute of selling is distinctly important because distributors may differ in the benefits they desire and because organizational buyers often differ in the criteria they use for selecting a supplier.

In general, six types of appeals may be employed in sales and distribution programs:

- Product appeals
- Logistical appeals
- Protective-provisions appeals
- Simplification appeals
- Price appeals
- Financial-assistance appeals

Product Appeals

Product appeals are the specific product-related benefits that buyers will gain from using a product or that distributors will gain from having the product in their assortments. The benefits of the product will almost always be important to the buyer or distributor. Accordingly, they will almost always be included in the sales message. However, in many cases a number of competing firms will be able to match product attributes or benefits. In those situations, other appeals are more likely to be determinant.

Product appeals are more likely to be determinant when non-economic-perceived risks are high. For example, if an industrial buyer purchases a component which is a major element in the quality of the final product, product quality and reliability will be the most critical attributes. For consumer goods, product appeals will be more important when social or psychological risks are paramount as the following example shows.

> BeautiControl Cosmetics has become the third largest direct selling women's cosmetics business, primarily by focusing on reaching career-oriented and professional women. The key appeal in the BeautiControl marketing plan is that the company offers free color analysis. This technique involves determining a women's skin tone and then identifying what color cosmetics will look best.[4]

In the case of industrial products, product appeals generally include quality control, reliability, distinctive performance features, the ability to meet computer specifications, or compatibility with existing products and systems. In the case of selling to distributors, product appeals are those which demonstrate the impact that carrying the product has on total distributor sales. For example, some products may help to build store traffic, provide prestige to the distributor, or enable the distributor to offer a more complete product line. Of course, not all of these product benefits can be easily demonstrated. As we shall discuss at the end of the chapter, the ability of the sales force to effectively and credibly communicate these benefits will be a major factor in the success of product appeals.

Logistical Appeals

In recent years, the cost of holding inventory has risen sharply because of an increase in the number of models and lines offered and because of the higher cost of borrowing money. Accordingly, logistical appeals have become increasingly effective in dealing with distributors and industrial buyers. These appeals include providing fast processing of orders, providing frequent delivery, and offering expedited delivery. Additionally, some manufacturers offer inventory-management appeals. For example, a buyer may guarantee a supplier that it will buy a minimum amount of a product over the course of a year. In exchange, the seller is responsible for providing very quick delivery (often within 24 hours) and also inherits the inventory-holding cost burden.

The primary effect of logistical appeals, therefore, is to help buyers or distributors reduce the amount of inventory they carry. This benefit is extremely important when any of the following conditions occur:

• Interest rates are high, so the cost of borrowing money to finance inventories causes a significant drain on profits.

• Demand for a product is difficult to predict, perhaps because demand is very sensitive to changes in economic conditions.

• The rate of product obsolescence is very high due to fashion changes, technological changes, or spoilage.

• Space constraints limit the amount of inventory that buyers or distributors are willing to carry.

---

[4]William Barrett, "See Dick and Jinger Sell," *Forbes*, Aug. 7, 1989, p. 48.

A variety of techniques are available for helping customers with inventory problems. Some of these can be seen in the actions taken by A. M. Castle & Co.

> A. M. Castle is an Illinois-based distributor of steel, aluminum, and other metal products to 30,000 industrial customers in a wide variety of industries and locations. During the 1990's, A. M. Castle will reduce from 18 to 12 the number of its regional warehouses. The surviving warehouses will be larger, however, and will stock more inventory to improve customer product selection. Additionally, improved locations for the warehouses will assure next-day delivery for the entire continental United States. At the same time, the company has linked its computer systems with those of customers to exchange information that enables Castle to help its customers track and manage inventory levels.[5]

Although logistical appeals may be very effective, the cost of these appeals can be very high. Accordingly, managers who wish to consider using these appeals should closely examine the profit impact that will result. Some procedures for evaluating this impact are discussed in Chapter 13.

Protective-Provision Appeals

Protective provisions represent specific policies designed to reduce buyer and distributor risk in accepting a product. For example, a supplier may offer *exclusive distributorships*. Under this provision, a wholesaler or retailer will know that there will be little (if any) competition with other distributors of a specific line. This policy tends to be most widely used when a distributor must provide a substantial amount of capital for facilities, service equipment, or inventory in order to sell the product.

To protect resellers against the risk of poor sales, manufacturers may offer the product on *consignment*. In this procedure, the title and the inventory risk remain with the seller until the distributor actually sells the product. Or the seller may provide liberal *return allowances*. This provision allows a distributor to return all unsold merchandise to a seller at a high percentage of the original cost.

To protect buyers against price increases, sellers may offer *long-term contracts* that specify future price levels in exchange for a minimum order volume. To an increasing extent, buyers are becoming willing to accept such contracts even when specific *escalator clauses* are included. These clauses permit the seller to add certain kinds of cost increases (such as labor or material cost increases) to the contracted price.

Finally, *private branding* may be the appeal employed for protective provisions offered to distributors. A private brand is a product manufactured by one firm yet sold under a brand name controlled by a distributor (such as Sears' Kenmore brand). Frequently, manufacturers of cash cows will offer to produce private brands as a means of using excess capacity without incurring the cost of supporting a brand through heavy promotion. Distributors may be successful with a private brand in the maturity stage of the life cycle if a large segment of the

[5]Flynn McRoberts, "Castle Fortified Metal Operations," *Chicago Tribune*, Aug. 7, 1989, p. B1.

market is price-sensitive. Additionally, by having a brand with no direct comparisons available, a distributor's risk of facing heavy price competition is reduced.

In many product categories, an issue of major importance to retail and wholesale distributors is the existence of *gray marketers,* unauthorized outlets which sell branded products far below list price and often offer no service. Gray markets can come about when large buyers take advantage of discounts of 30 to 40 percent and then resell the products to unauthorized dealers at less than what small retail outlets might pay. IBM has protected its dealers from such unauthorized competitors by insisting that dealers and large customers sign contracts agreeing not to resell to unauthorized dealers and by eliminating dealers or customers who violate these contracts.

Simplification Appeals

Simplification appeals are designed to enable the buyer or distributor to reduce the costs of handling, using, or promoting the product.

Manufacturers who sell to distributors often "preticket" merchandise (to save labor costs on the distributor's part) or provide specific promotional aids (sales training or displays). Some manufacturers offer distributors a complete plan for merchandising the product, providing inventory and space-allocation guidelines and promotional programs specifically tailored to the distributor's market. To illustrate, consider the following:

> Manufacturers of packaged goods products offer a variety of simplification appeals to enhance sales of their product. Some, such as Frito-Lay, place great emphasis on rotating the stock to assure that only fresh products are on the shelf. Others try to find ways of rearranging shelves and displays. For example, R. W. Frookies, a new entrant in the cookie business designed the packages so they could be stacked either vertically or horizontally and has designed a variety of shelf displays that the company can use to fit the spaces available in different stores.[6]

In the case of industrial buyers, the provision of special maintenance, repair and operating (MRO) services, and inventory assistance constitutes a parallel to such merchandising plans. This approach simplifies a customer's problems in using the product. As a result, the seller may be able to develop greater buyer or distributor loyalty, because these programs may enable the buyer to use the product more satisfactorily or because they may lead to an increased dependence on the supplier.

Price Appeals

As suggested in Chapter 9, basic price-level decisions are developed by product managers or marketing managers on the basis of cost, demand, and competitive considerations and on the basis of the marketing strategy. The sales force often has an important impact on the final price paid by each buyer, however.

[6]Paul Brown, "Cookie Monsters," *Inc.,* February 1989, pp. 55–56.

In the case of industrial goods, price *shading* is a commonly used appeal for closing a sale—especially when new accounts are being sought. That is, the sales force will often have some latitude on the actual price to be charged and may price "below list" if necessary. This practice is widespread among industrial goods firms. Additionally, under inflationary pressures, many firms develop price lists reflecting possible cost increases which might be incurred, and then systematically offer prices "off list" until cost increases catch up with the original list-price levels. In so doing, firms avoid the cost of frequent price-list revisions and also reduce buyer displeasure over rising prices.

Shading is not always an available option when manufacturers sell to distributors, because of the Robinson-Patman Act restraints on price discrimination that were discussed in Chapter 9. However, *quantity discounts* provide a mechanism for justifying lower prices to some distributors, and they also provide significant benefits to industrial buyers. The rationale for quantity discounts lies in the fact that buyers who order in large quantities do not require proportionately larger sales force, credit, or delivery costs to service the account. An additional possible benefit of quantity purchases to the seller is the reduction in inventory cost that results from shifting large volumes to the distributor or industrial buyer.

Financial-Assistance Appeals

In some cases, a buyer's working-capital, investment, or direct-expense requirements will be sharply increased as a result of a purchase. *Credit and cash discounts* are often provided when inventory requirements are large. Credit terms may range from 30 to 120 days (and often longer) and are designed to allow the distributor time to complete the resale of the product or to allow a buyer time for the production and sale of the final product in order to pay for the order. Cash discounts are designed to permit savings to firms that pay invoices quickly.

Additionally, sellers may offer special equipment free or at substantial savings to distributors in order to defray equipment and facilities investments. Signs, tools, service equipment, storage equipment, and many other inducements fall into this category.

More recently, new forms of financial assistance have been initiated that are designed to achieve special cooperation on stocking new products or building distributor sales support.

> In 1989, IBM began the Flexible Funds Program for its 1900 dealers. In contrast to the old practice of giving special discounts, the new program offers financial aid for things such as new showrooms, special seminars on topics such as computer-aided design, and even paying the salaries of distributor employees designated to sell only IBM products.[7]

[7]Susan Gelford and Maria Shao, "The Power Surge at Computer Dealers," *Business Week*, July 17, 1989, pp. 134–135.

TABLE 12-4   TYPES OF SALES APPEALS

Type of appeal	Examples
Product	Technical features Performance features Impact on distributor sales
Logistical	Speed of delivery Inventory management
Protective provisions	Exclusive distributorships Consignment selling Return allowances Long-term contracts Private branding
Simplification	Preticketing Merchandising assistance MRO services
Price	Price shading Quantity discounts
Financial assistance	Trade credit Cash discounts Special equipment Slotting allowances

On the consumer packaged goods side, the dominant new appeal in recent years is the *slotting allowance,* which is generally requested by supermarkets when the subject of stocking new products comes up.

Retailers initiated slotting allowances as a way of recouping part of the cost of setting up, handling, and stocking new products. In a typical supermarket, the number of items carried doubled between 1979 and 1990 and because many of these new items are line extensions or competing versions, the net gain in retailer revenue is usually modest. Accordingly, retailers have begun to require slotting allowances—upfront payments of $1,000 or more per store for each store in a chain to underwrite costs.[8]

The Relationship between Appeals and Objectives

As summarized in Table 12-4, a large number of appeals can be used as the focal point of the sales-force effort. Indeed, managers may elect to use several of these appeals simultaneously.

In general, nearly any type of appeal can be used to attempt to achieve a given sales and distribution objective. However, for a given type of objective, certain appeals do merit special consideration. For example,

[8]Lois Therrien, "Want Shelf Space at the Supermarket? Ante Up," *Business Week,* Aug. 7, 1989, pp. 60–61.

- Protective provisions, shading, and product appeals are very widely used for account development, especially if the buyers or distributors have limited knowledge of the seller's product.
- Simplification and financial-assistance appeals are widely utilized to build distributor support, because these appeals are effective in stimulating cooperative attitudes on the part of distributors.
- Logistical and simplification appeals are widely used in achieving account maintenance, especially if product features and prices do not vary a great deal among competing suppliers.
- Quantity discounts and long-term contracts are often effective for achieving account-penetration objectives because they focus most directly on the issue of increased volume.

However, in selecting specific appeals for a customer or a market segment, it is important that sales managers and sales-force personnel understand what motivates a buyer or distributor. As we suggested earlier, one advantage of using a sales force is the ability to adapt the marketing offer to meet particular buyer or distributor requirements. Additionally, the success of a given appeal will depend on the type of power or influence relationship that exists between a seller and a buyer or distributor. Buyer-distributor requirements and power relationships are both discussed in the next section of this chapter.

SELECTING AND IMPLEMENTING APPEALS

As we suggested at the outset of the chapter, the distinctive feature of sales-force activities is the personal interaction between the sales force and the buyers and distributors. This personal interaction has two basic functions:

- To develop an understanding of buyer or distributor requirements so that management can select appropriate appeals. (Figure 12-3 shows the process of selecting a sales appeal.)
- To maintain a power or influence relationship with buyers or distributors in order to successfully *implement* the appeals.

Buyer or Distributor Requirements

Requirements here refers to the various benefits that organizational buyers or distributors desire from a seller to satisfy the needs of their businesses. In Chapter 3, several kinds of benefits were identified. However, these can be expected to vary on a segment-by-segment basis, and often on a customer-by-customer basis—especially when a number of individuals are involved in the buying center. Accordingly, sales and customer service personnel must assess how their products and services fit the needs of *each* account. In order to do this, the sales force must be able to answer questions such as the following:

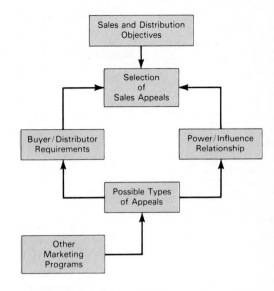

FIGURE 12-3   The process of selecting a sales appeal.

- How significant is the performance or quality of the product to the operation or performance of the buyer's business or to the distributor's assortment or image?
- What special problems does a buyer have in using the product or a distributor have in selling or servicing the product?
- What is the price-elasticity in markets served by buyers or distributors?
- What related costs must buyers or distributors incur in order to maintain inventory or to promote the product?
- What costs (such as lost sales or production bottlenecks) are incurred by buyers or distributors as a consequence of late delivery or stockouts by the seller?
- How can the sales force help the company's distributors meet their financial objectives (regarding inventory turnover or gross-margin return on inventory investment) or their sales-growth objectives?

Additionally, the salespeople who call on buyers or distributors must understand not only the buyer/distributor *product* requirements but the customer's sales process as well. That is, each buyer is likely to have individual preferences or be in special situations that condition the amount and kind of information needed to make a purchase. Some may desire a short sales presentation while others may need extensive information and materials to use in gaining approval from their managers.[9]

[9]David Szymanski, "Determinants of Selling Effectiveness: The Importance of Declarative Knowledge to the Personal Selling Concept," *Journal of Marketing,* January 1988, pp. 64–77.

TABLE 12-5 ALTERNATIVE POWER BASES AVAILABLE TO MANUFACTURERS, DISTRIBUTORS, AND BUYERS

Power base	To a manufacturer	To a buyer or distributor
Reward	Ability to offer product with low prices, quantity discounts	Ability to offer large buying volume
Coercive	Ability to withdraw product (with little loss in sales) when no comparable alternative is available to buyer or distributor	Ability to reject offer (with little loss in sales volume) when no equivalent distributors or buyers are available to seller
Expert	Ability to offer superior or needed technical assistance	Ability to provide unique distribution support
Referent	Ability to offer prestige brand name	Ability to offer image of quality retail outlet or to serve as prestige example of satisfied buyer
Legitimate	Contractual provision that requires distributor to carry full line	Contractual provision that requires seller to provide warranty, repair, exclusive distribution

Power Relationships

Power reflects the degree to which one firm can influence the actions and decisions of another firm. Power is significant in the selection of appeals because it reflects the degree to which sellers have real control over what appeals to offer. Some buyer or distributor requirements may be met in full simply because the supplier needs their selling support or buying volume. In such cases, the buyer or distributor can be viewed as more powerful than the supplier. Alternatively, buyers or distributors may be willing to accept a seller-determined appeal because of various sources of power possessed by the seller.

Theoretically, five bases of power exist. See Table 12-5 for a summary of the power bases available.[10]

• One firm may have power because of its ability to *reward* the other. By offering an economically desirable appeal (such as a high gross margin), a seller may be able to induce a distributor to provide greater selling support or increase inventories.

• Buyers or distributors that account for a large portion of a seller's volume may be able to demand specific appeals because of the *coercive* power they hold. That is, the fear of losing a key account may compel a seller to offer special delivery terms or service appeals.

• Product or service appeals are often desirable to buyers or distributors because of the seller's *expertise*. Similarly, distributors may accept simplification appeals because they believe the manufacturer has a greater knowledge of final buyer needs or of appropriate merchandising techniques.

[10]For an extensive discussion of the significance of power relationships, see Gary Frazier, "Interorganizational Exchange Behavior in Marketing Channels: A Broadened Perspective," *Journal of Marketing,* Fall 1983, pp. 68–78; and John F. Gaski, "The Theory of Power and Conflict in Channels of Distribution," *Journal of Marketing,* Summer 1984, pp. 9–29.

- Certain appeals may be acceptable or desirable because of one firm's *referent* power. That is, a buyer or distributor may want the prestige of working with an established, well-known supplier, and thus be willing to forego some normal financial requirements in favor of product appeals.
- *Legitimate* power usually exists when a seller and a distributor have a contractual relationship. For example, a franchiser's contract with the franchisee states the specific appeals (such as selective distribution, promotional aids) that will be used. When a supplier has legitimate power, the distributor fully accepts the legal or proprietary right of the supplier to specify certain levels of reseller support, and more or less standard appeals are established for all distributors.

To the extent that a supplier can measure the amount of power it holds relative to the amount buyers hold, some guidelines for selecting appeals can be developed. For example, if a supplier knows that it is perceived as having a unique technological advantage, management should emphasize its expertise by using product appeals. If a supplier has the ability to significantly reduce a buyer's costs or increase a distributor's profit by offering lower prices, management should use reward power by employing price appeals.

It is also important to recognize that power relationships can change over time. Indeed it appears that the relative power of manufacturers is in decline in many industries (both domestic and overseas) for a variety of reasons.

- In wholesale distribution, larger professionally managed firms are displacing smaller family businesses at a rapid rate. Moreover, these larger wholesalers are establishing strong on-going, long-term contractual relationships with final buyers, making it difficult for manufacturers to avoid dealing with them.[11]
- Large-scale retailers are also gaining a larger share of consumer goods sales, especially in the supermarket industry. This has enabled them to build their economic power base. But additionally, their expertise power is growing because of information technology. Expanded electronic scanning and computing capabilities combined with new statistical models for doing productivity analyses are allowing retailers to assess the profit performance of manufacturer brands more closely and to rely less on manufacturers' sales forces for advice on space allocation and in-store merchandising tactics.[12]
- Historically, manufacturers have held a strong power advantage in Japan because of the dominance of small retailers. In that nation, 1.6 million small stores control 53 percent of sales. (In contrast, only 3 percent of sales go through small stores in the United States.) In large measure, this power is a result of legislation which allowed small retailers to determine whether large stores could be introduced in their trading areas. But in spite of this tradition, large-scale retailing now appears to be gaining ground in Japan.[13]

---

[11]James C. Anderson and James Narus, "A Model of Distributor Firm and Manufacturer Firm Working Partnerships," *Journal of Marketing,* January 1990, pp. 42–58.

[12]Brent Felgner, "Retailers Grab Power, Control Marketplace," *Marketing News,* Jan. 16, 1989, pp. 1–2.

[13]Bruce Hirobayashi, "Winds of Change," *Age of Information Marketing,* A. C. Nielsen Co., Chicago, 1989, pp. 9–12.

Power and Relationship Building

As the power of a manufacturer declines relative to the power of strong distributors or large buyers, there is a greater tendency to pursue long-term *relational exchanges*. These kinds of exchanges occur when both parties have a high degree of dependence on the other and when they operate in highly uncertain environments (such as those dominated by fast-paced technological change or extensive competition). A high degree of joint planning, well-coordinated activities, and mutual trust characterize these exchanges.[14] As a consequence, sales and distribution programs in these settings are geared toward implementing relationship marketing strategies (as we discussed in Chapter 7). Illustrative of such programs is the one developed at Owens-Corning.

> Toledo-based Owens-Corning sells glass and building materials through building supply dealers to builders and contractors. To a large degree, Owens-Corning's success depends on its relationship with its retail dealers. Dealers depend on a strong supplier who will be reliable in deliveries and who provides fast response on order inquiries. Additionally, Owens-Corning provides its dealers with technical support when needed in calling on builders and architects to provide advice on the thermal value needed for a roof or on the appropriate grade of insulation.[15]

Regardless of the nature of the relationship, however, a power base cannot be effectively employed nor a relational exchange established except through the sales force. To a large extent, the salesperson is the personification of the company. If a given salesperson demonstrates a lack of expertise, the company's image on this potential power base will suffer. Thus, both in selecting and in implementing appeals, the individual members of the sales force have a major role to play.

The Critical Role of the Sales Force

In selling to organizations (whether distributors or final buyers), it is important to maintain effective relationships with each account. That is, the salesperson generally faces the same buyer over and over, selling the same type of merchandise each time and becoming the major link between a supplier and its customer or distributors.[16]

Furthermore, the salespeople generally have a dual role. They are not merely the company's representatives to the customers (providing product information), but in addition, salespeople are the customers' or distributors' representatives to the supplier, because they help buyers obtain on-time delivery, special services, or special product designs.

---

[14]See F. Robert Dwyer, Paul Schurr, and Sejo Oh, "Developing Buyer-Seller Relationships," *Journal of Marketing,* April 1987, pp. 11–27 for a discussion of how these relationships develop.

[15]"Owens-Corning Calls on Its Customers' Customers," *Sales and Marketing Management,* June 1986, p. 57.

[16]Benson Shapiro, "Manage the Customer, Not Just the Sales Force," *Harvard Business Review,* September–October 1974, p. 130.

These relationships are more or less continuous and involve the development of interpersonal relationships in which each individual (salesperson and buyer) is somewhat dependent on the other. Accordingly, the effectiveness of the salespeople is often dependent on the degree to which they are successful in communicating power.

Types of Salesperson Power The primary bases of power available to the salesperson are expert power, referent power, and reward power.

Expert power exists to the extent that buyers or distributors believe that the salesperson has knowledge or skills which can be valuable to the buyer. Forms of salesperson expertise that may be valuable to buyers or distributors include knowledge of how a product can be effectively used, the ability to set up an effective display, and a knowledge of the products and models that will appeal to a distributor's customers. Consequently, appeals that employ the expertise of the salesperson may provide that salesperson with a basis for influencing the buyer.

Referent power will exist to the extent that the buyer is attracted to the salesperson out of friendship or a feeling of shared identity because the salesperson is viewed as having similar values or interests.[17] Because shared identity often leads to an increase in the buyer's willingness to trust the salesperson, referent power will provide the sales force with a source of influence that is useful even when a high degree of technical expertise is not needed.[18]

Reward power can also be employed by the sales force. Entertainment or special favors performed for the buyer (especially those related to the salesperson's role as the customer's representative to the supplier) are illustrative of the use of reward power. When a reward power is used over a period of time, the salesperson may, as a result, develop a referent power base as well, because the buyer will be more willing to trust the salesperson.

Which Power Base to Use Individual customers are likely to differ in their frequency of interaction with the salesperson, the size of their order, the amount of risk they perceive in a given buying situation, and the kind of decision process employed (as was discussed in Chapter 3). Accordingly, the selection of a type of appeal and type of power should depend heavily on the specific selling situation confronting the salesperson. Additionally, the technical skills and personal characteristics of salespeople will vary. While one may be adept at using expert power, another may rely on referent power. Accordingly, no single approach may be superior. Rather, a given salesperson is likely to be most successful by

---

[17]See Gilbert Churchill, Robert Collins, and William Strang, "Should Retail Salespersons Be Similar to Their Customers?" *Journal of Retailing,* Fall 1975, pp. 29–42.

[18]Paul Busch and David Wilson, "An Experimental Analysis of a Salesman's Expert and Referent Bases of Social Power in the Buyer-Seller Dyad," *Journal of Marketing Research,* February 1976, pp. 3–11.

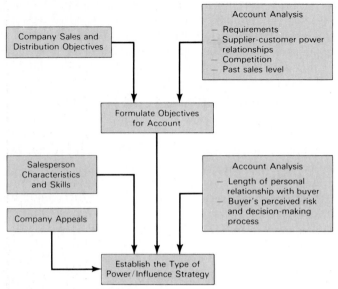

FIGURE 12-4   The salesperson's planning process.

adopting a behavior that is appropriate for his or her characteristics and skills as well as for meeting the buyer's or distributor's requirements.[19]

In sum, the salespeople must develop their own plan for the accounts they call on. A situation analysis should be performed for each customer, based upon that customer's requirements. An objective should be established for each account based on the current sales and distribution objective and on the salesperson's assessment of the opportunities for achieving that objective in each account. (This assessment will be based on competition, on the past level of success, and on whether the salesperson's company has the power to offer the necessary appeals.) Finally, the salesperson must adopt an influence strategy for each account based on his or her own capabilities and on the existing relationship with the buyer. Figure 12-4 portrays some of the elements involved in developing the individual account plan.

CONCLUSION

Sales and distribution programs provide the fundamental linkages between a firm and its buyers or distributors. The type of sales and distribution system a firm selects determines whether a product is sold direct or through wholesale or retail

[19]See Barton Weitz, "Effectiveness in Sales Interactions: A Contingency Framework," *Journal of Marketing,* Winter 1981, pp. 85–103; and Thomas Leigh and Patrick McGraw, "Mapping the Procedural Knowledge of Industrial Sales Personnel: A Script-Theoretic Investigation," *Journal of Marketing,* January 1989, pp. 16–34.

intermediaries and specifies the basic communication and customer service roles the sales force will play.

More specific direction for sales-force activities is provided by the program objectives that are established. These objectives should reflect the firm's marketing strategy and provide a basis for selecting the critical appeals offered to buyers or distributors. Additionally managers must consider buyer requirements and the existing power relationships among manufacturers, distributors, and buyers in selecting appeals.

Although sales managers have an important role to play in designing the sales and distribution program, it will be up to the salespeople as well as sales managers to identify achievable objectives and to select appeals that will be effective in each buying situation. In effect, the sales-force members may become marketing strategists for their market areas. However, in order to assure consistency among salespeople, managers should set the overall program objectives and determine the range of appeals that can be offered before individual sales-force members design their own plans and tactics for influencing customers. In this chapter, we have examined the types of objectives and appeals that managers may choose, the process for selecting objectives and appeals, and some of the major considerations involved in implementing appeals. Figure 12-5 summarizes the relationship among the topics in this chapter and their relationship to the preceding and following chapters.

As with any marketing program, sales and distribution activities cost money and do not always lead to the achievement of objectives. Accordingly, it is important to understand the mechanisms for budgeting, allocating, and evaluating expenditures on these activities. These are the major topics in Chapter 13. However, before proceeding to the next chapter, consider the following example to review some of the major elements of a sales and distribution program.

Amway Corp.: A Successful Sales and Distribution Story in Japan[20]

Amway Ltd. of Japan is an overseas subsidiary of the U.S. consumer-goods company of the same name. Currently it is the seventh fastest growing company in Japan with Japanese sales now equivalent to sales in the United States—over a half billion dollars. The company has 450 full-time employees and 700,000 individual distributors who sell 150 home care, houseware, nutritional supplement, and personal care products such as cosmetics on a commission basis direct to consumers.

A number of factors have contributed to Amway's success. First, the company competes with a traditional trade distribution system that is dominated by small, local retail and wholesale distributors who charge enormous markups to carry a product. These markups often lead to retail prices that are quadruple the manu-

[20]Developed from Ronald Yates, "All-American Amway Cracks Japanese Market," *Chicago Tribune,* Jan. 22, 1990, pp. B1, B4; and Ted Holden and James Treece, "Amway's Big, Happy Family Is All Smiles—In Japan," *Business Week,* Sept. 4, 1989, pp. 47–48.

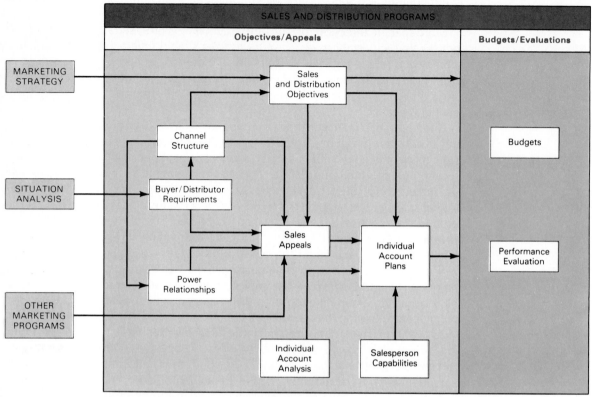

FIGURE 12-5   Relationship of sales and distribution objectives and appeals to marketing strategy, situation analysis, and other marketing programs.

facturer's price, and the small store size results in a limited selection for consumers. Second, Amway has established three automated distribution centers that receive computerized orders and ship within 24 hours to provide outstanding convenience. Third, because Japan is a compact market, it is easy to reach the customer. The independent salesperson-distributors service customers personally, distributing catalogs, making telephone calls, and conducting sales sessions and demonstrations in coffee shops. Customers can place orders by phone, by computer, and even by fax.

Recently, Amway has been very successful in marketing a small $265 induction range made by Sharp. The range heats only the ingredients in a pan and remains cool to the touch. It was a flop in the cramped retail stores but a big success for Amway whose salespeople were able to demonstrate its features.

1 Which type of sales and distribution system best characterizes the Amway system?

2 Discuss the types of sales and distribution objectives and appeals that appear dominant at Amway.

3 What is Amway's source of power in this system? What type of power do distributors have in dealing with Amway? With consumers?

QUESTIONS AND SITUATIONS FOR DISCUSSION

1 What type(s) of sales and distribution system(s) would be appropriate in each of the following cases? Explain.

   a A firm produces an expensive and technically complex piece of diagnostic equipment for hospitals.

   b A firm produces paper for use in duplicating machines.

   c A firm sells a wide line of canned food products to institutional buyers (such as nursing homes, schools, and factory cafeterias).

   d A firm operates a lawn-care service for homeowners.

2 For which of the following would direct response marketing be *least* effective? Explain.

   a A line of men's shirts

   b Videocassette recorders

   c Canned vegetables

3 Both firms that use trade sales forces and firms that use missionary sales forces employ distributors. Explain how these types of sales forces differ. Explain how the tasks performed by the distributors differ between channels in which the manufacturer uses each type of sales force.

4 Which type of sales and distribution objective would be most appropriate for each of the following firms?

   a A computer manufacturer operating at full capacity

   b A women's hosiery manufacturer with a product that is carried by a relatively small number of department stores

   c A bottler that wants to set up in-store retail displays for a new line of soft drinks

   d A manufacturer of automobile seat belts that is only one of several suppliers used by automobile manufacturers

5 In each of the following buyer-seller or buyer-distributor relationships, which organization would probably have the most power? Explain.

   a Haggar Slacks Inc. and a local store specializing in men's clothing

   b Kraft selling its newest cheese spread to a chain of 30 grocery stores

   c Isuzu and its largest automobile dealer

   d K-Mart and a manufacturer of work gloves

6 Which types of sales appeals are most likely to be effective in direct-response marketing programs? Explain.

7 Discuss how contractual systems and administered systems are likely to differ in terms of the kinds of power bases that manufacturers can use.

8 Assume that you are a salesperson in each of the following situations. Which type of power do you think would be most effective for you to use? Explain why.

   a Your company has come out with a new product that has been so well received that there is not enough production to meet customer demand.

    b Your company manufactures a product that must be customized to meet each buyer's needs.

    c Your company sells a product through distributors, and customer demand for the product is highly sensitive to economic fluctuations.

    d Your product is essentially an undifferentiated commodity that is not very complex. A number of competitors offer equivalent products and delivery appeals.

9 Gus is an account representative for a major computer manufacturer and is responsible for all sales and customer service activities at a major New York bank. Besides Gus, two sales managers, four salespeople, two trainees, and thirteen technical service reps are assigned to this account by the computer firm. When major acquisitions are being contemplated, the decision-making process in this bank may well take a year.

    a What are the probable reasons for selecting a direct personal selling system in this case?

    b Which sales and distribution objective will Gus and his team likely emphasize most?

    c Which appeals do you think will be most effective in this situation?

    d Discuss the most important factors a salesperson should consider in this type of selling situation.

SUGGESTED ADDITIONAL READINGS

Dwyer, F. Robert, Paul Schurr, and Sejo Oh, "Developing Buyer-Seller Relationships," *Journal of Marketing,* April 1987, pp. 11–27.

Frazier, Gary, and Jagdish Sheth, "An Attitude-Behavior Framework for Distribution Channel Management," *Journal of Marketing,* Summer 1985, pp. 38–48.

Gaski, John F., "The Theory of Power and Conflict in Channels of Distribution," *Journal of Marketing,* Summer 1984, pp. 9–29.

Leigh, Thomas, and Patrick McGraw, "Mapping the Procedural Knowledge of Industrial Sales Personnel: A Script-Theoretic Investigation," *Journal of Marketing,* January 1989, pp. 16–34.

Magrath, Allan, and Kenneth Hardy, "Avoiding the Pitfalls in Managing Distribution Channels," *Business Horizons,* September–October 1987, pp. 29–33.

Skinner, Steven, Alan Dubinsky, and James Donnelly, "The Use of Social Bases of Power in Retail Sales," *Journal of Personal Selling and Sales Management,* November 1984, pp. 48–56.

Stern, Louis, and Torger Reve, "Distribution Channels as Political Economies: A Framework for Comparative Analysis," *Journal of Marketing,* Summer 1980, pp. 52–64.

Weitz, Barton, Harish Sujan, and Mita Sujan, "Knowledge, Motivation and Adaptive Behavior: A Framework for Improving Selling Effectiveness," *Journal of Marketing,* October 1986, pp. 174–191.

CHAPTER 13

SALES AND DISTRIBUTION PROGRAMS: BUDGETS AND PERFORMANCE EVALUATION

OVERVIEW

In Chapter 12 we pointed out the importance of establishing sales and distribution objectives which would provide guidance for the design of specific sales and distribution appeals. We also noted that the specific appeals should be selected after an analysis of buyer-distributor requirements and of power relationships. As is the case with all marketing programs, however, a program which maximizes sales or the level of a program objective (such as new accounts developed) may not be optimal from a profit perspective. Like advertising and sales-promotion programs, sales and distribution programs cost money, and sales managers are generally expected to operate within a budget that is consistent with overall sales and profit objectives.

In addition to assessing the cost of various programs, sales managers are responsible for evaluating program performance on both sales-volume and non-sales-volume dimensions. These evaluations usually are made at various levels: The performances of individual salespeople, distributors, or sales territories are examined in addition to overall program performance. Such evaluations are then used to identify possible program modifications for improving performance.

In this chapter, we provide procedures for establishing the program budget as we examine the relationship between sales and distribution appeals and sales and distribution costs. Later in the chapter, we also present a number of methods for evaluating sales and distribution performance. In the next chapter (Chapter 14), we will discuss some of the sales management actions that are directed toward enhancing the performance of individual sales-force members.

ESTABLISHING THE SALES AND DISTRIBUTION BUDGET

In designing a program to achieve a sales and distribution objective, sales managers should attempt to estimate the budgetary consequences of the program. Specifically, managers should examine the *costs* that will be incurred by a specific program and the expected impact of the program on profitability. Then, managers can determine if the budget is consistent with the product objectives. That is, a sales and distribution budget that will lead to increased sales and market share may be appropriate for a problem-child product even if a decline in total contribution is expected in the short run. For instance, with those types of products/services, it is not unusual for companies to pay additional incentives to open new accounts in order to increase market share. In addition, travel and entertainment expenses associated with the sale of low-share products in high-growth markets often are higher due to increased competitive activity. Alternatively, sales and distribution budgets for cash cows should normally result in an increase in total contribution.

Figure 13-1 summarizes the elements in the budgeting process. As Figure 13-1 suggests, if the expected results of the proposed budget are inconsistent with the product objectives, revisions in objectives or in the appeals may be appropriate.

The first step in this process is to estimate the impact of the appeals on the profitability structure. As seen in Figure 13-1, sales and distribution programs can influence the direct costs of marketing a product or product line and the variable-contribution margin. Specifically, major budgetary factors that must be considered are

- Sales-force compensation costs
- Working-capital costs for credit and inventory
- Special transportation costs
- Prices and discounts

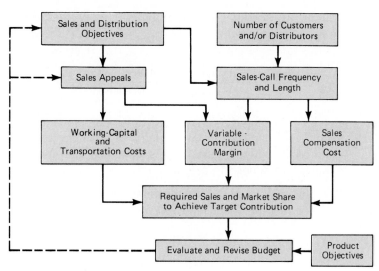

FIGURE 13-1   Establishing a sales and distribution budget.

Sales-Force Compensation Costs

The salaries of sales and customer service personnel and the travel expenses necessary for supporting them are a major expense category for the firms which employ company sales forces. Table 13-1 gives an indication of the cost per sales call associated with personal selling. The primary determinant of these costs is the size of the sales force.[1]

There are several ways in which the number of salespeople needed can be determined. Probably the easiest approach is simply to divide the dollars available by the costs necessary to support one salesperson. Although this method is simple to apply, it ignores the market conditions that should influence sales-force size. For instance, one would expect that early in the product life cycle it may be desirable to have more sales staff than would be necessary in the decline stage. Some firms practice the policy of hiring as many salespersons as possible as long as the gross profit on the new business they generate equals the costs associated with the additional salesperson. This can readily lead to overstaffing, with too many salespersons calling on too few customers. In addition, both economic and market conditions are overlooked when such an approach is followed.[2]

A more logical and systematic approach is to determine the size of the sales force necessary by considering the number of customer/prospects and their re-

---

[1]For a useful review of techniques for estimating the appropriate size of a sales force, see Arthur Meidan, "Optimizing the Number of Industrial Salespersons," *Industrial Marketing Management,* February 1982, pp. 63–74.

[2]Leonard M. Lodish, "A User-Oriented Model for Sales Force Size, Product, and Market Allocation Decisions," *Journal of Marketing,* Summer 1980, pp. 70–78.

quirements. A basic estimate of the number of salespeople needed can generally be made as follows:

$$\text{Size of sales force} = \frac{\text{number of accounts in target market} \times \text{required number of calls per year per account}}{\text{number of calls each salesperson can make}}$$

Note that managers may have to develop separate sales-force size estimates for different parts of the sales force. For example, when distinct selling tasks are required for different customers, specialized sales forces may exist. For example, managers may need to calculate separately the sizes of

- The sales force and the customer service force
- The new-prospect sales force and the sales force calling on established accounts
- The sales forces that call on accounts in different industries (this will often occur where a specialized knowledge of industry production processes or technologies is important)
- Sales force by territories

Whatever the relevant sales-force definition, the staffing plan must consider the number of accounts, the required sales-call frequency, and the call capacity of the sales and service representatives.

Estimating Required Call Frequency Managers should consider each of the following factors in estimating the required number of calls per account:

- The size of the various buyer or distributor accounts

TABLE 13-1 AVERAGE COST OF SALES CALL

	Type of sales force		
	Consumer goods	Industrial goods	Service
Average direct costs			
Compensation	$59,000	$69,000	$57,500
Expenses	$21,200	$21,250	$10,600
Total	$80,200	$90,250	$68,100
Average calls per year*			
High-frequency areas or policies	841.5	748.0	1122.0
Low-frequency areas or policies	561.0	561.0	654.5
Average cost per call			
High-frequency areas or policies	$133.87	$153.57	$85.63
Low-frequency areas or policies	$200.80	$227.61	$169.10

*Assumes 187 selling days per year.
Source: Developed from *1990 Survey of Selling Costs, Sales and Marketing Management*, Feb. 26, 1990, p. 8.

TABLE 13-2   AN ILLUSTRATION OF SALES-CALL FREQUENCIES BY ACCOUNT SIZE

Account group	Volume per month	Number of accounts	Planned frequency per account	Total calls
A	2000	100	24/year	2400
B	600	300	12/year	3600
C	50	600	6/year	3600
				9600

- The sales and distribution objectives
- The need for *unplanned* calls
- The estimated sales effects of increasing or reducing the number of calls per account

Account Size   An important consideration in estimating the required number of calls is the size of the account, because the sales manager will want to minimize the risk of losing large accounts. Large accounts, moreover, may be more profitable because of the size of their orders. It is a common practice of many firms to divide distributor or buyer accounts into account-size categories similar to the breakdown given in Table 13-2. As the table indicates, a small number of large accounts (the A accounts) generally represent a very large portion of sales. This is true whether the accounts represent final-buyer account or distributor accounts. Accordingly, those accounts will be called on more frequently than medium and small accounts.

An important issue in examining account size is whether to use *actual* sales or *potential* sales as the basis for classifying accounts. Firms that classify accounts on the basis of current sales are implicitly assuming that the company has reached its maximum level of achievement in each account. Yet, for most firms, some of the C accounts are very likely to become A accounts if additional effort is applied.

Sales and Distribution Objectives   The sales and distribution objectives for a specific program may force a modification of the basic call-frequency pattern, however. Although the frequency patterns given in Table 13-2 may be appropriate for account maintenance, if managers establish other objectives, then revisions in call frequency may be necessary. For example, if an account-development objective is established, sales calls on new accounts must be included in the staffing plan. For instance, Goodyear requires each salesperson to open five new accounts a year and bonuses are given according to the size of the new accounts.[3] Similarly, some sales or customer service calls to existing accounts are designed to fulfill a specific objective (such as demonstrating a prod-

[3]Bill Kelley, "How Much Help Does a Salesperson Need?" *Sales and Marketing Management,* May 1989, p. 35.

uct's superiority in order to increase sales penetration in key accounts or stimulating special reseller support on special programs).

Unplanned Calls   Emergency repairs or follow-up of an order may require unplanned calls. Usually the ratio of unplanned-to-planned calls can be established from historical sales-call reports. However, in developing a staffing plan, the number of unplanned calls should be considered, because they do take additional time from the sales force.

Estimated Sales Effects   As a final consideration in determining the required number of calls, managers should attempt to estimate the change in sales that will result from increasing or decreasing the current sales-call frequencies on each account. This analysis (which is incorporated in many computer-based systems for territory management) must usually be made on the basis of the joint judgment of the salesperson and the sales manager.[4] For example:

> Turner Warmack, Vice President of Sales and Marketing at Ziegler Tools holds an annual meeting with each of his 18 salespeople to discuss previous years sales, key accounts, account growth, and possible areas for new business. Warmack and his salespeople categorize accounts and decide how often to call upon them. If the salesperson believes that he/she can get more business from an account by calling on that account more frequently, they are encouraged to increase the call frequency.[5]

As was the case with the judgmental estimates we discussed in Chapter 6 (response of sales to advertising) and in Chapter 9 (price-elasticity), managers should seek to answer certain specific questions to gain insight into the relationship between sales calls and sales volume. Among these questions are the following:

- How frequently are buying decisions made?
- Is there a significant opportunity for account penetration?
- How frequently do competitors call on this account?
- Are new competitors, new products, or new technologies anticipated?
- How important is it to maintain referent power through frequent contact?
- How difficult or time-consuming will it be for buyers or distributors to change suppliers?
- How frequently do buyers or distributors need customer service support?

Estimating Sales-Force Call Capacity   In most organizations it is not usually a difficult task to estimate the average length of a sales call. However, the length of a sales call may differ significantly from new to existing accounts and from large

---

[4]Leonard Lodish, "Vaguely Right Approach to Sales Force Allocations," *Harvard Business Review,* January–February 1974, pp. 119–124. The impact of sales-call length and frequency is also examined in Raymond LaForge and David Cravens, "A Marketing Response Model for Sales Management Decision Making," *Journal of Personal Selling and Sales Management,* Fall/Winter 1981–1982, pp. 10–16.

[5]Kelley, op.cit., p. 32.

to small accounts. In addition, the length of call will vary if the purchase decision is made by a buying committee rather than an individual. Further, the possible number of calls will depend on the time required to travel between accounts. Accordingly, the sales-force call capacity will be significantly affected by the way in which the sales force is allocated to territories and to accounts. In turn, the number of salespeople and their travel costs will be determined by the allocation system.

Decisions regarding the assignment of *accounts to territories* are normally made only when several new territories are to be opened or when a major reorganization of the sales force is deemed necessary. In those situations, managers can use computer models to structure territories to minimize the cost per sales call. To implement these models, managers must first estimate the time and expense involved in calling on each account, the desired number of salespeople per sales manager, and the required call frequency.

Decisions regarding the *allocation of the sales force to territories* may be modified over time when management expects different territories to experience different rates of growth in potential. Accordingly, additions to the sales force should be allocated to territories in a manner that reflects these changes. (Indeed, it may even be necessary to shift salespeople from one territory to another.) The relative market potential of various territories may be a useful basis for allocating the sales force. However, in determining the size of the sales force actually required per territory, managers should also consider the required call frequency and the time per call on each account (old and new). Differences between territories in factors such as competition, travel time, or vulnerability to competitors are also often included in these decisions. It is important to keep in mind that although the goal of defining territories is usually to create comparable workloads and sales potentials while maximizing coverage and minimizing travel time, in some cases unequal territories and assignments may be desirable. For example, trainees may initially be assigned to small territories whereas proven salespersons are assigned larger responsibilities.

Decisions regarding the *assignment of individual sales-force members to particular accounts* may be required in certain selling situations. That is, if two or more salespeople or customer service personnel are sharing a geographical area, accounts may be assigned to each salesperson on some basis other than simply minimizing travel time. In particular, managers may assign salespeople to individual accounts on the basis of special expertise (such as knowledge of the buyer's or distributor's industry) or simply for the purpose of maintaining the continuity of interpersonal relationships when referent power is important to sales success.[6]

---

[6]See A. Parasuraman and Ralph Day, "A Management-Oriented Model for Allocating Sales Effort," *Journal of Marketing Research,* February 1977, pp. 22–23. For an expanded discussion of this issue also see R. W. LaForge, I. E. Young, and B. C. Hamm, "Increasing Sales Productivity Through Improved Sales Call Allocation Strategies," *Journal of Personal Selling and Sales Management,* November 1983, pp. 52–59.

Special Compensation Costs

Special compensation includes sales commissions, bonuses, and special incentives (such as merchandise and travel awards). These incentives are offered in order to achieve some specific type of performance on the part of sales-force members or distributors.

In the case of sales commissions, the incentive is directed toward sales-volume gains. Because the level of commission earned is determined as a percentage of sales or a fixed amount per unit of sales, the cost of this incentive is a *variable cost*. However, most special compensation costs represent increases in fixed direct costs and generally are tied to specific sales and distribution objectives. For example, bonuses or travel awards may be provided to salespeople who achieve a certain level of new-account openings or a certain level of retailer participation in a sales promotion.

Selling Costs and Manufacturer's Representatives

Because of the high cost of having a company sales force, a great many firms use manufacturer's representatives to perform the direct selling function. Manufacturer's representatives are independent businesses. They usually sell the product lines of a number of firms within a specific industry and operate on a percent-of-sales commission basis. Table 13-3 gives some examples of the level of commission paid on net sales to manufacturer's reps in some selected industries.

From a cost perspective, the decision to use a company sales force or a manufacturer's rep revolves around the company's total sales volume. A company sales force is a fixed cost with respect to sales volume, while the manufacturer's rep's commission is a variable cost. Thus, at very low sales volumes, the manufacturer's rep is the lower cost alternative. As sales volume (within a specific territory or market) grows, the fixed cost of the company sales force is gradually spread over more units.

TABLE 13-3 AVERAGE MANUFACTURER'S REPRESENTATIVES COMMISSIONS IN SELECTED LINES

Product or service	Average commission paid
Advertising products and services	16.17
Building materials and supplies	7.65
Computers	9.99
Electronic consumer products	5.64
Food products and services	15.00
Marine	9.81
Paper industry	11.16
Plastics	6.18
Sporting goods supplies and accessories	8.18

Source: Manufacturers' Agents National Association, *Survey of Sales Commissions,* as reported in *1987 Survey of Selling Costs, Sales and Marketing Management,* Feb. 16, 1987, p. 59.

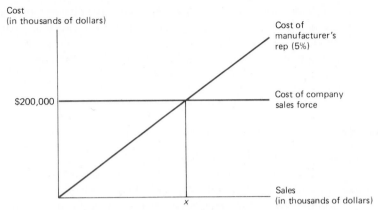

FIGURE 13-2 Relationship between sales volume and the cost of either a manufacturer's
representative or a company sales force.

Figure 13-2 demonstrates how the costs of the two alternatives behave as sales
volume increases. If the cost of a company sales force is $200,000 for a given
territory and if a manufacturer's representative charges 5 percent of sales, the
costs are equal when sales are equal to $4 million. The point of equal costs is
derived as follows:

$$\text{Cost of manufacturer's rep} = \text{cost of company sales force}$$
$$.05x = \$200,000$$
$$x = \$4,000,000$$

In this example, therefore, the cost of a manufacturer's rep is lower at sales volumes below $4 million, but the cost of a company sales force is lower at sales
volumes above $4 million. In addition to cost considerations, other factors must
be considered in the choice between a company sales force and a manufacturer's
representative. Among the major arguments made on behalf of the two alternatives, the following points are the most widely accepted.[7]

• Two critical advantages of manufacturer's reps are that they may have a better knowledge of customer or distributor needs and they may provide better coverage of small accounts. They are able to achieve these advantages because they
combine the lines of several suppliers and thus can justify more calls on such
accounts.

• The critical advantage of the company sales force lies in control over performance. While manufacturer's reps do not get paid unless they make a sale, a

[7]See Erin Anderson, "The Salesperson as Outside Agent or Employee: A Transaction Cost Analysis," *Marketing Science,* Summer 1985, pp. 234–254. For another view, see "Wal-Mart's War on
Reps," *Sales and Marketing Management,* March 1987, pp. 41–43.

company sales force can be motivated to perform nonselling or sales-development activities designed to build long-term growth or emphasize account maintenance. For instance, in West Germany, industrial salespeople seldom prospect, infrequently expedite orders, and rarely follow up on orders. However, the Germans excel at training their clients' employees, as well as helping install what they sell.[8]

Working-Capital Costs

Until recently, the costs associated with providing credit to buyers and distributors and with inventory incentives were seldom related to sales budgets. However, the cost of money has increased, and inventory and credit appeals have become more important to buyers and distributors. As a result, more organizations have begun to evaluate the additional working-capital costs that are incurred because of the use of these appeals.[9]

Credit Costs In examining the costs of offering a credit appeal, managers must consider each of the following factors:

- An estimate of the sales volumes generated under alternative credit policies
- The annual rate of turnover of accounts receivable
- The annual cost of providing trade credit (usually, the firm's cost of borrowing short-term capital plus costs of credit administration)
- The variable-contribution margin

For example, assume that a firm offers 30-day credit, a variable-contribution margin of 20 percent, and an annual cost of credit of 15 percent of the average amount of credit outstanding. If all credit customers pay their bills every month and if expected credit sales under this policy are $20 million, then the annual rate of turnover is 12 (that is, 12 months in a year divided by 1 month) and the annual cost of credit is

$$\frac{\$20 \text{ million}}{12 \text{ turns}} \times .15 = \$250,000$$

Now, assume that the same firm believes it can generate an additional $4 million in sales if customers are given 2 months to pay. Because the same credit terms must generally be offered to all customers, we can expected all credit customers to take the full 2 months to pay. Therefore, the account receivable turnover is now six per year (12 months divided by 2 months), and the cost of this credit policy is

[8]"How the Germans Do It," *Sales and Marketing Management,* Nov. 19, 1989, p. 25.
[9]William Crissy, Paul Fischer, and Frank Mossman, "Segmental Analysis: Key to Marketing Profitability," *Business Topics,* Spring 1973, pp. 42–49; also see R. D. Rutherford, "Make Your Sales Force Credit Smart," *Sales and Marketing Management,* November 1989, pp. 50–55.

$$\frac{\$24 \text{ million}}{6 \text{ turns}} \times .15 = \$600,000$$

Thus, credit costs will rise by $350,000 under the new policy. However, at a variable-contribution margin of 20 percent, the added $4 million in sales will increase the firm's dollar variable contribution by

$$\$4 \text{ million} \times .20 = \$800,000$$

Therefore, the net effect of the change in the credit policy will be

$$
\begin{array}{l}
\$800,000 \text{ (increased variable contribution)} \\
\underline{- \$350,000} \text{ (increased working-capital cost)} \\
\$450,000
\end{array}
$$

Salespeople need to know the direct cost of delayed payment terms. When salespeople are paid commissions based on sales orders rather than on paid-up sales, they are not appreciative of the direct cost to the company of delayed payment terms. However, many companies pay their salespeople when payment for the goods is received. In this way, salespeople quickly become as concerned about cash flow and the effect of credit terms on profitability as top management. Geolograph-Pioneer furnishes its salespeople with two statements each month. One is a statement showing collections from customers received during the prior month and the second shows all billings not paid. These two statements show each sales representative the status of each account every month which leads to a closer working relationship between sales and credit.[10]

Inventory Costs   Managers can employ a procedure similar to that used to examine the cost of credit appeals when they wish to identify the budgeting implications of inventory appeals. The major differences in the two analyses are that the annual rate of inventory turnover will be used in place of the annual accounts receivable turnover, and the annual cost of carrying inventory is used in place of the annual cost of providing trade credit. That is, for a given inventory policy,

$$\text{Inventory cost} = \frac{\text{annual sales}}{\text{inventory turnover}} \times \text{inventory carrying cost}$$

where

$$\text{Inventory turnover} = \frac{\text{annual dollar sales}}{\text{average dollar value of inventory held by the firm}}$$

[10]Ibid., p. 54.

Carrying costs generally incorporate short-term borrowing costs, administrative costs, product obsolescence, and breakage. Today, these costs are being watched more closely than ever.

As in the case of accounts receivable, increases in inventory costs that result from sales and distribution appeals should be considered direct expenses, and managers should consider the amount of these expenses in evaluating the profitability consequences of the program.

As we suggested earlier, many firms do not yet incorporate these costs when developing sales and distribution budgets. However, as product obsolescence becomes more significant (a particular problem in fashion and high-technology industries) more firms have begun to consider the impact of these costs. Consider, for example, the problems experienced by Dynascan.

> Dynascan was originally a manufacturer of electronic testing equipment but moved into consumer and office products with its Cobra-brand citizens band radios in the 1970s. Subsequently, the company produced lines of cordless telephones, radar detectors, answering machines, and other electronics products. While the company was highly successful with all of these products from a sales standpoint, it had severe profit problems with the CB radio and cordless phone products: When sales leveled off the company was awash in inventory. The company then recognized the impact of working-capital costs on its profits: $4 of working capital are needed to support every $10 of sales. So the company set up a system to continually analyze all sales programs for their impact on working-capital costs.[11]

Transportation Costs

Sales and distribution programs may cause increases in transportation costs when

- The sales force agrees to offer expedited (fastest-way) shipment of rush orders (requiring the most expensive transportation methods).
- More frequent delivery schedules (often entailing less-than-truckload or less-than-carload quantities) are offered.

Inventory management is of major concern to the international marketing manager. More multinational manufacturers are adopting just-in-time inventory policies. These policies minimize the volume of inventory that needs to be kept on hand for the production process. Usually, the ability to help a customer implement a just-in-time policy is a prerequisite to obtaining a sale.

To the extent that transportation-cost increases result from sales or customer service programs, the increased direct cost should be charged to the sales and distribution budget. Moreover, because transportation costs usually represent a large portion of total costs for products which are bulky or which have a high package-to-product weight ratio, it will be difficult to pass the increased transportation costs on to customers who require these appeals. Frequently, however, a change in the structure of the sales and distribution system may be useful in

[11]David Henry, "Death Wish," *Forbes*, Oct. 20, 1986, pp. 50–51.

providing improved delivery at the same (or lower) prices. As an example, consider the changes in distribution initiated by Perrier.

> Perrier naturally carbonated mineral water has been distributed in the United States since the turn of the century. However, until recently, sales in the United States had remained at a consistently low level relative to other beverages, while in Europe the product was outselling the leading cola 2 to 1.
>
> Through research, the company learned that the product did have good potential if the retail price could be cut and if product availability were increased. Accordingly, the company switched from direct sales and distribution to retailers to centralized distribution through soft-drink bottlers and beer wholesalers. Because these distributors were able to transport Perrier at a fraction of the former cost, the company was able to reduce prices throughout the channel. Retail prices dropped 30 percent and sales rose thirty-fold over a 2-year period.[12]

Variable-Contribution-Margin Effects

Managers often use price appeals (such as cash and quantity discounts or price shading) to achieve the program objectives. However, each of these appeals results in a reduction in the variable-contribution margin. Accordingly, to the extent that sales personnel have a role in setting prices, the profitability impact of price appeals should be closely evaluated.

Cash Discounts   Firms in most industries employ cash discounts as sales appeals. In fact, cash discount policies are often established more by industry tradition than through analysis. Although cash discounts may encourage faster payment of invoices (thus reducing working-capital costs), the costs of the discount often exceed the working-capital costs. For example, a firm that offers a 2 percent discount to buyers or distributors who pay in 10 days rather than 30 days is really paying 2 percent to gets its cash 20 days sooner. This translates into an annual interest rate of about 36 percent. (That is, 2 percent times 365 days divided by 20 days equals 36 percent.) If the firm's normal short-term borrowing cost is 20 percent, then the cash discount policy really increases total cost. Accordingly, unless the cash discount must be offered because of the buyer's or distributor's power, the discount should be reduced or eliminated if it results in increased cost.

Quantity Discounts   The seller may save in many ways through quantity discounts:[13]

- A possible shifting of inventory burdens and costs to the buyer or distributor
- Reduced sales-contact and order-processing costs

---

[12]"Perrier: Putting More Sparkle into Sales," *Sales and Marketing Management,* January 1979, pp. 16–17.

[13]An analytical approach for establishing quantity discounts is available in James P. Monahan, "A Quantity Discount Pricing Model to Increase Vendor Profits," *Management Science,* June 1984, pp. 720–726.

• More economical shipping costs because of increases in volume per shipment

• Improved production scheduling because larger, more economical production runs can be made

For instance, assume a firm has a buyer that orders 1200 units per year in monthly orders of 100 units each. Also assume that the seller's sales-contact and processing costs per order are $400, the inventory-carrying cost is 20 percent, the unit-variable-production cost is $80, and the price is $100 per unit. Further assume that the buyer will purchase in orders of 200 units if the price is lowered to $98 per unit. This means that only six orders per year must be obtained and processed (1200 units divided by 200 units per order). From the seller's viewpoint the two alternatives can be compared in terms of margin reductions and order costs, as indicated in Table 13-4.

The reduced direct cost of obtaining and processing orders offsets the lost contribution margin in this example. Note that this analysis does require several key assumptions:

• That order rates are fairly constant over the year

• That order-processing costs are actually lowered (that is, the sales calls are reduced and that reductions in order-processing costs are actually made)

• That buyers will perceive a gain from the lower prices which exceed their increased carrying costs

However, the seller is very likely to obtain additional benefits from reduced transportation costs and, in some cases, from reductions in the amount of inventory which must be held by the seller in order to satisfy customer requirements.

Cumulative Quantity Discounts   These discounts (also known as *volume rebates*) are given on the basis of the total volume of purchases over a period of time (usually 1 year) regardless of average order size. Some firms justify these

TABLE 13-4   EVALUATING THE PROFIT IMPACT OF A QUANTITY DISCOUNT

	At normal price	**At quantity discount**
Price	$100/unit	$98/unit
Variable cost	$80/unit	$80/unit
Unit variable-contribution margin	$20/unit	$18/unit
Sales volume	1200	1200
Dollar contribution margin	$24,000	$21,600
Order cost	$400/order	$400/order
Number of orders	12	6
Total order cost	$4800	$2400
Reduction in margin:		$24,000 − $21,600 = $2400
Savings in order cost:		$ 4,800 − $ 2,400 = $2400
Net profit impact		$ 0

discounts by showing that selling costs for large-volume accounts are proportionately less than for smaller accounts. However, the motivations for employing volume rebates are usually competitive. Volume rebates may be demanded by customers because competitors offer them. However, firms may offer the rebates because the rebates give better account penetration: With volume rebates, there is more incentive for a buyer or distributor to reduce the number of sources of supply.[14]

Price Shading Price-shading appeals are used when a lower price will enable the sales force to close a sale to a particular customer. Frequently, the lower price results in additional sales that otherwise would not be made. This is true especially when opening a new account or attempting to gain a larger share of the business of an existing account (account penetration). In those cases, price shading will increase profitability as long as excess capacity exists and as long as the price exceeds the variable costs plus the cost of delivery. However, the excessive use of price shading may mean that the sales force is not emphasizing other nonprice appeals to an adequate extent. By employing price shading on a broad scale, managers may ultimately find that dollar-contribution margins begin to decline and that competitors will begin to expand their use of price shading. Accordingly, some firms have begun to eliminate shading except for new accounts or very large buyers, and others have put greater limits on the sales force's authority regarding price, in order to ensure that minimally acceptable margins are realized.[15]

Finalizing the Budget

After a manager has identified the costs and margin reductions associated with providing a given set of appeals, a sales budget can be established. As indicated in Figure 13-3, several steps are involved in developing this budget:

1 Determining the required levels of sales and market share needed based on (a) increases in direct costs, (b) changes in variable-contribution margins, (c) the target contribution desired, and (d) the industry sales forecast
2 Determining whether the required sales and market share can be achieved on the basis of productivity judgments
3 Making revisions, if necessary, to the program objectives (such as the level of achievement required) or to the appeals in order to develop a more realistic budget
4 Assigning specific levels of achievement, if appropriate, for program objectives and sales quotas to individual sales territories, salespeople, and perhaps, to

[14]See Ashak Rao, "Quantity Discounts in Today's Markets," *Journal of Marketing,* Fall 1980, pp. 44–51 for a more extensive discussion.
[15]In one study, researchers found that salespeople with the greatest degree of pricing authority generated the lowest sales and profit performance. See P. Ronald Stephenson, William L. Cron, and Gary L. Frazier, "Delegating Pricing Authority to the Sales Force: The Effect on Sales and Profit Performance," *Journal of Marketing,* Spring 1979, pp. 21–28.

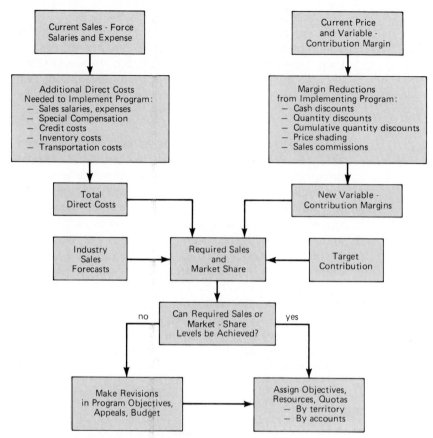

FIGURE 13-3   Finalizing the sales and distribution budget.

individual accounts, and allocating human and financial resources to each sales territory in a manner consistent with territorial potential, objectives, and quotas.

Note that steps 1 through 3 deal with the total sales and distribution budget. In assessing the likelihood that the required sales and market-share levels will be reached, the impact of other programs (such as advertising) must be known.

Consequently, the sales managers may not be the only managers involved in making the assessment about the reasonableness of the budget. (The process of coordinating program budgets is discussed in detail in Chapter 15.)

Managers may also have to develop separate budgets for different portions of the sales force. For example, a number of organizations separate the sales and customer service functions and budgets. That is, in some firms, customer service is viewed as a separate profit center—particularly when direct service charges are made to customers receiving maintenance, repair, and operating services. As a result, separate budgets may be developed for customer service.

Finally, as indicated in step 4, separate budgets may be established for individual sales territories and for specific customer or distributor accounts. Sales quotas may be established to indicate specifically the share of required sales that must be achieved in each territory or account in order to meet the budget requirements. Human and financial resources may be allocated to territories or to accounts to reflect differences in the potential for achieving the program objectives or for achieving sales-volume gains.

As the budget becomes finalized, then, the sales manager has effectively established a number of standards for monitoring and evaluating performance.

EVALUATING PERFORMANCE

In order to measure the effectiveness of sales and distribution programs and to identify opportunities for improved resource utilization, managers must employ some procedure for performance evaluation. Of course, measures of sales volume and total profit contribution are useful for measuring performance, but these measures may reflect the overall effectiveness of the marketing effort.[16] In evaluating sales and distribution performance, sales managers need measures and procedures that focus on the specific objectives, activities, and costs for which they are responsible. Further, sales managers usually need to evaluate performance at one or more of the following levels:

- Individual salesperson performance
- Individual distributor performance
- Sales-territory performance
- Sales segment performance

By examining performance at these various levels (as well as total performance), sales managers will be better able to understand the reasons for the overall total program results. Specifically, they will be able to identify the sales segments, territories, salespeople, and distributors that are strong and weak performers. Additionally, if the evaluation procedure is sufficiently detailed, managers should be able to understand the reasons for differences in performance and prescribe some corrective actions.

Individual Salesperson and Distributor Performance

Managers must evaluate the performance of individual sales and customer service personnel and individual distributors with several purposes in mind:

- Awarding incentives and bonuses
- Identifying personnel or distributors who may need additional training
- Identifying *problem* accounts or *problem* geographical areas covered by individual salespeople or distributors
- Determining whether new or additional distributors are needed

[16]Robert J. Freedman, "For More Profitable Sales, Look Beyond Volume," *Sales and Marketing Management,* August 1989, pp. 50–53.

TABLE 13-5   RESULTS-ORIENTED MEASURES FOR EVALUATING
DISTRIBUTORS OR SALESPEOPLE

1. Sales volume (total or by product or model)
2. Sales volume as a percentage of quota
3. Sales profitability (dollar gross margin or contribution)
4. Number of new accounts
5. Number of stockouts
6. Number of distributors participating in programs
7. Number of lost accounts
8. Percentage volume increase in key accounts
9. Number of customer complaints
10. Distributor sales-inventory ratios

TABLE 13-6   EFFORT-ORIENTED MEASURES FOR EVALUATING
DISTRIBUTORS OR SALESPEOPLE

1. Number of sales calls made
2. Number of MRO calls made
3. Number of complaints handled
4. Number of checks on reseller stocks
5. Uncontrollable lost job time
6. Number of inquiries followed up
7. Number of demonstrations completed

To be as widely useful as possible, measures of salesperson or distributor performance should help managers to determine whether the performance is due to individual or distributor actions or whether it is due to noncontrollable market forces. This means that performance evaluation should include *results-oriented* and *effort-oriented* measures. Tables 13-5 and 13-6 present some of the typical performance measures that are widely used by sales managers.[17]

When results-oriented measures are being used, the measure should have a logical and equitable basis. For example, if dollar-sales volume is being used, individual quotas should be established only after the sales potential in each distributor's or salesperson's account has been considered. Similarly, if the number of new accounts opened is the performance measure, then the number of potential accounts in each salesperson's or distributor's territory should be considered in evaluating performance.

In employing effort-oriented measures, the most appropriate measures are those that are most directly related to the sales and distribution program. For example, the number of inquiries followed up will be the most appropriate effort measure to use if the sales and distribution objective is to increase the number of accounts. However, the number of complaints handled will be a more appropri-

---

[17]The frequency with which managers use these various measures is examined in Donald Jackson, Janet Keith, and John Schlacter, "Evaluation of Selling Performance: A Study of Current Practices," *Journal of Personal Selling and Sales Management,* November 1983, pp. 43–51.

ate measure of effort when an account-maintenance objective has been established.

In general, however, management's primary concern is with results. Effort-related measures are primarily useful for diagnosing why performance is above or below average. That is, by comparing efforts and results, managers should be better able to assess whether poor performance is due to inadequate effort or misdirected effort. For instance, a salesperson or distributor may have a low performance measure in terms of account development because of a rush of customer complaints that had to be handled or because an inadequate number of sales calls were made. In the latter case, management can ascribe poor performance to a weak effort. But in the former case, the effort may have merely been misdirected because of circumstances beyond the distributor's or salesperson's control. By combining results-oriented and effort-oriented measures, therefore, sales managers can better diagnose the reasons for variations in performance and take the necessary remedial actions.

Sales-Territory Performance

Individual sales territories will differ in terms of sales potential and in terms of the resources they require for the firm to remain competitive. For example, some territories will have several well-established, high-volume accounts concentrated in a small area (so sales volume will be high and travel costs low). But other territories may have a large number of small accounts that are widely dispersed geographically, leading to a lower sales potential and higher travel costs. Because of these kinds of differences, managers cannot easily compare performance in several territories. However, each territory can be evaluated in terms of the degree to which sales and distribution objectives are achieved and in terms of profitability measures.

Achievement of Objectives   Measures of the achievement of objectives compare the level of performance of each territory with the objectives specified in the sales and distribution program. As we suggested earlier in this chapter, sales managers will usually assign specific levels of the program objective (such as the number of new accounts opened) to each sales territory.

Although managers often use these measures for awarding bonuses and other incentives, they also use them as diagnostic devices for identifying low performance territories. Once the low-performing territories have been identified, the sales manager can attempt to determine the causes of low performance. In some cases the territory objectives may have been set arbitrarily without adequate consideration of market potential and competitive conditions. Alternatively, inadequate effort, unexpected changes in local economic conditions, or a lack of necessary resources may be the cause of poor performance. An additional possible reason for variations in the achievement of objectives is that some territories may have reached their sales and distribution objectives simply because of excessive reliance on price appeals or delivery appeals, which may have resulted in negative profitability. Accordingly, sales-territory performance should also be evaluated from a profitability perspective.

Profitability   Measures of profitability at the sales-territory level can take several forms. Managers may compare territories to identify any variations in margins and traceable fixed selling costs as a percentage of sales. Additionally, margins and fixed selling costs may be related to sales and distribution objectives. For example, managers may want to measure the total dollars of selling cost per new account.

In addition to margins and selling costs, certain assets may be managed at the sales-territory level. Accordingly, territorial profitability may also be measured in terms of the return generated on those assets. Return-on-assets-managed ratios for different territories can be compared to find opportunities to improve allocation procedures regarding assets and direct expenses or to modify territorial budgets. Typically, accounts receivable, inventories, and warehouse assets are the assets that might be employed for calculating *assets managed*. To the extent that the sales territory determines credit policy and has its own warehouse for holding inventory, the assets managed may be substantial enough to warrant using this measure. Sales and cost analysis identifies the results achieved and the costs of obtaining those results. However, it is also necessary to consider the assets that are necessary to obtain those results. The formula for return on assets managed (ROAM) considers both the contribution margin for a given level of sales and asset turnover.

$$\text{ROAM} = \text{contribution as percentage of sales} \times \text{asset turnover rate}$$

Table 13-7 provides an illustration of the use of territorial profitability measurement.

By comparing profitability results and levels of achievement of program objectives in different territories, managers can obtain several insights on territorial performance. For example,

• A low percentage-variable-contribution margin may indicate excessive reliance on price appeals.
• A high ratio of shipping costs-to-sales or a low ratio of sales-to-average inventory may indicate excessive reliance on logistical appeals.
• A territory in which account development objectives are not being met may have a high ratio of new accounts per dollar of salary expense. The current sales force is doing an adequate job of generating new accounts, but is failing to capitalize on the total market opportunity, indicating that the territory may be understaffed.

In sum, the combined use of profitability-performance measures with a measure of the achievement or program objectives will enable managers to evaluate sales territories more fairly and will permit managers to more effectively diagnose the problems and opportunities in each territory.

TABLE 13-7   CALCULATING TERRITORIAL PROFITABILITY MEASURES

Sales	$1,500,000
Less variable costs	900,000
Variable-contribution margin	$ 600,000
Less direct costs	
Salaries of sales and customer service personnel	$ 200,000
Travel expense	50,000
Point-of-sale material	30,000
Expediting of shipments	20,000
Contribution to indirect costs and profit	$ 300,000
Assets managed	
Accounts receivable	$ 140,000
Warehouse	600,000
Finished-goods inventory	160,000
Total assets managed	$ 900,000

$$\text{Contribution as a percentage of sales} \quad \frac{\$\,300,000}{\$1,500,000} = 20\%$$

$$\text{Asset turnover} \quad \frac{\$1,500,000}{\$\,900,000} = 1.667$$

$$\text{ROAM} = 1.667 \times 20\%$$
$$= 33\ 1/3\%$$

Sales-Segment Performance

Frequently, managers find major differences in sales and profitability patterns when comparing different types of distributors and different types of customers. By recognizing these differences, managers can often identify possible improvements in the allocation of sales and customer service resources. For example, call frequencies, delivery policies, and discount policies may be adjusted for different types of sales segments. Two approaches can be used in examining these segment differences: sales analysis and distribution cost analysis.

Sales Analysis   Sales analysis is a term that covers a variety of procedures for examining sales performance and sales opportunities across various territories, customer groups, or distribution channels. Typically, managers use sales analysis to answer questions such as:

- How are sales distributed across sales segments?
- In which segments did sales exceed or fail to meet expectations?
- How effectively are sales resources being allocated to sales segments?
- Which products are being sold to which segments?

Essentially, sales analysis is the process of aggregating the sales reports of individual salespeople in a variety of ways. Consider, for example, the data in Table 13-8.

In this sales analysis report, each salesperson's unit sales results for the period October–December 1990 are aggregated by one of three model types and by customer group. (Note that this company sells direct to some customers, such as government agencies and banking and financial institutions, and indirectly through distributors to other buyers.)

The managerial value of sales analysis can best be examined by first inspecting the total sales figures for each model for the three customer groups and then examining the figures within customer groups. For example, Series 99 sales grew by only 8 percent over the preceding year and fell just shy of expectations. (Note that the performance index is just below 100, a level at which planned and actual sales would be equal.) However, these results mask some important sales results. When Series 99 sales are compared across customer groups, it is apparent the sales of this model were well below expectations in the government and banking and finance groups. Similarly, the banking and finance customer group is decidedly different from the other two in the sales performance for the Series 60 and Series 90 models.

TABLE 13-8   EXAMPLE OF A SALES ANALYSIS REPORT

Customer group and computer series	Unit sales of high-speed printers				
	Actual Oct.–Dec. 1990	Planned Oct.–Dec. 1990	Performance* index	Actual Oct.–Dec. 1989	Percent† change
1. Government agencies					
Series 60	8,000	6,000	133	4,000	100
Series 90	2,000	5,000	40	4,000	−50
Series 99	2,000	4,000	50	4,000	−50
Total	12,000	15,000	80	12,000	0
2. Banking and finance					
Series 60	3,000	3,500	86	3,000	0
Series 90	4,000	2,000	200	2,000	100
Series 99	1,000	1,500	67	1,000	0
Total	8,000	7,000	114	6,000	33
3. Distributors					
Series 60	23,000	18,000	128	18,000	28
Series 90	13,000	16,000	81	10,500	24
Series 99	4,000	2,000	200	1,500	167
Total	40,000	36,000	111	30,000	33
4. Total for 3 groups					
Series 60	34,000	27,500	123	25,000	36
Series 90	19,000	23,000	83	16,500	15
Series 99	7,000	7,500	93	6,500	8
Total	60,000	58,000	104	48,000	25

*Calculated as: (Actual 90 ÷ Planned 90) × 100
†Calculated as: (Actual 90 − Actual 89) ÷ (Actual 89) × 100

This type of information permits management to more readily identify areas in which performance is distinctly different from expectations or from past trends. Armed with such information, managers can focus their attention on these particular sales segments to determine whether changes in objectives, appeals, or sales-force effort should be considered. For example, the manager using the data in Table 13-8 would likely be concerned with determining why banking and finance customers are shifting from the Series 60 to the Series 90 while government agencies seem to be moving in a different direction.

It is important to recognize, however, that sales analysis only provides information on one dimension. As we suggested at the outset of this chapter, managers must also examine the costs involved in generating these sales and the profit implications of using alternative sales appeals. The most comprehensive approach for analyzing sales and distribution costs is known as *distribution cost analysis.*

Distribution Cost Analysis   Distribution cost analysis is a procedure for comparing the profitability of sales segments and for identifying possible approaches for improving profitability. Specifically, distribution cost analysis can be used to identify changes in sales and distribution appeals and budgets or in the structure of sales and distribution systems which may enhance the profitability of one or more sales segments. Although this procedure can be used for examining the profitability of sales territories, it is more widely used when the sales segments to be analyzed are

- Alternative systems (for example, direct response versus direct personal selling versus trade selling)
- Alternative distribution channels (for example, department versus discount chains or wholesale versus direct to retail channels)
- Alternative customer types (for example, buyers in different industries)
- Alternative account-size (sales-volume) classes

The basic procedure employed in performing a distribution cost analysis is to identify the sales revenues and costs attributable to each sales segment. Typically, managers allocated three types of costs to the various sales segments:

- Variable costs associated with manufacturing or selling the product (including sales commissions).
- Direct fixed costs which would not be incurred if a given sales segment were eliminated. (For example, if one or more salespeople sold only to a given sales segment, the salaries and travel expenses of those salespeople would be directly assignable to that segment.)
- Traceable, indirect costs which can be allocated (traced) to various segments on some logical, nonarbitrary basis. Operationally, firms will only allocate those indirect costs for which the level of costs can be influenced by the sales and distribution effort or appeals assigned to each sales segment.

The procedures and uses of distribution cost analysis can be illustrated by the analysis developed by Classic Apparel, Inc.

Classic sold a line of fashion-oriented lace blouses through quality department and specialty stores, using a small sales force. Each member of the sales force called on both large department store buyers and small independent women's apparel stores in a given geographic area. In 1990, Classic also began selling blouses via a direct response campaign in which mail-in order forms were distributed through a direct mail service targeted to higher-income households. Classic paid for shipments made to its retail distributors. However, direct response customers paid for the shipping costs of their orders. Table 13-9 presents a distribution cost analysis of Classic's sales and distribution systems.

The analysis revealed some significant differences in the relative profitability of the various systems.

• The percentage-variable-contribution margin on manufacturer sales for the direct response system was 60 percent, as opposed to 50 percent for the indirect channels, reflecting the elimination of retail margins in the direct response channel.

• Shipping, selling, and order-taking costs as a percentage of manufacturer sales were much higher for specialty stores than for department stores. A major reason for this was that specialty stores were large in number but purchased in smaller volumes. Department stores were able to order in quantities which were large enough to ship economically.

On the basis of these results, Classic's sales manager was able to identify some possible actions to take in order to improve profitability.

TABLE 13-9 DISTRIBUTION COST ANALYSIS: CLASSIC APPAREL, INC.
(Sales in Thousands)

	Department store chains	Specialty apparel stores	Direct response sales	Basis for allocation
Sales	$ 12,000	$ 4,800	$1,500	Sales receipts
Labor	−2,000	−800	−200	Unit cost
Material	−4,000	−1,600	−400	Unit cost
Variable contribution	$ 6,000	$ 2,400	$ 900	
Shipping	−800	−600	0	Delivery records
Order taking/billing	−10	−30	−60	No. of orders
Personal selling	−400	−800	0	Sales-call reports
Direct mail	−0	−0	−50	Invoices
Credit	−300	−200	−50	Average amount outstanding
Total contribution	$ 4,490	$ 770	$ 740	
Total contribution per $ sales	$ .374	$ .160	$ .493	

1 Classic could establish minimum order volumes for free delivery or impose delivery charges for small orders.

2 Classic could require cash payments on small orders to reduce credit costs.

3 Classic could reduce the frequency of sales calls on smaller accounts and thereby either reduce the size of the sales force or shift more selling effort to department store chains.

4 The fact that percentage-variable contribution margins are identical for the two indirect channels suggests that no quantity discounts are being offered. Classic might elect to raise prices but offer quantity discounts to large-volume buyers.

5 Classic might attempt to hire manufacturer's representatives to sell to specialty stores. Currently, personal selling, order taking, and credit costs account for over 20 percent of specialty store sales. If these functions could be performed at a lesser cost by using a second intermediary, profitability could be enhanced.

6 Classic could separate the specialty apparel segment into multiple subsegments based on purchase volume levels. This analysis might reveal that some accounts should be eliminated. It is important to note that a distribution cost analysis is useful in diagnosing where the profitability problems are but not necessarily in choosing the actions to be taken. That is, each of the alternatives under consideration would reduce or eliminate a sales and distribution appeal. Accordingly, before implementing any of these actions, Classic's marketing manager must analyze the sales consequences as well as the cost consequences. In other words, Classic must review the importance of these appeals in the context of distributor requirements and power relationships (as discussed in Chapter 12) in order to determine how specialty apparel stores will respond.

In our discussion of distribution cost analysis we have not taken into consideration what it costs to replace a "lost" customer. The Sandy Corporation has estimated the costs of replacing a customer can exceed $400 in the service industry. For instance, banks lose about $80 in unrealized revenue every time they lose a customer and this amounts to $322 for transportation companies. In addition, it is estimated that it costs approximately $100 in sales and marketing expense to replace customers in these industries. For this reason, some companies use "number of lost accounts" as a measure of sales performance.[18]

CONCLUSION

Sales and distribution programs incorporate a variety of activities linking the sales force, the customer service force, and distributors. Further, a number of different objectives and appeals may be employed by sales managers, and these objectives and appeals will affect the firm's cost and profitability structure in many ways.

The complexity of these programs does not mean that they are unmanageable, however. The purpose of Chapters 12 and 13 was to present a logical approach for developing and implementing these programs and to identify some of the conceptual and analytical approaches that managers can use to achieve effective

---

[18]"How Much Is a Customer Worth?" *Sales and Marketing Management,* May 1989, p. 23.

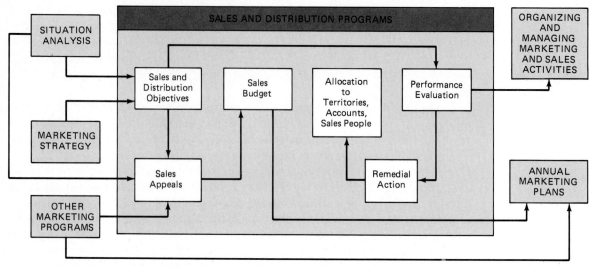

FIGURE 13-4   Relationship of sales and distribution programs with situation analysis, marketing strategy, other marketing programs, and coordination and control activities.

sales and distribution efforts. The relationship among these conceptual and analytical approaches and the relationship of sales and distribution programs to the other chapters in this book are summarized in Figure 13-4.

Because most marketing jobs fall into the sales and customer service categories and because the cost and effectiveness of these programs are critical to marketing success, an understanding of these approaches, concepts, and tools is of paramount importance not only to sales managers but to the members of the sales force as well. It is vital that managers recognize and use the various tools and concepts discussed in this chapter, as the following situation demonstrates.

Herman Volkert GmbH[19]

The Volkert company is a producer of bearings and sleeves used in a variety of industrial applications. Volkert bearings and sleeves are sold throughout Western Europe and exported to seventeen nations outside the European community. Sales and distribution in Western Europe are through Volkert's own sales force which works out of thirteen branch offices. Each branch provides warehousing for the Volkert product line.

Heinz Deitrich, sales manager for Western Europe, had recently begun to analyze branch-office operations preliminary to developing his sales budget. In reviewing the performance of the Frankfurt and Hamburg branches he had assembled the following information:

[19]Name of the company is disguised and the figures have been adjusted to provide confidentiality.

	Frankfurt branch	Hamburg branch
Sales	6,000,000 DM*	3,600,000 DM*
Cost of goods sold	4,800,000 DM	3,060,000 DM
Gross margin	1,200,000 DM	540,000 DM
Less variable branch expenses		
Salaries	372,000 DM	192,000 DM
Commissions	60,000 DM	24,000 DM
Office expenses	72,000 DM	48,000 DM
Travel and entertainment	96,000 DM	48,000 DM
Branch contribution	600,000 DM	228,000 DM
Branch investments		
Accounts receivable	1,200,000 DM	420,000 DM
Inventories	1,800,000 DM	480,000 DM
Total assets managed	3,000,000 DM	900,000 DM
Contributions as percent of sales	10.0%	6.3%
Asset turnover	2.0	4.0

*All figures in German Deutsch marks.

1 On the basis of profitability, which branch appears to have the better performance? What factors could explain this?

2 Given the assets necessary for each branch to produce these results, how would you compare the two branches?

3 How could Mr. Deitrich use the above information to further analyze performance and to make recommendations for improving the performance of the two branches?

QUESTIONS AND SITUATIONS FOR DISCUSSION

1 "In many companies, managers concentrate on ratios that indicate substandard performance. Given enough information, it is possible to find ratios that will make any unit of analysis look bad." Do you agree or disagree with this statement? Should this be the focus of sales and cost analysis?

2 After completing an analysis of their accounts, the M&N company found that many of their small accounts were unprofitable. Under what conditions would you recommend that they stop selling to these accounts and instead concentrate their resources on the more profitable medium and large customers?

3 Alpha Corporation sells $50 million worth of industrial repair parts to manufacturing companies each year, earning a 50 percent variable-contribution margin. Recently, customers representing 10 percent of Alpha's sales told Alpha that it must guarantee delivery in 2 days on all parts if it wants their business. Alpha's managers have figures that indicate they will have to increase inventory levels at their regional warehouses from an annual average of $12.5 million to $20 million in order to provide this service. Currently, Alpha's cost of carrying inventory is 25 percent of average inventory.
  a Determine Alpha's inventory cost of both average inventory levels.
  b Should Alpha submit to this request?

4 A manufacturer is reviewing its policy of offering discounts of 1 percent to distributors who pay invoices within 10 days rather than within the normal 30-day period. What specific issues should the manufacturer consider before making this decision?

5 At the beginning of Chapter 12, it was suggested that sales volume was generally inadequate as a program objective. However, in Chapter 13, we have indicated that sales volume is an important consideration in budgeting and in performance evaluation. Explain the relationship between sales volume and the four types of objectives established in Chapter 12. Then explain the roles of sales volume and of the types of sales and distribution objectives in the budgeting and performance-evaluation processes.

6 You are the sales manager for a three-state sales territory. Your sales force has been allocated to different geographical areas within the territory and you have just received the following information on two of your salespeople, Jan and Lee:

	Jan	Lee
Total sales, cases	10,000	15,000
Sales calls made	80	75
New accounts opened	3	0
Dollar contribution earned	$85,000	$120,000
Travel expense	$ 1200	$ 1000

Discuss how this information can be useful in evaluating the performance of each person, and indicate the additional factors or information you would need to completely evaluate their performance.

7 The national sales manager for your company has asked you to begin evaluating working-capital requirements in assessing the performance of sales territories. You have received the following data for the year just ended for two territories, A and B.

	Territory	
	A	B
Sales	$5,500,000	$6,800,000
Variable costs	3,300,000	4,488,000
Direct selling costs	300,000	350,000
Average inventory	2,040,000	2,125,000
Average accounts receivable	440,000	450,000

a Compare the two territories in terms of return on assets managed.

b Assume the firm's cost of carrying inventory and accounts receivable are 15 and 10 percent, respectively. Treating inventory and accounts receivable as direct costs, compare the total contribution of the territories.

c Which territory is the better performing one, and what factors account for the differences in performance?

SUGGESTED ADDITIONAL READINGS

Anderson, Erin, "The Salesperson as Outside Agent or Employee: A Transaction Cost Analysis," *Marketing Science,* Summer 1985, pp. 234–254.

Behrman, Douglas, and William Perrault, "Measuring the Performance of Industrial Salespersons," *Journal of Business Research,* September 1982, pp. 355–370.

Finkin, Eugene F., "Expense Control in Sales and Marketing," *Journal of Business Strategy,* May–June 1988, pp. 52–55.

Gates, Michael, "New Measures of Sales Performance," *Incentive,* November 1988, pp. 45–52.

Jackson, Donald, and Lonnie Ostrom, "Grouping Segments for Profitability Analysis," *Business Topics,* Spring 1980, pp. 39–44.

Kaplan, Robert S., "One Cost System Isn't Enough," *Havard Business Review,* January–February 1988, pp. 61–66.

LaForge, Raymond, and David Cravens, "A Market Response Model for Sales Management Decision Making," *Journal of Personal Selling and Sales Management,* Fall/Winter 1981–1982, pp. 10–16.

Levy, Michael, and Michael Van Breda, "A Financial Perspective on the Shift of Marketing Functions," *Journal of Retailing,* Winter 1984, pp. 23–42.

Lodish, Leonard M., "A User-Oriented Model for Sales Force Size, Product and Market Allocation Decisions," *Journal of Marketing,* Summer 1980, pp. 70–78.

Monahan, James P., "A Quantity Discount Pricing Model to Increase Vendor Profits," *Management Science,* June 1984, pp. 720–726.

Parasuraman, A., and Ralph Day, "A Management-Oriented Model for Allocating Sales Effort," *Journal of Marketing Research,* February 1977, pp. 23–33.

Schiff, J. S., "Evaluating the Sales Force as a Business," *Industrial Marketing Management,* April 1983, pp. 131–137.

PART 4

COORDINATION AND CONTROL

I n Part 3, we examined the various marketing strategies and programs that managers use to achieve product or product-line objectives. More specifically, we noted that product development, price, advertising, sales promotion, and sales and distribution programs can be used jointly or individually to stimulate demand in the desired fashion.

Because a variety of programs may be employed to carry out a marketing strategy and because more than one individual may be involved in managing these programs for a product or product line, some method of coordinating the programs is necessary. Further, the effectiveness of marketing strategies and programs will depend on how well they are executed. Nevertheless, even a well-designed, closely coordinated, and properly executed plan may fail to achieve the product objectives because of uncontrollable factors such as economic forces or competitors' actions.

In Chapters 14 and 15, we provide tools and procedures for

- Improving the coordination and execution of strategies and programs
- Monitoring results

• Modifying strategies and programs as necessary on the basis of performance or because of major environmental changes or both

Specifically, in Chapter 14 we present alternative approaches for structuring the organization and for managing human resources in order to achieve effective coordination and execution of strategies and programs. In Chapter 15, we demonstrate how managers can use annual marketing plans for coordinating the allocation of resources among marketing programs, for monitoring performance, and for adjusting the plan in response to gaps between planned and actual levels of performance.

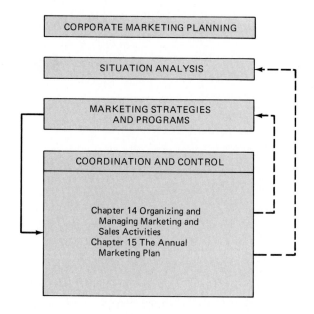

CHAPTER 14

ORGANIZING AND MANAGING MARKETING AND SALES ACTIVITIES

OVERVIEW

A central theme of this book is that managers should select strategies and programs that are consistent with the situation analysis and are designed to achieve specific objectives. However, a well-chosen strategy will still be ineffective if it is not properly executed. It has been said that it is much easier to think up marketing strategies than it is to make them work under company, competitive, and customer constraints.[1] Consider for example, the case of Tandy Corporation.

In 1986, Tandy Corporation's sales of personal computers showed strong growth. Sales of Tandys' low-priced home version PC was increasing while at the same time PC clones were gaining share from IBM. This was viewed by Tandy executives as an opportunity to further increase sales by selling direct to businesses. Tandys' strategy called for designating selected Radio Shack stores for direct computer sales and recruiting a direct sales force of 1500 persons. Radio Shack managers were assigned the responsibility for recruiting, training and managing this direct salesforce. Many of these retail managers initially hired the wrong people as trainees. These errors resulted from the managers' inexperience and their inability to effectively perform sales management activities while at the same time, continuing to be responsible for day-to-day store operations.

[1]The importance of paying attention to execution is discussed in Thomas V. Bonoma, "Making Your Marketing Strategy Work," *Harvard Business Review*, March–April 1984, pp. 68–76.

Trainees were given sales training over a period of eight Saturdays. This meant that they were selling for two months before they had completed their training. Within a year, all 200 college graduates hired for direct sales had left Tandy and the annual turnover of those remaining approached 65 percent. In an attempt to correct the situation, Tandy hired experienced direct sales managers to supervise those designated Radio Shack computer stores as well as assistants to handle administrative details. However, this did not result in increased performance. Tandy thus closed 103 computer centers and consolidated the remaining direct sales people under the most effective center managers. Experienced Regional Managers were assigned responsibility for hiring and a month-long sales training program was initiated. In addition, compensation programs were adjusted and a dozen sales veterans were recruited to concentrate on major corporations.[2]

As will be shown in Chapter 15, by coordinating the various marketing programs through annual plans, managers can improve the likelihood that the marketing strategy will be properly implemented. However, though the strategy may have been the appropriate one, given the situation, poor execution may have resulted in poor market performance. Therefore, it is important to coordinate and control marketing practices as well as the persons responsible for implementing these decisions.

Additionally, the success of the marketing effort will depend in large part on the degree of coordination achieved between marketing and the other functional areas of a business. Accordingly, the organizational structure that a firm uses to achieve coordination and the effectiveness of interpersonal relationships among managers in the various functional areas will have a major influence on the success of the firm's strategies.

The role of the sales force is particularly important in the execution of strategy. As we indicated in Chapter 12, the sales function will be effective only if appropriate sales appeals are communicated and if the sales force is structured for maximum efficiency in calling on customers or distributors. Accordingly, management must be sure that these human resources are effectively used if the strategy is to be properly executed.

In this chapter, we will examine some of the problems associated with executing marketing strategies. Since organizational design may be one of the key factors in determining the effectiveness of people in the firm, we will examine some of the types of organizational structures as well as factors considered in selecting the most appropriate type. Subsequently, we will examine the relationships between other functions of the business and discuss some ways of managing interfunctional conflict to improve coordination. The requirements associated with working with external agencies will also be discussed. Additionally, because the successful execution of marketing strategies is determined at the level of the individual salesperson, some of the actions managers can take to improve sales-force execution and effectiveness will be discussed.

[2]Todd Mason and Geoff Lewis, "Tandy Finds a Cold, Hard World Outside the Radio Shack," *Business Week,* Aug. 31, 1987, pp. 68–70.

EXECUTING MARKETING STRATEGY

Marketing practitioners know that successful performance depends both on strategy and the execution of that strategy. Consider, for example, the situation at Waterford Crystal.

> Waterford Crystal created an image of exclusivity by advertising in classy magazines such as the *New Yorker* and *Architectural Digest* and by limiting distribution to upscale retailers. However, at a time when the demand for crystal was booming, Waterford found its market share declining. The decline was partially attributed to the firm's failure to recognize the emerging market for crystal was made up of baby boomers with a taste for expensive household furnishings. Moreover, Waterford had failed to introduce new patterns, vary its advertising, or effectively service its 1500 U.S. retail accounts. The loss of market share resulted from a combination of inappropriate marketing strategy and poor execution of some of the major marketing functions.[3]

Marketing strategy and the execution of this strategy have a reciprocal effect on each other. Professor Thomas Bonoma of the Harvard Business School has concluded that strategy obviously affects actions; and execution also affects marketing strategies over time.[4] Problems in implementation can often disguise a good strategy. If the execution of the strategy is poor, it may cause marketing management to attribute the failure to a poor strategy and permanently change its approach. However, at the other extreme, one may find inappropriate strategies compensated for by excellent execution. In this situation, management may have time to recognize its strategic mistakes and adjust its strategy. At other times, it is possible that good execution of a poorly designed strategy can accelerate failure. Because poor execution may disguise whether the strategy was appropriate or inappropriate, it is necessary that managers look to marketing practices before immediately making strategic adjustments. These problems and practices can occur either with marketing functions, programs, systems, or policy directives.

Often poor execution is the result of the failure of management to pursue marketing fundamentals or to follow up on their implementation. Another cause of problems or failure comes about from the lack of a clear focus or from trying to concentrate on too many functions at one time. These faults typically result in what Bonoma has called "global mediocrity." It is not the way to earn a good reputation for some outstanding function, as Gillette did for its Personal Care Division's superior advertising or Hane's innovative packaging of L'eggs panty hose.

Marketing programs combine both marketing and nonmarketing functions for a certain product or market. Management attempts to blend functions such as sales promotion and production to sell a particular product or penetrate a target

---

[3]A. B. Wilson and Amy Dunkin, "Waterford Learns Its Lesson: Snob Appeal Isn't Enough," *Business Week,* Dec. 24, 1984, pp. 63–65.

[4]Professor Bonoma has argued that more often than not it is poor implementation rather than poorly designed strategies that result in failure to achieve marketing objectives. This section is based on Bonoma's investigations as described in Thomas V. Bonoma, "Making Your Marketing Strategy Work," *Harvard Business Review,* March–April 1984, pp. 69–76; and in Thomas V. Bonoma, *Managing Marketing,* The Free Press, New York, 1984, p. 552.

market. The combining of these various functions into effective marketing programs is often done poorly. Poorly executed programs may result from a company trying to go beyond its functional capabilities or from a lack of direction. Pepperidge Farm's decision to introduce Star Wars cookies, which didn't fit their upscale high-quality image, was a strategy that didn't match either marketing identity or product direction.

Poor marketing practice may be due to errors in formal organization, inadequate resource commitment, or in failure to depart from tradition. For instance, National Cash Register's profits lagged during the 1970s due to a marketing organization that had failed to adjust to the times. NCR focused on a few specific groups of customers—retail and financial—with a direct sales force. However, NCR was missing important sales opportunities, and decided eventually to use outside distributors. By 1986, 10 percent of sales came from these outside distributors. In addition, the direct sales force was then divided into two groups: one selling complete packages to small customers, the other selling stripped-down computers to those preferring to write their own programs.[5] The lack of adequate information may also result in poor execution. Too frequently, marketing managers lack the necessary information to determine the profitability by segment, product, or individual account—even though it is requested from other functional departments.

Several distinct characteristics seem to differentiate companies that execute marketing effectively from those that do not. First, in the best organizations there seems to be a sense of identity and direction. A clear theme and vision are present, and there is little uncertainty as to what the company represents and where it is going. For instance, Mag Instruments' manufactures and markets state-of-the art flashlights. This is a company that has been built on a philosophy and strategy of pushing quality to the limits. Premium quality permeates every aspect of the company's operations from its uniquely designed products to its manufacturing process and entire marketing effort. As a result the company can sell its best-selling flashlight for a retail price of $16.95, double the price of most flashlights. Mag products consistently appear in lists of best American-made products as well as on those that illustrate the finest in American design.[6]

A second characteristic is the concern for customers, including retail and wholesale distributors, that exists with those firms that consistently execute their strategies effectively. These firms view end users and distributors as partners and expect them to profit in terms of the value they receive as well as the lasting partnership that develops. Finally, in those companies that consistently seem to execute marketing well, followers are encouraged to challenge and question upper management.[7] For example, lower level managers are encouraged to provide suggestions for improvements to existing methods of operation. Delta Airlines, for

[5]Gary Slutsker, "Playing for the Long Haul," *Forbes*, Nov. 3, 1986, pp. 43–44.
[6]Paul B. Brown, "Magnificent Obsession," *Inc.*, August 1989, pp. 79–84.
[7]Thomas V. Bonoma, "Market Success Can Breed 'Market Inertia'," *Harvard Business Review*, October 1981, p. 115.

instance, is known for its open-door policy for employees and its willingness to make substantial policy changes as a result of these employee suggestions.

TYPES OF ORGANIZATIONAL STRUCTURES

Essentially, an organizational structure accomplishes two things:

1 It defines the formal allocation of work roles to identify the members of the organization who will perform each activity.

2 It establishes the lines of authority for integrating and coordinating activities.

In this section, our major concern is with the impact of the organizational structure on the execution of marketing activities. Specifically, we examine the ways in which a given structure can enhance or limit the coordination of marketing activities.

There is no single, ideal structure to fit all companies. A structure that may be effective for one firm will not necessarily work in another because of differences in size, in the number of products produced, in corporate strategies, and in management personnel. Accordingly, a company should select an organizational form that fits its own situation.

Essentially a firm can organize along one of three dimensions: the *functions* performed, the *products* and product lines offered, or the *markets* to be served. Although certain combinations of these forms can be used to fit the specific situation facing an individual firm, the primary basis for organization will be along one of these three dimensions.

Organizing by Function

The functional organization structure is a common approach to grouping marketing activities, especially among companies that offer a limited variety of products or services. In this type of structure, marketing activities are organized according to the type of duties performed, and decision-making authority and coordination are highly centralized. Because all functions are centralized, this structure is most applicable when the product line is relatively limited; when the products have similar manufacturing, research, and advertising requirements; and when the same sales force and distributors can easily be used for all the firm's products.

Although the centralization of the marketing effort reduces problems in coordinating marketing programs, it places a major responsibility for coordinating marketing with the other functional areas on the chief marketing executive. Additionally, when all decisions are centralized, decision making is often slow. Further, in large firms, the chief marketing executive may have difficulty in keeping abreast of market developments for every product. As a result, many firms have found that, as product lines expand, a completely centralized functional organization becomes unwieldy. For example, consider the changes initiated by Xerox.

When Japanese producers introduced low-price copiers in the mid-1970's Xerox was unprepared to compete for this market segment. Because of this competition, Xerox's share of U.S. copy revenues declined from 96 percent in 1970 to less than 45 percent in 1983. Product planning, design, service, and manufacturing had reported to separate executives at corporate headquarters and no one had the primary responsibility for seeing that new products were completed and introduced. To correct this, Xerox reorganized the copier business into four strategic business units. General managers of each unit set long-range strategy and oversaw product development while reporting to the head of the Reprographics Business Group who in turn answered to only one executive at headquarters. This resulted in an immediate 10 percent productivity gain. Further, engineering cycles for some new products were shortened by 10 percent.[8]

Essentially decentralization can be accomplished by organizing on the basis of products or markets.

Organizing by Product

To the extent that a firm has a large array of products and to the extent that the products are dissimilar in terms of their marketing requirements (so that each product requires specialized attention), a product-oriented organization can be structured in two ways: through product-manager systems and through autonomous product divisions.

The Product-Manager System   In a product-manager system, individual managers are assigned to coordinate the marketing programs of one or more products or brands. The key to the successful use of this form of organization is the effectiveness with which the product manager coordinates marketing programs with manufacturing and logistics. The product manager will develop and administer marketing programs; analyze and report on a business's progress; administer budgets, oversees sales, product development, and manufacturing functions; and train personnel. Although product managers have no line authority over the field sales force, they work closely with them to accomplish the necessary sales goals for their product. Although the product-management job differs from organization to organization, a frequently used arrangement is for the product or brand manager to be given a budget for the marketing of the brand and purchase sales support, advertising, marketing research or other services that the brand requires from the company.

The product-manager organization is not without its deficiencies, however. Among some of the limitations which have been cited are the following:

• The product manager may be knowledgeable about the product while lacking the expertise needed to make appropriate decisions in the technical areas of product research, manufacturing, and even sales and media.

• Product managers generally lack the authority commensurate with their responsibilities. For example, they must attempt to coordinate sales promotions

[8]"How Xerox Speeds Up the Birth of New Products," *Business Week,* Mar. 19, 1984, p. 58; and "The New Lean, Mean Xerox: Fending Off the Japanese," *Business Week,* Oct. 12, 1981, pp. 126–132.

with sales force and manufacturing schedules, but they have no authority over either activity. Accordingly, they must rely on their persuasive capabilities to gain the necessary cooperation.

- Many product managers find little time to perform the planning activities so critical to success because of the extensive time and effort involved in their daily interactions with other functional areas.

- Product managers spend considerable time on research and analysis, refining and executing minor changes and balancing quarterly marketing expenditures, but much of this activity deals with issues on which they can have only limited impact.

- If the product/brand manager has profit responsibility and is rewarded based on the profit performance of the brand, there may be no incentive to invest to build market share because this may be viewed as detrimental to short-term profits.

The Multidivisional Product Organization   Firms that have a very large number of products which differ in their manufacturing and R&D requirements as well as in their marketing requirements often employ a multidivisional product organization. In this organizational structure, separate divisions are formed, with products grouped into divisions containing similar products. Each division will have its own functional organization and, very frequently, will contain a product-management system.

In many firms, each division will be treated as a unique, autonomous business. Additionally, a recent study indicates that in well-managed companies, divisional managers are usually given responsibility for replenishing the new-product array and are usually allowed to reinvest earnings from the division's own products within the division. Although this practice appears inconsistent with the product portfolio approach (in which cash cow divisions provide the resources for divisions with greater growth potential), managers can still use the product portfolio concept to determine allocations of resources and product objectives among products within each division. More important, many of these firms believe that managers will not develop entrepreneurial skills in corporations that "give the fruits of one manager's labor to someone else."[9]

This organizational approach also has some limitations. In some cases, divisional lines can inhibit coordination and increase costs. For example,

Sara Lee made its first European acquisition in 1962 when it obtained a Dutch producer of canned foods. Since that time, Sara Lee has made numerous other international acquisitions. Included among these have been Douwe Egberts (Dutch coffee, tea and tobacco company), Nicholas Kiwi Ltd. (the Australian maker of shoe polish), Akzo N.V. (consumer products division) and DIM (French hosiery and underwear). Cornelius Boomstra, chairman of the company's main European unit in preparation for the European Community after 1992 initiated a program of standardization and reorganization. Douwe Egberts coffee was previously sold under different brand names in seven coun-

[9]Thomas J. Peters, "Putting Excellence into Management," *Business Week*, July 21, 1980, p. 200.

tries. Standardized packaging sizes and colors and a global advertising campaign was initiated to develop a European identity. By integrating the management structures of Adzo, Douwe Egberts and other European units Sara Lee expected profits to improve by $40 million a year. To avoid interdivisional disputes with existing megabrands, specialty products have been emphasized for Eurobranding. For instance instead of expanding *Prudent,* its top selling Benelux brand, Sara Lee selected *Zendium,* a Danish enzyme toothpaste that cost more. By combining administration and developing a coordinated approach, Boomstra anticipates Sara Lee will be better prepared to develop the European market and at the same time save enormous amounts of money.[10]

Organizing by Market

When customer groups have dramatically different needs and when these groups are large enough to justify individual attention, the organizational structure often includes market managers and separate sales forces. Note that the various market managers may share common manufacturing and research facilities because essentially the same product is being sold to different markets. However, there may be major differences in the quantities purchased, the appropriate channels of distribution, or the technical usage needs of the various customer groups. Accordingly, different packaging and pricing programs, sales forces, and customer service activities may be needed for each group. In these situations, many firms have begun to adopt these market-based organizational structures. For example, the Fonda Group sells to two markets. The consumer division sells disposable plates, bowls, and cups to supermarkets. The commercial division sells to restaurants, hospitals, and party goods stores, and includes in its product line "pails" for take-out food, popcorn cups, food trays, and hot dog holders.[11] At one time these two markets were served by the same sales force. However, management felt that the requirements of the customers in these two markets were different enough to warrant separate sales forces. Even though the product lines are similar, the ways in which they are sold are very different. Fonda had found individual representatives neglected that part of the business where they felt they lacked expertise. With the creation of separate divisions, expertise of the sales force was reinforced and sales rose 10 percent the first year.

As in the case of product managers, market managers seldom have authority over all the functional areas that are essential for implementing the marketing programs. Rather, market managers are responsible for planning and coordination, and sales managers are responsible for implementation. Mergers of large retailers have created a number of regional giants with immense distribution power. These large retailers require specialized attention such as Gillette's Safety Razor Division provides. Gillette chose to concentrate on the regional level rather than expand their national accounts department. Regional key account managers not only call upon headquarters but also upon chain division offices

[10]Steve Weiner, "How Do You Say L'eggs in French?" *Forbes,* Nov. 27, 1989, pp. 73–77.
[11]Rayna Skolnik, "Fonda Gets Feisty," *Sales and Marketing Management,* October 1986, pp. 49–53.

even if they are outside of the region. The regional sales manager's job becomes more of a business unit manager rather than just sales. This was accomplished by putting merchandising and sales planning under the regional sales manager. Salespeople, as a result of this restructuring, are now prepared to talk to their accounts about pricing distribution, promotion, and display.[12]

FACTORS INFLUENCING MARKETING ORGANIZATION

Although there is no single best way to organize, the presence or absence of certain conditions can influence the effectiveness of a given organization structure.

Corporate Strategy

A major purpose of structure in an organization is to assist in the implementation of corporate strategies. Accordingly, one type of structural form may be superior or inferior, depending on the strategic situation. A market-development strategy, for instance, might require a functional or customer-oriented organization if new markets are to be effectively developed. For example,

> Digital Equipment Corporation (DEC) was organized by product line for 19 years. Product managers were responsible for profitably developing and marketing one product line. However, the introduction of the VAX superminicomputers which were intended to be capable of automating entire corporations required a highly unified and coordinated marketing effort. To accomplish this marketing effort DEC dismantled the product line organization and organized along functional lines. The development of the VAX 9000 which directly competes with IBM mainframes brought additional organizational changes in 1989. In an effort to target specific industries, Regional Managers were put in charge of all employees—programmer system engineers and salespeople—who serve a given industry.[13]

Note that DEC's structure has changed as its strategy has changed. Consequently, management should allow the strategy to dictate the structure rather than the reverse.[14]

Needs of Target-Segment Customers

A firm's organizational structure should provide management with the most effective way to meet customer needs quickly. St. Regis Paper reorganized their Bag Packaging/Consumer Products Divisions for this reason. As competition became more aggressive, bids and answers needed faster response time for target market customers. Previously, bag packaging, the industrial side, was combined with consumer products. Five autonomous business units were established within

---

[12]"Gillette Hones Salespower to a Fine Edge," *Sales and Marketing Management,* June 1987, p. 59.

[13]Peter Petre, "America's Most Successful Entrepreneur," *Fortune,* Oct. 27, 1986, pp. 24–32; and "DEC Has One Little Word for 30,000 Employees: Sell," *Business Week,* Aug. 14, 1989, pp. 86–88.

[14]For further discussion, see Alfred Chandler, *Strategy and Structure,* MIT Press, Cambridge, 1962.

the division: (1) consumer goods—school, home, and office-supply products; (2) retail packaging—grocery bags; (3) specialty packaging—stretch film and semibulk containers; (4) multiwall east; and (5) multiwall west. The multiwall east and multiwall west divisions have complete operational control, including marketing, sales, and manufacturing for industrial products, and are responsible for profit and planning growth for their divisions.[15]

Customer considerations were also a major factor in the 1980 reorganization at General Foods. Three divisions (food products, pet foods, and beverage and breakfast foods) that formerly handled their own manufacturing and sales activities were restricted to concentrate only on the other marketing programs. Sales and manufacturing activities were placed in a separate function designed to serve all the divisions. Company officials believed that the new organization would result in more effective coordination and consolidation of those sales efforts which were focused on key distributor accounts.[16]

In sum, to the extent that customer needs differ among products and customers, the organizational structure should enable the firm to develop and execute marketing strategies to meet the needs of target customers. Further, the more dynamic a firm's markets, the greater the importance of being able to respond to customers' needs.

Management Philosophy and Resources

Management attitudes regarding concepts such as participative decision making, decentralization, and innovation will also influence the effectiveness of an organizational design. For example, in discussing Henry Ford II's decision to retire as chief executive officer of the Ford Motor Company, *Business Week* emphasized his desire to build a decentralized management structure similar to that of General Motors.[17] However, because of the strong personality of Henry Ford and his inability to relinquish control over certain decision areas, this effort was less than successful.

Unilever which was formed in a 1930 merger of Britain's Lever Brothers Ltd. with Hollands' Margine Union Ltd. was one of the first true global marketers. Most of Unilever's United States business is done by Lever Brothers. Unilever's unusual Anglo-Dutch structure gave it a multinational culture which resulted in a highly decentralized management. For the most part, Unilever's top management let local executives of its 500 subsidiaries in 75 countries run things as they chose. However, in the United States, the company set unrealistic profit objectives which led Lever Brothers managers to reduce advertising spending at the same time competitors were increasing expenditures and introducing new brands.

After Lever Brothers lost a total of $100 million from 1981 to 1986, Unilever took a more active role in the U.S. operations. One of Unilever's three cochair-

---

[15]"St. Regis Divides to Conquer," *Sales and Marketing Management,* Oct. 10, 1983, pp. 39–42.
[16]"GF Splits Marketing and Sales," *Sales and Marketing Management,* May 19, 1980, p. 10.
[17]"Ford after Henry II: Will He Really Leave? Absolutely," *Business Week,* Apr. 30, 1979, pp. 62–72.

men came to the United States and essentially dismantled Lever Brothers. Only household products were left with Lever Brothers. The personal products division was shifted to Chesebrough-Ponds' Inc. and the food division was made into a separate unit called VanderBurgh Foods. Each division now reports directly to Europe. This eliminated several layers of management and resulted in faster adoption of new ideas. Subsequently, Unilever's share of the U.S. household products market rose from 15 percent in 1980 to 25 percent in 1989. In addition overall operating profit increased 69 percent during this period.[18]

To summarize, the marketing organization must be structured so that corporate and marketing strategies can be effectively and efficiently carried out to meet customer needs. In addition, top management must be aware that both its philosophy and attitudes about the role of marketing and the availability of qualified middle managers can lead to the choice of an improper structure.

However, the structure of the total organization and of the marketing organization can never ensure the successful execution of strategies and programs. Organization charts do not coordinate activities—people do. And because of marketing's integrative role with the other functional areas, the ability to manage interorganizational relationships is essential, especially for product and market managers.

MANAGING ORGANIZATIONAL RELATIONSHIPS

In Chapter 1, we discussed the various ways in which marketing was related to the other functional areas of the organization. Because of these interrelationships, marketing managers must develop interpersonal skills to be successful in dealing with managers over whom they have no direct authority. Managers consistently cite the importance of their interactions with others, especially in coordinating efforts with other departments. In particular, marketing activities must be closely coordinated with R&D, manufacturing, physical distribution, and finance. We will now discuss the importance of achieving coordination with each of these functions.

Research and Development

In most product-development programs, marketing and R&D must work closely together. Accordingly, marketing managers should have an understanding of the technical problems and processes involved in the various stages of product development. Additionally, managers must be aware of the inevitable frustrations and exacting nature of the R&D activity and should share fully their knowledge of the needs of the market to provide useful guidelines for the work of R&D. Consider, for example, the experience of Colgate.

In 1985, Colgate started to adopt a system whereby managers of product cat-

[18]Walecia Konrad, "The New, Improved Unilever Aims to Clean Up in the U.S.," *Business Week*, Nov. 27, 1989, pp. 102–106.

egories would have direct profit responsibility. To provide them with the necessary authority, these category managers were given some control over other functions such as research, finance, and manufacturing. This system was designed to promote better planned and faster new-product introductions. A. Courtenay Shepard, Colgate's president in the United States, says that "by surrounding the marketing people with these multidisciplinary skills we make them instantly effective." This approach has been attributed as the reason that the company could take FAB 1 Shot detergent and fabric-softener from the idea stage to national introduction in only eleven months.[19]

But the sharing of knowledge between these two functions is often missing. One author has suggested four reasons for the lack of coordination between marketing and R&D.[20]

1 *Product-oriented company philosophy:* In many companies the orientation is an inward-looking one, dominated by products, properties, and processes. This attitude leads to the development of products that are designed around the organization's technological capability rather than around market needs.

2 *Deference toward R&D:* Marketing managers' lack of knowledge regarding the tools and techniques of the "scientists" may lead to permissiveness or great deference to R&D. As a result, some R&D efforts may lead to products that have little chance for commercial success.

3 *Search for perfect products:* R&D often attempts to achieve product perfection. But a technically perfect solution to the problem may be more than the market desires. Technically superior products may be unmarketable, because the complexity of these products may preclude high reliability or ease of maintenance. Alternatively, such products may have to be priced too high because of excessive production costs.

4 *Science versus art:* Although market satisfaction is derived from benefits (which are usually intangible), R&D is concerned with the tangible attributes of products.

A recent study by The Conference Board found that once new products had been developed, those persons in R&D and marketing went their separate ways. Because there is a tendency in most companies for marketing and R&D to view their jobs as very different from one another, it is almost impossible to get them to cooperate. However, some companies have effectively improved the relationship by a variety of formal and informal methods. Physical location next to each other and combined departmental meetings have worked for some firms. The key is having someone coordinate the effort—someone who has the necessary authority to get the two groups to cooperate.[21]

---

[19]Zachary Schiller, "The Marketing Revolution at Procter & Gamble," *Business Week,* July 25, 1988, p. 76.

[20]Mack Hanan, "Effective Coordination of Marketing with Research and Development," in Victor Buell (ed.), *Handbook of Modern Marketing,* McGraw-Hill, New York, 1970, pp. 3-17 to 3-28.

[21]Michael Duerr, *The Commercial Development of New Products,* The Conference Board, New York, 1986.

TABLE 14-1   MARKETING/MANUFACTURING AREAS OF NECESSARY COOPERATION
BUT POTENTIAL CONFLICT

Problem area	Typical marketing comment	Typical manufacturing comment
1. Capacity planning and long-range sales forecasting	"Why don't we have enough capacity?"	"Why didn't we have accurate sales forecasts?"
2. Production scheduling and short-range sales forecasting	"We need faster response. Our lead times are ridiculous."	"We need realistic customer commitments and sales forecasts that don't change like wind direction."
3. Delivery and physical distribution	"Why don't we ever have the right merchandise in inventory?"	"We can't keep everything in inventory."
4. Quality assurance	"Why can't we have reasonable quality at reasonable cost?"	"Why must we always offer options that are too hard to manufacture and that offer little customer utility?"
5. Breadth of product line	"Our customers demand variety."	"The product line is too broad—all we get are short, uneconomical runs."
6. Cost control	"Our costs are so high that we are not competitive in the marketplace."	"We can't provide fast delivery, broad variety, rapid response to change, and high quality at low cost."
7. New product introduction	"New products are our life blood."	"Unnecessary design changes are prohibitively expensive."
8. Adjunct services such as spare parts inventory support, installation, and repair.	"Field service costs are too high."	"Products are being used in ways for which they weren't designed."

Source: Reprinted by permission of the *Harvard Business Review* from "Can Marketing and Manufacturing Coexist?" by Benson Shapiro, September–October 1977. Copyright © 1977 by the President and Fellows of Harvard College; all rights reserved.

Manufacturing

Probably the most frequent conflicts between functions are those between marketing and manufacturing. Table 14-1 summarizes the various kinds of conflicts that typically occur between these two functions.

Although these conflicts can seldom be fully resolved, the level of conflict between these two groups can be made more manageable so that greater cooperation is achieved. Among the actions that managers may employ to manage these conflicts are the following.[22]

[22]Benson Shapiro, "Can Marketing and Manufacturing Coexist?" *Harvard Business Review,* September–October 1977, pp. 111–113.

- Clearly specified corporate strategies and marketing strategies should be developed to provide a common set of rules for both functions. For example, when the markets to be served are clearly specified, the number of models or product lines to be produced can be agreed upon more easily.
- Management can modify the evaluation and reward system to include interfunctional performance. For instance, marketing managers may be evaluated on sales forecasting performance and manufacturing managers on order response time as well as on inventory levels.
- By having manufacturing personnel attend sales meetings or marketing managers do "internships" in manufacturing positions, managers in each functional area may gain better insights into the problems facing managers in the other functional areas.

Physical Distribution

An effective and well-integrated physical distribution system can provide a firm with a significant competitive marketing advantage. Because a substantial share of the final price of a product is accounted for by physical distribution costs, any reduction in price resulting from more effective coordination will lead to more competitive prices or higher margins.

Allegheny Beverages' computerized order-entry system provides this type of advantage for its field sales force and production scheduling system. Allegheny's Desk and Furnishings Division's sales representatives are each equipped with a Hewlett-Packard Portable Plus laptop computer that allows them to dial into the headquarters' HP 3000 mainframe. Individual salespersons can check on the order status as well as shipment schedule for any customer. In this way they can assure customers of delivery dates or suggest alternatives. In addition, they can reserve inventory as well as place orders almost instantaneously.[23]

As we noted in Chapters 12 and 13, logistical appeals are becoming more desirable to customers, but the cost of providing these appeals is also increasing. Accordingly, coordination between sales programs and physical distribution is essential to building profitable sales-volume levels.

Coordination is also necessary to ensure that adequate supplies of the product will be made available to distributors during sales promotions. If supplies are inadequate, excessive transportation costs may be required to fill *rush* orders, and relationships with distributors may be damaged. Further, if there has been a history of poor physical distribution support associated with promotional programs, field salespeople may not enthusiastically support new sales promotions.

In sum, although an effective organizational structure can assist managers in the execution of corporate and marketing strategies, the development of interorganizational coordination ultimately will depend on the attitudes and actions of the managers in the firm. Essentially, marketing managers must "market

---

[23]Thayer C. Taylor, "Laptops and the Salesforce: New Stars in the Sky," *Sales and Marketing Management,* April 1987, pp. 50–55.

the marketing strategies and programs'' to other functional areas in order to obtain coordination. To be effective in performing this task, an understanding of the needs and aspirations of other managers, and an awareness of the constraints limiting their actions (such as the reward system they face), is essential. If marketing managers can develop this kind of understanding, they are more likely to develop programs that will receive support from managers in the other functional areas.

Finance

The marketing plan includes major financial inputs such as the cost and profit history for the business, pro forma financial statements, budgets, and the related marketing strategies. In developing and selecting the appropriate marketing strategies, management requires certain financial inputs. Many marketing decisions should be viewed as investment decisions. For instance, as discussed in Chapter 8, new-product alternatives should include a financial evaluation of the required investment and revenue stream. However, this shouldn't be limited to new products as the financial aspects of promotion, distribution alternatives, and pricing decisions must be considered by marketing management as well. In addition, financial considerations can often act as a significant constraint on the strategic options open to the marketer.

The failure of the computer ventures of RCA and General Electric in the 1970s are examples of the constraints financial considerations can place on marketing strategy. The market-share and growth objectives of both companies required a capital commitment to finance a large and rapidly growing leased-equipment inventory. However, the capital-generating ability of the marketing effort was inadequate in both cases.

Often, marketers fail to recognize the impact that their decisions have on such variables as inventory level, working-capital needs, financing costs, debt-to-equity ratios, and stock prices. Too often these are thought of as purely the responsibility of finance. Marketing management needs to be particularly sensitive to the impact various marketing strategies can have upon the financial well being of the company. The development of financial plans involving capital requirements, cash flow, and credit policies all require marketing input to work effectively with the finance department. It may be necessary for marketing to provide alternative strategies and environmental-condition scenarios to assist in financial planning. In addition, marketers must be willing to make the trade-offs necessitated by various financial considerations. This requires close cooperation and contact with the finance function as well as an understanding of the concepts and approaches utilized.

MANAGING EXTERNAL RELATIONSHIPS

The number of specialized skills, techniques, and information services necessary to effectively manage the marketing function has increased markedly in the past decade. As a result, there has been a rising demand and reliance upon marketing skills and expertise provided by outside organizations. To meet this demand, there are many individuals and businesses that offer advisory services. Among those frequently used are marketing consultants, advertising agencies, marketing research suppliers, international specialists, list brokers, and direct mail houses. Managers must have methods to establish, control, and effectively work with these outside individuals and organizations if such arrangements are to be profitable.

Advertising Agencies

The advertising manager working closely with marketing and product managers is generally responsible for selecting and working with the agency or agencies. Prior to the selection of an agency, managers should establish the tasks and functions the agency will be expected to perform. A list of available agencies should be compiled, the qualifications of each examined, and the one anticipated to do the best job selected.

After selecting and contracting with an agency, it is important to recognize that if there is to be a productive relationship, the agency must be considered an important part of the marketing effort. This may often mean that "confidential" material must be revealed to an outside organization. As discussed in Chapter 10, the agency needs to know and understand the overall marketing strategy if sound copy and media strategies are to be developed. It is also necessary that the advertiser be able to use the concepts discussed in Chapter 10 to evaluate the agency's work. Agency performance should be reviewed regularly and systematically and a number of evaluation procedures and forms have been developed for this purpose.[24]

Marketing Research Organizations

Many outside service agencies perform marketing research tasks. However, considerable caution must be taken in the selection of the agency best suited for the assignment. A number of organizations provide lists of research agencies, including those which specialize in particular research tasks and general research organizations.[25] The large number of research organizations serving marketers makes selection of the right one difficult. In making this selection, a number of steps and considerations are involved (see Table 14-2).

Once an agency has been selected, a firm agreement should be made covering such items as (1) quality controls, (2) subcontracting, (3) reports and presentations, (4) penalties for nonperformance, and (5) costs and method of payment. Managers should establish mutual points of contact in both organizations to fa-

---

[24]*Evaluating Agency Performance*, Association of National Advertisers, New York, 1979. In addition numerous related publications are available from the Association of National Advertisers, Inc.

[25]Two such lists include *Bradford's Directory of Marketing Research Agencies and Management Consultants* and the *Membership Roster and International Buyer's Guide to Marketing Services*, American Marketing Association, Chicago, 1986.

TABLE 14-2   CONSIDERATIONS IN SELECTING A MARKETING RESEARCH AGENCY

Steps in selection	Considerations
1. Requirements of the study	General statement of the problem and type of research required
2. Services available	General purpose or specialized Review agencies systematically
3. Check references	Prior experience vs. unknown
4. Preliminary discussions and comparison of proposals	Understanding of the problem Quality and quantity of work to be done Controls and validation of work
5. Cost	Evaluated in relationship to quality
6. Project responsibility	What individual(s) will be assigned

cilitate communication, and progress reviews should be conducted. Often it is beneficial to have a preliminary meeting to review findings prior to the final report. If the research company is used on a continual basis, it is important to provide it with feedback on the implementation of the research to enable it to provide more perceptive research in the future.

MANAGING THE FIELD SALES FORCE

Managing human resources is an important task in all functional areas. But within marketing, this task is primarily important for sales managers. This is true for three reasons. First, the largest number of marketing personnel are in sales positions. Second, the cost of personal selling is extremely high because sales salaries and other compensation are usually relatively high and because of the expenses associated with travel, training, and sales demonstrations.

Finally, effective sales-force management is important because the responsibility for execution of sales and distribution is highly decentralized. That is, the effectiveness of these programs depends on the performance of a large number of people. In contrast, other marketing programs (such as advertising) are normally executed by a relatively small number of people who have the opportunity to work closely with the managers responsible for the respective programs. Accordingly, sales managers must generally be far more concerned with human resource management than other middle-level marketing managers.

There are three kinds of sales-force performances that sales managers can influence in order to improve the execution of sales and distribution programs. First, sales managers can attempt to influence the *total number of sales calls* made in order to maximize the total selling effort. Second, sales managers can attempt to influence the *quality of the sales calls* by taking actions that enhance the expert and referent power of salespeople. Finally, sales managers can attempt

TABLE 14-3 HOW MANAGERS CAN INFLUENCE THE EXECUTION OF SALES AND DISTRIBUTION PROGRAMS

The salesperson can take the following actions:	These actions of the manager influence the salesperson:
Number of sales calls	**Number of salespeople**
	Training in territory coverage, routing, and time management
	Standard operating procedures for sales-force organization, territory coverage, and routing
	Tools for time saving
	Motivation and compensation
Quality of sales calls	
1. Message content	Training in product knowledge and customer operations
	Information flow on customer status, industry trends, and call planning
2. Communications effectiveness	Salespeople selection
	Training in sales skills, communications, listening, and group presentations
	Standard operating procedures for sales-force organization and call planning
	Visual sales aids
3. Interpersonal relationships	Salespeople selection
	Sensitivity training
	Motivation and compensation
Allocation of sales effort	
	Training in territory coverage, time management, and market planning
	Standard operating procedures for sales-force organization and territory coverage
	Motivation and compensation

Source: Reprinted by permission of the *Harvard Business Review* from "Manage Your Sales Force as a System," by Porter Henry, March–April 1975. Copyright © 1975 by the President and Fellows of Harvard College; all rights reserved.

to improve each salesperson's *allocation of selling effort.*[26] Table 14-3 summarizes the kinds of management actions that relate to each of these sales-force dimensions.

In Chapter 13, we reviewed some of the considerations involved in determining the number of sales calls, the size of the sales force, and sales-force allocation. In the remaining portion of this chapter, we examine sales-management actions that are directed more toward enhancing the performance of individual members of the sales force—especially regarding the quality of the sales call.

[26]Porter Henry, "Manage Your Sales Force as a System," *Harvard Business Review*, March–April 1975.

Selecting Salespeople

In many firms, efforts to recruit, select, and train sales-force members are almost continuous because of market expansion, promotions of salespeople into management, and resignations or retirements. A large investment in time and money is required to recruit and train new salespeople. Accordingly, it is important to develop selection procedures that enable a firm to hire people who will be successful. An improper selection can cost an organization $150,000 or more when all the efforts involved in selecting, training, developing, and managing are calculated. For example, consider the case of Wilkinson Sword USA.

In 1985, Wilkinson Sword made the decision to change from a selling system relying upon manufacturer's representatives and brokers to its own thirty-four-person sales force. Executive search firms and employment agencies were used to identify and recruit potential candidates. In some cases, this meant Wilkinson had to compensate an agency up to $15,000 to hire a single salesperson. The costs of recruiting and training the new sales force combined with salaries, bonuses, and selling expenses were over half a million dollars the first year. In addition, the recruiting and selection process took 8 months to complete.[27] Selecting salespeople would not be a difficult task if the characteristics that made a good salesperson could be readily identified. Moreover, each sales job has its own unique requirements. Formal tests, extensive interviews, and weighed applications are finding increasing use as firms attempt to improve their recruiting processes. Increasing use is being made of psychological assessment services in an attempt to reduce turnover.

For instance, Acme Fabrications estimates that they lose about $25,000 in salary, training, and recruiting cost each time they have to replace a salesperson. Each year they interview approximately 500 persons and hire 100 of them. Of these 100, about twenty will be terminated during the first year, resulting in a loss of $500,000. In an attempt to improve this performance, Acme has started to utilize a psychological assessment service. After preliminary interviews are conducted, they refer the best 200 candidates to an assessment firm to review at a cost of $150 a candidate. Acme feels that if the assessment service can reduce turnover by 2 percent, they get full payback in three-fifths of a year: two people times $25,000 (turnover cost) equals $50,000 as opposed to 200 times $150 equals $30,000 (cost of the assessment).[28]

Training Programs

To the extent that training provides the salesperson with product knowledge, customer knowledge, and special skills, the expertise power of the salesperson can

[27]Rayna Skolnik, "The Birth of a Sales Force," *Sales and Marketing Management,* Mar. 19, 1986, pp. 42–44.

[28]Lester L. Tobias, "Making Tests Pay," *Sales and Marketing Management,* Aug. 12, 1985, p. 80.

be enhanced. Similarly, training in interpersonal relations can improve a salesperson's ability to use referent power. Additionally, training sessions may help salespeople to better manage their time and thus be more productive.

Training can be costly and time-consuming, but more and more companies are recognizing the importance of this activity. For example,

> Bell Atlantic introduced its Top Gun program intended to position account executives to be better prepared for emerging technologies in the telecommunications-information services market. Bell selected 60 top sales producers for an intensive 13-week course to better equip them with solutions to solve customer problems. Goodyear has initiated a training center in which sales recruits spend approximately three months in training and veteran salespersons are brought back at regular intervals for refresher courses because the tire business has become more technical.[29]

Standard Operating Procedures and Selling Tools

Standard operating procedures are used to develop routines for those aspects of the sales function that lend themselves to standardization. If managers can routinize certain aspects of the sales function, more of the salesperson's time can be freed for the creative part of the selling task. Increasingly, firms are using automation and computerization for this purpose.

A variety of audiovisual sales aids and literature can be used to increase the communications effectiveness of the salesperson. In addition, technology is providing new ways for performing many selling activities. This has led to increased efficiency and improved quality of the selling function. Videodisc players, compact portable computers, telemarketing, and other electronic tools are becoming widely used in an effort to boost sales productivity. Video presentations, for example, can quickly and precisely show a complicated product's features. Gould Incorporated's Medical Products Division used video support on a new product (called a "disposable transducer") that translated blood pressure into readable electronic impulses. Two videotapes—a 6-minute sales presentation and a 9-minute user training film,—were produced at a cost of $200,000. An additional $75,000 was spent on video recorders for salespeople to take with them on calls. Gould claims this approach captured 45 percent of the $75 million transducer market in less than a year. This was a market Gould had previously been unable to penetrate because some salespeople couldn't convey the exact message the inventor and manufacturer had in mind when the product was designed.[30]

Hewlett-Packard has equipped all of its 2000 sales representatives with portable PCs and printers. Hewlett-Packard's goal was to increase sales productivity by 25 percent by increasing the actual amount of customer contact time. In addition this program increased the level of professionalism of their representatives by giving them direct experience with the solutions they sell to consumers. In the first

---

[29]Al Urbanski, "America's Best Sales Forces," *Sales and Marketing Management,* June 1988, pp. 25–45.

[30]"Rebirth of a Salesman: Willy Loman Goes Electronic," *Business Week,* Feb. 27, 1984, pp. 103–104.

10 months after the project was initiated, sales representatives increased their customer contact time by 27 percent.[31]

Motivation and Compensation

A central concern of any top- or middle-level manager is how to motivate people to achieve the desired level and type of performance. Unfortunately, research on motivation has not provided management with simple guidelines for selecting the best way of motivating the sales force.

In fact, most studies indicate that performance does not depend solely on motivational devices such as bonuses, awards, and promotions. Rather, performance also depends on factors such as quality of supervision, the realism of the selling objectives and quotas, the salesperson's need for achievement, the type of selling task (such as new-account development or account maintenance), and the type of sales job (such as trade selling versus missionary selling). Accordingly, the effectiveness of incentives will differ among industries, firms, and even salespeople within a firm.

It is clear that non-compensation-related forms of motivation should be a part of the motivational package in most firms. IBM wants its employees to feel like winners and has a 100-percent Club for those salespersons achieving their sales quota. About 70 percent of the sales force make the 100-percent Club. The reward for this is a 3-day trip that includes a recognition dinner, a blue and gold lapel pin, and the names of recipients posted on their respective branch office's wall.[32] Recognition is critical and, after a fair level of compensation, is a major motivational tool in many companies.

Compensation-based incentives are also widely employed and extremely effective in many instances. However, when incentive compensation plans are to be used, they should be designed to support the firm's particular sales-program objectives. An incentive based on dollar volume alone may encourage the sales force to emphasize low-margin products and may also lead to inadequate attention to any customer service or account-development objectives that have been established. In an attempt to overcome such problems, many firms in a variety of industries moved away from straight commission schedules and fixed salaries during the 1970s. Too much protection in a pay plan tends to favor the least productive salespeople and provides little stimulus for putting forth the extra effort to reach the sales objectives that have been established.

In a study of compensation plans, it was found the most frequently used was some combination of base salary plus incentive pay in the form of commissions, bonuses, or both. Only 12.4 percent of the companies studied used only salary

---

[31]Thayer C. Taylor, "Hewlett-Packard Gives Sales Reps a Competitive Edge," *Sales and Marketing Management,* February 1987, pp. 36–41.
[32]Patricia Sellers, "How IBM Teaches to Sell," *Fortune,* June 6, 1988, pp. 141–146.

and only 5.1 percent of the compensation plans were based on full commission.[33]

CONCLUSION

An essential ingredient to success in any business, government, or other type of organization are the individuals (and groups of individuals) who make and execute plans. Accordingly, if people are to be effective, managers must design an environment that will facilitate—not hinder—the efforts of individuals and enhance the coordination of efforts. Marketing strategy and the execution of this strategy have a reciprocal effect on each other. Inappropriate strategies can sometimes be compensated for by excellent execution. On the other hand, good strategies can often fail because they are poorly implemented. Several distinct characteristics differentiate those companies that seem to do a good job of implementation from those that do not. A well-defined direction, concern for customers' needs, and managers who encourage subordinates' ideas are among those major characteristics.

In this chapter, we discussed the impact of the organizational structure in facilitating the execution of strategies and programs. But we also recognized that no structure will ensure coordination. Interpersonal skills and cooperative attitudes must be developed to ensure effective coordination. Further, managers must learn to understand the factors that can hinder the performance of people within their own function. In marketing, this problem is most critical with respect to sales-force performance, because if programs are to be effectively implemented, the sales force usually has a major role to play. Although there is no "magic formula" for effective sales-force management, managers must consider the issues discussed in this chapter in order to build and maintain a quality sales effort.

It is important to be aware of the fact that organizing and managing human resources are activities that are an essential part of the planning process. Different organizational structures, different approaches for coordinating activities, and different devices for directing the sales-force effort will be necessary depending upon the types of strategies and programs selected. The relationships between these decisions and the other elements of the planning process are summarized in Figure 14-1.

It is particularly important to recognize that the corporate strategy and the product objectives have a special relationship to decisions regarding organization and human resources management. In fact, some managers believe that products require different managerial skills at various stages of the product life cycle.

In sum, an effective organizational structure and sound human resource management procedures can be of immense value in the execution of a marketing strategy. However, because a complex array of marketing programs are often em-

---

[33] *1986/1987 Sales Personnel Report,* The Alexander Group, Inc., New York, 1988; also see Robert J. Freeman, "For More Profitable Sales, Look Beyond Volume," *Sales and Marketing Management,* August 1989, pp. 50–53.

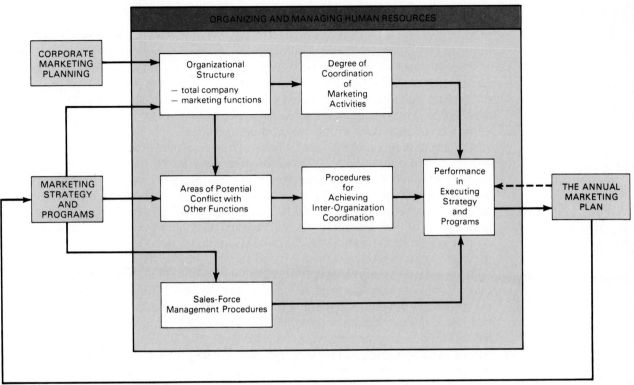

FIGURE 14-1   Relationship of organizing and managing human resources to the other elements of the marketing planning process.

ployed to implement the marketing strategy, annual marketing plans should be developed for defining and coordinating program plans. As we indicate in the next chapter, the specific type of plan used will depend in part on the organizational structure selected. Before proceeding to the chapter, however, consider the following situation in light of the issues discussed in the present chapter.

Procter & Gamble Reorganizes Its Sales Force and Brand Management System:[34]

In 1987, after a series of poor earnings, Procter & Gamble reorganized its sales, manufacturing, and distribution functions. This restructuring was a response to

---

[34]Arthur Bragg, "Wal-Mart's War on Representatives," *Sales and Marketing Management,* March 1987, pp. 41–43; "The Marketing Revolution at Procter & Gamble," *Business Week,* July 25, 1988, pp. 72–76; Laurie Freeman, "Procter & Gamble 'Teams' Serve Retailers' Needs," *Advertising Age,* Aug. 14, 1989, p. 21; Brian Dumaine, "Procter & Gamble Rewrites the Marketing Rules," *Fortune,* Nov. 6, 1989, pp. 34–43.

changes that had taken place in Procter & Gamble's traditional markets and reflected the company's long-term goal to be the market leader in each of their product categories. Among the major changes were a reorganization of the sales force and the addition of a new level of management called category manager.

Prior to this change, Procter & Gamble had eleven different national sales forces (4000 persons), each handling a product line such as detergents or foods. This meant that retailers had to deal with numerous Procter & Gamble salespersons, each with a different product line and many different promotions. However, consolidation among supermarket and drugstore chains combined with the widespread use of scanners shifted the balance of power from big manufacturers to the retailers. By the late 1980s, 100 chains accounted for 80 percent of Procter & Gamble's United States grocery sales where this had only been 15 percent 20 years earlier. At the same time, bar coding helped retailers build their own sales data and Procter & Gamble could no longer convince retailers to provide more shelf space for their brands based on Procter & Gamble figures.

In response to these changes, Procter & Gamble formed "key account" teams of two or three executives who were dedicated to serving the needs of major retail accounts. In addition, people from finance, distribution, manufacturing, and other functions were assigned to cover large retailers. The "total system efficiency" (TSE) program was designed to enable Procter & Gamble to work with retailers to remove hidden costs attached to moving a product onto retail shelves. For example, a team of a dozen is assigned solely to the needs of Wal-Mart. This has allowed Wal-Mart to set up a just-in-time ordering and delivery system for brands such as *Pampers* and *Luvs* disposable diapers. When inventory is low in a store, a computer sends an order to a Procter & Gamble factory which automatically ships the product directly to the outlet. The TSE program also reduces Procter & Gamble spending on trade promotions, payments, and allowances. In recent years, these expenditures have accounted for half of the company's marketing costs.

Procter & Gamble's traditional brand management system established strong incentives for managers to excel but also created conflicts over resources, such as marketing budgets and manufacturing capacity. So Procter & Gamble created the category management system in which thirty-nine product categories were identified and twenty-six category managers with direct profit responsibility were appointed. Advertising, sales, manufacturing, research, engineering, and other disciplines report to the category manager. This restructuring was designed to provide for the development of suitable marketing strategies by looking at categories and managing sets of brands rather than having competing brand strategies trying for resources. In the past, brand managers for competing brands such as Tide and Cheer might have made the same advertising claims. The category manager now decides how the brands should be positioned and such conflicts are avoided.

1 What are the disadvantages associated with the TSE selling organization?
2 What types of conflicts would you have expected to occur under the old

brand management system in decisions regarding budgeting, packaging, and manufacturing?

3 Would you expect the addition of the category manager system to result in better strategic planning? Why or why not?

QUESTIONS AND SITUATIONS FOR DISCUSSION

1 Xerox's Business Systems Group includes 3500 copier-duplicator representatives as well as an additional force of 500 to 1000 specializing in printing systems, office systems, information processing systems, facsimile, and sales engineering. Xerox, in an effort to improve its position in the more complex office automation market, has switched to a single, integrated general-line sales force. Ultimately, all salespeople are expected to sell all Xerox products to all types of accounts. What would you see as the major problems in such a shift from specialists to generalists? How would these be overcome?

2 Some manufacturers of pharmaceuticals prefer to hire and train inexperienced salespeople, while others attempt to hire experienced people from competitors. What would be some of the reasons for these two different approaches?

3 A leading marketing manager recently said that "as markets become more fragmented and companies keep developing multiple products, the key technical, manufacturing, and sales issues will become line-oriented rather than brand-oriented, making the involvement of product managers inefficient." Why would these factors prompt him to make such a prediction?

4 Would you expect sales-force compensation programs to vary over the product life cycle? Why or why not?

5 A medium-sized manufacturer of machine tools uses a top-management group for all major decisions. This group consists of the president and vice presidents of finance, marketing, manufacturing, personnel, and research and development. Assume you are the vice president of marketing and the top-management group is considering the following issues:

a Whether to expand warehouse capacity for finished goods at the existing home manufacturing facility or to establish four regional warehouses across the United States.

b Additional requests have been made for increasing staff by the research and development manager and by the sales manager. The vice president of finance indicates that only one of these requests can be funded at this time.

c A new alloy which is cheaper and more compatible with manufacturing processes has been proposed for use in a majority of products in the existing product line.

Would there be any difference(s) in the position you took if you approached these issues from the best interest of the company as a whole as opposed to those of your own function? Explain.

6 It has been said that threats to the effective implementation of a strategy generally come from three types of sources: company (internal), salesperson-related, and customer-related. How can salespeople be included as a source that adversely affects the implementation of an organization's strategy?

7 The role of sales in the credit decision had been a constant problem for the Throneberry Co. At one time, credit authorization and payment terms were decided solely by the credit department. However, after numerous complaints from the sales force that credit policies were overly restrictive, the credit evaluation process was revised. Sales representatives were asked to provide information used in credit decisions as it was felt because of their "closeness" to accounts and potential customers they could contribute valuable insight to such decisions.

After a few months, several representatives were openly complaining that there was no point in their providing information to the credit department as it usually was ignored or didn't seem to have any influence on the credit decision anyway. These salespeople felt that they should have total responsibility for credit authorization and terms since it was their personal compensation that was being directly affected by the credit decisions. What aspects, if any, of the credit process should the sales force play a role in?

8 "Marketers are expected and paid to be risk takers. Most financial people are expected and paid to be risk averse." Do you agree or disagree with this statement? Explain?

SUGGESTED ADDITIONAL READINGS

Avlonitis, George J., Kevin A. Boyle, and A. G. Kouremenos, "Matching Salesmen to the Selling Job," *Industrial Marketing Management,* vol. 15, February 1986, pp. 45–54.

Bonoma, Thomas V., "Making Your Marketing Strategy Work," *Harvard Business Review,* March–April 1984, pp. 68–76.

Eckles, Robert W., "The Seven S's of Successful Sales Management," *Business Horizons,* March–April 1983, pp. 14–17.

McAdams, Jerry, "Rewarding Sales and Marketing Performance," *Management Review,* April 1987, pp. 33–38.

Quelch, John A., Paul W. Farris, and James M. Oliver, "The Product Management Audit," *Harvard Business Review,* March–April 1987, pp. 30–37.

Ruekert, Robert W., and Orville C. Walker, Jr., "Marketing's Interaction with Other Functional Units: A Conceptual Framework and Empirical Evidence," *Journal of Marketing,* January 1987, pp. 1–19.

Shapiro, Benson, "Can Marketing and Manufacturing Coexist?" *Harvard Business Review,* September–October 1977, pp. 104–114.

Strahle, William, and Rosann L. Spiro, "Linking Market Share Strategies to Salesforce Objectives, Activities, and Compensation Policies," *Journal of Personal Selling and Sales Management,* August 1986, pp. 11–18.

Walker, Orville C., and Robert W. Ruekert, "Marketing's Role in the Implementation of Business Strategies: A Critical Review and Conceptual Framework," *Journal of Marketing,* July 1987, pp. 15–33.

CHAPTER 15

THE ANNUAL MARKETING PLAN

OVERVIEW

For virtually all organizations, the most basic planning mechanism is an annual plan which describes the goals or objectives the organization expects to achieve in the coming year and the budget required to realize these objectives. As we have indicated at several points in this book, many corporate and marketing strategies will take a long time (at least more than a year) to be implemented fully. Nevertheless, because the financial results for the total organization must be presented annually, budgets (and therefore the rationale for these budgets) must also be developed within this time frame.

In this chapter, we examine the annual *marketing* plan which is the mechanism by which the objectives, activities, and budgets for the various marketing programs (discussed in Chapters 8 through 13) are integrated. These plans serve three basic purposes.

• Like the various program plans, annual plans served as a communications device. They indicate clearly to the personnel involved in marketing what the planned objectives and programs are and thus should provide guidance to personnel on what activities to pursue.

• In an organization with multiple products, markets, or other divisions, annual plans serve as important inputs to the resource allocation process. As discussed later in this chapter, top management usually will review each annual plan within an organization, assess the corporate resources available, and approve or modify budgets based on their assessment of each unit's needs and contributions.

• Finally, once approved, the annual plan serves as a mechanism for control. That is, the annual plan establishes standards of performance against which the organizational unit's progress can be evaluated. Periodic evaluations of the performance-evaluation gap can be useful in making timely modifications to the plan, as we demonstrate later in this chapter. Additionally, the overall achievement of the unit is assessed largely on annual performance relative to the plan.

The major goal of this chapter is to identify the basic elements of a typical annual marketing plan, to demonstrate the use of the marketing plan for purposes of control, and to present some of the most important organizational issues associated with effective planning. Because managers must also assess the impact of environmental factors in setting standards and in evaluating performance, we also examine the process of environmental monitoring and its relationship to the marketing planning process. Before examining these concepts and procedures, however, we distinguish three major types of annual marketing plans and we indicate the various types of objectives that can be selected for the annual plan.

Types of Annual Marketing Plans

Organizations may have one annual marketing plan or several annual marketing plans. Additionally, the scope of the annual plan is not the same for all companies. Basically, the number of plans and the scope of the plans will depend on the diversity of the firm's products and markets and on the firm's organizational structure.

The Total Annual Marketing Plan In the simplest case, a firm or a division of a firm with a single product (or a single line of highly related products) sells through a sales force responsible only for that product. This situation is characteristic of many small- and medium-sized manufacturing firms, and in such cases, one annual marketing plan is developed by the general sales manager or the marketing manager of the firm or of the division. Similarly, limited-line retailers who specialize in a product category may develop a single storewide plan under the guidance of a merchandise manager or a store manager. Finally, a total marketing plan may be developed by a marketing director of a consumer services company (such as a bank or a health maintenance organization). These firms offer a large number of highly related services and do not normally employ sales forces.

The Annual Product or Department Plan Firms which are organized by product lines may require separate plans for each product (or, in retailing, for each department). In these situations, the number of programs included in the scope of the plans is more limited. For instance, a product manager typically develops the advertising and sales-promotion elements of a plan. But if a common sales force is used for several, separately managed products, the sales budget may not be a part of the annual plan. Although the product manager may attempt to influence these "noncontrollable" sales-force plans, the manager's only planning responsibilities with respect to the sales force will be to identify any special costs associated with their products (such as the cost of trade promotions). Finally, large service companies (such as large banks) may employ product plans if some products require special attention. For example, many banks develop separate annual plans to market services used only by corporate customers (such as certain pension trust services).

When individual product plans are developed, these plans must be integrated into other plans at higher levels in the organization. For example, in an organization with several divisions, each of which has several products, a divisional manager must develop plans reflecting the sum of the product plans. Subsequently, corporate plans must be developed on the basis of various divisional plans. And these corporate and divisional plans must be consistent with the corporate marketing-planning objectives discussed in Chapter 2.

The Annual Sales Plan   A third type of plan is the annual sales plan. If a sales force is responsible for several products in a division, a separate plan and budget covering only sales-force responsibilities may be developed by the sales manager. Sales-force salaries, commissions, and expenses will typically be the major elements in such budgets. However, to the extent that the sales force has decision-making power regarding discounts, credit, special-delivery terms, warranties, and merchandise returns, these may also be included in the scope of the plan. The annual sales plan will then be integrated with the various product plans in the divisional plan.

Because sales plans have already been discussed in Chapter 13, our discussion of the annual plan will center on the total marketing plan and the product plan. However, it is important to recognize that in multiproduct companies, each annual total plan will be reviewed at the divisional or corporate level, or both.

Figure 15-1 indicates how the various types of middle-management-level marketing plans may be integrated at higher organizational levels. As we suggested in Chapter 2, these product plans must be consistent with the product objectives established at the top-management level. However, the plans must also be developed in a way that reflects the situation analysis. In the next section we briefly review the major considerations influencing the marketing plan.

DEVELOPING THE PLAN

There is no single format or formula that is universally agreed on for every annual planning situation. In practice, each firm will develop a method, outline, or form that seems to best fit its own needs. However, there are two basic kinds of inputs to the planning process that should be a part of every plan: (1) a comprehensive situation analysis and (2) a statement of overall performance objectives.

Comprehensive Situation Analysis

As we discussed in the early chapters of this book, a firm should perform a situation analysis before designing its marketing strategy and programs. Specifically,

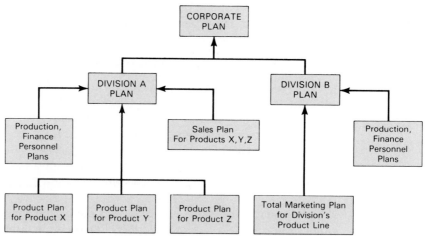

FIGURE 15-1   Relationship of annual marketing plans, product plans, and sales plans to divisional and corporate-level planning.

we argued that a marketing strategy should be based on a detailed market analysis, a competitive analysis, market measurements, and profitability and productivity analysis.

For an annual plan, it is not usually necessary to repeat each of these analyses (unless the annual plan will present a new marketing strategy). Assuming that a firm is continuing with its basic marketing strategy, the emphasis of the annual plan will be on the choice of and funding for individual marketing programs. Consequently, the situation analysis for an annual plan will focus on competitors' activities, industry trends (such as shifts in industry sales growth), and an analysis of the productivity of the most recent marketing programs. Consider, for example, Figure 15-2, which portrays a process that has been used at Procter & Gamble.

In this figure we see that the annual planning process begins about 12 weeks before approval with a review of the sales performance of a given brand and of competitive activity. Over the following weeks, the product manager develops estimates of the level of budgetary commitment required to achieve various unit sales volume and market-share levels. These productivity estimates (which are based largely on the analysis of historical ratios and judgments of competitive activity) are critical inputs to the budgeting process. In addition, however, managers involved in the planning process must have a clear sense of the objectives they are expected to achieve.

Annual-Plan Objectives

In Chapter 2, we examined *corporate objectives* and the process of establishing corporate strategies. On the basis of these corporate strategies and on the product portfolio analysis, *product objectives* are used to provide guidance to middle

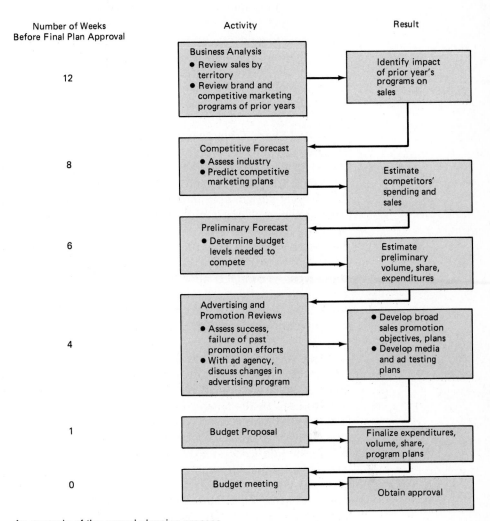

Number of Weeks Before Final Plan Approval	Activity	Result
12	**Business Analysis** • Review sales by territory • Review brand and competitive marketing programs of prior years	Identify impact of prior year's programs on sales
8	**Competitive Forecast** • Assess industry • Predict competitive marketing plans	Estimate competitors' spending and sales
6	**Preliminary Forecast** • Determine budget levels needed to compete	Estimate preliminary volume, share, expenditures
4	**Advertising and Promotion Reviews** • Assess success, failure of past promotion efforts • With ad agency, discuss changes in advertising program	• Develop broad sales promotion objectives, plans • Develop media and ad testing plans
1	Budget Proposal	Finalize expenditures, volume, share, program plans
0	Budget meeting	Obtain approval

FIGURE 15-2 An example of the annual planning process.

managers who develop the marketing strategies and programs that are needed to achieve the product objectives.

Because an annual plan must be developed for each product or product line, the plan must be consistent with the product objective. However, product objectives are usually stated in general terms (such as "increase market share"). Because a marketing plan must be expressed in detail, management must express the annual marketing-plan objective (or the annual product-plan objective) in specific terms regarding *time* and *level*. For example, a product objective stated as "increase the market share of product X" might be specified in an annual plan as "increase the market share of product X from 17 to 20 percent in 6 months, and to 22 percent in 1 year." When stated in this way, the objectives can provide more specific guidance on budget development and more measurable standards for evaluating achievement.

Essentially, there are three types of objectives that managers can establish for an annual plan: market-share objectives, sales-volume objectives, and profitability objectives.

Market-Share Objectives When management believes that a high market share will mean high profits, market-share objectives will be established. As suggested in Chapter 2, market-share growth is typically a product objective for problem-child products and for new products entering an established market. If the markets are growing rapidly, an increase in market share will lead to rapid sales growth and long-run profitability for these products. Further, growth in market share may be essential in order to achieve or maintain adequate distribution, because distributors may prefer to carry only the fastest selling brands.

Market-share maintenance may be the appropriate objective for stars. Because these types of products already have high market shares, it is usually costly and difficult to expand market share. However, because the market-growth rate is high, sales (and, it is hoped, profits) should be increased just by maintaining the current market-share level.

Sales-Volume Objectives Sales objectives are clearly related to market-share objectives. That is, if a firm has a market-share objective and an industry sales forecast, then a sales objective can be calculated by multiplying the industry sales forecast by the market-share objective. The primary advantage of converting a market-share objective into a sales-volume objective is that a unit sales-volume objective is needed to develop a complete budget. Without some estimate of the units to be sold, production costs cannot be calculated, and therefore profitability cannot be estimated. Accordingly, when a market-share objective is established, the sales volume that reflects that market-share objective should also be determined. Additionally, sales-volume objectives are appropriate when market share cannot be reliably measured because of a lack of industry sales data and when the annual plan is for a new-product form (where the market share is 100 percent).

Profitability Objectives As we discussed in Chapter 2, new products and problem-child products generally must receive extensive marketing support in order to build sales volume and market share. This means that, in the short run, profitability must be sacrificed in order to achieve a strong market position and long-run profitability. Accordingly, market-share and sales-volume objectives will take precedence over profitability objectives for these kinds of products.

However, cash cows and dogs are expected to be profitable for the reasons discussed in Chapter 2. Accordingly, profitability will be a primary objective for these products. Additionally, although stars are often not heavy cash generators, they are expected to be profitable. Finally, even in the case of new products and problem-child products, profitability cannot be totally ignored. There will be limits to the short-run losses that management can take on these products. In general, then, profitability will be either a primary objective or a secondary objective on all products. Any annual plan for a product, product line, or department will be expected to achieve some minimum target contribution (or some maximum negative contribution in the case of new products and problem-child products) to overall divisional or company profitability.

Returning to Figure 15-2, it is important to recognize that, in this particular process, all preliminary forecasts are submitted to top management so that the sum total of budget requests are known and can be prioritized before final budget meetings are held. Significant differences of opinion on budget levels between top management and the brand manager could well result in a directive to provide substantially revised goals or plans in the final budget proposal prior to the budget meeting.

To illustrate the development of an annual plan we will return to the Oswald Optical example first discussed in Chapter 6.

An Annual Marketing Plan: Oswald Optical

Oswald Optical management has developed an annual product plan for eyeglasses. Table 15-1 summarizes the basic elements of the plan. The essential feature of this plan is the attempt to build volume for eyeglass sales through a price promotion and through advertising emphasizing that Oswald Optical is convenient because of its good location, fast service, and in-house optometrists. The plan suggests that the combined effects of the programs will yield a 40 percent increase in eyeglass sales. These estimates were derived based largely on the company's prior experience and judgmental expectations of competitors' future actions.

Three specific features of the plan merit special attention:

- Historically, 35 percent of Oswald Optical's eyeglass purchasers received their prescriptions from Oswald's optometrists. In the annual plan, this percentage is expected to rise to 55 percent of customers because of the emphasis on convenience in the advertising plan. (Note that while 5000 eye examinations are projected for 14,000 eyeglass sales, the 14,000 eyeglasses are sold to 9000 customers.)
- The price promotion will result in some displaced sales. About 1000 of the second pair sales are expected to come from customers who would have purchased two pairs anyway at regular prices.
- Continued awareness advertising is needed because of customer turnover. (There is usually a 2- or 3-year gap between purchases.) To establish and maintain awareness at 80 percent, Oswald's ad agency believes it must generate 3000 GRPs over the course of 1991. In this community the target audience size is 200,000. Since one GRP is achieved by reaching 1 percent of the target audience one time, it takes 1 percent times 200,000 or 2000 impressions to generate one GRP. (Refer back to Chapter 10 to review the relationship between gross rating points and gross impressions.) The agency projects the local media costs to be approximately $7.50 per thousand. Therefore,

TABLE 15-1   OSWALD OPTICAL: 1991 ANNUAL PLAN FOR EYEGLASSES

Annual performance objectives

1. Increase sales of eyeglasses to 14,000 pair
   (from 10,000 in 1990)

2. Increase optometry examinations for eyeglasses to 5000
   (from 3500 in 1990)

3. Increase total contribution on eyeglasses to $60,000
   (from $50,000 in 1990)

Marketing strategy

Acquire new customers through head-to-head positioning
on price and convenience

Marketing programs

Program	Objectives	Budget
1. Television advertising: January–June, August–September	Achieve 80% awareness of Oswald Optical among eyeglass wearers by May 30	$45,000
2. Newspaper advertising: April–October	Achieve 50% belief of Oswald's claim as "most convenient"	$15,000
3. Price promotion: $20 off when you buy a second pair	Achieve second pair sales to 5000 customers	$20 discount on 1000 pair displaced sales

Oswald can obtain 2000 impressions (or a single GRP) for $15 ($7.50 × 2000), and the estimated budget for this program is as follows:

Size of target audience	200,000
× 1%	× 1%
Number of people reached for 1 GRP	2000
Cost of reaching 1 percent of audience (1 GRP)	$15
× Number of GRPs required	× 3000
Projected budget	$45,000

The process of putting the annual plan together is not a simple one because a variety of combinations of prices, program budgets, and costs may have to be considered. Consequently, managers will often go through a number of tentative plans before coming up with one that is satisfactory. However, the complexity and time involved in this process are substantially reduced if a manager uses one of the popular interactive electronic spreadsheet programs (such as Lotus 1-2-3) available on personal computers.

Finally, the plan should not assume that results will be achieved at a constant rate throughout the year. Seasonality of demand and variations in the timing of alternative programs are likely to exist in most plans. Where possible, therefore, monthly or quarterly breakouts should be established so that all managers will know when the various results are to be achieved and to facilitate control. (Table 15-2 provides monthly benchmarks for Oswald Optical's annual plan.)

USING THE PLAN FOR CONTROL

If managers were to simply forget about a plan once it was adopted, they would be failing to take full advantage of the planning process. That is, the annual plan serves not merely as a tool for coordination but also as a control device.

In fact, seldom will results go precisely according to plan. Changes in competitive actions, in buyers' willingness and ability to buy, or in other environmental factors may occur. Also, managers can seldom be absolutely certain of how productive the marketing programs will be in influencing sales—even in the absence of competitive reactions or other environmental changes. Finally, even costs are sometimes difficult to project.

Managers should recognize that there are at least two approaches to control. *Post-action* control can be used at the end of the planning period to review the degree of success achieved and to attempt to isolate the causes of any gaps between planned and actual performance. (For example, at the end of 1991, Oswald Optical could review its results, compare these to the planned sales and profit objectives, and try to determine why any performance plan gaps resulted.)

TABLE 15-2   OSWALD OPTICAL: BIMONTHLY PROJECTIONS FOR 1991 FOR EYEGLASSES

	Jan.–Feb.	Mar.–Apr.	May–Jun.	Jul.–Aug.	Sep.–Oct.	Nov.–Dec.	TOTAL
Optometry appointments for eyeglasses	800	900	1,000	700	900	700	5,000
Eyeglasses sold at regular prices	1,500	1,600	1,700	1,400	1,600	1,200	9,000
VCM—Regular sales	$45,000	$48,000	$51,000	$42,000	$48,000	$36,000	$270,000
Eyeglasses sold as second pair	700	900	1,100	800	900	600	5,000
VCM—Second pair	$ 7,000	$ 9,000	$11,000	$ 8,000	$ 9,000	$ 6,000	$ 50,000
Total sales of eyeglasses (pair)	2,200	2,500	2,800	2,200	2,500	1,800	14,000
Total variable-contribution margin	$52,000	$57,000	$62,000	$50,000	$57,000	$42,000	$320,000
Advertising expense	$10,000	$12,000	$14,000	$ 9,000	$15,000	0	$ 60,000
Other direct expense	$35,000	$35,000	$30,000	$30,000	$35,000	$35,000	$200,000
Total contribution	$ 7,000	$10,000	$18,000	$11,000	$ 7,000	$ 7,000	$ 60,000

The major purpose of this type of control system is to use the knowledge obtained from this analysis in developing future plans.

As an alternative, organizations can adopt *steering-control* models. This approach assumes that if performance deviations from the plan can be identified sufficiently early, managers can take corrective actions—that is, the plan can be adjusted (steered) to meet the original objectives.[1] From a marketing management standpoint, the steering-control approach certainly has important short-run advantages because the effectiveness of marketing programs in producing sales is always somewhat uncertain. Consequently, managers would prefer to have the opportunity to make adjustments to the marketing plan as soon as possible when it becomes apparent that annual objectives may not be achieved.

In order to implement the steering-control approach, managers must take the following steps.

1 Select the performance measures to be monitored
2 Compare actual and planned performance at appropriate time intervals
3 Specify the acceptable degree of deviation
4 Identify implications of the deviations
5 Modify the plan to steer it toward the objectives

Selecting Performance Measures

Because the primary objectives of a marketing plan are stated in terms of sales, market share, or profitability, managers would naturally want to monitor these performance measures. However, managers are likely to find that these measures are inadequate for a steering-control model for two reasons. First, information on these measures may not be available quickly enough. For example, manufacturers who sell through distributors often experience a lag between the timing of retailer sales and retailer purchases. Additionally, information on market shares may not be available on a regular basis. Second, and more important, managers who use the steering-control approach need information on *how* to change the plan to meet sales, market share, or profit objectives. Consequently, it is important to monitor program performance because deviations in program performance may serve as indicators that annual objectives are not being achieved. Table 15-3 lists some of the more common performance indicators which managers should monitor.

In many companies, the kind of information portrayed in Table 15-3 is also not available in a timely manner. In such cases, experienced managers often resort to developing their own measures using whatever data are available. For example one consumer-goods manager devised a weekly "Gimme Index" which was computed as the ratio of trade promotion expenditures-to-consumer promotion expenditures. The index served as a warning of either increased competitive activity to get shelf space (when the ratio is very high) or of weakening consumer

[1]Subhash Sharma and Dale Achabal, "STEMCOM: An Analytical Model for Marketing Control," *Journal of Marketing,* Spring 1982, pp. 104–113.

TABLE 15-3   SOME POSSIBLE PERFORMANCE MEASURES TO BE MONITORED FOR CONTROL

Overall performance measures

1. Unit sales
2. Dollar sales
3. Sales in specific market segments
4. Marketing costs
5. Production costs
6. Market share

Program performance measures

1. New-product programs	a. Rate of trial
	b. Repurchase rate
	c. Cannibalized sales
2. Pricing programs	a. Actual price charged
	b. Price relative to industry average
3. Advertising programs	a. Awareness levels
	b. Attribute ratings
	c. Actual expenditures
4. Sales-promotion programs	a. Redemption rates
	b. Displacement rates
	c. Stock-up rates
5. Sales and distribution programs	a. Direct response rates
	b. Number of sales calls
	c. Number of new accounts
	d. Number of lost accounts
	e. Number of distributors carrying the product
	f. Number of customer complaints
	g. Travel costs

sales (when the ratio declines). As a result, it signaled the manager that there was likely to be a deviation between planned and actual performance on either the level of distribution achieved or on sales.[2]

Comparing Actual Performance with Planned Performance

Performance comparisons should be made as frequently as possible so that managers can have the greatest opportunity for steering the plan. However, the intervals used to compare performance should be long enough to be meaningful. For example, because advertising programs generally work slowly, it will be more difficult to get useful indicators of advertising performance in a short period of time. On the other hand, sales promotion and direct response marketing work more quickly and can meaningfully be monitored on a monthly basis (or even more frequently if desired). Additionally, effort-based performance measures

[2]Thomas Bonoma, "Marketing Subversives," *Harvard Business Review,* November–December 1986, pp. 113–118.

(such as the number of sales calls or product demonstrations) can also be measured frequently. Finally, differences do exist across industries in terms of customer purchase frequencies. Consequently, sales performance may be meaningfully measured on a monthly basis in some markets, whereas in others quarterly comparisons may be more reasonable.

Specifying Acceptable Degrees of Deviation

The annual plan should also specify the acceptable degree of deviation from the performance standards. As noted earlier, managers do not really expect every performance standard to be fully attained. However, managers do want to identify significant deviations from the sales, market-share, and cost standards that have been set. Accordingly, it is generally useful to specify the acceptable range of performance in advance, so that management attention can be focused on the most important deviations. (For example, one firm may consider a 5-percent deviation in actual sales from planned sales acceptable, whereas another may only consider a 1 percent deviation acceptable.)

Additionally, the acceptability of a deviation should be considered in the context of the degree of reliability of the performance standard. For example, if managers want to impress their superiors there is always the chance they will set performance standards in too pessimistic a fashion so that the likelihood of achieving a standard (and any resulting bonus) is enhanced. On the flip side, some high-level managers push planners to set certifiably high-performance expectations. This may occur because top management is hoping for a good result (perhaps to justify an earlier decision) and thus is too optimistic or because these managers believe that the middle managers doing the product and sales plans have been setting conservative sales and profit goals so they can more easily meet the standard. While this problem is not easily solved, it can sometimes be made more manageable by getting managers to articulate their degree of certainty about various performance levels. For example, managers might be asked: "What share of market is 50 percent likely? 80 percent likely? 100 percent likely? for a given budget."[3]

Identifying Implications of Deviations

Depending on the specific performance indicators being monitored, managers will be faced with three related types of performance deviations to analyze: deviations in sales performance, program performance, and cost performance.

Observed deviations from planned sales performance may be due to uncontrollable factors (such as changing market conditions leading to a decline in industry sales or unanticipated competitive actions). If managers find no evidence

---

[3]For a discussion of these and other issues related to goal setting on marketing plans, see Thomas Bonoma, "Marketing Performance—What Do You Expect?" *Harvard Business Review*, September–October 1989, pp. 44–47.

that either type of uncontrollable factor is responsible for performance, then the logical next step is to analyze the performance of the marketing programs. (Additionally, as noted earlier, managers may want to examine indicators of program performance even before useful sales results are available.)

Program performance should be examined at two levels, where possible: the degree to which program *objectives* are being achieved and the degree to which planned program *effort* is being achieved. If levels of effort (such as actual sales calls or advertising coverage) are not being achieved as planned, then neither program objectives nor sales-performance objectives are likely to be achieved. However, if the planned level of effort is being achieved but program objectives (for example, number of new accounts or brand awareness levels) are not being achieved, then either the *design* of the program (for example, sales appeals, price level, advertising copy, value of coupon, and so on) is effective or the *budget* is inadequate. Further, managers may find that the performances of the various programs are all proceeding according to plan; however, sales performance is still below the planned level. Assuming that the manager has ruled out uncontrollable factors as a cause of sales deviation, the manager must conclude that the sales productivity of the various programs has been overestimated. (Figure 15-3 summarizes the steps involved in analyzing sales deviations.)

Finally, the actual direct marketing costs and variable costs may deviate from planned costs. Accordingly, reasons for these deviations should be identified. These reasons may include cost increases dictated by suppliers, inadequate estimates of the cost of reaching program objectives, or simply, faster achievement of program objectives than anticipated. For example, the sales force may call on some customers earlier or more frequently than planned. If so, sales costs may exceed the budget during the early periods of the plan.[4]

Regardless of the type of deviation being examined, managers must be able to distinguish environmental causes from "controllable" causes of poor performance. This is often very difficult because not all environmental changes are immediately recognized. Accordingly, a system for monitoring environmental trends and forces will assist managers in identifying uncontrollable effects and in attempting to make modifications to the plan. Some procedures and approaches to environmental monitoring are discussed later in this chapter.

Making Modifications to the Plan as Needed

Managers should make any marketing *program modifications* that are needed to get the firm back on track toward achieving the annual-plan objectives. If deviations between the plan and actual performance are relatively minor, then this is usually the only type of remedial action that managers must take. However, if the deviations are fairly large and if the likelihood of making up for these deviations during the rest of the year is relatively small, management may have to revise the

---

[4]Methods for identifying the sources of cost variance are presented in James Hulbert and Norman E. Toy, "A Strategic Framework for Marketing Control," *Journal of Marketing,* April 1977, pp. 12–20.

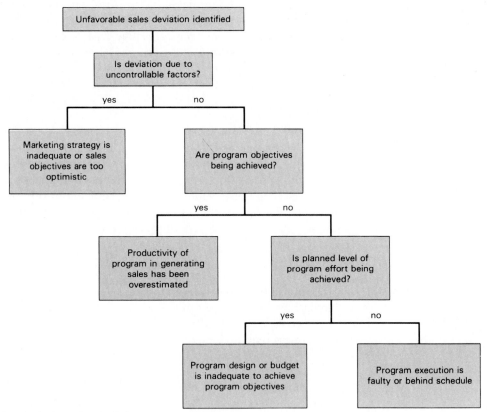

FIGURE 15-3   Analyzing sales deviations.

annual-plan objectives. (Of course, if actual performance exceeds planned performance, it may be desirable to revise objectives upward.) Finally, in the case of serious unanticipated competitive, cost, or other environmental changes, the entire marketing strategy and even the product objectives may have to be revised.

To illustrate the process of controlling the marketing plan, let us return to the case of Oswald Optical. Table 15-4 summarizes the overall performance of the product plan as of the end of June. Halfway through the year, the company is far behind its sales and profit projections. The eyeglass plan has not generated any increase in optometry appointments: The ratio of optometry appointments to eyeglass sales at regular prices is about the same as it was the previous year. Further, sales of second-pair eyeglasses are well behind the projected level. Since costs are being incurred according to plan, the deficiency in total contribution is due to sales effects.

In assessing the reasons for the failure to meet performance standards, management discovered the following:

TABLE 15-4   OSWALD OPTICAL ACTUAL VS. PLANNED PRODUCT
PERFORMANCE—JANUARY–JUNE 1991

Performance measures	Actual	Planned
Optometry appointments for eyeglasses	1,600	2,700
Eyeglasses sold at regular prices	4,700	4,800
Eyeglasses sold as second pair	1,600	2,700
Total eyeglass sales	6,300	7,500
Total variable-contribution margin (VCM)	$157,000	$171,000
Advertising expense	$ 34,000	$ 36,000
Other direct costs	$100,000	$100,000
Total contribution	$ 23,000	$ 35,000

• Competitors began reacting to the discount offer on the second pair of glasses almost immediately after the policy was initiated. Most large optical stores offered comparable prices by March.

• While awareness of Oswald Optical reached a level of 75 percent by the end of May (very close to the planned level of 80 percent), the newspaper advertising campaign appeared largely ineffective. After 3 months, only 6 percent of the target market believed that Oswald Optical was "the most convenient" optical store. Although the target level of 50 percent was not expected to be achieved until October, the weak early results suggested that the advertising was ineffective. This was viewed as the major cause of Oswald Optical's failure to achieve a greater number of optometry appointments.

Based on this analysis, Oswald Optical's management decided to take the following actions:

• The second-pair discount was reduced to a $10 (rather than a $20) reduction. Based on competitors' prices, this would keep Oswald Optical competitive while improving profit margins. Management assumed that sales of the second pair of eyeglasses during the remainder of the year would follow the same ratio of one second pair for every three regular-priced pairs sold.

• The advertising plan was completely revised. The awareness campaign planned for August and September was dropped in favor of a new television campaign emphasizing "one-stop optical needs" including eye examinations.

Based on these modifications, the revised plan presented in Table 15-5 was established. Note that if Oswald Optical can achieve the levels of performance stipulated in the revised budget, the company will have made up part of the January to June shortfall in sales and total contribution. In other words, management will have begun the process of steering the plan toward the original objectives. Although these initial objectives are no longer viewed as achievable, the process at least enabled management to spot the effects of uncontrollable factors and an ineffective program before the entire year was wasted. Clearly, the earlier the detection of such problems, the more effective a steering-control system will be.

TABLE 15-5   OSWALD OPTICAL: REVISED PLAN FOR JULY–DECEMBER 1991

	Original July–Dec.	Revised July–Dec.	New Total* for 1991
Optometry appointments for eyeglasses	2,300	2,000	3,600
Eyeglasses sold at regular prices	4,200	4,200	8,900
Eyeglasses sold as second pair	2,300	1,500	3,100
Total eyeglass sales	6,500	5,700	12,000
VCM—Regular eyeglasses	$126,000	$126,000	$267,000
VCM—Second pair	$ 23,000	$ 30,000	$ 46,000
Total VCM	$149,000	$156,000	$313,000
Advertising expense	$ 24,000	$ 28,000	$ 62,000
Other direct costs	$100,000	$100,000	$200,000
Total contribution	$ 25,000	$ 28,000	$ 51,000

*Includes January–June (actual) and July–December (planned).

It is also important to note that the effectiveness of steering control will depend in part on the degree to which a firm can be effective in making modifications. If deviations are primarily due to noncontrollable environmental factors, managers cannot modify their strategies without thorough consideration of the effects of further environmental changes. Thus, the process of environmental monitoring is an important adjunct to the process of steering control.

ENVIRONMENTAL MONITORING

Environmental monitoring consists of searching for and processing information about changes in an organization's environment. While some analysis of the environment is a prerequisite for the development of corporate and marketing strategies, the marketing environments faced by most firms are dynamic. Thus, in order to analyze deviations in performance from the basic plan and in order to make any necessary adaptations in strategy, managers should have access to systems which continually monitor the environment.

Strategic Environment Monitoring Systems

Strategic environmental monitoring systems are formalized approaches for monitoring change on a continuous and systematic basis. These systems can be effective if management has clearly defined the system's purpose to ensure that crucial information will not be overlooked.

Montgomery and Weinberg have proposed three kinds of purposes for such systems.[5]

[5]David B. Montgomery and Charles B. Weinberg, "Toward Strategic Intelligence Systems," *Journal of Marketing*, Fall 1979, p. 42.

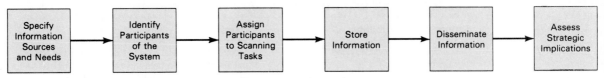

FIGURE 15-4   Organizing a strategic environmental scanning system.

1 *Defensive:* This intelligence is obtained in an effort to avoid surprises. That is, the purpose of environmental monitoring is simply to determine if the implicit and explicit assumptions upon which current strategies are based will continue as anticipated.

2 *Passive:* This intelligence is used to provide benchmark data for an objective evaluation of a firm's policies. For example, a firm might gather industry sales compensation data in order to reward sales performance in a manner comparable to the firm's competitors.

3 *Offensive:* This kind of intelligence is designed to *identify* opportunities.

By establishing the purpose of a strategic environmental monitoring system, management can be more certain that the kinds of information required will be collected and avoid what is irrelevant. Once the information sources and needs have been established, the participants who need this environmental information must be identified. Since a variety of individuals and departments are involved in providing the necessary strategic information, definite assignments for the acquisition of specific types of intelligence must be made.[6] Figure 15-4 summarizes the major elements that would be necessary in a strategic environmental scanning system.

Environmental Information Sources

In establishing a formal environmental monitoring effort, managers must identify the information sources likely to be of most use for its stated purposes. In Chapter 4 we discussed some sources that were especially pertinent to competitive analysis and in Chapter 5 we identified some sources for general market-measurement data. Additional useful sources are presented in the appendix.

Perhaps the most important development in recent years with regard to environmental monitoring is the on-line information bank. There are now over 1400 data bases that can be reached through telephone-computer modem links to one or more of over 200 organizations.[7] Some of the better-known organizations and the data they make available are listed in Table 15-6.

---

[6]David B. Baker, "Organizing a Strategic Information Scanning System," *California Management Review,* January 1983, pp. 76–83.

[7]See Daniel Seligman, "Life Will Be Different When We're All On Line," *Fortune,* Feb. 4, 1985, pp. 68–72 for a discussion of these bases.

TABLE 15-6   MAJOR DATA BASE DISTRIBUTORS OF BUSINESS INFORMATION

Service and distribution	Description
DIALOG Information Services (Lockheed Corp.)	More than 200 data bases containing over 55 million records; article indexes and financial data; annual reports of publicly held U.S. corporations.
Dow Jones News Retrieval (Dow Jones)	Business and economic news, stock quotes, investment information; complete and unabridged articles from *The Wall Street Journal*, *Barron's*, and Dow Jones News Service.
The Source (Reader's Digest/Control Data Corp.)	General news, air schedules, retail catalogs, market quotes, research tools, employment data bases.
Compuserve Information Service (H&R Block)	Financial information, banking, encyclopedia, newspaper abstracts.
Bibliographic Retrieval Service (Thyssen Bornemisza)	Multiple data bases covering agriculture, business, management, engineering, and other academic indexes.
Data Resources (McGraw-Hill)	Business and economic data and Japanese Economic Information Service.
LEXIS (Mead Corp.)	Full text of state and federal court decisions, statutes, regulations.
PROMPT (Predicasts, Inc./Lockheed)	Citations and abstracts on new products, technology, markets from over 2000 U.S. and foreign publications.
DRI-VisiCorp	58 data bases, economic forecasts, foreign exchange, individual industries.
Executive Information Service	*Harvard Business Review* management contents, John Wiley publications, and Academic American Encyclopedia business data bases.
Legi-Slate (*The Washington Post*)	Current status of federal legislation, voting records of members of Congress.

Other Sources of Intelligence

In addition to data-based sources of intelligence, there are several sources that are reliant on the skills and expertise of human experts.

Technological Forecasting   Technological forecasting includes a variety of procedures that managers may use to predict the probability, timing, and significance of future technological developments regarding products or processes. Among the procedures that firms use for technological forecasting are Delphi probes, scenarios, and trend extrapolation.

The *Delphi probe* is a systematic method for analyzing independent expert opinion. A panel of experts are questioned individually about some future event or trend. All responses are combined and summarized, and the results are returned to the participants. After the results have been communicated to all participants, the experts are asked to respond again to these questions. This process is repeated for three or more rounds until a consensus is reached. The Delphi method may be used not only for identifying relevant changes but also for identifying the most appropriate actions the firm should take.[8]

Scenarios are composite descriptions of possible future technological events or conditions that may have an effect on the decisions made by an organization. Usually multiple scenarios are developed to represent possible alternative environments. In effect, scenarios are "what if" exercises that force managers to consider certain technological challenges they may face. Given a set of alternative scenarios, strategic planners can then develop and evaluate the alternative strategic responses that the firm should be prepared to make if a given technological development materializes.

Another method of technological forecasting is to *extrapolate historical trends*. The primary assumption is that the trend of technological advances in the past will remain fairly constant in the future. Particularly in very high technology industries such as electronics, past rates of advance (such as cost per bit of information processed) can be projected into the future with some degree of reliability.

Social Trend Analysis   Individuals, groups of individuals, and society at large are constantly changing in terms of what is considered a desirable and acceptable way of living and behaving. These changes can have a profound impact on individuals' attitudes toward products and toward marketing activities. In particular, it is important for managers to understand and predict changes in consumer values and changes in the social issues that groups within society feel are important. To track such changes, Daniel Yankelovich, Inc., a major independent research firm, measures thirty-five social and value trends on issues such as materialism, sexual freedom, and religion. Other organizations, such as Arthur D. Little's Impact Service, Predicasts, Inc., and The Future Group, also provide subscription services for monitoring social trends and related economic trends.[9]

ORGANIZING FOR PLANNING

Because the annual marketing plan may involve different program elements in different organizations, there is no single best way to assign responsibility for the annual marketing plan for an individual product.

Although a number of larger firms have planning staffs, these individuals are primarily involved in long-range planning and in providing information regarding short-run forecasts and market conditions. Thus, the role of a planning staff in developing the annual plan is to provide basic inputs into the short-run situation

---

[8]Harper Q. North and Donald L. Pyke, "Probes of the Technological Future," *Harvard Business Review*, March–April 1969, pp. 29, 68–82; and D. D. Wilmot, "A Comparison of the Methods of Technological Forecasting," *Industrial Marketing*, Sept. 1, 1971, p. 97.

[9]Myron Magnet, "Who Needs a Trend Spotter," *Fortune*, Dec. 9, 1985, pp. 51–56.

analysis and objective setting. Additionally, these individuals may participate in the process of reviewing proposed plans to ensure that the key market assumptions (and sometimes the manufacturing cost assumptions) are reasonable.

Most planners seem to feel that planning should be delegated as far down the organization as possible, so that one person is responsible for achieving each program objective. The reasoning behind this view is that the manager most closely involved with a program is in the best position to estimate the costs and productivity of the program and to identify possible changes in market conditions.[10]

However, in many firms this will mean that planning for an individual product will rest in the hands of more than one person. That is, unless the plan is confined strictly to one marketing program (such as sales), some organizational mechanism is needed to coordinate program plans into the overall annual plan. In firms with a broad product line, the product manager or brand manager will typically assume this role, and that manager's plans will be reviewed by a higher level marketing manager. In other firms, the sales manager may perform this role—especially when selling costs dominate the budget, when the sales manager is responsible for sales promotions (often the case in industrial marketing), and when advertising focuses on the corporation as a whole rather than on individual products and thus is managed at the corporate level. Finally, the senior marketing manager may perform this role when program responsibilities are widely dispersed among a number of managers.

It is clear, however, that in the modern, large organization the marketing planning process is bidirectional. Research on how firms develop marketing plans indicates that it is rare to find a situation where the total marketing budget is developed simply by summing the requests of various product or sales managers. More typically, these requests are reviewed and revised to fit total corporate needs. In still other cases the total marketing budget is decided centrally (usually with excessive influence by the finance department) and allocated to individual products or departments.[11]

CONCLUSION

Because of the array of different programs that managers may employ to implement the marketing strategy for a product or a line of related products, the annual plan is a critical element of coordinating activities and budgets. Further, because the marketing environment is dynamic and because the effectiveness and costs of marketing programs are always somewhat uncertain, annual plans are necessary for monitoring results and directing corrective actions. Individual programs must also be monitored because in most cases each program makes only a partial contribution to product objectives such as sales or market share or to total profitability. Consequently, the annual plan is necessary in order to evaluate the total mar-

[10]Harold Koontz, "Making Strategic Planning Work," *Business Horizons*, April 1976, pp. 37–47.
[11]Nigel Piercy, "The Marketing Budgeting Process: Marketing Management Implications," *Journal of Marketing*, October 1987, pp. 45–59.

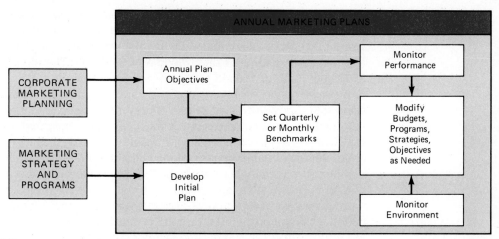

FIGURE 15-5   Relationship of annual marketing planning to other elements of the marketing planning process.

keting effort as well as the contributions of the various program elements. (Figure 15-5 shows the relationship of annual planning to other aspects of the marketing planning process.)

Moreover, because program performance is heavily influenced by environmental changes, an effective control system cannot be developed unless managers have access to strategic intelligence regarding customers, competitors, or other relevant environmental forces.

Ultimately, the effectiveness of the annual marketing planning process depends on the quality of the efforts made by those who do the plans. But the degree to which the organization facilitates market-driven planning is also important. In organizations that are truly market-oriented (as discussed in Chapter 1) not only is the annual marketing plan likely to be viewed as a very important management activity, it is also likely that the plan is primarily designed by the manager most knowledgeable about the market. To gain more insight regarding this process, consider the challenge faced by management at Time Warner Inc. in developing a plan for *Entertainment Weekly*.

Time Warner Inc.: Developing a Marketing Plan[12]

In February of 1990, Time Warner Inc. launched *Entertainment Weekly*, a magazine designed to review movies, videos, records, books, and television shows. In addition to reviews, several in-depth features on the entertainment business were to be part of each issue.

[12]Developed from Susan Duffy, "Can the People Who Brought You *People* Do It Again," *Business Week,* Feb. 12, 1990, p. 34; and Daniel Cox, "Criticism in Small Servings," *Chicago Tribune,* Feb. 12, 1990, sec. 4, p. 4.

After 2 years of direct mail testing, the company was able to identify the market to which it had the greatest appeal. The expected profile of the readership was 36.8 years of age, equally divided between male and female, 72 percent college educated with a median income of $41,800. The magazine was priced at $1.95 per issue or $51.48 for an annual subscription.

Because magazine revenues come from two sources—subscriptions or newsstand sales and advertising sales—Time Warner needed to develop two separate yet consistent plans. The size of the circulation base (which was targeted at 600,000 per week for the first year) would obviously impact magazine sales revenue. But the circulation base, along with the profile of the readers and the actual number of readers (which might be five times the circulation) would all be important to prospective advertisers.

To get subscribers, Time Warner offered a sales promotion involving four free issues of the magazine. The promotion was bolstered by $30 million in advertising through television and Time Warner's other magazines. Simultaneously, the advertising sales force was making calls on potential advertisers and advertising agencies, with a goal of signing up 100 advertisers to 2-year commitments.

1 Develop a list of the annual performance objectives that could be included in the annual plan(s).

2 What program performance measures should Time Warner use for control?

3 Approximately how frequently should performance be assessed?

4 Most new publications take a couple of years to be profitable. So should Time Warner really bother with an annual plan for this product? Explain.

QUESTIONS AND SITUATIONS FOR DISCUSSION

1 For each of the following situations, indicate the kinds of annual plans that should be developed to coordinate and monitor the marketing effort.

   a A division of a consumer-goods company uses a single sales force to sell all the following products: a shampoo, a toothpaste, a deodorant, and a hair spray.

   b A medium-sized corporation sells only a line of cellular telephones.

   c An automobile dealer sells the full line of Honda cars and trucks and offers a service department for maintenance and repair of any automotive vehicle.

2 Explain why a market-share-growth objective should be accompanied by a sales-volume objective and a target-contribution objective.

3 Explain the difference between postaction control and steering control.

4 In each of the following situations, would you tend to establish performance benchmarks at rather short intervals (such as weekly or monthly) or at rather long intervals (such as quarterly)? Explain your answers.

   a A consumer-goods firm relies heavily on sales-promotion programs to achieve a sales-volume objective for its line of cookies.

   b A typewriter manufacturer is introducing a new line of products for its commercial and industrial buyers. Advertising in industrial magazines and personal selling are the primary programs being used to achieve a sales-volume objective.

c A food company is attempting to improve the profitability of the product line it sells to institutional customers. The marketing effort is primarily designed to increase the volume purchased by large, existing accounts through more frequent sales calls and the use of quantity discounts.

5 What differences, if any, are there between a strategic environmental monitoring system and marketing research.

6 In some firms, marketing budgets are primarily determined by top management and in others by middle managers. In what circumstances should top management be the initiator of the budget as opposed to primarily acting as a reviewer of the budgets submitted by middle management?

7 The Bramble County Credit Union had been established in 1963 to serve employees of Bramble County government and the Bramble County schools. By 1990, 6320 employees had become members of the credit union.

The credit union offered share savings accounts, share draft (checking) accounts, certificates of deposit, and a variety of types of loans. At the end of 1990, the board of directors voted to offer a VISA credit card to the membership.

During January of 1991, a subcommittee of the board met with the executive director of the credit union to construct a marketing plan for the VISA credit card. The executive director, Ms. Ingram, had developed some data on the cost of a credit-card program. She believed that the credit union could attract nearly 2000 members to the credit-card program during the first year based on the experiences she had heard about from other credit union directors. To do this, she expected that the credit union would need to offer a rate of 14 percent on the unpaid monthly balance and avoid any annual fixed fees to cardholders. This would provide a 2 percent interest rate advantage against local banks.

Ms. Ingram also was planning a direct mail advertisement campaign for March, April, and May designed to achieve 90 percent awareness that Bramble County Credit Union now offered a credit card and 80 percent awareness of the 14 percent interest rate. The target market included all members and all 8000 county employees who were still nonmembers. Based on the experience of other credit unions, Ms. Ingram anticipated that approximately 15 percent of members and 5 percent of potential members would sign up once they were aware of the availability of a VISA card, as long as the price was competitive.

A telephone campaign was planned for the period June 1 to October 30. The telephone campaign was designed to remind members and potential members of the availability and price of the card and to get the member or potential member to (at least) agree to receive the application packet. Employees would be used to do the telephoning and would receive overtime pay as applicable. It was expected that 100 calls per week would be completed, that 60 percent of the calls would result in the mailing of a packet, and that half of these application packets would actually be completed and returned.

Based on industry averages, Ms. Ingram estimated that the credit union's fixed operating cost for this product would be $10,000 per year. Additionally, the variable cost per account was expected to be $54 per year. Marketing costs were projected as $1500 for direct mail and $200 per week for the telephone campaign. Beginning in August of 1991, one new clerical person would need to be hired in the operations department at a salary of $1300 per month to help in processing these accounts. Monthly revenue per account was expected to average $6.72 after the account was established for one month.

Develop a marketing plan for the VISA card for the period March 1 to December 31, 1991, following the general approach given in Tables 15-1 and 15-2. State the reasons behind your estimates of the number of accounts the credit union will have at the end of each month.

SUGGESTED ADDITIONAL READINGS

Bonoma, Thomas, "Marketing Performance—What Do You Expect?" *Harvard Business Review,* September–October 1989, pp. 44–47.

Cooper, A. C., and Daniel Schendel, "Strategic Responses to Technological Threat," *Business Horizons,* February 1976, pp. 61–69.

Daniells, Lorna M., "Sources on Marketing," *Harvard Business Review,* July–August 1982, pp. 40–43.

Hulbert, James, and Norman E. Toy, "A Strategic Framework for Marketing Control," *Journal of Marketing,* April 1977, pp. 12–20.

McLeod, Raymond, Jr., and John Rogers, "Marketing Information Systems: Uses in the Fortune 500," *California Management Review,* Fall 1982, pp. 106–118.

Piercy, Nigel, "The Marketing Budgeting Process: Marketing Management Implications," *Journal of Marketing,* October 1987, pp. 45–59.

Sharma, Subhash, and Dale Achabal, "STEMCOM: An Analytical Model for Marketing Control," *Journal of Marketing,* Spring 1982, pp. 104–113.

Stasch, Stanley F., and Patricia Lanktree, "Can Your Marketing Planning Procedures Be Improved?" *Journal of Marketing,* Summer 1980, pp. 79–90.

APPENDIX

SELECTED SOURCES OF INFORMATION FOR MARKETING MANAGERS

SOURCE DESCRIPTION CODE

A General industry conditions, competitors, trends
B Consumer market characteristics/buying power
C Consumer purchasing patterns
D Advertising and promotion statistics
E Sales tracking and marketing effectiveness studies

ABI/INFORM:(A)

Data Courier, Inc.

620 S. 5th St, Louisville, KY 40202; (502) 582-4211

Online service. Provides access to business information. Contains abstracts of articles on accounting, economics, information science, marketing, and other related subjects.

ADTRACK:(D)

Corporate Intelligence, Inc.

P.O. Box 16073, St. Paul, MN 55116; (612) 698-3543

A computerized index to advertising appearing in major consumer and business magazines. Advertising of ¼-page size or larger are indexed by fourteen data items. Data coverage includes company name, product name, description, color, date, page number, magazine name, and spokesperson.

Advertising and Marketing Intelligence (AMI):(C,D)

New York Times Information Service, Inc. and J. Walter Thompson Co.
Mt. Pleasant Office Park

1719 Route 10, Parsippany, NJ 07054; (800) 631-8056

Includes abstracts from advertising, media and marketing covering new products, consumer trends, people, research, media planning and buying, and sales promotions. Each entry consists of a brief statement on the subject, product, or person with the relevant bibliographic citation.

Advertising Age-100 Leading National Advertisers:(D)
   Crain Communications
   740 Rush St., Chicago, IL 60611; (312) 649-5200

> Marketing reports for each company provide useful facts about their marketing operations, such as sales and earnings, leading product lines and brands, how they rank nationally, share of market, advertising expenditures; also names of marketing personnel and agency account executives, both for print company and for principal divisions (found in the mid-September issue).

Adweek's Marketer's Guide to Media:(B)
   ASM Communications, Inc.
   49 E. 21st St., New York, NY 10010; (212) 477-4533

> Quarterly. Includes audience data for various kinds of media.

American Profile:(B)
   Donnelley Marketing
   1515 Summer St., Stamford, CT 06905; (203) 348-9999

> Profiles over 70 million households. Coverage includes household population, income, dependents, and other demographic variables. This data base also maintains an excellent array of socioeconomic data including number and type of businesses, number of employees in area, banking activity, and other demographic area profiles.

American Statistics Index:(A,B)
   Congressional Information Service, Inc.
   4520 E-W Highway, Bethesda, MD 20814; (800) 638-8380

> This is a comprehensive guide and index to the statistics published by all government agencies, congressional committees, and statistics-producing programs.

Annual Study of Advertisers:(D)

> Provides information on the 100 U.S. firms that spend the most on advertising. For each advertiser, provides estimates of total advertising and promotional expenditures, total sales, and total earnings. Contains extensive descriptions of each firm's products, markets, corporate planning, and strategy. Ranks the top 100 advertising spenders, and includes general descriptions of trends in advertising spending, strategy, and techniques of these firms.

Audience Measurement by Market for Outdoor (AMMO):(B)
   342 Madison Ave., New York, NY 10173; (212) 986-5920

> Available through the Institute of Outdoor Advertising. Reports reach and frequency by market for all four sizes with demographic breaks by age, sex, and income.

BAR (Broadcast Advertising Reports):(D)
   BAR, Inc.
   500 5th Ave., New York, NY 10036; (212) 221-2630

Maintains monthly data on network television commercial activities and expenditures by product, network, parent company, and mean estimate per commercial minute. Includes the relationship between a particular commercial and the others aired in the preceding and succeeding time slots.

Brand Preference Change Measurements:(E)

Audience Studies, Inc. (ASI)

The ASI measurements are made during and after exposure of the test commercials to a recruited, captive audience gathered in a theater. Various aspects of viewer response to television commercials are measured.

CACI:(B)

330 Madison Ave., New York, NY 10017; (800) 366-6600, Ext. 7807

This service provides demographic information and is accessible on nine time-sharing networks. Offers a sales potential system that measures consumer spending in any area of the United States. Information can be used for site selection, market entry planning, market share and penetration decisions, promotional planning, store performance analysis, and so forth. Updates U.S. Census data regularly and provides many specialized reports.

Consumer Economic Service Data:(B,C)

Data Resources, Inc.

29 Hartwell Ave., Lexington, MA 02173; (617) 861-0165

Offers vast amount of detailed demographic and economic data in five report areas: (1) Current Population Survey Annual Demographic File; (2) Consumer Expectations Survey—a diary and interview of 40,000 households; (3) TGI-Brand specific purchasing and media penetration data; (4) Longitudinal Retirement History Survey; and (5) Consumer Markets Services—personal consumption, retail sales, and associated prices.

Consumer Expenditure Study:(C)

Bureau of Labor Statistics, Department of Labor

441 G St. NW, Washington, DC 20212; (202) 523-8165

Bulletins and/or reports. Annual. These studies are based on personal interviews from a sample of 20,000 consumer units and record-keeping by a sample of 23,000 consumer units. These samples offer income and expenditure analysis by income class, family size, and several other demographic parameters.

Consumer Expenditure Survey:(B)

National Technology Info Service, U.S. Dept. of Commerce

5285 Port Royal Rd., Springfield, VA 22161; (703) 321-8525

Report. Eight volumes. Covers seven demographic parameters and presents consumer expenditure statistics for each area by demographic type. Coverage includes family income, size, age, race, education, tenure, and composition.

Demographic Research Company:(B)

233 Wilshire Blvd., Suite 995, Santa Monica, CA 90401; (213) 451-8583

This data base provides demographic, marketing research, and multivariate analysis assistance as well as a ZIP Code Data Base that organizes U.S. Census data in terms of income, occupation, and housing in ZIP code areas.

DIALOG:(A,B)

3460 Hillview Ave., Palo Alto, CA 94304; (800) 334-2564

This online service covers more topics than almost any other data base. The DIALOG Business Connection is a menu-based information service that offers quick and easy access to high-quality business information from a collection of respected sources. Available information includes share of market data, analysts' reports on industries, sales prospecting, and much more

Editor and Publisher's Market Guide:(B,C)

11 W. 19th St., New York, NY 10011; (212) 675-4380

Useful for market planning and selection, setting sales quotas, planning advertising and merchandising programs, and selecting store/plant/warehouse locations; this guide contains standardized fourteen-item surveys of market data for over 1500 daily newspaper markets in the United States and Canada. Also includes estimates of total and per household disposable income and offers current retailing data for nine sales classifications based on U.S. Census of Retail Trade. Published annually.

Government Market Studies:(A)

Washington Researchers

918 16th St. NW, Washington, DC 20006; (202) 733-2230

Book. Provides information on how to find and obtain over 5000 industry studies and reports. 1980.

Industry Reports:(A)

U.S. Dept. of Commerce, Superintendent of Documents, U.S. Government Printing Office

Washington, DC 20402; (202) 783-3238

Reports. Quarterly. Presents summaries on selected industry trends.

Information Access Corporation:

404 Sixth Ave., Menlo Park, CA 94025; (800) 227-8431

America Buys:(C)

Annual book. Indexes information on over 40,000 products, including evaluations, brand name references, consumer buying information, and brand comparisons.

Business Index:(A)

This data base indexes and abstracts information from more than 300 business periodicals, *The Wall Street Journal* (cover to cover), *Barron's* (cover to cover), *The New York Times* (Financial Section), business articles from more than 1000 general and legal periodicals, and business books from the Library of Congress's MARC data base. It provides extensive special indexing of information on corporations, their divisions, executives, and profits.

Leading National Advertiser, Inc. (LNA):
136 Madison Ave., New York, NY 10016; (212) 725-2700

Company Brand Report:(D)
Records the advertising expenditures of national advertisers. Lists parent companies alphabetically, showing total advertising expenditures by brand along with expenditures in each of the following media: magazines, newspaper supplements, network television, spot television, network radio, and outdoor advertising. Also lists the leading national advertisers, the top-ranking spenders in each of the six media, media tools for the ten previous years, magazine totals by group, total industry class expenditures, and industry class expenditures in each of the six media.

Multi-Media Report Service:(D)
Quarterly. Analyzes advertising expenditures of about 15,000 companies.

Publishers Information Bureau:(D)
PIB/LNA Magazine Advertising Analysis
Three volumes (monthly service). This is a service that provides detailed month-by-month advertising expenditures and linage by brand and by name of specific magazine. It is arranged in the following sections: volume 1 contains data for apparel, business/finance, and general/retail; volume 2, drugs/toiletries, food/beverages, home building, transportation, agriculture; volume 3 gives magazine totals, class totals, and an index.

Market Profile Analysis:(B)
Dun & Bradstreet, Inc.
99 Church St., New York, NY 10007; (212) 285-7000
Annual. Loose-leaf. Detailed profiles of U.S. metropolitan areas.

Market Statistics, Inc.:(B)
633 Third Ave., New York, NY 10017; (212) 986-8000
This data base includes demographic and retail sales information on each of 3100 American counties, including data on income, buying power, demographic profiles, and more. Four basic data packages are available: (1) Demographic Data Base I (basic demographic information); (2) Demographic Data Base II (basic demographic information plus ethnic characteristics); (3) County Commercial and Industrial Data Base (covers industrial and business characteristics); and (4) Planner's Data Base (includes television, geographic, and market information necessary for strategic planning and forecasting).

Mead Data Central, Inc:(A,B)
P.O. Box 933, Dayton, OH 45401; (800) 227-4908

Through one of its two main data base families known as Lexis, Mead Data Central provides electronic access to the full text of hundreds of business data bases. Available information includes wire services, company annual reports, investment firm reports, periodicals, newsletters, and selected newspapers.

Media Market Guide:(B,D)

322 East 50th St., New York, NY 10022; (212) 832-7170

Published by Conceptual Dynamics, Inc. Provides marketers, media sellers, media buyers, and advertising executives with a description of the physical dimensions, population characteristics, and major media opportunities in each of the top 100 metro markets.

Merrill Lynch Economic Regional Database:(A,B)

Merrill Lynch Economics, Inc.

One Liberty Plaza, 165 Broadway, New York, NY 10080; (212) 766-6200

Maintains demographic and economic data for individual statistics and SMSAs on labor force trends, population, tax payments, individual profiles, retail sales, construction, income, and housing starts.

MRI:(C,D)

Mediamark Research, Inc.

341 Madison Ave., New York, NY 10017; (212) 599-0444

This is a syndicated research organization that compiles information showing relationships between media use, product use, and demographics. Advertising agencies, magazines, and other media utilize the information to guide strategy and target markets. Reports include those on magazine audiences, multimedia audiences, and product volumes.

Nielsen, A. C.
Nielsen Plaza, Northbrook, IL 60062; (312) 498-6300

Retail Index:(C)

This index measures the buying patterns of consumers by store type, brand/product, sales area or region, and price. Data are indexed by major media advertising expenditures, in-house advertising support, retailer's gross profits, and retail inventory profiles.

Station Index:(B)

This index keeps track of family viewing habits by tracking the results of each family's diary. The results are used by advertisers in buying time and stations for program evaluation.

TV Index:(B)

The Nielsen Television Index measures the number of homes in which television sets are in use, the channels to which these sets are tuned, and reports these measures in terms of total homes and percentage ratings and shares. Data are developed for those demographic characteristics that reflect household data such as geographic area, county size, household size, household income, presence of nonadults, and so forth. The NTI reports measurements of 4-week cumulative program audience and frequency, in addition to many other breakdowns and analyses.

NPD Research:(C)
9801 W. Higgins Rd., Rosemont, IL 60018; (312) 692-6700
Offers four syndicated research services: (1) The CREST Report (Consumer Reports on Eating Share Trends) on consumer buying habits in restaurants; (2) The Gasoline Market Index on national and regional gasoline and allied products; (3) Textile Apparel Market Index on household textile, apparel, and home sewing markets; and (4) The Toy Market Index on the national toy market.

Online Site Evaluation System (ONSITE):(B,C)
Urban Decision Systems, Inc.
2030 Armacost Ave., P.O. Box 25953, Los Angeles, CA 90025; (213) 820-8931
Provides trade-area demographic data of more than 600 aggregate data items. Coverage includes such demographics as consumer expenditures, updated income, population, and household equipment and figures.

Predicasts:
Predicasts, Inc.
11001 Cedar Ave., Cleveland, OH 44106; (800) 321-6388

Basebook:(A)
Comprehensive, loose-leaf volume containing approximately 29,000 time series, arranged by modified 7-digit SIC #; and including also statistics for economic indicators. The industry statistics usually include production, consumption, exports/imports, wholesale price, plant and equipment expenditures, wage rate.

PROMT:(A)
Monthly. Quarterly and annual cumulation. Abstracts of market information grouped into twenty-eight major industry sections. International coverage.

Terminal System (PTS):(A)
This data base contains over 3 million summaries of information taken from over 2500 U.S. and foreign trade journals, newspapers, and general business publications. It offers article summaries, statistical data, and one- or two-line indexing services to provide users with background information on companies, products, industries, or marketing trends.

Prospects:(B)
The Futures Group
76 Eastern Ave., Glastonbury, CT 06033; (203) 633-3501
A data base for consumer forecasting. Sample data coverage includes households, families, marriage, divorce, education, labor force, popula-

tion, and lifestyle indicators. Forecasts are accompanied by a list of projected events based on historical trends and related events. Forecasts may contain over 100 indicators used to describe American consumers and their behavior. Also used for forecasting the hospital supply and pharmaceutical industries.

Rand McNally's Commercial Atlas and Marketing Guide:(B,C)
Rand McNally & Company
P.O. Box 127, Skokie, IL 60676; (800) 284-6565

Of particular use in allocating sales effort, this volume presents detailed maps of the United States and provides information about population; households, retail sales, auto registration, sales for consumer goods, food stores, drugstores, and other census statistics for counties, principal cities, and Standard Metro Statistical Areas. Published annually.

Rezide/1980 Update:(B)
Claritas Corp.
1911 N. Fort Meyer Dr., Arlington, VA 22209

1981. National edition. (ten volumes). For each ZIP code in the United States, shows population, number of households, household income in seven intervals, and median household income.

SAMI/BURKE:(E)
800 Broadway, Cincinnati, OH 45202; (513) 381-8898

Maintains data on warehouse distribution activity to supermarkets. Data coverage includes consumer prices by dry goods, household supplies, health, and beauty supplies. Many specialized reporting functions are available for data analysis.

Simmons Study of Media and Markets:(B,C)
Simmons Market Research Bureau
219 E. 42d St., New York, NY 10017; (212) 876-1414

Consists of detailed descriptions of the characteristics of users of individual products, brands, and services and of audiences of individual media. Descriptions include detailed information regarding age, sex, education, occupation, income, geographic location, household description, lifestyle and psychographic data (including hobbies, recreational and leisure activities), respondent self-concept, buying style, and social position.

Site Potential:(B,C)
Caci, Inc.
1815 N. Fort Meyer Dr., Arlington, VA 22209; (703) 841-7800 or (800) 336-4752

Provides estimates of the demand (consumer expenditures) by residents within a defined area for approximately 140 product and service items. This data base generates reports covering sixteen different retail stores and three financial institutions. Coverage includes apparel stores, appliance stores, auto service stores, department stores, drugstores, footwear stores, grocery stores, hair salons, home improvement stores, ice-cream stores, optical centers, commercial banks, financial companies, and savings and loan associations.

Social Indicators:(B)
    Government Printing Office, Washington, DC 20402

> Triennial. Charts and tables on population; the family; housing; social security and welfare; health and nutrition; public safety; education and training; "work," income, wealth, and expenses; culture, leisure, and the use of time; social mobility, and participation. International data are provided for comparison. Extensive technical notes accompany each section. Includes references for further reading and a subject index.

SRI Values and Lifestyles (VALS):(E)
    Menlo Park, CA 94025

> SRI International-VALS is a research service that tracks marketing-relevant shifts in the beliefs, values, and lifestyles of a sample of the American population. The VALS system divides the population into segments consisting of three major groups of consumers, in turn divided into nine specific segments. Tracking the shifts in the values and behavior of these segments can help in understanding the target segment one is appealing to.

Standard & Poor's Industry Surveys:(A)
    Standard & Poor Corp.
    25 Broadway, New York, NY 10004; (212) 208-8000

> Separate pamphlets for 33 industries, updated quarterly and annually. This is a valuable source for basic data on thirty-three industries, with financial comparisons of the leading companies in each industry. For each industry there is a "Basic Analysis" (about forty pages) revised annually, and a short "Current Analysis" (about eight pages) published three times per year. Received with this is a four-page monthly on "Trends and Projections," which includes tables of economic and industry indicators, and a monthly "Earnings Supplement," giving concise, up-to-date revenue, income, and profitability data on over 1000 leading companies in these thirty-three major industries.

Starch Recognition Tests of Print Advertisements:(E)
    Starch INRA Hooper, Inc.
    566 E. Boston Post Rd., Mamaroneck, NY 10543; (914) 698-0800

> Starch Readership Studies make three basic measurements among persons who claim readership of specific magazine issues: the noting score, the seen associated score, and the read most score.

Statistical Abstract of the United States:(A,B)
    U.S. Bureau of Census, Department of Commerce
    Washington, DC 20230

> This guide provides a general overview of statistics collected by the federal government and other public and private organizations. Some of the topics covered include geography and environment, labor force, communications, population, employment and earnings, business enterprises, vital statistics, transportation, energy, manufacturers, foreign commerce and aid, standard metro area statistics, and more.

Statistics Reference Index:
Congressional Information Service
Washington, DC 20230

>Monthly in two parts, with annual cumulations. A comprehensive, selective guide to American statistical publications available from sources other than the United States government, such as trade, profit, and other non-profit associations and institutions; business organizations; commercial publishers (including trade journals); independent and university research centers; state government agencies.

Survey of Buying Power:(B)
Sales & Marketing Management magazine
633 Third Ave., New York, NY 10017; (800) 543-3000

>Presented in the July issue, this guide contains information on all Standard Metropolitan Statistical Areas in the country and covers population, households, effective buying income, retail sales, and a "Buying Power Index" useful in allocating marketing and promotional efforts. Also includes national and regional summaries; and metro area, county, and city rankings. Published annually.

Survey of Current Business:(A)
Bureau of Economic Analysis, Department of Commerce
Washington, DC 20230

>This publication presents monthly and quarterly statistics on several business indicators for national income, from income and marketing, inventories, industrial production, commodities, advertising, and wholesale and retail trade by product category. Published monthly. Order from: U.S. Government Printing Office, Superintendent of Documents, Washington, DC 20402.

Target Group Index:(B,C)
Axiom Market Research Bureau, Inc.
420 Lexington Ave., New York, NY 10017

>Report. Supplies sample demographic data for users and nonusers of various products and services. Includes market shares for such things as product brands, TV programs watched, and magazines read.

U.S. News & World Report's Study of American Markets:(B,C)
2400 N. St. NW, Washington, DC 20037; (202) 955-2000

>It covers customer characteristics, buying behavior, purchase influences, and media exposure for such products as liquor, life insurance, hand-held electric calculators, automobiles, watches, cameras, home entertainment products, travel.

ZIP Code Demographic Database (ZDDB):(B)
Demographic Research Co.
233 Wilshire Blvd., Suite 995, Santa Monica, CA 90401; (213) 451-8583

>Provides completion of the latest statistics on population, education, income, and housing by postal ZIP code.

INDEX